The Mask of Enlightenment is the most detailed textual and thematic study of one of Nietzsche's most important but least understood works: *Thus Spoke Zarathustra.* In this book Nietzsche was laying the groundwork for a fundamental philosophical and political revolution on a global scale. One of the difficulties that the text poses is Nietzsche's prophetic style; Stanley Rosen unravels the complex threads that form the rhetorical voices of the work, and so explains the style in an accessible manner. He rejects recent skeptical, deconstructionist interpretations of Nietzsche and reveals a coherence underlying the multiple and apparently incompatible intentions embedded in the text. There is extensive interpretation of the doctrine of eternal return, of the nature of the philosophical prophet, and of the dialectic of philosophical revolution. Professor Rosen is also concerned to provide an adequate contextualization of *Zarathustra,* and he thus devotes considerable space to the Greek and Christian background to Nietzsche's thought, to Nietzsche's relation to Plato, and to Nietzsche's relationship with the Enlightenment in one direction and with postmodernism in the other.

Nietzsche is a figure whose influence on contemporary thought in the humanities and social sciences continues to be enormous. This book is sure to become the definitive study of *Zarathustra;* it will have broad appeal to philosophers and students of modern philosophy, intellectual historians, political scientists, and literary theorists.

THE MASK OF ENLIGHTENMENT

MODERN EUROPEAN PHILOSOPHY

This series comprises a range of high-quality books on philosophers, topics, and schools of thought prominent in the Kantian and post-Kantian European tradition. The series is nonsectarian in approach and methodology and includes both introductory and more specialized treatments of these thinkers and topics. Authors are encouraged to interpret the boundaries of the modern European tradition in a broad way and to engage with it in primarily philosophical rather than historical terms.

THE MASK OF ENLIGHTENMENT

Nietzsche's *Zarathustra*

STANLEY ROSEN
Boston University

CAMBRIDGE
UNIVERSITY PRESS

PUBLISHED BY THE PRESS SYNDICATE OF THE UNIVERSITY OF CAMBRIDGE
The Pitt Building, Trumpington Street, Cambridge CB2 1RP, United Kingdom

CAMBRIDGE UNIVERSITY PRESS
The Edinburgh Building, Cambridge CB2 2RU, United Kingdom
40 West 20th Street, New York, NY 10011-4211, USA
10 Stamford Road, Oakleigh, Melbourne 3166, Australia

First published 1995
Reprinted 1996

Printed in the United States of America

Typeset in Baskerville

A catalogue record for this book is available from the British Library

Library of Congess Cataloguing-in-Publication Data is available

ISBN 0-521-49546-6 hardback
ISBN 0-521-49889-9 paperback

CONTENTS

PREFACE

In the following pages, I propose to study in considerable detail the philosophical teaching of Nietzsche's most problematic work, *Thus Spoke Zarathustra* (hereafter abbreviated as *Zarathustra*). Despite Nietzsche's current popularity, and the almost unending stream of books and articles devoted to his thought, one could not say that *Zarathustra* has been subjected to extensive analysis. More precisely, we have been presented for the most part with instances of two extreme (and unsatisfactory) kinds of commentary: the paraphrase of selected passages in the language of academic scholasticism and the translation of Nietzsche's already perfervid quasi-poetry into the deliquescent obliquities of postmodernism.

My own approach will differ from these extremes while attempting to capture something of the virtues associated with them. There is no point in writing a book on *Zarathustra* that offers to explain the obscure by the still more obscure. At the same time, it has to be acknowledged that Nietzsche was neither an analytical philosopher nor a professor engaged in the technical exploration of causality, perception, or performative utterances. What I am calling postmodernism for convenience is surely right to claim Nietzsche as its decisive ancestor. Nietzsche, more so than Feuerbach, Marx, or other great figures of the nineteenth century, initiates what Heidegger called the *Destruktion* of the tradition, and it is of course Heidegger's version of Nietzsche's *Destruktion* that underlies the deconstruction disseminated by Derrida and his students to the English-speaking world. When Nietzsche speaks of causality, perception, and other traditional philosophical topics, it is with the intention of subjecting them to radical dissolution. When Nietzsche is pertinent to the self-styled analytical philosophy, it is to accentuate the incapacity of that movement to preserve itself from deconstruction because of an adherence to the deepest postulates of late-modern thought, in particular to the identification of Being with thinking.

And yet it is quite misleading to approach Nietzsche from the perspective of postmodernism or deconstruction. One cannot understand the father of a revolution by composing florid celebrations of his unorthodoxy that reduce him to the orthodoxy of the florid. Ideology is one thing; philosophy is something else again. I do not mean by this to recommend the ostensibly neutral prose of the academic specialist in opposition to the pyrotechnical rhetoric of the *École normale*. Both are to be avoided, the first as an unconscious residue of positivism and historicism, the second as narcissism. Nietzsche did not prepare his revolution as an unconscious trace of difference, but in full cognizance of the historical moment of late modernity, and so too of the alternatives facing the resident of that moment.

This point is clearly grasped by Lawrence Lampert in his extremely valuable study *Nietzsche's Teaching*. Although I disagree with Lampert's formulation of Nietzsche's intentions, and am in particular disagreement with him about the coherence and success with which those intentions are executed, I recognize the strength with which Lampert addresses in a genuinely philosophical manner the task of reading Nietzsche. As will shortly become apparent, Lampert and I are in considerable agreement about the relation of Nietzsche to Plato. We disagree, however, in that Lampert's Plato is too close to Heidegger for my taste. In somewhat different terms, Lampert exaggerates the retrospective epochal importance of Nietzsche, just as he is overly enthusiastic about the soundness of Nietzsche's critique of the modern tradition. Nevertheless, I recommend his book to the reader as a contrast and supplement to my own study.

I see no point in citing the various attempts to translate Nietzsche into the jargon of analytical philosophy. There is no doubt that the latter school (or, better, set of related schools) shares important principles with Nietzsche, of which the most fundamental is the unexamined conviction, derivative from Kant and in particular from Neo-Kantianism, that the world is a construction of human feeling, perception, and discourse. The difference between Nietzsche and the analysts, however, is overwhelming. Nietzsche rejects both mathematics and the syntax of ordinary language as paradigms of philosophical analysis. For the unexamined grammatical world view of analytical philosophy,

Nietzsche substitutes a radical critique of the solipsistic and so nihilistic consequences of the modern post-Kantianism from which, as we shall see, he cannot free himself. It is a guiding thesis of this study that most of the incoherences in Nietzsche's doctrines stem from his unsuccessful attempt to combine a poetic version of Kantian world constitution with a Platonic conception of the philosopher as prophet and lawgiver who understands human nature and how its fundamental types are to be rank-ordered.

The poetic strand in Nietzsche's teaching is closely connected with his acceptance of the thesis, common to pre-Socratic speculation and modern natural science, that rest is an illusory derivative of change. Since Nietzsche deviates from Neo-Kantianism, or let us say belongs to its historicist wing, and treats the ego not as transcendental but as itself the product of chaotic accumulations and discharges of points of force, he is in no position to validate his Platonist understanding of rank-ordering or to justify his distinction between noble and base nihilism. But one cannot correctly understand Nietzsche by simply overlooking his emphasis on rank-ordering and finitude. This is the crucial mistake committed by those commentators who have been influenced by Gilles Deleuze. Deleuze simply falsifies Nietzsche's doctrine when he claims, very early in his *Nietzsche and Philosophy,* that the eternal return is not the return of a particular arrangement of things, and so that "only action and affirmation return" (p. xi).

A much better interpretation of Nietzsche from the postmodernist camp, unfortunately not well known in the English-speaking scholarly community, is Gianni Vattimo's *Il soggetto e la maschera* (*The Subject and the Mask*). Vattimo shares the Heideggerian thesis that Nietzsche is a critic of metaphysics who cannot himself elude the language of metaphysics; in what I find an amusing example of this thesis, Vattimo holds that Nietzsche's rejection of socialism leads him to use aristocratic models for the superman, thereby falling back into the language of metaphysics (pp. 373–75). Fortunately enough, this is not typical of the level of Vattimo's analysis, although it does fairly illustrate his tacit political presuppositions. He gives us a close textual analysis which emphasizes the central role of the mask in Nietzsche's entire corpus. My major objection to his book is that, despite his rejection of Deleuze's emphasis on genealogy as the central Nietzschean method (p. 147), his own reading overlooks the coherent and quite explicitly Platonistic, but certainly not metaphysical, political framework of Nietzsche's various uses of the image of the mask. Vattimo finds the coherence of Nietzsche's thought in the process of a continual changing of masks as man becomes progressively more free. But this is to equate freedom with aesthetic play, a doctrine that Nietzsche shares to some extent with Schiller; it misses the difference between philosophical and poetical play.

To turn to a more general hermeneutical problem, which follows directly from the weaknesses of postmodernist (and ultimately Heideggerian) readings of Nietzsche, one cannot understand him, or for that matter anyone, unless the sense of a text is in principle accessible to the philosophical intelligence, despite all ambiguities of interpretation and the impossibility of equating the final significance of an author's theme with his discursive elaboration of it. It is true that Nietzsche is the champion of perspectivism, but perspectivism is a doctrine which may be adopted or rejected, and this is because the doctrine of perspectivism, like all doctrines, is accessible to philosophical *sunopsis*. A perspective, after all, is a viewpoint, and viewpoints may be assumed by a variety of observers because they are defined by a structure that provides them with a stable identity. Viewpoints differ from one another, but not fundamentally or continuously from themselves; there is nothing to prevent one person from regarding the spectacle of existence from a series of viewpoints. Indeed, existence might be described as that series itself, but this does not entail a vitiating relativism, provided that one can say what one has seen from each member of the series and thereby make the view accessible to others.

If one cannot say this, then there is after all nothing to be said, and the ostensible replacement of vision by writing is in fact a reversion to scribbling. In this fundamental sense, Nietzsche was as much a Platonist as Plato, albeit he entirely rejected the so-called doctrine of Ideas or pure forms. Otherwise put, Nietzsche's Platonism amounts to the conviction that he understands human nature and how it is to be transformed by the philosopher in his role as prophet and lawgiver. As I noted above in criticizing Deleuze, on this point Nietzsche is explicit; the evidence is unequivocal and can be denied only by doing violence to the texts, published and unpublished.

In previous publications I have argued at length that Nietzsche was neither the last Platonist metaphysician nor the first Heideggerian but something that combines elements of both ways of thinking. This combination results in an unstable attempt to produce what is intended as at once a true interpretation of traditional philosophy and the revelation of a new epoch of historical existence. To repeat, what is valid for Nietzsche in Platonism is the conception of the philosopher as prophet and lawgiver, not a doctrine of Being or eidetic structure. The doctrine, or, more accurately, the metaphor, of the eternal return has nothing to do with a conceptual articulation of the structure of totality, but in effect reassimilates the Hegelian Absolute into the rhetorical language initiated by Plato's myth of the reversed cosmos. As to the content of the revelation, it is not so much a proto-Heideggerian attempt to deconstruct Western history in order to uncover a new beginning for *Seinsgeschichte* (the history of Being) as a reprisal of what has already eventuated and a celebration of the heroic ages of the past as paradigms intended to justify the destruction of the present decadent epoch. Nietzsche teaches the acceptance of the noble nihilism as a surgical instrument suited to the excision of the base nihilism that disguises itself as progress, egalitarianism, and enlightenment.

At the heart of Nietzsche's complex teaching is the maxim he assigns to Zarathustra: He who would create must first destroy. Neither destruction nor creation can be understood in narrowly hermeneutical terms, and they certainly have nothing to do with metaphysics or ontology, except on the one crucial point that they are made possible by the identification of Being as chaos. Nietzsche belongs to what Socrates calls in the *Theaetetus* Homer's army, or to those who believe that rest is a disguised version of motion. It is a double corollary of this belief that art is worth more for life than the truth and that war is the father of all things; hence Nietzsche's replacement of the Platonic philosopher-soldier by the poetic warrior, or what he calls more ambiguously "Caesar with the soul of Christ." If Being is chaos, then ontology or metaphysics is certainly nonsense; it must be replaced by rhetoric. But this is not the same as to say that philosophy is replaced by art. Nietzsche has not the slightest intention of retreating to the private existence of the aesthete. He conceives himself not as a character in a novel but as the author of a philosophical revolution in which art plays the role of stimulus and, in a deeper sense, of narcotic.

In recent times there has been a concerted effort to illuminate the doctrine of the eternal return on the basis of modern physics. Without in any way denying the obvious fact that Nietzsche was intrigued by the possibility of finding support for his revelation in physics, it has to be emphasized that mathematics, logic, and so too physics are at bottom for Nietzsche human perspectives. By this term he means a way of perceiving, that is to say interpreting or making rather than discovering or grasping, the accumulation and discharge of points of force. Physics is thus a species of art, which is in turn an expression of will to power, an exoteric expression (as Nietzsche tells us in his *Nachlass* [Notebooks]) for the random fluctuations of chaos. Like all reductionists, Nietzsche is faced with the impossible task of giving value to life, consciousness, and intentional activity on the basis of the perturbations of energy, or, as he would have put it, of force: in a still older expression, of matter in the void. This in turn leads Nietzsche to identify chance with necessity and value with power. The result is an incoherent synthesis of *amor fati* (love of fate in Spinoza's sense) and a doctrine of creative transvaluation. Nietzsche provides us with a reinterpretation of Spinoza's definition of freedom as knowledge of determinism. He thereby reproduces at the level of art and *die grosse Politik* (politics in the grand manner) what Spinoza expresses metaphysically: the common doctrine of modern philosophy as decisively shaped by modern mathematical and experimental science.

In order to find one's way through the Nietzschean labyrinth and to mitigate the distraction induced by his conflicting doctrines, we must hold firm to his comprehensive intention to liberate humanity from the sickness of decadence by what one might properly call homeopathic medicine. The decay into nihilism is to be accelerated by the revelation of the false foundations of the tradition of which we are the latest manifestation and, as such, already infected with the sickness unto death, but in the potentially long-lasting form of the doctrine of progress that masks the advent of the last man. The first stage of Nietzsche's political revolution is to assert not merely that our values are decadent but that life, and indeed Becoming, is valueless. What Nietzsche euphemistically refers to as "the innocence of Becoming" is a salutary pseudonym for the illusion of the value and significance of human existence. But this poses an apparently insoluble problem for the second, or positive, stage of the revolution. If Becoming is chaos and values are transient human creations, indeed, noble lies, then so too must be the noble and virile values of the superman. In slightly different terms, the doctrine of radical freedom and creativity is flatly contradicted by the finitude and necessity of the eternal return.

There is a rather simple way in which to make sense of, if not to render fully coherent, Nietzsche's apparently inconsistent set of doctrines, which I put forward as a useful hypothesis, with the warning that it should not be taken as a license for oversimplification. I want to underline here that the hypothesis does not overlook the finally incompatible nature of the crucial elements of Nietzsche's teaching. What it purports to do is to make intelligible Nietzsche's comprehensive intentions. The hypothesis is rooted in Nietzsche's diverse texts, published and unpublished, and so in his explicit statements rather than in the doctrines of Heidegger or recent French speculation. It is also based on the evidence of Nietzsche's extraordinary artistry and his complex rhetoric, decisive features of his thought that are wholly ignored by the analytical or orthodox-academic schools of interpreters. If one does not take into account Nietzsche's mode of writing, one will no more be able to understand him than Plato or Kierkegaard.

Unlike many twentieth-century scholars, Nietzsche was entirely familiar with the long tradition of esotericism, or concealment, by philosophers of dangerous truths with salutary myths. He refers frequently to the distinction between the esoteric and the exoteric, at length in *Beyond Good and Evil,* and throughout his writings, published and unpublished. There is no question about Nietzsche's endorsement of this distinction, which can be briefly expressed in his epigram "Everything deep loves the mask." Nietzsche also unquestionably believed that order and life are valueless modifications of chaos, and so that meaning as well as value is a human creation.

This belief can serve both to liberate us for new acts of creation and to paralyze us with a despairing acknowledgment of the emptiness of life. Simply stated, my hypothesis is that Nietzsche takes the bold step of attempting to establish the first of these alternatives on the basis of premises that underlie the second. As I have already indicated, the first step in this attempt is the most dangerous; Nietzsche must destroy all foundations, whether natural or transcendental, of traditional value, in order to free us of every restriction on our creative powers. This is the ancestor of contemporary efforts, mediated by reference to Heidegger, to deconstruct the Western tradition and so to prevent the reification of the human spirit. The price Nietzsche pays for liberation, paradoxically enough, is bondage. Whereas Kant teaches that freedom is the spontaneous manifestation of rationality, Nietzsche reduces rationality to the spontaneity of chaos. It is this reduction that Nietzsche must disguise, especially from himself, by the rhetoric of creation and transvaluation. And this is why we find throughout Nietzsche's writings the operation of what I shall call a double rhetoric, implied by the already cited assertion that he who would create must first destroy.

The rhetoric of destruction is a radicalizing of the skepticism and materialism intrinsic to the modern European Enlightenment, with the decisive difference that Nietzsche is much more thoroughgoing, or, as he himself would say, more honest, than the great figures of the scientific Enlightenment, because he reduces mathematical science itself, the mainspring of the Enlightenment, to chaos. The rhetoric of creation, however, is also a radicalizing of the libertarian humanism of the Enlightenment, a humanism that derives from the Renaissance and which Nietzsche purifies or intensifies, but which he also modifies in two ways: first, with a dose of archaism that looks to the Pre-Socratics for inspiration; and second, because of his inability to liberate himself from Wagnerian melodrama and nineteenth-century Romanticism.

In sum: Nietzsche is a Platonist in the following sense. He provides us with a noble lie, but with a much more explicit account than Plato's of the fact that he is so providing us. He is not a Platonist, because there is for him no domain of Ideas by which the philosopher may take his bearings and to which he may escape from the winds of history. Nietzsche attempts to rise to the Platonic level of what he calls the land of the Hyperboreans, citing Pindar. The Hyperboreans cannot be reached by land or by sea, because they dwell above history and have achieved the *skopos,* or perspective, of all perspectives assigned to the divine demiurge in Plato's myth of the reversed cosmos. Absent the Ideas, however, Nietzsche's *skopos* is itself a historical event; in place of an ontology of Being, Nietzsche gives us, like so many thinkers of the nineteenth century, a philosophy of history.

My hypothesis, then, is that Nietzsche attempts to escape from the limitations of temporality and human finitude by a vision of the eternal return of the same. This vision is both destructive and, at least in Nietzsche's eyes, liberating. All fundamental ambiguities in Nietzsche's writings stem from his efforts to balance the destructive and liberating aspects of his central vision by means of a double rhetoric. Nietzsche destroys in order to create; the problem is that he must destroy those whom he wishes to persuade that they are creators. This problem applies to Nietzsche as well; his *skopos,* or Hyperborean residency beyond good and evil, the vantage point from which Nietzsche is vouchsafed his vision of eternity, is reduced by the details of that vision to the status of critical historical event, or what one could call, adopting an expression from Heidegger, the perspective of all perspectives. As such, however, the vision is prey to the dissolution of the random motions of chaos.

It is in the light of this hypothesis, for which I have offered elsewhere extensive attempts at confirmation, that I approach *Zarathustra.* I see *Zarathustra* as an example of Nietzsche's *grosse Politik,* and in that sense his Platonism. Whereas Plato as it were establishes Western European history on a basis of philosophy by writing the *Republic,* Nietzsche publishes *Zarathustra* in order to destroy a Western Europe that has been enervated by a deteriorated, historically exhausted Christianity, or Platonism for the masses. But *Zarathustra* is not and cannot be a simply destructive book. For reasons which I have now introduced, it must also contain a noble lie, or invocation to create. This invocation is compromised by the obvious fact, made obvious by Zarathustra, that all disciples are inferior, or that supermen cannot be produced by doctrines and revelations. Nietzsche's dilemma is that he can destroy only in the hope that out of the ashes of the present will arise an infant who is also a creator of a new table of values. Nietzsche knew, as his letters show, that his invocation to creativity would be radically misunderstood or at least radically misapplied by those who believed themselves to be at once supermen and his disciples. He nevertheless took this chance, presumably in order to rescue us from the stagnant reign of the last men. *Zarathustra* is thus at once a handbook of revolution and a confession by its author that revolutions must always fail. A careful study of *Zarathustra* has much to teach us, not only about the origin and nature of postmodernism, but also about the last consequences of the Enlightenment, or the attempt to free mankind by enslavement to an incoherent reliance upon two finally incompatible principles: mathematics as the expression of eternal order and subjectivity as the locus of the spontaneous manifestation of order. I have written this book not as a philological exercise in the history of philosophy but in the attempt to understand, or at least to illuminate, the problem of the relation between philosophy and politics.

This is not the same as the problem of the relation between theory and practice, which is internal to philosophy and which cannot be solved so long as we persist in regarding the two, theory and practice, as independent elements in a synthesis. One could of course argue that philosophy and politics are dependent on one another, but the situation is altogether different from that of the mutual implication of theory and practice, as for example in the constructive discovery of intelligible order. The philosopher, as a distinct human type who is motivated by ends that detach one from politics, must decide upon the proper mode of dependence; and by "proper" I mean the mode that allows philosophy to exist in contrast with ideologies and the fashions of intellectuals. As is obvious from a knowledge of history, the philosophical temptation to remake history in order to preserve philosophy is very great. This temptation (if that is the right word) was especially strong at the beginning of the Western European tradition, and it has been even stronger at what I will call the end of that tradition in the second half of the nineteenth century and much of the twentieth. Whether we take this renewed activity as the travails of birth or the death throes of an epoch, there can be no doubt that Nietzsche is crucial to our understanding and to our political destiny.

I have therefore approached *Zarathustra* with maximum seriousness and in the light of the entire Nietzschean corpus, thereby disregarding as patently absurd the two extreme schools of Nietzsche interpretation. The first school insists that Nietzsche was primarily an epigrammatist and littérateur, incapable of coherent analytical thought; the second school, following Heidegger, sees *Zarathustra* as the antechamber (*Vorhalle*) to his genuine and most important teaching, which is to be found only in the fragments of the late *Nachlass*. I myself share the view of Karl Löwith, whose book *Nietzsches Philosophie der ewigen Wiederkehr des Gleichen* (*Nietzsche's Philosophy of the Eternal Return of the Same*) is now neglected but who remains one of the sanest guides to Nietzsche. According to Löwith, all of Nietzsche's later doctrines are to be found in *Zarathustra*. I intend to show the degree to which *Zarathustra* is a carefully constructed work that contains an intricate teaching couched in a double rhetoric, as noted above. At the same time, it has to be acknowledged that *Zarathustra* is not a treatise on epistemology or ontology; it is a work of art, and like all such works it contains strong elements of inspiration and pure poetry to which there are no easily decipherable discursive equivalents. I should also say that I am no admirer of Nietzsche's poetry, nor am I a partisan of his doctrines. But this is irrelevant to the central task of the present volume: to understand as precisely as possible not only Nietzsche's revolutionary teaching but the problem of philosophical revolution itself.

I see no point in engaging in a long preliminary essay on methods of interpretation. *Zarathustra,* a book for everyone and no one according to the subtitle, is written in a mixture of public and private discourse. Many of Nietzsche's symbols are self-evident, but some are no doubt obscure products of the poetic unconscious. One has to navigate between the Scylla of aesthetical obtuseness or overinterpretation and the Charybdis of underinterpretation or failure to penetrate what has been intentionally masked. A book like *Zarathustra,* very much like the Hebrew and Christian Scriptures after which it is in part modeled, will say whatever each reader asks of it unless we are able to determine the author's intention. By invoking this today unfashionable expression, I do not mean to deny that there are always alternative interpretations of imaginative texts. As I have already indicated, the alternatives open up only when we are able to grasp the author's controlling viewpoint. Without this grasp, so-called alternatives are mere arbitrary fantasies and as such have nothing to do with the text that is presumably under interpretation.

However one looks at it, a book like *Zarathustra* requires a large amount of paraphrase. It is all very well to complain about the violation of poetic integrity, and I have already acknowledged the strong element of inspiration in Nietzsche's rhetorical effusions. But inspiration either fills its recipient with spiritual and intellectual illumination or it is merely the hot air of the whirling dervish. The test of the rationality of Nietzsche's rhetoric will be in the success of my interpretation. Nor is this interpretation arbitrary or a mere perspective to be placed in contrast with countless others. In its central contention and broad outlines, it must be sound or unsound. I begin from the unmistakable Nietzschean intention to present the human race with a new revelation. However masked may be the expression of the details of this revelation, it cannot help but be stated in its main points in a more or less explicit manner. Zarathustra teaches the coming of the superman through two irreconcilable means: creative revolution and the continuing rotation of the circle of the eternal return. This irreconcilability is puzzling, but it is not unintelligible. The primary task of the interpreter is to remove the irreconcilable element or to demonstrate in a persuasive manner why it cannot be removed.

I shall begin with a general account of Nietzsche's intentions and follow with a detailed analysis of the Preface to Part One, which in fact serves as an introduction to the entire work. I then turn to extensive studies of selected sections of the four parts of the work. There is a great deal of repetition in *Zarathustra*, in part no doubt for the practical purpose of inducing a hypnotic state in the potential disciple (who is of course not the superman), but partly because Nietzsche seems to have been carried away periodically by his rather unsteady Muse. Something must be said of the overall architecture of the work, and enough sections must be scrutinized to avoid the risk of omitting what is essential. I have passed by those passages that add nothing substantially new to another deeper or more detailed presentation of the same topic. As a consequence of the desire to avoid repetition, the length of my treatment of the successive parts of the text is uneven; by far the longest sections of this study are devoted to the Preface and to the individual episodes of Part One.

The amount of space required to unwind the intricacies of Nietzsche's argument and to assess its philosophical merits with respect to the larger question of philosophical revolution has made it impossible for me to engage in a running commentary on the secondary literature. I have tried to indicate how I stand with regard to important examples of Nietzsche scholarship, both here and in the Introduction. But nothing is gained from cataloguing one's agreements and disagreements with a panoply of experts on this or that textual detail. I add that, with very few exceptions, although I have enjoyed many books on Nietzsche, my interpretation is grounded in a reflection on his own texts. In this connection, I should say that I have made no attempt to provide a history of the explicit influences on the young Nietzsche; in particular, the reader will find no discussion of Schopenhauer's treatment of the will. In my opinion it is much more important for grasping the significance of Nietzsche's thought to uncover the inner relation to Plato, and the perhaps unconscious but very deep influence of Kant, as well as the curious presence of Hegel in Nietzsche's central doctrines. My study, in other words, is not a history of Nietzsche's development but a philosophical assessment of his mature teaching, and in particular of the teaching of *Zarathustra*.

I have included a number of brief comparisons between points made by Nietzsche and analogous or homologous points in other thinkers, especially Plato, Kant, Hegel, and Heidegger. One otherwise sympathetic anonymous reader of my study has complained that these comparisons, although conducive to fruitful development, are too cryptic as they stand. I am sensitive to the criticism, but upon mature reflection have allowed these comparisons to stand, precisely because I hope that the reader is correct in finding them useful for further thought. The main topic of this book is after all Nietzsche's *Zarathustra,* not the history of philosophy. But part of the process of understanding *Zarathustra* is to think on one's own about the connections between it and other relevant philosophies. Those who find the remarks unhelpful are asked to ignore them.

Two last points. In the early chapters of this study, I have provided extensive citations from works by Nietzsche other than *Zarathustra,* in order to buttress my general account of his teaching. Once that intention has been accomplished, the number of footnotes is drastically reduced. Second, "man" and the pronouns "he" and "him" are employed in their general sense to signify the human being, not the male sex, in deference to Nietzsche's own use and because of the absurdity of the contemporary assumption that sexual prejudice can be ameliorated by lapsing into incorrect or incoherent English (as though the author could change his sex from paragraph to paragraph).

THE MASK OF ENLIGHTENMENT

INTRODUCTION: THE MASK OF ENLIGHTENMENT

The title of this book refers in the first instance to the role of rhetoric in the revolutionary movement known as the Enlightenment. Speaking very generally, but not inaccurately, the various versions of the Enlightenment constitute an attempt to free mankind from the superstitions of religion and traditional philosophy, or metaphysics, as well as from the monarchical or aristocratic political and social institutions for which they provide the foundation. As such, the Enlightenment is a radicalization of the sixteenth- and seventeenth-century revolt against ancient thought by modern scientists and philosophers. The symbolic general of the modern army is Descartes, who advocates the mastery of nature by means of mathematical physics and experimental science. In its initial impetus, the modern revolution was forced to employ a rhetoric of accommodation to the dominant religious, philosophical, and even scientific thought it hoped to replace. This accommodation is represented by the expression of the youthful Descartes, who refers in his private papers to his appearance on the philosophical stage as *philosophus larvatus,* the masked philosopher.[1] The mask of enlightenment is thus at first that of a new foundation for traditional doctrines. To take the outstanding example, Descartes disguises the revolutionary implications of his call to mankind to become masters and possessors of nature by advertising his new physics as a foundation for Christian doctrine that is superior to Scholastic metaphysics.[2]

Despite all precautions, one easily detects in Descartes and his fellow revolutionaries an extraordinary confidence in the powers of the new science to transform human existence, with the subsequent postpone-ment if not outright conquest of death. By the end of the eighteenth century, this confidence, although not entirely free of the need to accommodate to local political exigencies, has on the one hand ac-quired more powerful technical tools to implement the revolution, and on the other succeeded in routinizing the seventeenth-century rhetoric of liberation into an ideology shared to one degree or another by the great majority of educated Europeans. By the nineteenth cen-tury a routine of revolutionary optimism is further extended and vul-garized into the doctrine of bourgeois progress. As Nietzsche poses the rhetorical question in *Twilight of the Idols*, "Is not the nineteenth cen-tury, at least in its conclusion, merely a stronger, brutalized eighteenth century, that is to say, a *décadence* century?"[3]

This dissemination and consequent vulgarizing of the revolutionary doctrine carries with it an ongoing revision of the rhetorical stance of its principal spokesmen. In all stages of the modern revolution, how-ever, one factor remains constant. The scientific and philosophical doctrines that are the basis of the rhetoric of freedom and enlighten-ment serve also as a basis for the dissolution of confidence in the solidity, even in the actuality, of the everyday world. The poetical intuition, already explicit in Sophocles and the Hebrew Scripture, of the insubstantiality of human existence, and the philosophical distinc-tion between a genuine world of Ideas or species forms on the one hand and their images in genesis and history on the other, are radical-ized by the new scientific version of classical atomism and the associ-ated distinction between primary and secondary attributes. In the older doctrines of the transience of human affairs and the inferiority of genesis to formal structure (with the exception of the atomistic phys-ics), the forms of pure cognition are the basis for the achievement of value and meaning in human life. Even the escape from the world of images to Platonic Ideas or Aristotelian essences serves to provide significance to the life of the philosophical individual, as well as ends by which to distinguish between noble and base political orders and individual lives. And it goes without saying that the emphasis on the vanity of temporal life by the religious tradition is part of a deeper teaching concerning temporal virtue and eternal salvation. With the advent of modern physics, the situation changes dramatically.

The distinction between primary and secondary attributes reduces not only everyday subjective experience but also the entire religious and philosophical superstructure to the level of an illusion. Genuine Being, in the standard account, consists of matter in the void, or in other words of the primary attributes of the extension, motion, posi-tion, and geometrical shape of particles of matter. We are indeed such stuff as dreams are made on, as Shakespeare puts it, and our little lives are rounded with a sleep. However Shakespeare may have understood this, the immediate implications of the scientific version of the doctrine are clear. Man is not only caught, in the famous expression of Pascal, between the two infinities of the macroscopic and the microscopic; the interval allotted to him is itself an illusion. Even granted the genuineness or independent actuality of extension, motion, position, and geometrical shape, nothing whatsoever follows from this that is pertinent to human life as it is lived, not only by ordinary mortals but also by giants like Descartes and Newton. Whether we speak of the creation of new values or adherence to old traditions, the significance of this discourse evaporates in the reduction effected by mathematical physics. What does not seem to have been clearly perceived by the enthusiastic exponents of scientific revolution is that science itself, as the speech of ghosts, has nothing but ghostly significance. It is absurd to describe a dream life, one that is nothing but an unintelligible epiphenomenon of matter in motion, as an existence rooted in freedom and mastery.

This absurdity is intensified rather than mitigated by the Kantian attempt to fix a domain of freedom and morality in the noumenal domain of "as if," itself a phantom dimension both distinct from and the same as the determinist, Newtonian domain of the phenomenal, which includes the everyday world insofar as it is perceptible and intelligible. On the one hand, Kant is unable to demonstrate that we are free; his maximal claim is that he has cleared a space for the possibility of freedom. On the other hand, this possible freedom must be mysteriously enacted within the determinist domain of the phenomenal, to which not only our bodies but also our faculties of cognition restrict us. As if this were not enough, Kant derives order and intelligibility from a set of faculties, the famous transcendental ego, which is not a separate consciousness, but the conditions for the possibility of perception and cognition under which beings like us must function in a world governed by Newtonian mechanics. Kant makes the dual error of attributing the actualization of order and intelligibility, and so necessity, to the spontaneous activity of our cognitive faculties, and of identifying order on the basis of Newtonian physics, Euclidean geometry, and Aristotelian logic. When these conceptions of order come to be revealed as historical approximations to, rather than as eternal manifestations of, the truth, the priority of spontaneity to eternity becomes a license to construct new mathematics, logics, and physics. The transcendental ego deteriorates into "historical reason," to employ the paradigmatic expression of Dilthey; in the still more radical thought of Nietzsche, doctrines of structure and value are redefined as perspectives or arbitrary interpretations of the perturbations of chaos, not by independent and coherent subjects but by an unstable and continuously dissolving differential of multiple body-egos, to coin a phrase for what is itself only a temporary organization of the accumulation and dissolution of points of force.[4]

From the standpoint of the presumed integrity of ordinary human existence, there is then no difference between the nihilism of modern scientific enlightenment and the radical hermeneutics of postmodernist Nietzscheans. Nietzsche is the point of confluence of two separate but intimately related streams of modern thought, which streams are still plainly visible today in what is called "analytical" and "Continental" philosophy. Both those who believe themselves to be sophisticated computing machines and those who prefer the more romantic terminology of traces of *"différance"* agree in their repudiation of what they call "the myth of the given." Both identify necessity with chance; both liberate contradiction from physical necessity and give priority to the imagination over reason; both speak incoherently of freedom and mastery (or what comes to the same thing, of the free abolition of mastery in a utopia in which everyone is a master and no one is a slave).

What stands between freedom and bondage, or more generally between enlightenment and nihilism, then, is rhetoric. As Nietzsche understands the historical situation in the second half of the nineteenth century, the rhetoric is one of scientific, political, and spiritual progress: This is the initial visage of the mask of enlightenment. But that visage is itself illusory and conceals the deeper grimace of a steady decay into impotence and vulgarity. The rank-ordering of aristocratic virility has been replaced by egalitarianism; the ruthlessness that is the necessary accompaniment of creation has evaporated into liberal sentimentality; science and technology have combined with secular or effeminate Christianity to produce a society of bourgeois philistines. The love of danger gives way to the love of comfort; the desire to overcome is replaced by the pursuit of comfortable satisfaction, both physical and spiritual.

According to Hegel, modern man prays by reading the morning newspaper; Nietzsche fixes at an early stage in his development upon the newspaper and beer as suppressors of the German spirit and later notes the destructive consequences of reading the newspaper in place of morning prayer.[5] The newspaper is a confluence point of the industrialization of technology and the values of the average or even below-average person. When everyone votes or has a political voice, the level of political discussion is lowered, and so necessarily are the standards of general cultivation. The Christian doctrine of salvation is thus replaced by the doctrine of secular or political salvation. The link between democracy and the newspaper is expressed as "the general vulgarization of the European spirit."[6]

These references to the newspaper serve as a symbol of Nietzsche's aristocratic condemnation of the Enlightenment and will suffice for introductory purposes. From this standpoint, Nietzsche advocates the replacement of the globally degenerative consequences of the Enlightenment by a transvaluation of values that is not at all, as the more extreme rhetoric of *Zarathustra* would suggest, a radically new creation of the unique individual but rather a reappropriation of the aristocratic spirit of the archaic Greeks or Renaissance Italians, to give only two examples. As is guaranteed by the doctrine of eternal return, there cannot be a radically unique creation. "Every elevation of the type 'man' was previously the work of an aristocratic society – and so will it always be again."[7] The fundamental task is one of rank-ordering "human types that have always occurred and will always exist."[8] In this context it is important to notice Nietzsche's remarks in the Notebooks of 1880 to the effect that most original thoughts are foolishness and that the Germans suffer from a rage for originality.[9] However various the external forms, the spirit of an aristocratic rank-ordering is always the same: life enhancement or power.[10]

These examples will suffice as indications of the diagnostic stage of Nietzsche's doctrine. They also make evident the impossibility of finding in Nietzsche a basis for democratic egalitarianism or of liberation from the so-called structures of domination of the past. The will to power liberates only in the sense of changing masters. To continue with Nietzsche's diagnosis, whether we call it decadence or nihilism, late-modern European society believes itself to be progressing on all fronts but is in fact steadily declining.[11] Stage two of the doctrine is that this decline must be accelerated. Having exposed the grimace beneath the mask of progress, or, in his own terms, having been the first to state openly and honestly the psychological essence of all human spiritual activity, including philosophy, as well as the chaotic interior of all ostensible order and intelligibility, Nietzsche must now himself assume the mask of revolution. Otherwise put, he shifts from the open visage of historical and psychological analysis to the mask of revolutionary ideology. These are the two fundamental forms of what I called previously Nietzsche's double rhetoric.[12] But there is a further distinction to be drawn between the destructive and creative stages of the revolutionary ideology. In order to destroy, Nietzsche must invoke nihilism; in order to create, he must overcome it.

In a notebook entry dating from 1887, Nietzsche distinguishes between active and passive nihilism. Active nihilism is the maximum of relative force that functions as a "masterful force of *destruction,*" namely, of the passive nihilism that is inseparable from if not identical with decadence.[13] The most intense manifestation of active nihilism is Nietzsche himself, who has transformed the extreme decadence of his own nature into the power by which we may overcome the passive nihilism of the next two hundred years.[14] This point must be emphasized. Nietzsche is in a position to forecast the history of the coming two hundred years because he is "the first complete European nihilist, who has however already lived nihilism to its end in himself."[15] I am reminded of Hegel's observation in the preface to *Lectures on the Philosophy of History* that "the whole is already known by me" and hence can be communicated to his students.[16] Whereas Hegel describes, however, Nietzsche prescribes. "A pessimistic mode of thought and teaching[,] an ecstatic nihilism can possibly be indispensable to the philosopher: as a mighty blow and hammer with which he breaks up denatured and dying races and out of these ways creates, ⟨in order to⟩ make a road for a new order of life, or in order to provide a longing for the end to that which is denatured and dying."[17] The purifying or active nihilism is identified by Nietzsche in a fragment from 1886/87 as the eternal return: "The *value* of such a crisis is that it *purifies.*"[18] And again, the eternal return is "the most extreme form of nihilism; nothingness (the 'meaningless') forever!"[19]

I have now distinguished three stages of Nietzsche's teaching. The first stage is that of honest diagnosis of the decay of the West; Nietzsche speaks here with no other mask than that of the juxtaposition of subtlety and refinement with exaggeration and bombast. The second stage, as I have just sketched it, is revolutionary and consists of two substages, one of destruction and the other of creation, or at least of the prophecy of creation. It is this stage that is characterized by a double rhetoric in which the alternation of subtlety and bombast previously employed for descriptive or analytical purposes is now directed toward persuasion. Otherwise put, Nietzsche employs the same crucial doctrines, will to power and eternal return, in an intrinsically inconsistent manner, corresponding to two distinct ends. First we must be liberated from the past by the active nihilism. Next we must be stimulated to overcome the nihilistic dimension of activism in the creative act of overcoming or transvaluation. The problem is that the second, or creative, substage is already vitiated by the destructive force of the first substage.

"My demand: to bring forth a nature that stands exalted over the total race 'man': and to sacrifice to this goal myself and 'those who are nearest to me.' "[20] This reference to self-sacrifice is an indication that Nietzsche understands the impossibility of the prophet's entering into the promised land. The danger of the entire enterprise is warranted, however, by the destiny into which we have already begun to dissolve.[21] In sum: Nietzsche is the intellectual and spiritual precursor of those twentieth-century forms of terrorism that justify their acts by rejecting the fatal alternative of acquiescence in a corrupt society. As such a precursor, he enlightens us with respect to the inner darkness of the Enlightenment. Nietzsche is inevitably himself a figure of the Enlightenment, but of an Enlightenment that has turned on itself, like the snake that swallows its own tail. The mask of the Enlightenment thus turns out at bottom to be the Enlightenment itself. The instruments of illumination, in the first instance mathematical physics and experimental science, are also the instruments of darkness. Despite his love of the archaic Greeks and his unique celebration of the blending of philology and psychology, Nietzsche is decisively stamped by the same scientific materialism of the nineteenth century that will produce Freud as his intellectual successor.

I want to end this section with a brief remark. It seems to me that a good part of Nietzsche's criticism of the consequences of the Enlightenment is sound. But this is not on my view a sufficient reason to disown the Enlightenment. Not the least of Nietzsche's merits is that his rhetoric serves as an ideological emetic that purifies us of the imperfections of modernity. The risk that modernity will be rejected *tout court* is at least mitigated by Nietzsche's constant recognition of the impossibility of arriving at the past by any route other than that of the future. The danger of Nietzsche's thought does not lie in his conservatism, as many of his most characteristic views would today (erroneously) be labeled, but in his extremely radical appropriation of the mask of enlightenment, which leads the most gifted of those who wear it into the temptation to transform society by overcoming entirely the split between theory and practice.

The Pagan Models: Pindar and Plato

The text we are about to study was regarded by Nietzsche as his most important work.[22] It is written in a peculiar style that evokes the Bible[23] and also the *Thousand and One Nights*. Differently stated, the book does not resemble a Western philosophical treatise, but is a cross between two species of Oriental writings: revelations of a prophet and adventure stories in the form of parables. There is no doubt that the book is by a Westerner or that it deals primarily with Western European civilization. But there is also no doubt that Nietzsche is approaching the theme of the destiny of the West from a standpoint of detachment, in a way reminiscent of Montesquieu's *Persian Letters*. This is a European literary convention: to criticize Europe from the assumed standpoint of an Oriental or outsider.

This peculiarity of the form has an important doctrinal implication. As a Persian and a prophet, Nietzsche claims to view Western civilization from an external and higher perspective. I have referred to this previously as Nietzsche's Hyperboreanism. But Nietzsche does not claim in an unambiguous manner to be a philosopher of transcendent or superhistorical vision. This claim is indeed made in certain texts, published and unpublished during Nietzsche's lifetime, as well as in his correspondence. In *Zarathustra,* however, Nietzsche presents himself, at least initially or on the surface, as outside the philosophical tradition.[24] The first observation required for an understanding of Nietzsche's enterprise is that *Zarathustra* is not primarily a philosophical book, at least not in the usual sense of that expression.

Nietzsche does not present argued doctrines in *Zarathustra*. He is not providing us with a philosophical system as an alternative to the traditional systems of the great Western philosophers. To the contrary, Nietzsche offers us an alternative to philosophy. And yet he cannot do so except as a philosopher. Let me first explain the nature of the alternative. Philosophy is the pursuit of the truth about *phusis;* as an inquiry, it is primarily an activity of discovery, of discovering that which presents itself to, but also that which conceals itself from, our intellect. The activity of discovery cannot be carried out without recourse to production, as is evident from its fundamentally linguistic nature. Languages may be grounded in intellectual perception of eternal structure, but they are themselves historical artifacts by which we are forced to modify our initial perceptions in order to bring them into the domain of discursive reason. Nietzsche insists that the laws of logic, tables of categories, and conceptual schemes are all productions or artifacts that reflect the particular historical perspective embodied in a language, as well as the inflection imposed on that perspective by the individual thinker whose will prepares the structures of order that philosophy supposes itself to discover.[25]

As evidence of this previous contention, I will cite a passage that is of special importance in view of the contemporary tendency to interpret the doctrine of the eternal return on the basis of modern physics. "In fact, everything that can be numbered and conceived is for us worth little: Where one cannot arrive through concepts, that counts for us as 'higher.' Logic and mechanics are applicable only to the *most superficial.*"[26] And yet, even on this extreme hypothesis, the production is oriented toward the discovery of what underlies order. In Nietzsche's teaching, what we discover is chaos or illusion.[27] This discovery justifies us in our productive effort to replace someone else's illusion with our own. In that sense, production continues to be oriented by discovery. But there is a decisive difference between Nietzsche and, say, Platonism. The difference is as follows. The purpose of philosophical production is to make explicit a cosmos that we ourselves have not made, not even in our persona as makers. It is only within the horizon of that cosmos that freedom, spontaneity, and so the creative embellishment of *phusis* take place. In however refined or attenuated a manner, our creations are subordinated to the given.

Nietzsche, on the other hand, in his persona as antiphilosopher, represents the crucial stage in the history of the denial of the primacy of the given. But we have to be precise in stating the nature or content of this denial. The turn toward the primacy of productive activity is conditioned by our "deconstruction" or dissolution of the illusory forms of givenness, of *phusis* or cosmos. To that extent, Nietzsche remains a philosopher of history, and so he continues to be bound by the *phusis* or nature of the illusion itself. Before we can produce, or return to the origin of chaos, we must first destroy the antecedent productions. But the past continues to be the theoretical if not creative paradigm for the future; what we can produce has already been given or produced. As we have already seen, the invocation to the future is at the same time a praise of archaic Greece, Renaissance Italy, or some other historical age. Whereas the past, to repeat an earlier formulation, can only be reached via the future, it is precisely the past that we reach when we enter into the future.

In sum: Nietzsche makes production higher than discovery because production is the expression of energy, life, and growth, and so nobility. Furthermore, the great creator does not "discover" his production by deriving it from his study of past creations, with one crucial exception to which I shall return in a moment. The creator must be viewed both as a force and as a resident within a historical epoch. As a force, the creator is spontaneous. But the spontaneity of this force is necessarily shaped by history in two senses. First, all possible creations have already been produced within the eternal return. Second, the forcefulness or nobility of our creation is obviously conditioned by the historical circumstances within which we live. To take the extreme instance of this second condition, a time of extreme decadence is one of debilitated creative force, and yet it is precisely in such an epoch that the most forceful creation occurs.

This brings me to the aforementioned exception. The philosopher remains free from the deconstruction of the illusion of the history of philosophy (and with it of Western civilization) in the vision or understanding of the entire enterprise by which human beings shape chaos into perspectives.[28] But this freedom is not that of the pure

contemplative. It is a freedom that as it were discharges itself in prophetic activity: in the descent from the mountaintop in order to cultivate a new breed of humanity.

Why must the philosopher descend from the mountaintop? Why
must he create? Nietzsche's answer is as follows: He must create a world
in which to live both as a philosopher and as a citizen. In other words,
what philosophy sees is the whole, the circularity of history (but not, as
in Hegel, the circularity of the concept). But this vision occurs in a
period of maximal decadence, as the conditions of spiritual vision are
deteriorating. The act of creation of a world takes place in the preceding period of decadence, of the self-destruction of the previous world.
It does not take place *ex nihilo*, as in the story about the Christian God.
This is because there are no gods, but only humans. The land of the
Hyperboreans is inaccessible to ordinary human beings, but it is still a
land on the earth, of however isolated or exalted a location. The act of
creation, hence of the lawgiving of the philosopher-prophet, takes
place within the jurisdiction of other laws, inside a world or perspective. The condition for this act of creation is to live simultaneously in
two worlds: the world of decadence and the world of the Hyperboreans. Residence in the world of decadence is thus not simply the precondition for, but is actually the same as, residence in the land of the
Hyperboreans.

It is worth comparing Nietzsche's analysis with the analogous interpretation of human existence by Plato. In the *Statesman* (268d5ff.),
Plato assigns to the Eleatic Stranger the myth of the reversed cosmos.
According to this myth, there are two cosmic cycles, one of them our
own and the other a reversed cycle in which everything, including the
chronology of human existence, moves in the direction opposite to
ours. The shift from the normal to the reversed cycle occurs through
divine mediation when the normal epoch grows decadent and is on
the verge of dissolution. In the epoch of normal existence, where both
political life and philosophy occur, human beings generate sexually,
develop to maturity, support themselves by the sweat of their brows,
age, and die. During this epoch, the cosmos moves on its own, assisted
by a gradually failing memory of its generation by the demiurge. When
the god sees that the cosmos is about to dissolve, he leaves his divine
lookout, takes up the helm of the cosmos, and guides it backward in a
cycle of rejuvenation. During this cycle, humans spring up as old men
from the earth, grow young, and return to the soil. There are no sexual
generation, no political life, no work, and obviously no philosophy.
Eros is not present in the reversed cycle. Otherwise stated, rejuvenation
depends on forgetting rather than on recollecting.

I note here only the most relevant points in the Platonic myth.

Human existence in the usual sense of the term is independent of divine intervention. Political life and philosophy are special types of human labor of which the prototype is sexual reproduction. But this independent existence brings with it old age and dissolution; freedom, as it were, can be preserved only by its periodic surrender to divine governance. All human beings, and not the Hyperborean philosophers alone, exist in both cycles, which represent two simultaneous phases of human existence. The philosopher or prophet is distinguished from the multitude by the ability to remember both cycles; in so doing, he encompasses the eternal return of the same, or, more precisely, of the same and the different. Recollection is thus the Platonic version of the transcendence of history. It is also the horizon or limitation on the creation of new worlds or the opening of new perspectives.

For Plato, decadence is the ground or condition of renewal. Nietzsche radicalizes renewal by equating it with origination, which is transferred from the level of the divine or cosmic to that of human existence.[29] The dialectic of recollecting and forgetting continues to be present, but in a way that differs from Platonism. Apollo is the symbol of recollection and Dionysus of forgetting. Apollo is the god of the Hyperboreans and represents philosophical lucidity as well as the comprehensive vision of the continuously circling sun. But Dionysus is also pagan and represents the destructive force of the forgetfulness induced by intoxication, rather than the Christian doctrine of creation *ex nihilo*. The famous death of God refers to the deity of the Judeo-Christian tradition, not to his pagan predecessors, who in fact eternally recur, regardless of the presence or absence of the rival God.

The pagan nature of Apollo and Dionysus makes manifest a fundamental problem in understanding Nietzsche. Are we to view his paganism as religious or philosophical? Is the intoxicated and destructive frenzy of Dionysus also to be understood as the positive force of creation? Zarathustra never mentions Dionysus by name. How are we to understand his assertion that he who would create must first destroy? Creation is a power of the Judeo-Christian God; Plato's cosmic demiurge devises the heavenly motions from the eternally enduring sameness and difference. Otherwise put, the demiurge does not create the Platonic Ideas. On this point, Nietzsche transfers to mankind the power assigned by the Judeo-Christian tradition to God. In so doing, however, he also reinvokes the pagan deities, thereby blurring the difference between Athens and Jerusalem, but without endorsing the institutions of Christian Rome. Is it for Nietzsche a part of what Plato assigns to forgetting that we must believe ourselves capable of radical creation, of creation *ex nihilo*, even though the creator God is dead? Is this death the condition of our own deification, or a premise in the rhetorical consolation of the human, all too human, by the resident of the land of the Hyperboreans?

There is of course no such land as that of the Hyperboreans. Their story is a myth about certain extremely decadent individuals who transform their dissolute spiritual residence into the land of the Hyperboreans by virtue of their comprehensive understanding of decadence. This is the basis for a philosophical myth of epoch-making proportions. The myth is that of a creator who is produced by the spiritual institutions of his time; but these institutions affect his peculiar spiritual energy in such a way as to liberate him, to transform him into a destroyer. On this understanding, creation turns out to be a noble lie, or a salutary interpretation of the eternal return of the same. Nevertheless, as salutary, it has a certain liberating power: the power to represent the old as the new. Whereas it may be true that reproduction is disguised as production, it is also true that the disguise, which Nietzsche often refers to as "art," is worth more than the truth as a stimulus to life.[30]

Creation is also destruction. And both creation and destruction are productive rather than acquisitive or discovering activities. Those who simply theorize or contemplate the cosmos are in fact reacting to the creations of others: They discover their own bondage, not their mastery. All of this being so, it is a serious error to look for traditional philosophical doctrines in Nietzsche. *Zarathustra* contains no ontology, no epistemology, no ethics. At the same time, there is no *Kunstlermeta- physik*, no aesthetical metaphysics or philosophy of creativity.[31] Nietzsche teaches simply that the plasticity of genesis, and so the illusory nature of natural and historical world orders, is evident from the possibility of willing them away. We can obey the Nietzschean imperative (taken from Pindar) "Become what thou art" only by becoming what we will ourselves to be. We must understand the submissiveness of previous creations to the will, and thereupon we must determine who we are by deciding who we will be.

Thus far I have emphasized those elements of Nietzsche's teaching that are associated with his invocation to creation or overcoming. It would, however, be a serious mistake to assume that Nietzsche is nothing but a philosopher, or, if you prefer, an anti-philosopher, of liberation. This is already evident in his appropriation of the motto from Pindar. Nietzsche indicates his disagreement with paganism, or his own view of the priority of production to discovery, by editing Pindar's assertion "Become what thou art through understanding."[32] Zarathustra tells us merely to "become what thou art," thereby implying that we must fulfill ourselves through the overcoming of our humanity by an act of will rather than intellect. On the other hand, to be told that we must become what we are is to remain within the orbit of the pagan doctrine of nature. As Alexandre Kojève puts the point in his commentary on Hegel's *Phenomenology*, the Christian ideal is "Become what thou art not."[33] The Christian doctrine of salvation is one of rebirth in a transformed nature. Nietzsche's doctrine of salvation, despite its explicit appeal to the Christian doctrine of transformation, or to the notion of the overcoming of nature by the supernatural, is pagan rather than Christian. The ascent to the superman is not an ascent to the supernatural, and not an overcoming of, but a return to, nature. It should be added immediately that "nature" in Nietzsche represents an amalgam of pre-Socratic doctrines of *kinēsis* and modern scientific doctrines of force (*Kraft*).

The limitation on the concept of creation is already evident in the necessary finitude of the eternal return. In a complicated sense that I have already mentioned, the appeal to the eternal return is in the service of a repudiation of eternity and a comprehensive affirmation of historical existence. There is obviously some truth to the assertion that the eternal return is an existential imperative;[34] but it is also true that this understanding of the doctrine fails to do justice to its cosmological role as an interpretation of nature.[35] Expressed in terms of natural science, the eternal return is the regular pulsation or fluctuation between the expansion and contraction of the physical universe.[36] Expressed in metaphysical or philosophical terms, there are a finite number of human types and associated stages of historico-political existence. Strictly speaking, there is not only no unending creativity or radical uniqueness, there is no creation at all. Creation is the illusory or phenomenal manifestation of the actual or noumenal fluctuations of chaos (i.e., intrinsically random motions of points of force, or of what are today called energy distributions).[37]

The Christian Paradigm

Despite Nietzsche's paganism, one can easily identify the substantive influence of Christianity in his thought, by way of German Idealism and, more specifically, Kantianism. This can be brought out by a citation from Karl Löwith's book on Nietzsche. Löwith states the contradiction in the doctrine of the eternal return as one between the expression of completeness and the invocation to a decision. Löwith claims that Nietzsche attempts to overcome this contradiction through the identification of his own will to overcome with the self-willing of the heavenly or natural world in an ecstatic *Einklang* (harmony) that anticipates and culminates in madness, a madness in which Nietzsche identifies himself as God.[38] I cite the opening lines from Nietzsche's last letter to his former colleague at Basel, Jakob Burckhardt, dated 6

January 1889: "Dear Professor, In the last analysis I would rather be a Basel professor than God, but I have never dared to indulge my private egoism so far as to abstain for its sake from the creation of the world."

Without denying the fact of Nietzsche's madness, it has to be said that this is not a useful basis for interpreting a philosophical teaching. If the teaching is a consequence of, or culminates necessarily in, madness, then it is hardly worth taking seriously, except perhaps by psychoanalysts. I myself believe that we can take Nietzsche's statement to Burckhardt with complete literalness as the inner meaning of *Zarathustra*. Nietzsche genuinely believed himself to have created the world of the future – in other words, the world as it would be understood by the coming generation of his disciples. This belief is compatible with Nietzsche's paganism, because if Being is Becoming, or in other words if rest is the limit state of motion, and so merely an unusually slow motion, then everything is changing, war is the father of all things, and human existence is nothing but a series of transient interpretations of chaos. Order is just a tentative concatenation of points of force, one that can be retained through an act of will. The instrument for the enactment of will is not philosophical argumentation or scientific discovery but prophetic rhetoric.

It is entirely erroneous therefore to attempt to analyze the inner conceptual structure of the doctrine of the eternal return as if it were a complex and harmonious set of rational arguments, whether philosophical or scientific.[39] This is not to say that the expression does not summarize a series of doctrines. But the doctrines are of two distinct levels or directed toward two distinct stages in Nietzsche's revolutionary program. The difference between the two levels is both manifested by and concealed through Nietzsche's double rhetoric. On the one hand, he must persuade us to jettison all forms of Platonism and its vulgar equivalent, Christianity, according to which the source of value lies in eternity or heaven, and thereby to be courageous enough to create a new table of values by which we repudiate the nihilistic decay in which the European tradition has sunk. On the other hand, the shift in the locus of value from heaven to earth, or from eternity to history, is understood by Nietzsche to require on his part an affirmation of all of earthly or historical existence. If any part of actual human existence is repudiated, a space is opened for "Idealism": in other words, for dreams about what might have been or ought to be, and so in effect for a return to the traditional dualism between imperfect or valueless human existence and a transhistorical utopia like that of Plato's hyperuranian *topos* or the Christian heaven.

As a consequence, in order to prevent his own prophetic invocation to the coming generation of supermen from being understood as a utopian appeal to transhistorical Idealism, Nietzsche is forced to insist on the historical actuality of the future. The overcoming of mankind is not a dream of the future but a retrospective prophecy of what has already occurred an infinity of times. We can become supermen because we have already become supermen an endless number of times in the past. Otherwise stated, the superman is not an ideal, but the fulfillment of human existence at its best, and has been achieved to one degree or another by a variety of previous historical epochs, including that of archaic Greece, the Scandinavia of the Vikings, and the Italian Renaissance of the artist-warriors. At the same time, Nietzsche knows that we cannot simply sit still while awaiting the inevitable coming of the superman. Just as the chance of chaos looks like necessity to the mathematical physicist, so the inevitable rotation of the circle of history looks like creative initiation to the warrior-artists who embody the essence of noble and vital ages. We must be moved to act; but what is required to make us act, that is, to assume responsibility for our own lives, amounts both to the equation of value with life and the denial that life, in its generalized form of historical becoming, has any value at all.[40]

In sum, it has become evident that there is a serious ambiguity in Nietzsche with respect to the status of eternity. The repudiation of Platonism and the turn toward temporality is not sufficient to count as a decisive repudiation of eternity. Nietzsche's philosophical vision of totality retains a Platonist tinge; his interpretation of totality as the eternal return, however, is Christian rather than Platonist because it temporalizes formal structure. Nietzsche's eternity, for which Zarathustra plaintively declares his love and which he identifies as the only woman by whom he wishes to have children, is not simply the stimulus of fecundity, as in Plato's *Symposium*. It is itself the emergence process of creative acts.

As such, however, Being is Becoming, and Becoming is innocent; it is neither good nor bad. We can impose on its random motions whatever value we will. Creation, when viewed *sub specie aeternitatis*, is indistinguishable from chaos. Cosmological nihilism is therefore the precondition for the conquest of historical nihilism. But this means that cosmological nihilism is the inner truth of the illusion of human existence; this is why Nietzsche says that, for life, art is worth more than the truth. What I may regard as my own creation of value in the form of the superman is in fact chaos or the accumulation and discharge of points of force, just as in the philosophical interpretation of modern physics, reality consists of primary attributes like figure, motion, and number, whereas human existence consists of subjective secondary attributes that have no existence independent of our own self-deluding interpretations.

One can therefore say that Nietzsche's doctrine is intrinsically incoherent, but it is so because of his coherent perception of the nature of things, not because of an inner confusion or madness. Nietzsche is forced to lie for the sake of the salvation of humanity from the noble nihilism of the unmitigated truth. His problem is rendered more complex by the fact that he is also forced to tell the truth in order to clear away the rubble of a dying tradition that is carrying humanity inexorably into the long night of base nihilism.

This is the basis for penetrating the double rhetoric employed by Nietzsche in writing *Zarathustra.* It is also the basis for relating the pagan and Christian paradigms in Nietzsche's thought. But by making this relation, we note a lacuna in the analogy between the doctrine and its paradigms. The pagan model corresponds to the descriptive or analytical aspect of Nietzsche's teaching, whereas the Christian model corresponds to its creative aspect. But there is no paradigm for the destructive element. This element is the genuinely original part of Nietzsche's teaching, and by "original" I do not intend to be flattering. Nietzsche's originality is also the cause of his extraordinary danger.[41]

To come back to *Zarathustra,* the particular chapters of the work are critical commentaries on aspects of European civilization. But the work as a whole is itself an illusion: the illusion that Nietzsche is in fact Zarathustra, a Persian and the founder of the epoch of good and evil. Zarathustra comes down from the mountaintop to destroy what he has himself created. Those who dwell within the chapters or episodes are thus finally figments of his imagination or will. That is, since Zarathustra is himself a mask for Nietzsche, the author assumes in writing this book that he has himself created Western European civilization: He takes full responsibility for it, or enacts what he calls elsewhere *amor fati.* In words taken from *Zarathustra,* he says: "Was that life? Well then, once again!" In order to liberate himself from the totality of Western civilization, Nietzsche must assume full responsibility for it, must accept it *in toto;* he must will it to be *once more,* which is the actual implication of each act of epochal creation, because each such act starts the next cycle of the eternal return instead of allowing things to run down into chaos.

Nietzsche's Platonism consists in his acceptance of the myth of the reversed cosmos. His anti-Platonism consists in a new interpretation of that myth and, more precisely, in a new interpretation of recollecting and forgetting. In the sense just indicated, Nietzsche provides us with a new interpretation of the noble lie. This, I believe, is what Nietzsche means when he refers to himself as the first honest philosopher. His honesty consists in the revelation of the superiority of falsehood to truth. And yet, in order to deliver this revelation, he must speak the truth.[42] As an antiphilosopher, Nietzsche is forced to remain a philosopher. In so putting the point, however, I have already gone beyond the boundaries of *Zarathustra,* which, despite its appearance of excessive frankness, differs from all other Nietzschean texts in the degree to which it is an exercise in concealment. It is the only work by Nietzsche in which he does not speak in his own name but, like Plato, conceals himself behind the mask of a dramatic hero. This is enough to suggest to us the degree to which the interpretation of *Zarathustra* is an exercise in rhetorical subtlety.[43]

The Structure of the Work

In addition to emphasizing the greatness of *Zarathustra* with respect both to its content and its literary style, Nietzsche also predicted that it would take many generations before the work was understood.[44] This praise notwithstanding, questions have been raised, in particular by Heidegger, as to the status of *Zarathustra* in Nietzsche's writings.[45] Heidegger cites the following passage from a letter to Overbeck, dated from April 1884, in which Nietzsche says: "I have now resolved to devote the next five years to the working out of my 'philosophy,' for which I have built an entrance hall (*Vorhalle*) via my Zarathustra."[46] An analogous statement occurs three years later, in a letter to Carl Fuchs dated 14 December 1887: "My entire 'up-to-now' is to be laid to rest ... Now when I must go beyond to a new and higher form, I need above all a new estrangement (*Entfremdung*), a new separation from human beings (*Entpersönlichkeit*) ..." and so on.[47]

There is no necessary contradiction between the two sets of texts. Nietzsche could well have regarded *Zarathustra* as the greatest of all his works, precisely because it offers to mankind an entrance into the final and stylistically quite different formulation of his philosophy. One could perhaps compare the relation between Nietzsche's unfinished final statement and *Zarathustra* to that of a detailed commentary on the Bible to the Bible itself, a commentary written by God in his capacity as philosopher rather than as prophet. As Nietzsche writes in his Notebooks in 1883: "It is not enough to bring a teaching: One must also transform mankind by force, in order that they accept the teaching! – Zarathustra finally understands this."[48] The word "finally" is very important here; I will gloss it by citing some passages from the Notebooks that discuss the structure of *Zarathustra.*

In 1881 Nietzsche made the following sketch of the structure of the four books (called "parts" in the published version) of *Zarathustra.*[49]

Book One: "Chaos sive natura: 'of the dehumanization of nature.' "
The expression *chaos sive natura* refers to Spinoza's *deus sive natura;*
Nietzsche replaces "God" by "chaos." But Part One also refers to
Nietzsche himself, to his spiritual existence. In a letter to Overbeck
dated 10 February 1883, Nietzsche says of Part One, which he wrote in
ten days, that "it contains with the greatest precision a picture of my
nature, how it is, as soon as I have discarded my entire burden. It is a
poem and not a collection of aphorisms."[50] In other words, Nietzsche
presents Zarathustra in Part One as freed of the burden of preparation,
as the exuberant prophet who sings his teaching of self-overcoming
but who has not yet completed the process for himself or understood
the resistance of those to whom he preaches. The reference to dehumanization means that there is a certain frankness in Part One that
makes it unacceptable to its audience. To say the same thing in another
way, Zarathustra is singing to himself in Part One; he has not yet
adopted the rhetoric of accommodation that is essential for every
successful prophet. I should add that it will remain a problem whether
Zarathustra ever manages to make contact with human beings in the
later parts. But the problem does not arise in Part One, which contains
the full impetus of the energy accumulated by Zarathustra during his
ten years on the mountaintop.

Coming back to the sketch of 1881, Nietzsche says of Part Two:
"Fleeting – skeptical – mephistophelian . . . about the corporealizing of
experiences." In this part, Zarathustra will come into closer contact
with human existence; the enthusiasm of Part One is tempered by a
lower perspective, namely, that of the body.[51] To cite only the most
important example, the fact of death is overcome in Part One by the
purity and innocence of Zarathustra, whereas in Part Two Zarathustra
will indicate through the interpretation of dreams that death presents
an inner limitation in the doctrine of self-overcoming. Part Three, says
Nietzsche, "is the most interior of all that I have thus far written; it
hovers over the heavens: 'of the last happiness of the solitary.' "

In a sense, the work ends with Part Three; in it, Zarathustra replaces
God, who is said in Genesis to hover over the waters prior to the
creation of the world. Nietzsche shows in this part something analogous to what Hegel says of his *Logic,* namely, that it contains the
exhibition of God's nature (and so the thinking of his thoughts) as it
is prior to the creation.[52] But the thinking is that of humanity, not
God; Nietzsche says in a letter of 3 September 1883 to Köselitz, "In the
third part, poor Zarathustra really sinks into gloom – so much so that
Schopenhauer and Leopardi appear to be merely beginners and nov-
ices in comparison with his 'pessimism.' "[53] The last happiness of the
solitary is thus equated with the deepest gloom and pessimism.

In the earlier fragment, Nietzsche says finally of Part Four: "Dithyrambically comprehensive, Annulus aeternitatis."[54] So, on this account, Part Four is the poetic exterior that binds together the whole like the ring of eternity that binds together the eternal return of the same. It should also be noted that Part Four was not originally intended for general publication; forty copies were printed for distribution to friends "and with every degree of discretion."[55] On 8 January 1888, Nietzsche writes to Brandes that Part Four is "an *ineditum* of mine that belongs to the most personal of which I am capable."[56] One might conjecture that Part Four adds nothing to the substance of the first three parts but contains the final integration of Nietzsche's teaching with his self-comprehension. I believe that this conjecture is mistaken; as we shall see at the appropriate point, Part Four expresses Nietzsche's need to overcome pity for the higher man, and so for himself, an overcoming that is effected by a strange blending of cynicism and rhetorical exaltation.

In a note from 1883, slightly later than the one previously cited, Nietzsche says that Part Three shows Zarathustra's self-overcoming as a model for the self-overcoming of mankind. "For this the overcoming of morality is necessary."[57] This is at a lower level than the description of 1881, but it is consistent with the general account, according to which Part Three takes us back to a higher level than Part Two, but without the innocence or initial creative impetus of Part One. As to Part Four, Nietzsche now says that Zarathustra dies when he sees the pain of his friends. "But after his death, his spirit comes over them."[58] How does this square with the assertion that Zarathustra finally understands the need to transform mankind by force, so that it will receive his teaching? I believe that there is a note of deep ambiguity here. In 1881, the force is anticipated as the creation *ex nihilo* or its revision as a reshaping of chaos. He who would create must first destroy. In 1883, on the other hand, creation is replaced by death; Zarathustra destroys himself in the process of destroying the old civilization and its tablets of commandments. Zarathustra returns to his friends as a spirit, but we are not told of the consequences. This is in keeping with the 1883 letter in which the earlier reference to happiness is replaced with a statement of gloom and pessimism.

With this in mind, I may suggest that Nietzsche initially presented his thought in personal terms but that by 1884 he came to see the need for a new and different statement of his "philosophy"; this in no way requires us to attribute to him a new philosophy, one with a content that differs radically from the teaching of *Zarathustra*. This new statement requires both self-transcendence and self-comprehension. It seems evident that Nietzsche came to see his own spiritual existence as the exemplification of his discursive teaching, and furthermore that this exemplification is both a success and a failure. As I shall contend, the success of philosophical revolution is necessarily a failure, since success depends upon vulgarizing the original doctrine. This is true not simply of Nietzsche but of all philosophical revolutions. From this standpoint, my study of Nietzsche is intended as a very detailed exemplification of a general philosophical thesis.

I close this introduction with a preliminary remark concerning the title. Nietzsche himself points out that the style of *Zarathustra* imitates Luther's translation of the Bible, and the title clearly identifies the book as a collection of speeches by a prophet. But Zarathustra is neither a Jew nor a Greek. Not only is he antecedent to the Western religious tradition, but there is no subordination of Zarathustra to a creator god. There are discussions of the debility and even death of the Judeo-Christian God, as well as metaphorical appearances of pagan gods, but there are no appearances of gods in their proper personae in this prophetic work. Zarathustra is himself neither a man nor a god; he is the prophet of the superman but not himself a superman. Zarathustra has no fixed identity; he is an indeterminate human being, somewhere between a man and a superman. We can tentatively identify him as a personification of the human spirit in its effort to overcome. This effort is incompatible with belief in a god, as Zarathustra will make explicit.

The imitation, or rather parody, of the Bible is thus a single element in the constitution of the work as a whole, the significance of which is to do away with religion as the Bible understands that phenomenon. Gods are repudiated because they would restrict man's overcoming; but *Zarathustra* is not a celebration of humanism, because man is something to be overcome. It is easy and even tempting to say that Nietzsche intended to found a new religion of which Zarathustra is the prophet, but I believe that this is finally an error. It remains to be seen whether Nietzsche himself committed that error. If we take him at his best, however, by which I mean on the basis of his most daring and consistent formulations, Nietzsche abolishes religion as a restriction on the creativity of life, which is itself a euphemism or noble lie that stands for the fluctuations of chaos.

The subtitle of *Zarathustra* is *A Book for All and None*. The book is for all, because it is directed to the human race, or, more modestly, to the European representatives of humanity. It is a rhetorical attack on Christianity, an attempt to make a new race of human beings and in particular a new type of philosopher (the philosopher of the future). But it is also for none, because no one is ready to understand, let alone to accept, Nietzsche's teaching. He has to prepare his audience, and this requires a double rhetoric: One kind is needed to accelerate the destruction of already decaying European civilization, in other words to clear the ground of rubble in order to make possible an act of radical creation; another kind is needed to produce artists of the requisite degree of creative strength. Nietzsche's central problem is already visible. It is possible to produce disciples who are instruments of destruction, but no rhetoric will suffice to create the superman. The most Nietzsche can accomplish is to prophesy the coming of the superman; the danger is that this prophecy will itself result in the production of disciples who are phantasms or simulacra of the superman and who in fact make impossible his coming.[59]

It is the duality of Nietzsche's intentions, I believe, that accounts for the strange mixture of excessive clarity, platitudinous incantation, and even rabble-rousing on the one hand, and extreme refinement, subtlety, and concealment beneath veils of allegory on the other. In my opinion, too much has been made of the mysteriousness, intoxicated obscurity, and inaccessibility to rational explanation of *Zarathustra*. Nietzsche himself encourages this kind of attitude by his account of the inspired circumstances under which he composed the work. At the same time, his *Nachlass* reveals how carefully he revised his manuscripts, and we would do well to refrain from appealing to ineffable inspiration or impenetrable obscurity whenever discursive analysis is possible.[60]

In sum: The title and language direct us toward religious analogues, thereby insulating Nietzsche from the charge that he is a littérateur rather than a philosopher. As I have already suggested, he is the founding father and the greatest exemplar of what has come to be known as the postmodernist stance. Yet Zarathustra is curiously Hegelian in his teaching that God is dead and that the structure of intelligibility is the eternal return of the same.[61] Perhaps we can say that, as a first approach, the book is best understood as a philosophical meditation and a political document. As a philosophical meditation, it is a critical commentary on the history of European culture; as a political text, it is an incitement to revolution, to the overthrowing of the old order and so to the preparation for a new order. This new order is not described in any detail, but it is evoked: We can infer some of its general characteristics from Nietzsche's criticism of the old order. It is an order of existential types, or what Nietzsche calls a *Rangordnung*, and not an order of laws and institutions.

Let me finally emphasize that as the first and best postmodernist, Nietzsche exemplifies the reappropriation of the Western philosophical tradition, not in the manner of the historian or polymath, but as an artist of the deepest refinement. The previous remark about the reminiscence of Hegel can be repeated with a preparatory observation about Nietzsche's assimilation of Plato. As will become obvious, the descent of Zarathustra is like the descent of the philosopher into the cave in Plato's *Republic*. The *Republic* begins with Socrates describing how "I went down yesterday to the Piraeus." Socrates goes down to found a city ruled by philosophers, which Nietzsche takes as the underlying theme of Western European civilization, with the intrinsic complication that the exoteric version of Platonism replaces philosophers with priests. In this light, it is doubly significant that Nietzsche's doctrine of the eternal return is reminiscent of the Hegelian doctrine of the perpetual recurrence or circularity of the fully developed Concept. Nietzsche thus "recuperates" (in the contemporary jargon) the history of European philosophy. In both the beginning and the end of that history, the circularity of history is the recurrence of all possible philosophical positions, or what Nietzsche might call comprehensive perspectives, fundamental tables of values.

In Hegel, the internal excitation of chaos or negativity organizes itself to produce the totality of genesis, or Becoming. In Nietzsche, chaos organizes itself into perspectives or worlds, which also recur perpetually. In Hegel, the central difficulty is to explain how God and man, or the eternal and the temporal, coincide. How can the finite consciousness, or self-consciousness, coincide with the Absolute while retaining its finite self-identity? In Nietzsche, there is a similar problem. The free spirit or philosopher of the future must become a radical creator and a new type of human being. In order to do so, however, he must learn that subjectivity and self-consciousness are illusory projections or perspectives of the underlying "Absolute," often called "will to power" but at bottom chaos. In Hegel, the solution to the problem results in an identity of finite and infinite as the truth of totality. In Nietzsche, however, there seems to be no solution, since the truth of chaos cancels the significance of each finite creation or perspective.

In sum: Zarathustra is a "younger and stronger" representation of Nietzsche himself[62] as the prophet of a new doctrine, or rather of a new version of an old doctrine, that of the philosophical lawgiver or revolutionary founder of a new order. As Nietzsche writes to Overbeck on 22 October 1883, "In the reading of Teichmüller I am ever more transfixed with wonder at how little I know Plato, and *how much* Zarathustra *platonizei*."[63] By 1884, Nietzsche is ready to put Zarathustra to one side and prepare a new version of his philosophy in which he speaks directly: "Resolve: I want to speak, and no more Zarathustra."[64]

THE PREFACE

The Holy Man

Part One begins with a long preface that sets the stage for the entire work. The major themes of Nietzsche's teaching are introduced in a series of connected dramatic episodes that illustrate Zarathustra's destiny as prophet of the death of God and the coming of the superman. A careful analysis of this preface gives us a coherent view of the inner unity of what appear in the sequel to be discontinuous meditations, revelations, and dreamlike events. We are thereby prepared for the subsequent peripeties in Zarathustra's prophetic career, peripeties that arise from the misunderstandings engendered by its very success.

We first encounter the prophet in his thirtieth year: the age of Christ as his mission comes to fulfillment (11).[1] But Zarathustra does not attempt to save mankind at the age of thirty. Instead, he goes up to the mountaintop for ten years of additional ripening.[2] The work begins effectively when Zarathustra is forty; as a classical scholar, Nietzsche would have known that the Greeks regarded forty as the peak of human life. Greek culture, which is represented obliquely in the opening passage as the sun or Apollo, is required in order to overcome Christian decadence.

Zarathustra goes up in order to prepare himself for his descent. The way up is not the same as the way down; one must be different and riper in order to descend successfully. Bear in mind that Zarathustra's descent will not be successful, in the obvious sense that it is too soon for the revolution to triumph. But it can be successful in the task of introducing the revolutionary doctrine: of initiating the process by which decadence is accelerated. Next, the ascent from the lowlands to the mountaintop is a rising "beyond good and evil," but not beyond good and bad. It is a rising above the leveling, or herd morality, of modern Christian Europe. The level terrain stands for the levelers or egalitarians, those who deny what is noble.[3]

Zarathustra spends ten years enjoying his *Geist*, which I will translate as spirit, and which must be distinguished from soul, or *Seele*. Normally, *Geist* refers to the general life force, whereas *Seele* designates the personality of the individual.[4] Nothing is said about thinking or talking during these ten years, which in itself does not mean that none occurred. But enjoyment, "basking in the sun," is not the same as discursive thinking. Zarathustra is being refreshed, storing up his energy. *Geist* is broader than *nous*, or intellect, and includes what Plato calls Eros. The soul loves the Ideas, but the intellect sees them; it is the eye of the soul. The soul must be open to the vision of the intellect, which it can also influence and guide. In Nietzschean terms, the *Geist* must be rejuvenated by a creative reappropriation of Greek nobility. Zarathustra enjoys his spirit and his solitude. The enjoyment of spirit is not that of civilized intercourse, conversation, or *Bildung*. It is a turning inward and, through that turning, a return to nature.

"Finally, however, his heart changed": his *heart*, not his spirit. The heart stands for love and pity for mankind, to which Zarathustra will frequently refer. But that is not the way in which he puts it initially; here he says that he is "distressed" or "burdened" by his wisdom, which he needs to share with, to distribute among, human beings. This is an expression of his own need, not of his desire to benefit mankind, which is derived from the creative impulse rather than defining it. Zarathustra compares his wisdom to bee's honey; he gathers this wisdom from the sun by instinct or nature, not by intention or for moral ends. The point is clarified by his remark to the sun: "What would thy happiness be if thou hadst no one to illuminate?"[5]

Natural forces require to act, and so to spill over, to act on what is outside themselves. This is often called the will to power. Note that the effect of the will to power need not be destructive; it can be invigorating or fructifying. But this has nothing to do with benevolence or morality. In Nietzschean terms: Power cannot be exerted without subjects or witnesses.

As far as we are informed, this is the first speech addressed by Zarathustra to the sun during his ten-year sojourn on the mountaintop. In fact, the speech is not the initiation of a conversation; Zarathustra is talking to himself in the presence of the sun. This is a fundamental characteristic of Zarathustra as we know him: However silent he may have been prior to the opening of Nietzsche's account, and despite his continued sense of solitude or loneliness, Zarathustra cannot keep silent. On the contrary, he is marked by an excessive garrulity that corresponds to his excess of pent-up energy. Speech is the medium of Zarathustra's action. This action is initiated by the cumulative effect of the sun, which, as the recreative power of nature, is like Socrates' Idea of the Good. But Zarathustra's sun is nature itself, not *epekeina tēs ousias* (beyond Being). It is moving, changing, repeating itself by manifesting its inner diversity (which has a limit of some sort).

Also, by speaking to the sun, Zarathustra presents an interpretation of nature, just as Nietzsche does by writing his book. Speech does not here create the sun, but explains it, and in particular, it explains Zarathustra's relation to the sun. This explanation is an *Auslegung*, an interpretation and so a perspective, albeit a comprehensive perspective on what is real in itself or for human beings everywhere, waiting to be interpreted, namely, nature. It is the sun to which Zarathustra speaks, not to the moon or the stars. Speech to the moon or the stars would carry an altogether different significance and fail to convey Nietzsche's authorial intentions, which are the basis for all valid interpretations. There is, after all, despite the intrinsic chaos of things, some natural order that is the basis for intelligibility; and this must guide our production of perspectives as well as our interpretations. Interpretations are various, but they are not completely arbitrary.

A small but important point: Zarathustra addresses the sun as *du*. He is on terms of intimacy with it. Intimacy with nature replaces intimacy with a personal God. The happiness of the sun requires it to have beings that it illuminates. This is also true of Zarathustra. Compare here Aristophanes' *Birds:* The gods are nourished by feeding on the smoke of human sacrifices. Hence Zarathustra emphasizes the fact that the sun has risen to his cave for ten years; it has come up to him. The image is one of anthropocentrism rather than heliocentrism. Zarathustra gives the sun its significance. This expresses very well Nietzsche's synthesis of ancients and moderns, or the peculiarly modern way in which he attempts to return to the early Greeks. Nietzsche advocates a return to nature, but from a human perspective. For this reason the pagan gods, and in particular Apollo the sun god, are useful to Nietzsche as the *deus absconditus,* or transnatural God, of the Judeo-Christian tradition is not.

The return to nature is artificial; it is required in order to restore humanity to health. If we can return to nature, it cannot be simply as Greeks; we return as moderns. So the imitation of the Greeks is as it were restricted to the abstract fact of return. The Greeks do not return to nature; they are *there.* Hence, in returning, we are unlike the Greeks on the very point on which we attempt to imitate them. The upshot is that Nietzsche is not advocating a genuine return to antiquity. He directs man to the future, not to the past. But we can move forward in a healthy manner only by adapting to our own situation something fundamentally pagan. The ostensible return to nature is the destruction of Christianity (and so too Platonism) in order to come back into contact with nature in the sense of the will to power, the source of creativity and the sense of nobility.

The sun would have become fatigued with its light and with the trip to Zarathustra's cave, "without me, my eagle, and my snake." Animals play a crucial role in this work. The eagle soars high in the sky, and the snake crawls on the surface of the earth. The eagle exhibits strength and cruel nobility; the snake exhibits cunning and deceit (as in the Garden of Eden). The animals are associated with Zarathustra, not with the sun. It is obvious enough that they are metaphors for human attributes, but this is only part of their significance. Animals are not human, but natural; they do not construct themselves. Zarathustra will refer later to man as the not yet completely constructed animal. But the eagle and the snake are completely constructed; they are not open interpretations of human attributes, but natural paradigms. As such, however, they are also deficient; their very specificity makes it impossible for them to overcome what they represent, and so they will never fully understand Zarathustra. In sum: The animals, precisely as Zarathustra's favored companions, express his loneliness and inability to make genuine contact with human beings.

In this context, we should consider Machiavelli, *The Prince*, Chapter 18, and Chiron, the centaur who is said to have tutored Achilles. According to Machiavelli, who is one of Nietzsche's two favorite authors (Thucydides is the other),[6] a prince has to know how to use the natures of both beast and man (as was taught covertly by the ancients). Zarathustra and his animals receive the overflow of the sun's light and bless the sun for it; this is part of the reinterpretation of Christianity. "Look! I am weary of my wisdom, like the bees who have gathered too much honey; I require hands that stretch out" (i.e., toward me). Presumably the animals had some role in the production of Zarathustra's wisdom; at least they shared in the reception of the sunlight. But it is Zarathustra, not the eagle or the snake, who is weary of his wisdom. Animals do not possess wisdom and cannot be wearied by it. This is equivalent to my previous statement that animals are incapable of self-overcoming. Wisdom is a property of human *incompleteness* because it is active or productive. Wisdom is here the creative projection of new values; but it is also the contemplation of the eternal return.

The bees stand for instinctive productivity rather than for contemplation; the doctrine of the eternal return is not yet explicit, although it is present implicitly in the circular orbit of the sun. Honey is made by bees via a natural process; the sweetness of honey represents the happiness of creativity. But this happiness fatigues us and becomes cloying if we do not share it or use it to transform others and so to make them happy as well. This process of bringing happiness to others is undertaken as an expression of a natural process or will to power, not because of moral principles. But the hands of human beings must stretch out to receive the honey, or wisdom. And as we shall soon see, this does not occur naturally. Hence the necessity for the rhetoric of revolution.

To this one must add immediately that the happiness of honey, or in other words of the hive or (in human terms) the people (*Volk*), is not the same as the happiness of the creative individual. Honey cloys in excess; it becomes the happiness discovered by the last men (19). In Part Four, Zarathustra will make it explicit that he is concerned with his work, not with happiness. The eudaimonism of classical Greek philosophy is replaced by a radicalized version of Hegelian satisfaction (*Befriedigung*), that is to say, by the repudiation of personal happiness for the sake of world-historical construction.

"I should like to give away and distribute": Whereas Heidegger speaks of the "gift of Being," Zarathustra refers to his own gift; he thereby indicates a more radical version of Heidegger's own assertion in *Being and Time* that without man there is no Being.[7] Heidegger, however, restores the priority of Being to human thinking in his later work. For the later Heidegger, Being completes man within each epoch; for Nietzsche, man completes Being in each epoch. Zarathustra's gift is a transvaluation of values: The result of his gift is that "the wise among men will once more be happy in their foolishness and the poor once more in their wealth." In other words, Zarathustra is playing with Christian expressions but gives them a quite different meaning. "Foolishness" is here the overcoming or destruction of traditional wisdom; hence, it is becoming poor but thereby rich because no longer impoverished by the decadent wisdom of modern secularized Christianity.

"Therefore I must ascend into the depths" (*in die Tiefe steigen*). This is a striking expression. *Steigen* means to climb, ascend, mount a horse, and so on. By going down the mountain into the valley, into the city of the Motley Cow, Zarathustra will be ascending into the depths; compare here the Biblical expression *de profundis clamavi*. Mankind calls out of the depths to God for salvation, which Zarathustra will offer in the absence of God. In so doing, he will become the spiritual equivalent to the sun, which also ascends into the depths and goes down to illuminate the cities of mankind. "I must, like thee, go under, as human beings call it" (12): The sun does not call it anything. Zarathustra both is and is not a human being; he is an anticipation of the superman, or philosopher of the future. He can "go under" only because he is already up above; he is not a genuine resident of the depths below. Also: His going under is an exit from the cave, whereas Socrates goes down into the cave. Zarathustra brings the sunlight into the city; Socrates locates the sunlight up beyond the city.

"So bless me then, thou resting eye that can see without envy even an all too great happiness!" Yahweh and the Christian God are both jealous; they will not allow mankind to worship other gods, and they also deny wisdom to human beings. One thinks here of Aristotle, who contradicts the Greek poets by saying that God does not begrudge wisdom to human beings.[8] Nietzsche is thus not simply returning to Greek poetry, which on this point is, so to speak, Judeo-Christian. To say this in another way, the association with the sun is intelligible only as one between Zarathustra and Apollo. Nietzsche cannot be understood simply as a worshiper of Dionysus, who is not even mentioned in *Zarathustra*. Apollo is the god of wisdom and lucidity; Dionysus is the god of intoxication and creativity. For human beings, to be submerged in the wisdom of sunlight is to share in the sun's bliss (*Wonne*).

In the last statement of the first section of the Preface, Zarathustra wishes once more to empty himself of his wisdom and thereby to become a human being again. The sun cannot do this. Zarathustra is an intermediate creature, a spirit that can become a man, and so a replacement for Christ. With all due respect to the pagan gods, they cannot overcome the separation between the human and the divine. Nietzsche's values are expressed by pagan gods, but his revolutionary activity is expressed by Christian metaphors. This point is contained in Nietzsche's famous invocation of "Caesar with the soul of Christ" in a fragment of 1884,[9] as well as in *The Genealogy of Morals,* where he says that a creative *Geist* will redeem reality by plunging into it.[10]

In the second section, Zarathustra begins his descent. He meets no one between the mountaintop and the forest. This is the distance between him and other living beings. In the forest he comes upon an old hermit, who stands for the Christian holy man. The hermit has left the city but cannot emerge from the obscurity of the forest into the clearing that leads up to the sunlight. This indicates the mixed status of Christianity: It is by no means simply bad, because in its original impetus it expressed the will to power of Jesus, the attempt to raise mankind upward. In *The Gay Science* Nietzsche praises the religious men and points out that the struggle against the church is one of superficial against profounder natures.[11] The point is developed in *Beyond Good and Evil,* in which Nietzsche condemns the modern scholar as an arrogant dwarf and vulgarian compared with the religious man he looks down upon.[12]

The holy man recognizes Zarathustra from the time of the latter's ascent. It is of some importance that Zarathustra is well known even to those whom he seems to be encountering for the first time. Zarathustra stands for creativity, but not for the uniqueness with which his twentieth-century disciples so frequently credit him. The teaching of overcoming or creativity is not unique or original; if anything, it has grown stale through repetition. Nietzsche's tactical problem is precisely how to rejuvenate the doctrine of creativity that underlies every expression of human greatness but that becomes decadent and even common through the very act of publication.

According to the holy man, Zarathustra has changed since their last encounter: "Then thou carried thy ash to the mountain; willst thou today carry thy fire into the valleys?" Zarathustra left the city ten years ago, burned out by his experience among human beings. This image confirms my previous comment about Zarathustra's notoriety. Neither Zarathustra's doctrine nor Nietzsche's mode of presentation is radically new. Just as Zarathustra comes and goes throughout the four parts of Nietzsche's text, so he has come and gone previously and will come and go in the future; this is demanded by the doctrine of the eternal return. What is "unique" is the particular situation of the present moment, as contrasted with the particular structure of previous moments on the circle of history. At this moment, the doctrine of uniqueness will serve a rhetorical function that it could not fulfill in other moments.

This is because of the difference between historical and cosmological time. There are finite historical epochs on the unendingly rotating circle of temporality; it is obviously a mistake to equate the infinite points of temporality with the finite forms of human history. The present form of human history is penultimate in the sense that it closes the historical, but not the cosmological, circle. Within this historical epoch, all fundamental human types have been manifested, exactly as Hegel claimed. This makes it possible for the emergence of Nietzsche, who has incorporated all of these types into his own soul and therefore understands the comprehensive truth about human nature and historicity: "I want to live through all of history in my own person and make all power and force my own."[13] But if the closed circle of fundamental human types has been fulfilled, then it is time to begin again. If Nietzsche were to translate his determinism, or *amor fati,* into the domain of historical prophecy, the next stage would be identified as the repetition of a particular antecedent within the sum of historical types. But this would make revolution or human action superfluous; indeed, impossible. Hence the rhetorical appeal to uniqueness, which means nothing more than that we do not know and cannot prophesy what form the next manifestation of human history will take.

The hermit understands very well the essentially negative content of Zarathustra's doctrine, which he compares to the activity of the arsonist. Zarathustra is recharged by the sun, but his ostensible gift or creative act is to spread the sun's fire through the habitations of European society. There can be no positive doctrine, since this would result in disciples, not in unique or creative supermen. The residents of the cities of the plain, represented by the city of the Motley Cow, are therefore right to fear innovation as a destructive force. Zarathustra's eye is pure, and no disgust hides in his mouth. He sees neither good nor evil, nor has he come to judge or condemn mankind, but instead to transform men with the free gift of his wisdom. But this gift cannot be offered, and certainly not accepted, without the destruction of the existing civilization: In order to create, one must first destroy. So this defines the rhetorical problem of the work. Zarathustra is in fact not going to save the people to whom he presents his teaching, but rather their descendants or successors. He brings a clear-eyed, noncondemnatory message of destruction to his immediate audience.

The hermit then asks: "Does he not walk like a dancer?" I take this in a double sense. Zarathustra is of course spiritually graceful, and he leaps from peak to peak without building intermediate bridges of dialectic or argumentation.[14] But the dance is also a form of deception. It is designed to charm his audience by masking the heaviness of the body with a veil of music.[15] In a slightly different image, Zarathustra has become a child, one who is awake among the sleepers: "What are you doing among the sleepers?" This continues the same theme. To be a child is to be purified and so to exemplify the principle of a new cycle. Zarathustra will himself make this very point in the first speech of Part One. Sleep stands for decadence. On the other hand, a child cannot practice the rhetorical cunning required for the project to succeed. The only weapon against decadence is philosophy, and this weapon functions only in the case of philosophers. If Zarathustra is in fact a child, then his failure is indicated in advance.

The holy man continues: Zarathustra lived in his solitude as in the sea, and now he wishes to step up on land: "Woe! thou willst drag thy body thyself?" The sea represents genesis, the source of life. The land is the home of already existing life, the civilization that requires to be dissolved once more by the sea. But dancing will not be possible on this land; Zarathustra will have to drag his body around. He cannot swim or float; that is to say, he cannot walk on the water. He must become like the land-dwellers in order to converse with them. The holy man is no doubt speaking here from the bitterness of his own experience. He himself was forced to drag his body around in the city, whereas he had wished to be a pure spirit: Hence his retreat to the forest.

Zarathustra replies: "I love mankind."[16] This is an apparently simple but in fact ambiguous statement. To begin with, it recalls Christ, who so loved mankind that he died for human sins. But Zarathustra's love has no divine reference above himself, as does the love of Christ. Is Zarathustra's love Platonic rather than Christian? Platonic Eros is directed toward the Ideas: Man is only an occasion for this love. Whatever Nietzsche's agreement with Plato, there are no Platonic Ideas in *Zarathustra*. We will see later that love is for Zarathustra a euphemism for the will to power. From this standpoint, mankind is only an occasion for Zarathustra also, just as in the case of the Platonic Eros. We can see the inner relation between Nietzsche and Plato, all question of the Platonic Ideas to one side, as follows. In the *Symposium* (210d3 – e1), Eros leads to the production of beautiful speeches in the light of the beautiful. Zarathustra's "Eros" is for the production of beautiful human beings in the light of beautiful speeches. In this decisive sense, Nietzsche, very far from opposing logocentrism, shares the implicit Idealism of late-modern philosophies of language.

The holy man replies: "Why did I go into the forest and the desert?" What desert? This is the first mention of it. How can a forest also be a desert? In this sense: The trees conceal from the holy man their own intermediate function as a pathway up to Zarathustra's cave or down to the city. The holy man is lost, or trapped, in a solitude that is quite different from that experienced by Zarathustra on the mountaintop. Even though he lives in the forest, as a failed Christian he is not in touch with nature. The desert is in his heart, despite his love for God, the holy ghost. The hermit loved man too much; "now I love God; I do not love mankind. Man is to me too incomplete a thing. Love for man would destroy me." Zarathustra will later state that man is the not yet completed animal. What is for him the condition of creativity is for the holy man the condition for destruction. Love of God leads to the loss of creative power.

As if corrected by this speech, Zarathustra replies: "What did I say of love! I bring mankind a gift." Zarathustra's "love" is in fact the need to overflow, to fecundate, to transform. It is the expression of a natural force, and in that sense the will to power. It is not Christian because,

entirely apart from the question of God, it is not personal. But it is also
not genuinely Platonic because of the absence of the Ideas. On the
other hand, the Ideas have a *dunamis* to attract human beings and thus
to lead them to generate. So too Zarathustra represents here, or is
rather himself the medium of, a higher power, one that comes from
above. But finally, the "above" lies within man's own nature. Man is the
aperture, shaped by chaos, through which the will to power flows from
chaos into the shape of a world.

Let me restate this crucial point: Being is Becoming, and Becoming
is intrinsically chaos. There is no permanence except for the recurrence of perspectives or worlds, the so-called eternal return. This
means that although one can speak of fate or necessity in the sense of
the recurrence of finite worlds, human existence as a whole is radically
contingent and finally without meaning. Mankind is just one of the
possible outcomes of the random collocation of matter or force. But
once formed, mankind itself becomes a producer. This is our nature;
we are incomplete or chaotic, but also partly complete, shaped by
chaos itself as a productive animal. Hence to create is also to transmit
the virus of chaos; whatever comes into being must decay and die.
Traditional philosophy is a false inference from the appearance of the
stability in creation. This means that traditional philosophy is bad art.
Good art is an illusion that enhances life and keeps us fecund for as
long as possible. The highest illusion is not just the creation of a world,
but the promulgation of the teaching of creativity. In this way, one
identifies with the will to power or the force of chaos itself, which is
both destruction and creation. In sum: The presentation of a gift to
humanity is the exhibition of one's own divinity.

It is important to be clear at the outset that despite this criticism of
traditional philosophy, Nietzsche regarded himself as a philosopher
and never subordinated genuine philosophical thought to art. In June
of 1878, Nietzsche writes to his friend Carl Fuchs with respect to
Human, All Too Human: "Now I attempt to pursue wisdom itself and to
be myself a philosopher; previously I honored the philosophers."[17]
Ten years later, toward the end of his productive life, he writes in *The
Case of Wagner:* "What does a philosopher demand first and last from
himself? To overcome his time; to become 'timeless' . . . I am as well as
Wagner a child of this time, that is to say a décadent, except that I
defended myself against the concept and against myself. The philosopher in me defended himself against it."[18] When Nietzsche writes that
art is worth more than the truth,[19] he is referring to art as a stimulus
to life.[20] As a work of political rhetoric, *Zarathustra* is a work of art; as
the expression of Nietzsche's understanding of human existence, it is
a work of philosophy.[21] The same distinction holds with respect to

Zarathustra's assertions of love. The content or vision embodied in the gift is Apollonian; the gift as act is Dionysian.

The holy man is opposed to giving anything to mankind; he recommends instead that Zarathustra take something from it, that is, take away part of the burden of human existence by sharing it as did Christ, who died for the sins of mankind. Suddenly his mood shifts and he becomes very bitter: "And wouldst thou give them anything, give nothing more than alms; and let them beg for it!" In other words, treat them as they treated me! The holy man's love has been transformed into a desire for vengeance; more precisely, into an extension of the desire for vengeance against life that led the priests to invent the Christian God in the first place. But Zarathustra refuses to give alms; he is not poor enough. He lacks the Christian poverty of spirit that is on the one hand humility but on the other vengeance or ressentiment.

In a characteristically rapid shift of mood, the holy man laughs. He lacks inner stability. Or, perhaps more accurately, he is upset by the arrival of Zarathustra, who is no doubt the first person he has conversed with for some time. Zarathustra's mission, as well as his appearance, has upset the holy man: Those who are disillusioned resent people with strong hopes. The old man warns Zarathustra of the suspicious nature of human beings and in particular of their mistrust of hermits and those who walk the streets during the night. They do not want the customary order to be altered. Nighttime signifies for hermits the solitude in which they approach mankind, but for mankind it represents a time of danger, from which they must hide in their beds.

"Do not go to human beings, but stay in the forest. Go rather to the beasts! Why dost thou not want to be like me, – a bear among bears, a bird among birds?" An eagle is a bird, but a special type, a king among birds. The holy man generalizes this into the multitude. The cunning of the serpent is replaced by the lumbering strength of the bear, who is known for hibernating during winter. The holy man does not speak of "his" animals, but rather of himself as an animal. Zarathustra is protected from this degeneration by his link to the sun. This distinction leads us to a general observation about the geographical setting of the opening scene of the Preface.

The forest is between the mountaintop and the city in the plain. It is a place of half-light, whether from the sun or the moon and stars. The inhabitant is a holy man who represents not Christianity but the decay of Christianity. Zarathustra has been living in the open sunlight, alone on a mountaintop with his animals. He talks both to the animals and to the sun, but not to human beings. Zarathustra is outside human existence when on his mountaintop. But he is not outside nature. His conversations with nature, in its animate and inanimate forms, are evidently a part of his preparation for bringing a gift to mankind. In general, Nietzsche does not "repudiate" nature on behalf of art, convention, or history. To the contrary, he attempts to strip nature of philosophical, scientific, and artistic interpretations, to return to nature or to bring mankind back to nature as the source of vision, boldness, power, cunning.[22]

The forest is the place for failed prophets. I regard it as a symbol of Nietzsche's criticism of the Enlightenment as it exists in the nineteenth century; consider again the previously quoted passage "Is not the nineteenth century, at least in its conclusion, merely a stronger, brutalized eighteenth century, that is to say, a *décadence* century?"[23] The age of illumination is in fact an age of obfuscation, half-light, and loss of faith, a dissolution of the fictions that are needed for human existence, and hence too not a discovery or mastery of nature but a loss of nature. In other words: Nature is represented accurately for the higher purposes of civilization, not by mathematical science but by the animals of human fables. Whereas it is true that all accounts of nature are perspectives or interpretations, and so that the animals are as much an interpretation as is mathematical science, there is a difference between life-enhancing and life-diminishing interpretations.

The forest is a transitional or intermediate zone. One may arrive in the forest from the mountaintop or the city; conversely, one may emerge from the forest either by going up or going down. And contrary to Heraclitus, the way up is not the same as the way down. Furthermore, as a transitional zone, the forest represents the stage through which civilized mankind – the residents of the city – must pass in order to reach the mountaintop, just as Zarathustra passed through the forest ten years ago. In other words, decadence is the necessary precondition for an understanding of the truth of the human situation, for philosophy, and so for the preparation of the gift to mankind: "No one is free to be a crab. There is no help for it: One must go forward, I mean *step by step farther into décadence* (this *my* definition of modern 'progress' . . .)."[24]

One cannot move directly from the city to the mountaintop. But there is no evidence that the entire population of the city can move from the city into the forest and so up to the mountaintop. This can be accomplished only by individual prophets, whether failed prophets like the holy man or potentially successful prophets like Zarathustra. And this means that the residents of the city would have to be converted, that is, to accept Zarathustra's gift, while remaining in the city. Their conversion would thus be an accommodation to, or a vulgarization of, the truth. Truth is for prophets or lawgivers, not for the multitude of mankind. The forest is a boundary between the city and the sun.

The significance of the forest is further developed in the next exchange. Zarathustra asks the old man: "And what does the holy man do in the forest?" He does not ask: "What are *you* doing in the forest?" This is a generic question. The holy man replies: "I make songs and sing them, and when I make songs, I laugh, cry, and *brumme*," that is, grumble, mutter or buzz like a fly, hum like an insect. Here are three modalities of nonarticulate expression: laughing, crying, humming. So the songs have no words, no lyrics. They are like the half-light of the forest, an attempt to articulate or to speak that succeeds only in expressing a mood or emotion. And they also prepare us for the humming of the last men, or of what awaits us in the event of the failure of Nietzsche's philosophical revolution.

This emotive noise of laughing and crying is self-negating: Laughing and crying cancel each other, and the result is humming or buzzing: "Thus I praise God." This is important. The disillusionment with mankind is not a complete abandonment of God. We should take this together with the fact that there are animals in the forest as well as the holy man. If something should happen to render articulate the holy man's songs, if he could communicate with his animals as Zarathustra does with his, then the holy man would be revitalized and could emerge from the forest. Note also that he praises the god "who is my God." Nietzsche is a polytheist in the pagan sense; whether the holy man understands the full significance of his words is unclear. But *his* God is too weak to get him out of the forest.

The impetus for the holy man to emerge from the forest must come from the mountaintop. Hence he asks Zarathustra: "What hast thou brought us as a gift?" *Us:* for me and for my God. We need a gift of your strength in order to emerge from the twilight zone of the forest. "When Zarathustra had heard these words, he saluted the holy man and spoke: 'What would I have to give you! But let me leave quickly, so that I take nothing from you!' And so they separated from one another, the old man and the younger one, laughing, just as two boys laugh" (13–14). Zarathustra cannot give anything to the holy man; he can only rob him of his twilight contentment. Why is this? In other words: Zarathustra is heading into the city in order to bring a gift, to transform mankind by a transvaluation of values. Why doesn't he start with the holy man? This is connected to the inarticulate singing of the holy man. We have to consider separately the conversation between the holy man and Zarathustra and the decadent prophet's songs to his God.

The conversation is part of the dramatic representation of the distinction between decadent and healthy prophets. The description of the singing, on the other hand, is a representation of decadence itself. In this light the request by the holy man for a gift in no way stands for the recognition that Zarathustra is a potential savior. It shows the childishness of the holy man, his senility. It is true that both men, the *Greis* and the *Mann,* as Nietzsche distinguishes between them, laugh like boys. But this means something different in the two cases. The holy man is a "boy" in the sense that he is senile; Zarathustra is a "boy" in the sense that he brings renewal of life. He is at the beginning of his descent from the mountaintop. But this does not exclude the certainty that he will become decadent during his sojourn among human beings.

At a more general level, Zarathustra cannot save the holy man or reinvigorate him, because the latter is a spokesman for a false god. The holy man is not mankind, nor is he the exceptional individual who has passed through the forest and up to the mountaintop by his own efforts. He is the detritus of the failed attempt by mankind to transcend itself. Hence he must be bypassed; Zarathustra must convert the people, that is, mankind as it lives and acts in the city. This is extremely important: The city, and neither the mountaintop nor the forest, is the place for the renewal of mankind. This renewal is political; it is not a matter for multitudinous individual prophets or unique creative individuals, as so many of Nietzsche's twentieth-century disciples have assumed.

The section concludes as follows: "When Zarathustra was alone he spoke to his heart, 'Can it be possible? This old saint has not heard in his forest that God is dead!'–" I remind the reader of Nietzsche's terminological distinctions: *Geist, Seele, Herz.* "Heart" involves emotions, concern for others; here, a certain pity for the old saint. On the death of God, one should also consult *The Gay Science*, section 125.[25] This book was published in 1882, the year before the first two parts of *Zarathustra*. The holy man has presumably not heard that *his* God is dead. But is it correct to say that all gods are dead? In other words, how can Zarathustra bring a divine revelation if there is no god to sustain it? Heidegger cites Hölderlin to make the point that "the gods have flown away from this parlous epoch." He reiterates that we must await the coming of a new god. But it is not at all clear that Zarathustra announces the coming of a new god. At the same time, his doctrine could not be called humanism, as I noted above. I suggest that nature is the replacement for this or that god; nature is the source of gods, it is the divine, exactly as for the early Greeks. Hence the importance of Apollo and Dionysus for Nietzsche.

Theoretical Preparation for the Rope-Dancer

Zarathustra leaves the holy man and arrives at the city nearest to the forest. The city is on the edge of the twilight that marks the period between historical cycles in the eternal return of the same. Now the question arises: What is the exact relation of the city and the forest? This question cannot be answered until we study the speeches and deeds of the residents of the city. By way of orientation, it is already apparent that the forest is a kind of ghostly emanation of the city and that the holy man who dwells within it represents the old age of Christianity in nineteenth-century Europe. The holy man's ignorance concerning the death of God should not be taken to mean that Nietzsche's critique of Christianity is novel, or that cultivated Europeans require the revelation of Zarathustra in order to be informed of their spiritual condition. This is historically and dramatically false. Despite Nietzsche's solitary existence during his creative years and the initial neglect of his works by the educated public, it did not take long for him to become a cult figure among the European intelligentsia.[26] Zarathustra's message is received enthusiastically by an ever-increasing number of advanced thinkers and artists because it corresponds to the contemporary spiritual situation and seems to provide a way of reversing it.

Stated with greater precision, Zarathustra's message corresponds to the inner disorientation and spiritual emptiness of the political dissemination of the conquest of nature and the associated rise of industrial bourgeois society that is the dominant heritage of the Enlightenment. At the same time, his message is sufficiently general to appeal to the most diverse manifestations of dissatisfaction, even to those who believe themselves to be representatives of the Enlightenment rather than its opponents. Nietzsche speaks to the needs of the left as well as the right, to revolutionaries and counterrevolutionaries alike. The common denominator of Nietzsche's diverse audiences is a perception of the decadence of Christianity and the steadily increasing irrelevance of the traditional culture associated with it. The holy man is a generalized figure who represents the effect of this perception on Christianity. He both knows and does not know, or is unable to sustain coherently his knowledge of, the fate of Christianity. The dreamlike character of the residents of the city is partly explained by their spiritual schizophrenia: Their souls are already lost in the twilight of the forest. They rise up like phantoms in Zarathustra's path, but there is no genuine encounter or dialogue.

But this is not the whole story. Part of the message of *Zarathustra* is that prophets are not only misunderstood in their own time, but that they must themselves misunderstand their own time. Zarathustra does not understand until after his speeches and adventures that he has come too soon. And in fact, prophets must come too soon. This is what it means to be a prophet: to deliver a teaching about the future that will not be correctly understood by the present. A part of Nietzsche's teaching from the outset, as distinguished from the gradual development of Zarathustra's self-consciousness, is just this mutual misunderstanding. When judged from the highest standpoint, every revolutionary success is a failure. The philosophical equivalent to the terror of the French Revolution is the mutual destruction of Nietzsche's disciples.

The prophet sees the future within the present; that is, he sees the present as the future. And this means that he does not see the present as the present. Instead he comes to see the present as the past. I mean by this that he understands the present *qua* present only retrospectively, after it has rejected him. Hence the partial detachment of the prophet from his own time, his lack of "realism" or "common sense," his strangeness, but also his charismatic appeal to certain imaginative individuals, who are themselves partially detached from the present but sufficiently attached to it to be able to set to work to carry out the prophet's teaching. At the same time, the force of the imagination that leads to partial detachment is political and social alienation, which in turn makes impossible a realistic or sensible modification of existing conditions. The prophet is the voice of doom addressing those who are doomed to intensify the chaos they seek to avoid. This by way of anticipation. Let us now continue with the Preface.

Zarathustra finds a multitude of the people (*Volk*) gathered in the public square, "for it had been promised that a rope-dancer would be seen" (14). The holy man is a personification of the *Geist* of the people of the city. The rope-dancer is a step down from the level of the holy man but still above the people themselves, who look up to watch his skilled and daring performance. The difference between the holy man and the rope-dancer is best stated as follows: The rope-dancer entertains the people, whereas the holy man bores them. The holy man loved the people too much; that is, he expected too much from them. But they disappointed him, and so he went into the solitude of the forest. The people want a secular expression of their inner state. One's first inclination is to regard the rope-dancer as an expression of *panem et circenses*. But this should not be understood in an entirely vulgar way. Rope-dancing represents the cleverness and daring of the late-modern spirit as it balances over an abyss. This is not the peak of spiritual refinement, but there is something to be admired here.

The rope-dancer is the popular understanding of the superman.

The balance of the section is devoted to Zarathustra's announcement of the coming of the superman, or, more precisely, to his invocation to mankind to overcome itself. His audience initiates the process of misunderstanding, partly anticipated by the holy man, with which Zarathustra will be received. They assume that he is announcing the approaching performance of the rope-dancer.

Zarathustra begins with great directness and emphasis: "*I teach you about the superman.* Man is something that ought to be overcome." The use of the plural *Übermenschen* shows that Zarathustra is not prophesying the coming of a single superior being, but a new human type. And his prophecy is not a prediction, but an invocation; man *ought* (*soll*) to be overcome. This is our first solid indication that the overcoming is not necessary, not something that will follow automatically or as the next stage of the eternal return. As in the case of all famous prophecies, we have to do something in order to make it come true. And this will be one of the hardest points of Nietzsche's own doctrine. How are we to reconcile the appeal to human choice, hence to our freedom to decide the future, with the *amor fati,* or doctrine of necessity, intrinsic to the doctrine of the eternal return? Note that the same problem was intrinsic to Marxism, which attempted to persuade mankind to enact historical necessity.[27] Both Marx and Nietzsche are materialists who uphold the thesis that life is an epiphenomenon of motion. Does this thesis entail necessity? Only if one claims that knowledge of the laws of motion is possible. According to modern physics, the laws are mathematical. For Marxism, the laws of physics are themselves dialectical. What is Nietzsche's contention?

The sciences to which Nietzsche regularly appeals are psychology, physiology, physics, and philology. Psychology and physiology can be reduced to physics, but philology cannot. Philology is the science of the interpretation of life as it is lived, and so of life as an illusion or work of art. If human beings reduce in their variety to some finite number of distinct types, then it is possible to claim that there is a set of rules that may be inferred from the behavior of these half-dozen types, rules by which to interpret all interpretations or perspectives. These rules are scientific, but they are not rules of physics. They cannot be mathematicized. Even if we ignore Nietzsche's later statements that mathematics, physics, and logic are all themselves interpretations, there is a fundamental dualism in the scientific attitude that corresponds to a diremption or dualism in materialism itself. Physics (or mathematics) and philology are the irreducible sciences of the whole, as we could express this point.

Suffice it to say that we must be on the alert from the outset for the evocative or rhetorical nature of Zarathustra's prophecy. Despite all talk of fate and necessity, despite all denial of subjectivity and the integrity of the ego, we have to do something that can only be done by subjects or integral egos. But this does not entail the conclusion that there is a fundamental difference between *Zarathustra* and Nietzsche's late teaching. The key points in Nietzsche's later writings, published and unpublished, are all to be found in *Zarathustra*.[28] What I will call for convenience the doctrine of will to power, which is grounded in the interpretation of Becoming as a random self-modification of chaos, is for Nietzsche both necessity and freedom. Chaos is not only the inner truth of subjectivity; it is also the precondition for the freedom of the postsubject, or superman. But a postsubject is not the comprehensive negation of the subject, any more than postmodernism is a comprehensive negation of modernity. Nietzsche requires a new doctrine of what is called subjectivity in modern philosophy, and this helps to explain why he wishes to return to the Pre-Socratics. The superman is as much an ancient as a postmodern. But he is not a spiritual cipher. Nietzsche's account of human beings, in other words, cannot be understood simply as a description of the perturbations on the surface of chaos.

"Man is a rope tied between beast and superman – a rope over an abyss." The rope-dancer is not the rope; he is the dancer on the rope, or the spirit of late-modern European man. I begin my interpretation of this famous image with a further remark about postmodernism. This expression can be understood as an interpretation of the result of the performance by the rope-dancer. If the rope-dancer reaches the correct end of the rope, he is transformed into the spirit of a superman, and the rope is itself transformed. If he goes backward to the opposite end, he becomes the spirit of a beast. But he can also fall from the rope and break his neck, as is about to happen in the continuation of the text. And there is a fourth possibility: The rope-dancer can remain poised approximately in the middle of the rope. This is, I believe, our historical situation today. The advocates of postmodernism repudiate the aristocratic and Platonist nature of the superman; but they refuse to identify themselves with the last men. The result is an impossible attempt to combine uniqueness and creativity with the emancipation of the late-modern mob.

The rope-dancer represents the desire to excel, to surpass, to overcome (*überwinden*). "Every being thus far has created something that goes beyond itself." This may sound initially like social Darwinism. In fact, Nietzsche criticizes Darwin by denying that the fittest, in the sense of the highest human types, always survive.[29] For Nietzsche, nature is extravagant, cruel, and wasteful of superior types.[30] There is no natural guarantee that the higher type will survive. The desire to overcome is usually thwarted or corrupted. This is why he says, "Das überwunden werden soll" ("That ought to be overcome"). Man must act against the thoughtless extravagance and wastefulness of nature in order to overcome himself, even though the desire to overcome is natural in the sense of being an expression of force, of the will to power. In other words, Nietzsche's criticism of the wastefulness of nature is based on his aristocratic values, or on a quite different interpretation of nature from that of Darwin. The coincidence of cruelty and extravagance with spiritual excellence is reflected in the squandering of higher human types by the profligate violence of nature.

This line of analysis reveals an ambiguity in Nietzsche's account of overcoming. It is not enough to overcome; one ought to overcome in the right way. Since life is continuous change, existence is always the replacement of one form by another; but not all these forms are expressions of the highest rank-ordering. Once again we see Nietzsche's inconsistent attempt to appeal to freedom in the interstices of necessity or (what amounts to the same thing) chance. We can attempt to make his doctrine coherent as follows. Nietzsche's call to action is not the same as his theoretical understanding of human existence. Thought occurs at Nietzsche's level, in the understanding of the natural process. What Nietzsche understands, however, is that the natural order is contingent, continuously being created and recreated, or that there is no natural order, but only the process of spontaneous production. Nature provides us with the raw materials, in the crucial instance with ourselves as beings who strive to overcome.

This brings us to the delicate point. We must supply the interpretation of the raw materials of nature. Yet this interpretation is not purely spontaneous or ungrounded in natural processes. In order for Nietzsche's doctrine to preserve a minimal coherence, it is essential that the aristocratic conception of value be made to coincide as closely as possible with the existential consequences of chaotic perturbation. The intended link between these two aspects of Nietzsche's teaching is the will to power. By "will" Nietzsche is not referring to a psychological faculty; we recall that the ego or subject is for him an illusion, and so too must be the human faculty of the will. On the other hand, the will is not an ontological concept; there is no *logos* of chaos, and all structure is itself a consequence of the will to power, not its ground or explanation.

Nietzsche's problem is now easily stated. Whereas it is plausible to maintain that the high and the noble must exercise power in order to preserve its ascendancy over the low and the base, the mere exercise of power is an insufficient criterion by which to distinguish the high and the noble from the low and the base. This is directly visible in the extravagance of nature, which often brings it about that lower versions of overcoming predominate over higher forms; it is visible in particular in the imminent threat of the last men. Nietzsche associates spiritual weakness with the debasement of aristocratic values, but it does not follow from this that the accumulation of power will suffice to reinstate those values in a purified form. The striking failure of Nietzsche's thought is that although it is dedicated to rank-ordering and the reinstitution of aristocratic values, nowhere in his writings, published or unpublished, is there any satisfactory analysis of the concept of value. Nietzsche justifies his rank-ordering by example: by powerful rhetorical appeals to the will to power that ostensibly animates the high and noble expressions of the human spirit and in that way exhibits them as manifestations of cosmic forces.

Nietzsche could of course reply that there is no noncircular analysis of value, or that one cannot demonstrate the high and the noble but only affirm it. And this is precisely what he often does, disdaining argument as a kind of shopkeeper's device for masking philistine tastes. But this kind of invocation to spiritual refinement is itself subject to corruption in the mouth of the vulgar, who also speak of the will to power. At one extreme, Nietzsche personifies the modern repudiation of the salutary rhetoric of the ancients, who also understood that no arguments can be advanced to generate nonexistent spiritual refinement, but who offered instead one version or another of compromise with human nature. At the other extreme, Nietzsche himself engages in salutary rhetoric, and never more so than when he seems to be most candid. By shouting his demands for refinement, he provides us with the paradoxical spectacle of a man who attempts to destroy vulgarity by recourse to a rhetoric of vulgarity. I do not mean by this that Nietzsche is always vulgar, but it is the bombast of Zarathustra on which Nietzsche relies to destroy the restrictions on the profound subtlety and exquisite refinement that he reveals in his private voice.[31]

To come back to the text, everything overcomes itself; man is a being that "ought" to be overcome. Comprehensive overcoming is thus an illusion that obscures the surface of comprehensive change. Whether or not it can be explained ontologically, Nietzsche demands that we guide this change in keeping with our highest aspirations. Since very few of those whom he addresses are capable of the highest aspirations, Nietzsche assigns to Zarathustra a vulgar account of subtlety. This explains what I have already called the bombastic style of the book, which is a direct consequence of Nietzsche's revolutionary intentions, as well as of his own distinction between the "happy few" and the unhappy many. Yet it is a further peculiarity of the work we are studying that Nietzsche reveals within it his own recognition of the inevitable failure of his intended revolution.

The few must take the appropriate action to insure their survival. This is not a kind of selfish disregard for the welfare of the multitude. To the contrary, the many will also benefit from the overcoming of mankind or the coming of the superman by participating in the nobility of the new order to be established by the few. This is very similar to Hegel's contention that the many, or the nonphilosophical, will share in the Absolute by way of the laws and institutions of the state.[32] This constitutes a difference between antiquity and modernity, or (let us say for greater specificity) between Plato and Hegel. In Plato, there is a sharp difference between the guardians (that is, the philosopher-kings and warriors) and the class of workers and farmers. The lowest part of the soul can never be reconciled with the two higher parts; it can only be ruled by them. This rule is fundamentally one of restraint. Differently put, it is impossible for the workers to participate in the higher functions of the best city. Thus they are not subject to the peculiar institutions of the upper classes, such as the possession of women and children in common, and they do not receive the same education. Despite living in the city of philosopher-kings, the workers do not participate in philosophy. There is, so to speak, no Platonic Absolute. That the good shines differently on the many than on the few is shown by Aristotle, who observes that in Plato's city the guardians are an occupying army.[33]

Hegel, however, is a Judeo-Christian in the technical sense that he wants all citizens to participate in the "Holy Spirit." That there is a Judeo-Christian dimension in Nietzsche's teaching is unmistakable: Hence the impression he generates of liberating everyone by transforming mankind into a race of supermen. Nietzsche's doctrine of perspectivism and spontaneous creativity is a secularized version of the Judeo-Christian conception of the equality of all mortals in their distance from God. Nietzsche of course suppresses God; hence he seems to liberate human beings, each of whom is equal to every other human being as an expression of spontaneous creation, as a focal point of a comprehensive interpretation, as a summation of an infinite series of subinterpretations.

If this impression corresponded to the essence of Nietzsche's doctrine, then all human beings would be potential supermen. This is the manner in which Nietzsche is read by his admirers on the political left, but it is flatly contradicted by all of Nietzsche's cardinal doctrines, including rank-ordering, aristocratic values, the pathos of distance, the masked esotericism of the few, and so on. The couching of the appeal to the extraordinary individual in such a way as to make it seem applicable to all readers of *Zarathustra* is accordingly required for the task of revolution, for instigating and guiding the destruction of decadent European civilization. In this light the unique individual is revealed as the foot soldier of Nietzsche's infantry.

To approach the same point from another direction, we have to interpret Zarathustra's speeches in terms of their immediate audience. Zarathustra talks to the multitude, to selected human types either individually or collectively, to the animals, to natural phenomena like the sun, and to himself. The problem is complicated by the fact that the book as a whole must be written in a rhetoric of exaggeration, suitable for moving diverse audiences to direct revolutionary action. Even Zarathustra's speeches to himself are therefore also delivered to the potential reader, both as a private person and as a member of a social group. When put in the context of multiple audiences, the problem of interpreting *Zarathustra* may seem more difficult than it in fact is. Most of Zarathustra's speeches are generally intelligible to the educated reader, in much the same way that we read the Bible, myths, fairy tales, or poetry. In addition, we have Nietzsche's discursive writings of the same epoch, in particular *Beyond Good and Evil* and *The Genealogy of Morals,* which were written as commentaries on *Zarathustra,* as well as the extremely frank *Twilight of the Idols;* all these may be supplemented by Nietzsche's extensive correspondence and his Notebooks.

Above all, however, we must rely upon the one indispensable principle of every hermeneutical enterprise, a principle that has today gone out of fashion largely on the basis of Nietzsche's own authority. The principle is that authors write and publish books with the intention of influencing the speeches and deeds of audiences that are selected in advance by the nature and content of the writings. This principle does not deny that texts may say more, but also less, than the author explicitly intended or recognized. But "more" and "less" are here measured by what the text testifies. It is simple nonsense to claim simultaneously that there is no authorial intention, or that such an intention is irrelevant to the hermeneutical activity, or that there is not and cannot be a canonical interpretation of any writing, or that there is no single text but only a congeries of perspectives, while at the same time offering one's own reading of that text. It is entirely correct to say that a book like *Zarathustra* has a multitude of meanings, that different meanings are addressed to different audiences, that Nietzsche's language is often incantatory and subject to a wide range of possible construals. But it is a sign of thoughtlessness or incompetence to deny that the book encompasses its perspectives within a synoptic teaching. To say that this teaching is finally incoherent, as I myself claim, is something quite different from a failure to perceive it. There are, of course, no quasi-mathematical demonstrations of the validity of interpretations, beyond the coherence and comprehensiveness of the interpretation itself. But to those for whom there are no authors and no intentions, there are also no readers and no texts.

So much for the principles of hermeneutics. In preaching to the multitude, Zarathustra accommodates his teaching to the popular understanding, exactly like the Author of Holy Scripture. Mankind must be overcome or else sink back into the bestial. The reference to the ape is an allusion to Darwin, but the characterization of the ape as an embarrassment to mankind is pure Nietzsche. Darwinians emphasize our relation to the apes at the price of human transcendence, as is obvious today from the criticism directed at the attempts by Alfred Wallace, Darwin's anticipator and collaborator, to show that science and morality are peculiarly human and so peculiarly divine. Nietzsche cites the same relation to shame us into overcoming it. That this is not his last word on the topic is evident from his own relation to the eagle and the snake.

Reflection on this point shows us that it is not satisfactory from Nietzsche's own standpoint to exaggerate the importance he subsequently places upon genealogy.[34] The Socratics arrive at the Ideas, or pure forms, in their return to the origins; but the Nietzschean will arrive at chaos. The origin, in other words, is ambiguous. In the case of human existence, whether private or political, the origin for the Socratics is myth, not formal clarity. Nietzsche is on this point a Socratic; his myth is one of overcoming, which points to the future, not to the past: to development, not to the origin. Every attempt to reduce the myth of overcoming to the will to power and the eternal return, rather than to understand these two principles as themselves part of the comprehensive myth of overcoming, renders human existence unintelligible. Interestingly enough, all such "ontological" interpretations of Nietzsche, paramount among them Heidegger's, are very much in the spirit of scientific rationalism. But it must never be forgotten that with *Zarathustra* we are in the domain of myth and fairy tale.

This means that the origin is ambiguous rather than simply good or bad, noble or base. What counts is the direction of development, the incrementing of power. As the ape is to man, so ought man to be to the superman: a source of laughter or of painful shame. Why both, or is this an alternation of exclusion? I understand Zarathustra to imply that the superman will laugh at his low origins, but that he will also be shamed by them because he cannot entirely repudiate them. And even the superman must shoulder the burden of the knowledge that he himself is as an ass in comparison to what transcends the superman. "You have made the path from worm to man, and much in you is still worm. Once you were apes, and man is still more ape than any ape." Here Zarathustra uses Darwinian language to make his own point. The ape itself cannot overcome itself; but man, who has already overcome the ape, nevertheless retains the apelike nature of fixity unless he overcomes humanity itself, or, more precisely, the present type of humanity.

"He who is the wisest among you is still only a disunion and a hybrid of plant and ghost." Here Zarathustra omits the animal component. Our spirit is ghostly because it is still Christian, and our body is a plant, stuck in the earth, rooted in position, not overcoming but decadent. "The superman is the meaning (*Sinn*) of the earth. Say to your will: Let the superman be the meaning of the earth!" As we can put this, the superman is closer to the earth than to the ghost. The earth is the source of life, hence of evolution, as opposed to heaven, the domain of ghosts or death. Zarathustra here tactfully overlooks the fact that we bury our dead in the earth. The earth is a graveyard as well as a womb. But he will return to this point shortly.

There follows one of the most famous of Zarathustra's invocations: "I adjure you, my brothers, *remain true to the earth* and believe not those who speak of supernatural (*überirdischen*) hopes" (15). The repudiation of Christianity is obvious enough, but we must not forget that the earth is also the domain of the worm and the plant; to exaggerate fidelity to the earth is to put overcoming at risk. In a striking image, Zarathustra says that once the greatest sin was against God; today it is the sin against the earth, namely, to honor the intestines of the inscrutable more than the significance (*Sinn*) of the earth. This is not without its rationalist implications; whereas there are no scientific investigations of the interiority of the divine, the earth falls within human scrutiny. Fidelity to the earth thus leads naturally to the discovery of the afore-mentioned duality of its significance. And this is an enduring problem for Nietzsche. There is no transcendence or overcoming of death, which, especially in the absence of Christianity or as a consequence of the death of God, reestablishes the dominance of nature over the human will.

The rest of Section 3 is now perfectly intelligible. Man, the human type of the Judeo-Christian tradition, is today a dirty stream and must be washed away by the ocean of chaos, which is also a force of purification. "The hour of the great contempt": This is the hour in which we recognize not merely the radical decadence of our Judeo-Christian persona but also the self-repudiation that is the necessary prerequisite to a new race of mankind. The expression will recur in a passage of extreme difficulty and importance, "The Pale Criminal," to which I shall devote considerable attention. Suffice it to say for the moment that in his sermon to the townsfolk, Zarathustra speaks as if they are all capable of the great contempt. It would be more accurate to say that there is a public, or exoteric, and a refined, or esoteric, version of this emotion. The truly contemptible are incapable of self-contempt. It might seem that those who are capable of it are not truly contemptible, but we shall see later that this is a superficial view of the situation. For the time being let me suggest only that the great contempt is a kind of Dionysian intoxication purged by Apollonian lucidity, in which Nietzsche mocks the presumption with which Christ takes responsibility for human sins and dies on our behalf.

The happiness of our present condition is poverty and filth and wretched contentment. "But my happiness ought to justify existence itself." Existence is not justifiable in its own terms: This is what Nietzsche calls elsewhere "the innocence of becoming."[35] Becoming has no intrinsic ends; it is not guilty of the sins of European mankind, but neither does it posit a higher end to human affairs. In itself it is neither good nor bad but can become whatever we make of it: It is therefore not only innocent but also seducible. Otherwise stated, if Becoming is innocent, then it is we who are guilty. Zarathustra's happiness will justify existence, or (what comes to the same thing) he will undergo genuine happiness, if and only if he can bring about the coming of the superman. By parity of reasoning, his failure to bring this about must produce the great contempt against himself.

We see here one of Nietzsche's most pervasive doctrines. Becoming is chaos, which both deprives nature of a teleology and makes possible human creativity, referred to in his later writings as "interpretation" (*Auslegung*).[36] At the same time, our interpretations must "justify" existence, and this leads back to the problem of the standard of justification. The very conception of value and rank-ordering is unintelligible except on the basis of a natural distinction between the high and the low. "What is noble? Thoughts on rank-ordering," writes Nietzsche in a characteristic fragment of 1885/86.[37] And again, the extremely important fragment from 1886/87: "My philosophy is directed to rank-ordering: not to an individualistic morality. The sense of the herd ought to rule in the herd – but not to extend beyond it."[38] If the noble is itself just an interpretation of nature, then we generate an infinite regression, and all talk of rank-ordering is unsustainable; in particular, talk of the superman reduces to an empty celebration of the accumulation and discharge of points of force.

The same problem can be stated in more explicitly political terms. In order to produce a new order, Nietzsche must overthrow the old one. But if he overthrows it completely, we return to chaos, and Nietzsche will have no control over the consequences, that is, over which stage of the eternal return will arise. But nineteenth-century civilization is a decadent stage in the history or devolution of early-modern Europe from the Renaissance forward, just as the Middle Ages were a decadent version of classical civilization, which in turn may be regarded as a decadent version of archaic or Homeric times.[39] In general, the beginnings or origins are for Nietzsche (as for his student Heidegger) better than the (late) consequences, because the creative forces are more concentrated. There is no experience of diversity, hence no tolerance for or enjoyment in experiencing other modes of life. In the original stage of human society, the human being is more virile, more cunning, more creative, because it is closer to the enmity of nature, to a clear perception of the harshness of existence and the identity of might and right, to the concentrated egoism of the child and hence to the ability to make use of the bestial, and to a freedom from excessive pity, from the liberalism that comes from too much diversity of experience: In sum, the origin is the moment of maximum will to power.

Decadence is accordingly not some alien growth that has superimposed itself upon initial virility; it is virility grown old and weak. Tolerance is a kind of skepticism or freedom from superstition; excessive pity is a tacit recognition of the merciless and bestial character of nature and hence of human existence as the attempt to survive in a hostile world. Corrupt hedonism is a hypertrophied version of the return to the earth and the body that in times of innocence is associated with virility; the decay of traditional customs and the corruption of traditional institutions is the necessary precondition for their destruction and replacement by new, life-enhancing forms of existence. In short: Decadent narcissism is the flaccid or enervated version of the egoism of the child, which is why we speak of the second childhood of senility.

This complex situation explains why Nietzsche, whether in his own varied voices or behind the mask of Zarathustra, can carry out a double rhetoric so effectively. The critique of decadence is necessarily an invocation to create a new beginning, to return to the origin. The decadent accordingly believe themselves to be the new race of mankind for whom Zarathustra calls, just as the townsfolk believe that the rope-dancer is the superman. If the townsfolk are moved to action, they engage in the unfolding and dissemination of modern progress; revolution is for them the institution of the age of the last men against which their sons and daughters must be persuaded to rebel. Hence the leaders of revolutions are the children of the upper middle class, the artists and intellectuals, the *bien pensants* who so love their fellow human beings that they are moved to terrorism and political nihilism and thus to self-destruction, sustained by the illusion that they are themselves either supermen or the progenitors of a race of supermen.

We can now move to the end of Section 3: "Behold, I teach you the superman; he is this lightning, he is this madness!" (16). This sounds like a combination of Apollo (light) and Dionysus (madness). The crowd replies: "We've heard enough about the rope-dancer; let us now also see him!" and laugh at Zarathustra. Why? Undoubtedly because they are amused by his inflated rhetoric. We cannot explain this simply by attributing it to the coarseness of their perceptions. In fact, Zarathustra's prose is bombastic and offends the good taste and common sense of the liberal and progressive bourgeoisie. But it is not addressed to them directly; Zarathustra is speaking in the first instance to those who are bored by liberalism and progress and who are therefore peculiarly susceptible to overheated invocations to radical transformation, even at the price of destruction.

We turn next to Section 4. "Zarathustra, however, observed the people and was surprised. Then he spoke as follows: 'Man is a rope, tied between beast and superman – a rope over an abyss.'" The rope-dancer is the instinct in mankind to go beyond; the rope represents that which is to be surpassed and, as such, the path from one stage to another. We cannot become supermen except by traversing the destiny of our own human nature. This destiny is partially contingent: The rope stretches over an abyss. So the rope-dancer, in his traversal, could fall into the abyss; mankind could be destroyed by the very attempt to overcome itself.

If the rope-dancer successfully traverses the rope, it will not be destroyed; it merely becomes useless at that point unless the dancer is required to return to his point of origin. In other words: Zarathustra implies that self-transcendence is not self-destruction. This is his reversal of Socrates' noble lie. That is, he tacitly identifies self-overcoming with the expression of excellence that is normal to a decadent people. The rope-dancer thinks that he is the superman and so begins his performance, which, whether successful or not, will result in his transformation. But by persuading the rope-dancer that he is the superman, Zarathustra moves him to risk his life, to participate in his own destruction while under the impression that he is fulfilling himself. This epitomizes Nietzsche's double rhetoric.

After emphasizing the dangers of the crossing, Zarathustra notes that man is great because he is a bridge, not an end: This is straightforward and poses no problems (17). As a bridge, man is an *Übergang* and an *Untergang*, both a transition and a decline. The rope is a bridge from one stage to the next, from the subhuman to the superhuman. Man must traverse his own nature if he wishes to surpass himself; he cannot bypass his own decline. On the other hand, he cannot be allowed to carry that decline to its conclusion, the epoch of the last men. Better to turn more directly to the partial chaos engendered by the destruction of decline. It would seem that Zarathustra must orchestrate the rope-dancer's fall into the abyss. In his present persona, the rope-dancer cannot traverse the rope; what will appear to himself and to his audience as progress will in fact be a continuously decelerating spiritual motion, or in other words an extended decline.

This raises the following difficulty. The death of the rope-dancer leaves us with a rope between beast and superman, a bridge with no one to traverse it. At this point, Nietzsche's image breaks down; the rope, as it were, must itself break when the rope-dancer falls into the abyss. There is then no continuity. We return to chaos in either case, quickly if Nietzsche's acceleration succeeds, slowly if it does not. Let us assume that Nietzsche succeeds. What is to insure the transition to the stage of the superman? The rope is at this point an ineffective and meaningless image; it is a modality, like the stages of the beast and the superman: three possible consequences of chaos.

Our choice, then, is between a rapid return to chaos in the hope of a creation *ex nihilo* or continuous decadence, the slow return to chaos. Either Nietzsche believes that it is possible to manipulate historical circumstances in such a way as to make likely, if not to guarantee, the desired outcome. Or he intends merely to destroy decadent Europe and leave what will follow to chance, on the ground that any beginning, as an expression of the origin, must be more vital, life-enhancing, virile, and aristocratic than what exists in his own time. We could unite these alternatives as follows: By "superman" Nietzsche means no particular cultural or spiritual configuration: not archaic Greece, not the Renaissance, but simply *a new beginning*.[40]

If this is a more or less accurate reconstruction of Nietzsche's inner intention, then we can reconcile two features of Zarathustra's rhetoric that seem initially to contradict one another. Zarathustra both speaks very vaguely about the next stage, the way of life of the superman, and also regularly implies that the superman is somehow a continuation of humanity at a higher level of activity. A "superman" sounds like a superior man. But if mankind is in decadence and has already reached the peak of its possibilities, the next stage, in order to be both higher than the present and nevertheless discernibly human, must in fact be a *reversion* to some earlier condition or to some approximation of an earlier more creative and virile epoch. This in turn suggests that whereas man may be a rope over an abyss, it is misleading to talk about going from bestiality to the superman as if this were a progression entirely beyond, albeit by way of, mankind itself. In fact, the edge of the abyss, the stage called "superman," is located somewhere along the rope called "man." And this forces us to rethink the advisability of driving the rope-dancer to his destruction. Nietzsche is faced with a dilemma. Even in order to retrogress, say to the Renaissance or to archaic Greece, or to some approximation of those epochs, he must destroy contemporary culture but not the human spirit. If mankind is destroyed, there is no guarantee that the next stage to emerge from the chaos of origination will not be that of the beast.

In Section 1, Zarathustra begins his *Untergang* or descent; in Section 4, he invokes an *Übergang* that is also an *Untergang*. Zarathustra descends from his mountaintop to deliver his revolutionary prophecy to mankind, but he does not cross over. Mankind is told to descend in order to cross over; this descent is a destruction of the condition antecedent to the crossing. It is not a descent from a mountaintop to the city, but from the tightrope into the abyss. When his prophecy is rejected, Zarathustra does not descend into the abyss; he goes back up to the mountaintop cave. In other words, Zarathustra will be neither destroyed nor transformed; he comes and goes, but always as himself. Zarathustra, the teacher of the eternal return, himself eternally returns. He represents an eternal possibility for mankind. More straightforwardly, Zarathustra's perspective is Hyperborean, or beyond the circuit of fundamental historical perspectives. Nietzsche's understanding of historical possibility, of the human *Geist*, is not itself a perspective except in the sense of the perspective of all perspectives: It is a Platonic *sunopsis* or vision of the whole. And yet, even as such, it remains a historical event.

The distinction between Zarathustra and his immediate audience is evident in the structure of Section 4. Zarathustra begins by addressing mankind in general: "Man is a bridge." In the second assertion, he addresses a portion of mankind: "those who do not know how to live, except by going under; for it is they who cross over." This refers to whoever will become Zarathustra's disciple and lead the way toward the fulfillment of his prophecy. In the third assertion, the exact nature of the addressee is unclear: It could again refer to his disciples, but it could also refer to himself or, by extension, to the philosopher *qua* prophet and lawgiver. The great despisers long for the other shore: They long to surpass, to cultivate a new breed of mankind. From the fourth assertion on, Zarathustra speaks to himself and to his disciples.

The balance of Section 4 consists of a series of statements about what Zarathustra loves. It would be possible, but it is unnecessary, to study each of the assertions in the section in order to distinguish which statements of love refer to the projected disciples and which to Zarathustra himself. I note only the following:

(1) Assertion 6: "I love him who lives in order to discern [*erkennen:* not "to know" in the sense of having scientific or factual knowledge] and who wants to discern in order that some day the superman may live. And so he wants his descent (*Untergang*)." This refers to the prophet; Zarathustra loves himself and whoever (if anyone) is like him. This descent is not a crossing over; Zarathustra has already crossed over. Otherwise he would be unable to deliver the true prophecy. But Nietzsche, who invokes and is filled with the spirit of Zarathustra, will not cross over in the literal or historical sense. He has dedicated his life to preparing for the crossing, and in that sense has sacrificed himself for the earth so that the earth may some day belong to the superman.

(2) In assertion 9, Zarathustra says, "I love him who does not retain a drop of spirit (*Geist*) for himself, but who wishes to be entirely the spirit of his virtue; so he crosses over the bridge as spirit." In other words, he does not cross over as flesh. Zarathustra has crossed over in his thought and in his will. Let us distinguish again between Zarathustra and Nietzsche. Zarathustra is the spirit of the crossing-over itself; Nietzsche incarnates that spirit within his own historical epoch but will not cross over in the flesh; he will go under with the decadent race to which he belongs.

(3) As the section progresses, the reference to "going under" evolves into "zu Grunde gehen," a phrase used by Hegel to mean not only perishing but also "going back to the ground." I am not suggesting that Nietzsche is tacitly quoting Hegel here, but rather that the underlying thought is similar to Hegel's. It is suggested by the German expression itself. The "ground" here is chaos. We return to chaos in order to initiate a beginning, in this instance ostensibly of the superman. In this segment of Section 4, it would be impossible to say that Nietzsche has intentionally constructed it in such a way as to allow us to distinguish sharply between admonitions to mankind, to his human disciples, and to himself and his fellow prophet-philosophers. The mood is exalted, even intoxicated, and the emotion has clearly blurred the exact identities of Nietzsche's addressees. But the general structure of his thought is nevertheless visible. Zarathustra "goes under" or descends to be "a herald of the lightning," namely, of the superman (last assertion). Mankind "goes under" in the sense of "crossing over" the bridge to the next stage of development. This crossing over is to be led by Zarathustra's human disciples, in the sense that they must consciously sacrifice themselves by accelerating the destruction of their decadent age.

The upshot is as follows: None of Zarathustra's "actual" or "contemporary" addressees will cross over in the flesh. In that sense, they are themselves the rope or bridge over which mankind must cross. This is evident in the equation between "going to ground," or perishing, and crossing over the bridge. To cross the bridge is to die in the flesh so that the spirit may be transformed into that of the superman.

I append some additional comments on Section 4. (1) In assertion 12, "too many virtues" probably refers to the four cardinal virtues: wisdom, justice, courage, and moderation. In this context, Zarathustra approves of courage only, the noose on which the catastrophe of self-destruction or self-sacrifice hangs. (2) There is a kind of inverted Platonism in Zarathustra's invocation to dying, or going to ground. For Socrates, philosophy is a preparation for death. For Nietzsche, death is a preparation for philosophy. More specifically, for Nietzsche this epoch must perish so that the next epoch may come into being. (3) Note Nietzsche's terminology: (i) He wants the *Geist* to cross over (assertion 10) and (ii) the *Seele* to squander itself (assertion 13) and to go over by perishing (assertion 18), to forget itself by becoming all things and thus to go under (assertion 19); (iii) he loves him who is free *Geist* and free *Herz*, whose head is the entrails of his heart and whose heart drives him to go under (assertion 20). *Geist* does not perish or go under; it crosses over (assertions 17–18).

The Rope Dancer

I begin with a comparison between the opening lines of Sections 4 and 5: "Zarathustra, however, looked at the people ... then he spoke as follows" and "When Zarathustra had spoken these words, he looked once more at the people and was silent." The passionate speech of Section 4 was delivered between looks; that is, Zarathustra was not looking at the people as he spoke. In the strictest sense, Zarathustra's speech is not addressed to his contemporaries; as he says, "They laugh; they do not understand me, I am not the mouth for these ears." What is the obstacle? The people are proud of their *Bildung*, their formation or education, their cultivation. To them, the rope-dancer is not a vulgar circus performer but an expression of their highest accomplishments.

What of Zarathustra's potential disciples, not the prophet-philosophers of other epochs, who do not require or who are immune to Zarathustra's speeches, but the members of the present generation who are accessible by his rhetoric and will become instigators of his revolution? At first glance it might seem that these persons lack *Bildung*, or cultivation. But this would be going too far; in fact, as I noted previously, Nietzsche's cause was taken up by some of the most

advanced artists, thinkers, and political activists of the day. This brings
to light an ambiguity in Nietzsche's conception of art. On the one
hand, the artist is thoroughly political because he or she speaks to the
audience of the day; more generally, artists "were in all times valets of
a morality or philosophy or religion."[41] On the other hand, "art is the
great stimulus to life."[42] This is an ambiguity but not a contradiction.
Even as a stimulus to life, art is intrinsically political. Art is worth more
than the truth in the preparation of a world that is habitable by human
beings. Perspectives are human artifacts, but the teaching concerning
perspectives is philosophical, not artistic. Nietzsche's rhetorical or political use of art as an instrument for the production of the revolution
has confused many readers into believing that the conception underlying its production is also an artifact.[43] As to individual artists themselves, in some ages they are spokesmen of established social and
political doctrine; in others, they are especially sensitive to contemporary decadence and welcome prospective change. But even this openness to change is for Nietzsche an extension of the artist's role as
subservient to the philosopher's.[44]

Once the distinction between master and servant is made, we can
say that the utility of the servant is in this case precisely his propensity
to welcome change. The artist cannot captivate his audience unless he
presents old doctrines in new clothes. It would, I believe, be wrong to
say that from Nietzsche's standpoint the artist is intrinsically revolutionary. What one can say is that the artist is for technical reasons peculiarly
susceptible to revolutionary rhetoric. It is easy to persuade artists that
they are themselves original thinkers and revolutionaries, or masters
rather than servants. Art has a more immediate access to the human
soul, even in its avant-garde forms, than does philosophy. No one
can doubt that Nietzsche's own artistic gifts are responsible for his
extraordinary popularity and influence. Art is better suited than philosophy to employ the rhetoric of violence that is required in order to
attract the attention of the conventionally educated European. "Must
one smash their eardrums in order that they may learn to hear with
their eyes?" Those who "hear" with their eyes will see the lightning
mentioned at the end of Section 4, namely, the superman.

The people are proud of their *Bildung* and do not want to hear the
word "contempt" applied to them (19). That is, they do not want to
hear Zarathustra's criticism of their enlightened and progressive age.
Accordingly, he will address their pride by assuring them that they still
have the opportunity to avoid what is truly contemptible: the last man.
Nietzsche means by "the last man" a kind of human analogue to
physical entropy, someone who does not strive to overcome, to rise to
a new intensity and fecundity of existence. But we cannot overcome or

rise higher unless we possess a *Rangordnung*, a hierarchy of values. We must be able to distinguish the low from the high; we must also despise the low and esteem the high, or else we shall ourselves become despicable.

The activity of the creator is his judgment of the present. Creation, we recall, is for Zarathustra gift-giving, or what he here refers to as love. The inability of the last man to judge is expressed in the following passage: " 'What is love? What is creation? What is longing? What is a star?' – so asks the last man, and blinks." The "What is *x*?" question is of course a cryptic reference to Socrates or to Platonism. Underlying the last man, and so too the postmodern, for whom all perspectives are valid, is the neutrality of Western theory, which does not evaluate, but defines. To ask, "What is . . ." is already to cut oneself off from the possibility of understanding human existence, which is not a sequence or system of "what's" but a hierarchy of "what for's" and so of "good for's" or values.

The last man is no longer familiar with stars as symbols of distant goals, because he has no goals, no Eros; and this is because Socrates directed the human Eros of Western man toward lifeless Ideas. The merit of this point, if any, depends on our putting to one side the fact that the Platonic Ideas are also hierarchical and so express a table of values. For Nietzsche this is negated by the detachment of the Ideas from historical or generated existence and from concentration on the nature of the thing *as* thing, or, as Aristotle puts it, on "being *qua* being." For Nietzsche, on the contrary, the Ideas are present only as the fundamental human types whose successive epochs of domination constitute the humanly accessible structure of the eternal return.

I do not want to overemphasize the link between the description of the last men and the Platonic Ideas. Perhaps the most salient point here is homogeneity. This is evident in the repetition of the reference to blinking: Vision is analyzed into atoms of sight, thereby destroying the cumulative structure and so the purpose and value of vision itself. The earth has become small. Man is accordingly reduced in spiritual magnitude to the status of the beetle who does not walk but hops, just as the last man blinks rather than gazes upon or sees the whole. Homogeneity is not the Eleatic One, but discontinuity, or what is today called *"différance."* The reduction of sameness to difference is merely the reinstitution of the tyranny of sameness.

The reference to the beetle is important: Man is reduced to the level of the insect; in other words, to the lowest level of the bestial, or subhuman. At the same time, the last man, precisely as an insect, believes that he has invented happiness. The beetle associates happiness with caution, with peace, with socialism (rubbing against one's neighbor to keep warm), with egalitarianism or the absence of suspicion: "One no longer becomes rich or poor; both require too much exertion. Who still wants to rule? Who obey? Both require too much exertion. No shepherd and one herd! Everybody wants the same, everybody is the same: Whoever feels different goes voluntarily into a madhouse," and so on (20). This is all self-explanatory. Instead of parsing the obvious, let me interpolate a general remark about Nietzsche's political thinking.

Interlude: Politics and Psychology

In the broadest sense of the term, Nietzsche is not an ontologist or metaphysician but indeed a political thinker. His most comprehensive intention is to transform the collective circumstances of human existence in order to breed a new race of mankind.[45] It is in this radical and comprehensive sense that Nietzsche is a prophet or lawgiver.[46] It is also true that Nietzsche has political views in the more restricted sense of the term: He despises socialism, is a critic of Bismarck, speaks inconsistently on nationalism, and so on.[47] These views are a consequence of Nietzsche's comprehensive politics. But they are also affected by contingent circumstances, which is to say that they may vary with local historical conditions; they are not simply determined by his global or comprehensive political intentions.

One could also say that although Nietzsche accepts the traditional Platonist view of philosophy as synoptic vision and hence as the discovery of the truth about the whole, he normally approaches questions of a purely theoretical or metaphysical sort from the standpoint of human nature; this is what he means when he describes himself as a psychologist. Nietzsche wishes to give a *logos* of the psyche, and this is an essential part – indeed, it is the basis – of his comprehensive political teaching. As part of my general remarks about Nietzsche's political thinking, let me give a brief account of his psychologism.[48]

It is certainly true that in his later writings, published and unpublished, Nietzsche speculates on what look like metaphysical or ontological questions. At the risk of some (but not much) oversimplification, we could say that his main thesis with respect to these questions is as follows: Heraclitus was correct and Parmenides incorrect: Being is Becoming, everything is in motion, stability is a ratio of changes, ratios are changing perspectives, changes emerge from chaos and not in accord with a plan or fundamental order. Note what follows from this "ontological" thesis: There is no ego, no subject, and hence no will. The will to power is in fact an infinite regression of points of force. This is what Nietzsche means when he refers to the will as an exoteric concept.[49] No apparent cohesions, or what one might call fields of force, have a unifying identity. Hence personal identity is an illusion. It follows further that there can be no explanation of *illusion* itself, of why we experience ourselves as finite personalities, why we perceive things or objects, why our experience is organized as if it were a coherent whole. This is what Nietzsche means by his acceptance of Heraclitus's reference to Zeus as a "playing boy" (*pais paizōn*). The cosmos, or what we take to be order, is just the purposeless play of chaos. Nietzsche's enthusiastic adoption of Spinoza's *amor fati* comes to the same thing. Nietzsche is not a genuine Spinozist except for one point: He denies teleology, or divine purpose.

All this being so, ontology or metaphysics is entirely worthless as a basis for explaining human existence as human or as lived. Not only is it worthless, but it is dangerous, since the derivation of all apparent order from chaos must also apply to rank order. Lawgiving, or the establishment of a rank order, may be said to express the ontological condition of chaos as the play of forces in the sense that the formulation of laws is an attempt by the lawgiver to force human beings to perceive chaos from his own perspective. "Might makes right," in the words of Spinoza. What Nietzsche calls noble or aristocratic is then simply an expression of power or force, given human significance by Nietzsche's own preferences in art, conduct, social and political institutions, and so on. When he refers to the will to power as "the last fact," or step, in the reduction of human life,[50] he is speaking of "the origin of motion" or the points of force that are the expression of chaos.[51]

In sum, Nietzsche arrives at his ontological conclusions not by a scientific or formal analysis of the structure of Being but through a psychological analysis of lived experience. Traditional philosophy, religion, and metaphysics are rejected as an illusion because they have lost their power to convince us, not because Nietzsche possesses a theoretical demonstration of their falseness or invalidity. As one could also put this, the tradition is false as tradition, because the traditional is the decadent. Whatever decays loses its power to create persuasive and fecund structures of force. In human terms, through excessive familiarity laws lose their power to compel. Civilizations, or more precisely their underlying principles, wear out in time. Articulate *logos* changes into the humming of the holy men.

Furthermore, what we call nature demonstrates its own chaotic interior independently of our philosophical, religious, or scientific beliefs. Nature is ruthless, extravagant, indifferent to our perception of excellence, and fundamentally hostile to permanence and hence to the survival of humanity. In essence, Nietzsche accepts the implications of the Cartesian scientific revolution, or attempts to make man the master and possessor of nature. But he rejects the thesis that science is an expression of intrinsic natural order. Instead, he claims that science is itself an artifact of human perspective, an expression of our will to dominate. Very far from being an antiscientific or antimodern thinker, Nietzsche simply draws out the last consequences of the modern enterprise. The last man is a product of the Enlightenment, not of obscurity.

As an instrument of power, or an expression of man's lawgiving nature, science is a version of art. "Art" is not here a term of aesthetics but rather an expression of the fundamentally constructive character of human experience. In a famous passage, Nietzsche refers to the world as a work of art that gives birth to itself.[52] Strictly speaking, however, the world is born in human experience: It exists because we perceive it. And this in turn means that chaos arranges itself haphazardly in fields of force which yield human consciousness, or the illusion of personal and cosmic stability. This is Nietzsche's late-modern version of Kant's transcendental doctrine of the world: Haphazardness replaces purposiveness. One may therefore say that chaos gives birth to the world, one aspect of which is consciousness of the world, a consciousness that again organizes in clusters of points of consciousness, which clusters give rise to the illusion of self-consciousness or personal identity.

Nietzsche's psychologism consists in this: He moves toward chaos by a progressively deeper dissolution of the appearance of order in all aspects of human experience. His starting point is man, and he moves in all cases from man the discoverer or contemplator of order to man the maker of order. Nietzsche's radicalism consists in the further reduction of man the maker to the status of artifact or contingent modification of chaos. Nevertheless, he regularly defends or advocates a set of values, a way of life, virility against decadence as expressed not ontologically but in concrete human creations, speeches, and deeds. The middle term between these concrete or historical human preferences is health, also interpreted as virility, fecundity, growth, self-transcendence, and increase in power. Health, in other words, is an everyday or colloquial expression for the will to power, which is itself an anthropomorphic expression of the chaotic play of forces.[53] Nietzsche's first principle, so to speak, is this: Chaos is not primarily dissipation, but the interplay of accumulation and discharge.

From the standpoint of eternity, discharge is no better than accumulation. But from the human standpoint, accumulation is superior; discharge itself assumes a positive identity only when regulated by accumulation. "Only by creating are we able to negate."[54] Health is better than sickness; hence healthy life is better than death. The sick, on the other hand, if they cannot be cured, deserve to die.[55] Human existence is discharge and accumulation of force: This, we may say, is its ontological structure. But as lived or experienced, human existence has a curious double structure that consists at once in our perception of the ontological structure, although not necessarily in such abstract terms as accumulation and discharge, and also in experience in the traditional sense of speeches and deeds: the activities, communal and solitary, of self-subsisting, self-conscious persons bound together in ethical, religious, cultural, political, and historical associations, and so too differentiated by these same groupings.

We must not infer from this that the scientific and philosophical analysis of the everyday leads us directly to what I am calling only for expository purposes the ontological structure of accumulation and decay of force. Science and philosophy are for Nietzsche themselves structured by the human need to conceal inner chaos with spiritual productions that impose anthropomorphic order on the play of forces.[56] At the same time, the need to conceal, which arises both from the hostility of nature (an anthropomorphism for chaos) and from our unwillingness to perceive ourselves or to perceive perception itself as an illusion, is at bottom a recognition of the human plight. To conceal is also to reveal; our love of masks – and everything deep loves the mask[57] – is a recognition of the impossibility of emerging into the light of the sun, as Socrates urges in the *Republic*.

To remove the masks, to emerge into the sunlight of honest recognition, is to acknowledge the hostility of nature, the hypocrisy of our religious doctrines and moral codes, the emptiness of our metaphysical theories, the dependence of our scientific explanations on the forcefulness of our own invented methods and so of our will to power and hence the true nature of science as an expression of power rather than of eternal truth: It is also to acknowledge the solace that we seek, and that we obtain, from art. Art is the comforting illusion that life is beautiful, meaningful, orderly, within our control. It is important to see that the difference between the philosophical removal of the mask and the institution of the epoch of the last men is quite tenuous. It rests on little more than the courage of the philosophers, but how this courage is to be translated into popular terms is not easy to see. Perhaps the answer is that the last men still believe in progress, which therefore serves as their ignoble lie.

Nietzsche's explanation of human existence is thus of an illusion that is saturated with fragments of clarity concerning the transitory status of every mask of chaos. As a philosopher, he is engaged in the task of the destruction not of the history of philosophy but of human existence and the human personality: of the psyche. It is in this sense that he is a psychologist. *Logos* does not synthesize or "gather together"; it dissolves. Clarification is thus destruction.

I come back now to Nietzsche's political thinking. It consists in the attempt to make use of the ontological doctrine, the ostensible truth about the illusory nature of our experience or order and stability, but hence too of belief in the stability of values, to clear the path of history for a return to the fructifying origin, to chaos itself, understood as the source of all new forms and hence rejuvenation. Nietzsche wishes to remove the tattered mask of late-modern European civilization from the face of chaos in order to replace it with a new and vital one. This requires of Nietzsche that he enlighten his own contemporaries by accelerating their dissolution; remember that clarification is destruction. The return to chaos as origin will make possible the birth of a new race of mortals and so another cycle of the eternal return. The preliminary step is to obliterate the coming of the last men. But all of Zarathustra's bombastic rhetoric fails to conceal from the sober reader the disconcerting fact that the last men share with the Nietzschean philosopher the modern spirit of the scientific Enlightenment.

Perhaps Nietzsche believed that a new and vigorous age of warrior-artists would be conducive to the growth of free spirits, or philosophers of the future. But he must also have known that such philosophers could never exist publicly without masks, that their speeches could never be understood by their fellow citizens, and certainly not by the warrior-artists, that if by chance their speeches *should* be understood, they would lead to the destruction of the new epoch, that unmasked speech must be punished by the same ostracism endured by Nietzsche in his own lifetime. It is an illusion to think that the crowd in the marketplace who laugh at Zarathustra and who assume that the description of the superman refers to the tightrope-dancer will be replaced in the new epoch by a race of careful auditors of clarifications of the illusory nature of their own life force.

The Rope-Dancer *(continued)*

" 'We have invented happiness,' say the last men, and they blink." One thinks here of the last line of T. S. Eliot's *Hollow Men:* "This is the way the world ends, not with a bang but a whimper." Eliot's poem is a commentary on what Zarathustra means by the last men: the complete trivialization of human existence, or an infinite extension of nineteenth-century liberal progress.[58] All facts are known. Pleasure has been accommodated to the digestion. The crowd in the marketplace is delighted with this prospect, and interrupts Zarathustra with demands that he give them the last men in exchange for supermen. "And the

entire folk rejoiced and clicked their tongues." Clicking is here an
anticipation of blinking and an echo of the humming of the holy man
in the forest; these sounds represent the dissolution of significance.

Zarathustra ends his first speech (in Section 5) with a reference to
blinking. The speech is identified by Nietzsche as "The Preface." Why
this odd device of a preface within a preface? It calls our attention to
the distinction between Zarathustra's official speeches and the events
of his sojourn among human beings. As is already apparent from the
scene in the forest, Zarathustra's conversations are different from
his prophecies. We can expect a greater degree of frankness in
these spontaneous encounters with individual persons or animals
than is suitable in a public oration. In the same way, Nietzsche
gives us accounts of Zarathustra'a reactions to the reception of his
speeches; the contrast in mood is often quite striking, and this should
warn us against surrendering to the enthusiasm of Zarathustra's inflated rhetoric.

Zarathustra is saddened and speaks to his heart: "They do not understand me; I am not the mouth for these ears." At this point, the actual
conclusion of Zarathustra's adventures is already anticipated: failure.
The heart is the symbol of love and passion. Zarathustra is a rejected
lover. Nevertheless, he continues by saying that he has lived too long
in the mountains: "I listened too much to brooks and trees; now I
speak to them as to goatherds."

There are a number of interesting echoes of Plato's *Phaedrus* in
Zarathustra on which I shall comment from time to time. The two works
are related by the fact that both describe the efforts of a philosopher or
prophetic teacher to communicate a new doctrine of the human soul
or nature through the mediation of the "intellectual" (as he is now
called) or *vox populi*. Phaedrus is no more a philosopher or superman
than are Zarathustra's disciples. The difference between him and Socrates is perhaps too obvious to mention; and yet it is usually ignored by
students of the dialogue, who fail to explain why he is the addressee of
the Socratic revelation. Any such explanation must begin with the fact
of Phaedrus's mediocrity.[59] It is not by chance that Socrates employs a
bombastic rhetoric to convey his meaning to Phaedrus.

Phaedrus calls our attention to the difference between himself and
Socrates when he says that Socrates doesn't seem to go outside the city
walls at all. Socrates replies that "I am a *philomathēs;* the country places
and the trees do not teach me anything . . ." (230d3). Zarathustra
comes into the city from the country; Socrates goes into the country
from the city. Zarathustra speaks like a rustic; he lacks the *Bildung* or
the idiom of the city-dwellers. Socratic philosophy is an urban activity;
even the study of nature begins in the city. So too the revolutionary

speeches of philosophy (with the decisive exception of the *Phaedrus,* in which the transpolitical nature of philosophy is especially apparent) take place within the city walls, even those in the *Republic.* Zarathustra speaks as though his wisdom comes from outside the city, from nature. Even the study of the city begins in nature. This is a fundamental point in Nietzsche and should not be obscured by the emphasis on art. Chaos is nature; it is not an artifact.

The difference between Socratic urbanity and Zarathustra's solitude is also reflected in the difference between the lives of Plato and Nietzsche. Plato turned away from politics but toward philosophical education and friendship. Nietzsche had no philosophical companions, no teacher and no students who were at his level. His attempt to establish a philosophical relationship with Lou Salome was a failure; one has only to read his letters to see that he regarded himself as entirely alone in his philosophical activity.[60] Not only this, but he insisted, increasingly so with the passage of the years and the intensification of his illness, that it was necessary for his work that he avoid all genuine human contact. This need for solitude is a metaphorical expression of Nietzsche's return to the origin. Isolation is an anthropomorphism for chaos. But Nietzsche resists the primacy of chaos by continuing to practice philology. He continues to read, to observe his fellow human beings, and to study the tendencies of the forces emerging from chaos.

Nietzsche's intentions constitute order within chaos. His theoretical investigations are guided by a political plan, which is for all practical purposes the same as that of Plato. But to the extent that the practical plan must be in accord with chaos, Nietzsche continues to live in accord with the nature of modern science. His substantive link to the Greeks is by way of the Pre-Socratics and Thucydides. Nietzsche belongs to Homer's army, as Socrates calls it in the *Theaetetus* (152e1–9), namely, to those who believe that change is fundamental and all-encompassing. The regular course of the sun, the flow of water, the growth and decay of plants, the cycle of the seasons, the characteristic behavior of animals (which provides the basis for their function as symbols of human traits): This is the order within chaos, the basis for Nietzsche's understanding of the ebb and flow of human existence, and the structure intrinsic to chaos, which we humans call genesis. It is this structure that underlies the intelligibility of human speech and so of the books that Nietzsche the philologist read throughout his productive life.

As rooted in nature, Nietzschean philology is distinct from the *Bildung* of decadence: Knowledge of the laws of growth and decay is itself immune to decay. This is represented dramatically by Zarathustra's link with nature rather than with books. "My soul is unmoved and as bright as the mountains in morning." Note the distinction between the heart and the soul: Zarathustra tells his heart of his sadness, which does not extend to the soul. The difference between the heart and the soul is expressed by what the crowd takes to be Zarathustra's coldness. The fire of prophecy is perceived by the crowd as ice; they discern that Zarathustra is not one of them, that he is, precisely as someone who attempts to transform them, outside or beyond, and that he is indifferent to the very attributes for which they admire themselves. Hence they turn to ice in response to the ice of an alien fire (21).

Even as Zarathustra delivers his sermon to the folk, the rope-dancer has begun his performance (see the last sentence of Section 3). There is no indication in Sections 4 and 5 that anyone is watching him. It seems that Zarathustra has become the center of the crowd's attention; despite their misunderstanding of its content, the onlookers are attracted by the rhetoric. Unfortunately, this attraction pulls them in precisely the wrong direction. This is an important hint about the destiny of philosophical revolutions. The rope-dancer represents the higher aspirations of the crowd, of late modernity. He has been moving forward on the rope during Zarathustra's speech and is now exactly halfway across. Again I remind the reader of the *Phaedrus:* The sun is at high noon as the discussion of Eros begins. High noon is the moment of greatest clarity. Nietzsche uses a similar device to make a different point. The rope-dancer has reached the point of no return, but he has not crossed it. He can go backward as easily as forward. So this is a decision point.

We can sharpen this: The midpoint is the most dangerous point, because each end of the rope is equally far from it. In this sense, the rope-dancer cannot return to safety. The point of decision is the point of maximum danger. This point is reached simultaneously with the conclusion of Zarathustra's revelation and with the crowd's icy reaction to it. A door opens in the tower from which the rope-dancer began, and "a fellow in motley costume, like a jester, leaped out and moved with quick steps toward the rope-dancer." If the townsfolk had accepted Zarathustra's prophecy, it would have led to their destruction through replacement by the race of supermen. Just as Zarathustra's prophecy constitutes a danger to the crowd, so the jester is a distraction and a danger to the rope-dancer. The jester is the projection onto the rope, that is, to the level of the spirit or higher aspirations of the crowd, and so of Zarathustra himself, who is regarded by his audience as a fool or jester, an entertainer who distracts them from the rope-dancer. (To anticipate, in Section 8 the jester reappears to Zarathustra and says to him: You talked like a jester.)

The jester moves quickly; this was not said of the rope-dancer. He is also scornful of his predecessor and abuses him with an idiomatic vocabulary that is a satire on the exalted vocabulary of Zarathustra's prophecy. Furthermore, he jumps over the rope-dancer with a cry "like a devil" and causes him to fall to the ground. I think that this episode has two closely connected meanings. First, it represents the fatal consequences of Nietzsche's teaching for his contemporaries. Second, it is the abuse and the rhetorical tricks, symbolized by the jester's jumping over the rope-dancer, that does the damage, not the exalted poetry and high-flown rhetoric of Zarathustra's speeches.

The rope-dancer loses his head and the rope when he sees the triumph of his rival. "He threw his pole away and fell faster than it, like a whirlpool of arms and legs, into the deep. The market and the people were like the sea when a storm passes over it. Everything flowed apart and together, and especially on the spot where the body must hit the ground." This is a marvelous description of the dissolution of the aspirations of late modernity and the return to chaos. In this scene, Nietzsche prophesies the consequences of his vitriolic attack on contemporary *Bildung*. But he also indicates a degree of respect for the rope-dancer, who falls at his feet and regains consciousness just before dying. A brief conversation follows in which Zarathustra explains to the dying man that there is no devil and no hell: His soul will die before his body (22). One could say that the rope-dancer is dead as soon as he falls from the rope. His function is aborted; the temporary return from chaos is required dramatically in order to show that Zarathustra pays homage to the noble aspects of a dying epoch.

"By my honor, friend . . ." It is incompatible with Zarathustra's honor that there should be a devil and hell, that Christianity should be true. (The jester is "like a devil" but not the devil.) And this honor is extended to the dying rope-dancer to assure him a peaceful sleep: There will be no punishment, no vengeance for the deeds and speeches of this life. The rope-dancer is uneasy; his life is evidently nothing, and he is no more than a trained beast. Zarathustra denies this: To live and die for danger is not to be despised. The distinction between man and beast is this: The beast cannot choose to live dangerously, but does so by its nature; it can only be tamed or civilized. But man can choose to adapt the qualities of the beast to the ends of *Bildung*. As a mark of his respect, Zarathustra will bury the rope-dancer with his own hands.

The unmistakable general significance of the scene we are studying is that the death of the rope-dancer represents the death of a stage of human *Bildung*. It is also evident that both Zarathustra and the jester have something to do with this death. The role of the jester is plain; it is his verbal abuse and his deed of jumping over the rope-dancer that causes the latter to lose his head and that precipitates his fatal fall. This fall is not simply an unwilling response to the jester; the rope-dancer participates in his own demise out of chagrin at the triumph of his rival. But who is his rival? In the fundamental sense, it can only be Zarathustra, the prophet of the superman, of a superior rope-dancer. This suggests the inner connection between the jester and Zarathustra. The difference between their speeches and deeds can then be explained by a consideration of the two kinds of rhetoric required for the separate deeds of destroying one manifestation of man's desire to overcome and of explaining the significance of this destruction.

At the beginning of Section 7 the townsfolk scatter, and Zarathustra sits by the corpse of the rope-dancer. Night comes, and Zarathustra speaks to his heart. I note four main points in this speech. (1) He compares himself to a fisherman, the symbol for Christ. But Christ is a fisher of souls, whereas Zarathustra has caught a corpse; again, destruction precedes creation. (2) "Human existence is uncanny and still without sense (*Sinn*); a jester can become its destiny (*zum Verhängniss werden*)." The contingency of life is also its absurdity; this absurdity is accessible to a destructive rhetoric of absurdity. (3) "I will teach men the sense of their being." This sense must express the nature of chaos in positive human terms: The superman stands for the positive accumulation and discharge of force, the lightning out of the dark cloud of man, that is, the destructive illumination that emerges from shapelessness. (4) Zarathustra is still far from men: "My sense does not speak to their senses. I am still a mean for mankind between a fool and a corpse ." What lies between a fool and a corpse? I believe that Zarathustra refers to the figure of the jester. The jester is not just a simpleton, or alternatively not just a clown or harmless entertainer, but a bitter expression of the absurdity of late-modern *Bildung*. He is not dead, not a corpse, but the anticipation of death, the sign of the destructive interior of decadence.

From the very beginning of his contact with the city-dwellers, Zarathustra is aware that he has come too soon. He knows in advance, as is appropriate for a prophet, that he will fail to reach his contemporary audience. Why then does he not return immediately to the mountain-top? This is a crucial question, because it bears on the central problem of Nietzsche's intention. To begin with, one could of course say that Zarathustra must promulgate his message among mankind in order for it to take hold in future generations. This is no doubt true; but how can that message take effect, how can it persuade those who do not hear it? Could not Zarathustra have articulated a more persuasive message? In my opinion, the purpose of Zarathustra's continuing adventures is to educate himself, not the human beings with whom he comes into contact. Let me again distinguish between the public and private rhetoric of Zarathustra. He regularly tells the truth to his heart, that is, to himself as personality, as an agent of love, not simply of will to power; to himself as philanthropist, but not just in the general or abstract sense of one who wishes well to mankind as a race. The heart represents Zarathustra's longing to live himself as a superhuman man and in a society of the future.

In this respect, Zarathustra stands for Nietzsche's own loneliness and longing for spiritual and intellectual companions. Nietzsche must learn through extensive experience that it is impossible not merely to effect a rapid transformation of mankind – this, after all, is obvious enough – but also to find friends or companions to share the task of preparing for this transformation.[61] He must also learn that the time is not ripe even for satisfactory disciples. Zarathustra is the dramatic projection of the fact that Nietzsche has neither friends nor genuine students. The writing of the book *Zarathustra* is thus in the first instance a catharsis of Nietzsche's own heart. This is why the book is so personal in tone and so precious to its author.

But it is not simply a personal document or confession. In the second place, the book is a testament to those potential philosophers of the future whom Nietzsche will never know but who will be in a position to benefit from his experience and knowledge. In order to serve as such a testament, the book must be preserved; it must be read. And this is to say that it must have political influence. There is a third point to be made here. The fact that the people inside the text are not able to listen to Zarathustra does not prevent Nietzsche's genuine audience from understanding him. I believe that the *Phaedrus* comes to our assistance on this point also. After having concluded his Stesichorean ode to the soul as a winged charioteer, Socrates prays to Eros and asks to be forgiven for his fancy rhetoric, which was necessary in order to retain Phaedrus's interest (257a3ff.). In my opinion, Nietzsche has a similar intention that underlies the excessive rhetoric of *Zarathustra*. It is designed to attract the attention of as large an audience as possible among those intellectuals and aesthetes, romantics, idealists, and so on who are dissatisfied with the vulgarity of late-modern European *Bildung*. But it is also addressed to the quasi-religious, to those who are dissatisfied with life as such, who long for transcendence but lack the power to believe in the gods of traditional religion. *Zarathustra* is addressed to those who long to believe in something but have no clear focus to this longing.

This helps us to understand the peculiar quasi-Biblical nature of the rhetoric and style of *Zarathustra,* which is unique in Nietzsche's writings. It hardly suffices as an explanation to say that Nietzsche was carried away by a divine revelation while writing *Zarathustra*. He does tell us in his letters that he was inspired when writing the book, and that he produced each of its parts in a remarkably short time. In my opinion, this refers to the totality of the work, to its effectiveness in carrying out his intentions, and so to the complexity of its rhetorical style. It should not be taken to mean that the exalted style reflects the fact that Nietzsche wrote the book in a trance or as a man possessed who did not know what he was doing.

Post-Mortem

The balance of the Preface is concerned with the events following upon the death of the rope-dancer. The main figures here are the jester, whom we have already encountered, and the gravediggers (23). The connecting thread is the corpse of the rope-dancer, which Zarathustra is carrying, in order to bury it with his own hands, as he said at the end of Section 7. After a hundred paces, Zarathustra hears a voice in his ear; it is that of the jester, who has sneaked up from behind and who warns him to leave the town: "There are too many here who hate you. The good and the just hate you, and they call you their enemy and despiser. The believers in the true faith hate you," and so on. All this is clear enough; Zarathustra is an enemy of Christianity, of Platonism for the masses. He was spared because he talked like a jester and hence was laughed at, and also because he showed pity in lowering himself before the dead rope-dancer.

Zarathustra bows down before the fallen spirit of a decadent age. He honors the spirit of overcoming as such, not the particular manifestation of that spirit in contemporary *Bildung*. This is not the same as to show pity toward the weak, the humble, and the poor. Furthermore, Zarathustra did not intend to entertain the people; their laughter is a sign of their own baseness. But it is also a sign of the inappropriateness of Zarathustra's rhetoric, if the purpose of that rhetoric is to transform the multitude. I have just indicated why I believe that this is not its purpose. The absurd character of Zarathustra's rhetoric preserves him from destruction because the crowd finds it amusing, but the "enlightened" members of the crowd will be seduced by this rhetoric.

The jester continues: "But go away from this town, or tomorrow I shall leap right over you, a living man over a dead one." In the sense that the jester is the absurd manifestation of his prophetic mission, Zarathustra runs the risk of having the public, or exoteric, side of his teaching triumph, rather than the private, or esoteric, side. I believe that Nietzsche was aware of this risk, namely, that his rhetoric would fail by virtue of succeeding too completely at the vulgar level. And this is in fact what has happened. After delivering this warning, the jester vanishes, and Zarathustra continues. He is prepared to take the risk.

We recall that Zarathustra is carrying the corpse of the rope-dancer. The jester did not allude to this. If the crowd was mollified by what it interpreted as Zarathustra's pity toward the dead man, why would this pity not be extended by knowledge that Zarathustra is also going to bury him? And this leads us to ask: Why did the crowd disappear, thereby leaving the corpse alone with Zarathustra? One could hardly say that they were so panicked by the fall from the tightrope that they forgot to discharge their duties of pity as well as of civic responsibility. In other words: If they are moved by Zarathustra's compassion, where is their own compassion?

This question is reinforced by the next episode (24). Zarathustra meets the gravediggers at the gate of the town. They have not been sent to attend to the corpse of the rope-dancer; Zarathustra has presumably encountered them in their precinct, no doubt at the public cemetery located at the edge of the town. The gravediggers make it explicit that to them the corpse is "a dead dog" that they would not themselves bury: "For our hands are too clean for this roast. Will Zarathustra steal this bite from the devil?" The gravediggers are already an expression of a low stratum of society; the task both is unpleasant and requires little skill besides a strong back. On the other hand, they acquire a certain cynicism that passes for wit because they dispose of the high as well as the low: One could say that the vanity and the emptiness of life are all too visible to them, whereas they are not in a good position to see what is virtuous and honorable in human existence. Just as the rope-dancer represents what is highest in the people, the gravediggers represent what is lowest. The rope-dancer is the most idealistic element of the people; the gravediggers are the most cynical.

Why do the gravediggers refuse to bury the rope-dancer, and why, like the jester, do they refer to him as "the dead dog"? The cynical and the sordid pay no honor to what is noble in the human spirit. They consign the corpse to the devil, who is able to claim it without their mediation. To the gravediggers, all men are equal because equally dead; all are corpses without the spirit of differentiation or distinction. In this respect, the gravediggers are lower than the devil, who would honor the rope-dancer by eating his corpse, and so too Zarathustra by eating him alive. We received an indication earlier, in Zarathustra's exchange with the dying rope-dancer, that the devil and hell do not exist. The gravediggers, of course, do not know this. It is interesting that neither Zarathustra nor the gravediggers refer to God in this connection, although of course Zarathustra has previously spoken of the fact that God is dead. It is entirely possible that the gravediggers know this. The universe is to them a charnel house, not a cathedral. They are accordingly immune to Zarathustra's exalted rhetoric. They laugh at him, just as the crowd did in the public square. And if tomorrow the crowd should kill Zarathustra, will the gravediggers bury him, or leave him to lie beside the rope-dancer like another dead dog?

The latter alternative seems the likely one: To the gravediggers, Zarathustra's rhetoric is as vain as the aspirations of the rope-dancer. As long as Zarathustra is masked by his ability to inspire laughter, he will be left unharmed. As I have indicated with respect to the figure of the jester, Zarathustra will become the rope-dancer of the next epoch, rather than, or rather precisely as, the prophet of the superman. After walking for two hours in the woods, still burdened by the corpse of the rope-dancer, Zarathustra is made hungry by the hungry howling of the wolves, as he was not by the events of the long day. Zarathustra comments on the oddness of his hunger, which often comes to him only after a meal. Eating represents an increase in energy; this leads to the desire for more energy rather than to repletion. During the episodes with the rope-dancer, jester, and gravediggers, Zarathustra was neither augmenting nor expending his force: We were here at a moment between two epochs, a moment that prefigures the much later scene in which Zarathustra speaks of the moment (*Augenblick*) that connects the future and the past.

Zarathustra knocks on the door of the old man's house and asks for food with the following observation: "He who feeds the hungry refreshes his own soul: Thus speaks wisdom." This complements the previous discussion. The statement could be given a traditional Christian interpretation as praise of charity. But the act of nourishing to which Zarathustra refers is that of the prophet who overflows like the sun. The old man replies: "This is a bad region for the hungry; that's why I live here. Beast and man come to me, the hermit." Not only does he make no distinction between beast and man, but he ignores the difference between the living and the dead. "Whoever knocks at my door must take what I give him. Eat and be off!" (25).

The forest is the zone in which distinctions are blurred or suppressed. Feed no one or everyone: Zarathustra gave nothing to the first hermit, and he takes nothing from the second; he leaves without eating. Revolutions, or the establishment of rank-ordering, take place in cities; so too prophecies are delivered in cities, although revelations occur on mountaintops. What happens in forests? Nothing definite. But there is a difference between the two hermits. The first still believes in God and has rejected mankind. The second neither believes nor disbelieves; he simply feeds. Perhaps the first hermit represents the decadence of Christianity, whereas the second has a secular or political significance: the decadence of progressive democracy or egalitarianism.

Zarathustra walks another two hours; he likes to look in the face of the sleeping. He can see without being seen. Next he hides the corpse in a hollow tree trunk to protect it from the wolves, lies down on the ground, and sleeps. What protects him from the wolves? There is a peculiar affiliation between Zarathustra and the beasts. In some sense he is closer to them than he is to the citizens of the town, although he has no gift for the beasts; he makes no attempt to feed them, but associates with and talks to them. They are totemic representations of the return to nature that is the necessary transition between one political epoch and another.

In the next section (9), several important points of Nietzsche's doctrine are introduced. Zarathustra sleeps through the night and the following morning; in other words, he awakens toward noon (25). This should remind us of the opening section, where he announces his descent at the dawn of a new day, and so too of the *Phaedrus;* there is greater clarity at noon than at dawn. "Then he saw a new truth." This truth corrects the initial revelation. Note the double occurrence of "ein Licht gieng mir auf" as well as the previous comparison to a seafarer who suddenly sees land.[62] The illumination concerns the type of companions that Zarathustra requires for his own voyage through the cities of mankind. A *Gefährte* is someone who travels with us. It could be a friend or a disciple. But thus far it is not clear that Zarathustra can have either.

Zarathustra needs living companions, not corpses: This of course refers to the rope-dancer. In the previous part of the revelation, Zarathustra also stated that he requires a certain type of human being who will prepare the act of "going over" the rope, or the transition to the superman. The transitional type will remain faithful to the earth and will repudiate the heaven of Platonism and Christianity: In the words of the sermon (Section 3), "Let your will say, the superman *shall* be the meaning of the earth." Zarathustra wills, or tries to will into being, a transitional type that will itself *will* the superman into existence. Thus far, as the scene in the town has shown, Zarathustra fails; his words are not for contemporary ears. He has been too precipitate; the transformation requires time and planning. It requires further voyaging on his part. Hence he now needs companions. The problem is of course this: There are not yet any supermen, and the highest representatives of the present type are "dead," or decadent, as represented by the corpse of the rope-dancer. In Section 3, Zarathustra spoke to those in the crowd who were already in a position to assist him, and there were no such persons. He cannot simply locate them; he must produce them.

Zarathustra can carry corpses wherever he wishes, but they would be useless to him for his ultimate enterprise. In other words, had he wished to excel by the contemporary standards, Nietzsche could easily have done so. But this is not his intention. "I need living companions who follow me because they want to follow themselves, and there, where I will." That is: A companion is one who wills to follow himself and so who regards himself as already a superman but who is in fact just following the directions of Zarathustra, which have been assigned to him by Nietzsche.

The new illumination continues: "Let Zarathustra speak, not to the people (*Volk*), but to the companions. Zarathustra shall not become the shepherd and dog of a herd!" This sustains the previous interpretation and is self-explanatory. The shepherd of a herd is also the shepherd's dog: This refers to Plato and to traditional philosophers, who from Nietzsche's standpoint are all Platonists because all are lawgivers to sheep, not to human beings, who are "supermen" in comparison with the herd animals of the tradition. Nietzsche seems to have believed that he could interrupt this process of wise shepherds. Differently stated, he seems to have believed that it is a matter of effective tactics to exaggerate what can be done. If one cannot replace the shepherd with the superman, the next best thing is to hypnotize the sheep into believing that the replacement has been effected.

I suspect that this is a serious error. For one thing, it is never enough to hypnotize the sheep; one must also hypnotize the shepherd. Since this is impossible, Nietzsche is in effect attempting to induce the sheep to rise up and kill the shepherd. But this is also impossible by his own doctrines. The philosophical rhetoricians of the past are all shepherds; they start from the inescapable distinction between the few and the many. Nietzsche obviously starts from the same point but prepares a rhetoric of exaggeration that asserts the intention, and hence implies the possibility, of transforming the many into the few. Nietzsche's hyperrhetoric resembles that of Marx. But Marx, or at least Marxists, were aware that the transformation of the many into the few, the abolition of differences between the gifted and the average or below average, requires a scientific transformation of human nature, not one that is rhetorically induced.

Despite his celebration of the will to power, Nietzsche puts too much trust in the power of speech. This is also evident in his emphasis on philology. Nietzsche is a logocentrist despite himself. But there is a difference between rhetoric and scientific *logos* that has a bearing on the correct interpretation of chaos. Thus Nietzsche attempts to reduce physics, and indeed all of the mathematical and experimental sciences, to the role of speeches or interpretations. He also tries to reduce these interpretations to the status of effects of physiology; but physiology is itself a science and hence an interpretation of the effects of affects, namely, of speeches produced by physiological sensations. Unfortunately, affects are also effects (sensations are interpretations). So this is circular in the vicious sense of the term.

Whether or not science is a speech or interpretation, it goes entirely beyond rhetoric by altering rather than merely conditioning human nature. The only way in which to transform human beings from sheep into supermen is by natural, as distinct from hermeneutical, science. The hermeneuticists or philologists may believe that it is they who control the scientists, because it is they who explain the sense of science. But this is irrelevant and mistaken. Once science effects a transformation of human nature, the interpretations prepared by the antecedent generation of prophets or hermeneuts become invalid. One cannot define in advance what will be the speeches and deeds of the new race, a race that is produced by altering the genetic code. What we sheep regard as the speeches and deeds appropriate to supermen may be regarded by the supermen as the speeches and deeds that are appropriate for sheep. It is true that science is also speech, or, otherwise put, that philosophy guides scientific investigations. But the results of science are not themselves simply speeches or interpretations; by altering our relation to nature, science alters us and so alters our potential speeches.

Nietzsche certainly saw this point more clearly than do his excessively garrulous postmodernist disciples. Hence his emphasis on destruction, cruelty, pitilessness, the blond beast, the warrior as higher type, and so on. Cruelty and mercilessness are the human properties that most closely approximate to the procedures involved in a scientific transformation of mankind. They may, of course, be put into play in what is described as a philanthropic desire to improve the human stock. But this is a euphemism for the destruction of mankind as presently constituted. In sum: Nietzsche seemed to discern that the coming of the superman would in fact be the coming of the superbeast, or, perhaps more precisely, of a beast made sub-bestial through its possession of genuinely human qualities, as opposed to the totemic attributes of Zarathustra's animals. Evidently he thought this to be a necessary component of the rejuvenation of the human spirit. This was his fundamental error.

Zarathustra develops the theme of the herd and its shepherds; he is himself a robber of the herd who comes to steal away those sheep who may be transformed into companions (26). The shepherds call themselves the good and the just. "Whom do they hate most? He who breaks their table of values, the breaker, the criminal – but he is the creator." This is now entirely intelligible. Note again that Nietzsche makes explicit and thereby exaggerates a Platonic theme. The philosopher, as the lawgiver or founder of a new city, is a traitor to the laws of the city in which he resides. The shepherd is first a criminal who breaks the old table of laws in order to substitute his own.

The destruction of the old laws is not followed immediately by the institution of the new ones. There is an interregnum, a period of lawlessness, chaos, hence a period that is not so much "beyond" as "between" good and evil. We can now distinguish three purposes underlying *Zarathustra*: (1) to announce the new order; (2) to accelerate the destruction of the old order; (3) to lead us from Egypt to Jerusalem, or to prepare the transition from the old to the new, but without the divine tablets vouchsafed to Moses. The transitional period is in this sense a period of nihilism. But we can also look at the book in another way. It is intended not merely as a document addressed to, or for the production of, companions, disciples, and supermen, but also as an account of the plight of the prophet.

The prophet-philosopher is a member of the race of Hyperboreans, who worship Apollo and live far to the north; they cannot be reached by land or sea: This corresponds to Zarathustra on his mountaintop. In order to deliver his prophecies, he must descend into the cities of mankind, or enter into history. To anticipate an image from a later passage in the text, Zarathustra's relation to the circle of Apollo (the rising and setting sun) is that of the philosophical vision of the eternal return, a circle that reappears later as the gateway of the moment. His descent into the city of the Motley Cow is a dramatic representation of the need to enter into historical time by passing through the gateway. All of Zarathustra's adventures can be understood as consequences of his efforts to reconcile the conflicting demands of the Hyperborean and the historical dimensions of philosophical existence.

The great obstacle to any proper understanding of *Zarathustra* is the tendency to succumb to the explicit dimension of Nietzsche's rhetoric by exaggerating the Dionysian element. It must constantly be borne in mind that the purpose of the explicit rhetoric is not to share a vision, but to transform, to produce certain types of human beings: companions, disciples, supermen. The chaotic interiority of things does not in itself lead to the submergence of Apollonian vision in Dionysian intoxication. Those who are intoxicated cannot see accurately; they cannot even stand up properly, let alone produce a global historical revolution. If creation and so lawgiving were purely or essentially Dio-

nysian, it would be entirely pointless, unconscious, haphazard, or chaotic. But not even the intended production of a race of beings who are
dedicated to purposeless play can be carried through by a drunken
madman or by purposeless play. This is why the book begins with a
vision of Apollo rather than of Dionysus.

As Zarathustra himself puts this point, "The creator seeks co-
creators, those who write new values on new tablets." This cannot be
done in a trance. The writing of new values is an intentional act
requiring forethought. "The creator seeks companions, those who
know how to sharpen their sickles." They will be called despisers of
good and evil because they cut down the wheat or corn of tradition.
But this cutting is rooted in knowledge, such as knowledge of how to
sharpen one's sickles, knowledge of how to adjust one's rhetoric. One
must be sober in order to sharpen sickles without cutting oneself.

In the last part of Section 9, Zarathustra addresses a final word to
the corpse of the tightrope-dancer. By burying the corpse in a hollow
tree, Zarathustra has protected it from the wolves of the forest. The
valuable element in the rope-dancer's existence is saved by Nietzsche's
doctrine from dissolution into the indeterminateness of the forest. The
tree stands for enduring nature as modified by burial, or the human
interpretation of death. The wolves, on the other hand, represent the
violence of nature, or, in human terms, what Hegel called the slaughter
bench of history. "But I part from you, the time is up. Between dawn
and dawn a new truth has come to me. I shall be neither shepherd nor
gravedigger. I shall never again speak with the people; I speak for the
last time to the dead."

From this point onward, Zarathustra speaks only to selected individuals. The fate of the rope-dancer has apparently purged him of the
revolutionary zeal – indeed, of the naiveté – with which he initially
descended from his mountaintop. I say "apparently" because there
will be resurgences of hope, and especially at the end of the work;
nevertheless, it is a striking fact that the Preface directs Zarathustra
away from the townsfolk and introduces the body of the work with
an elaborate portrayal of the failure of direct political action by the
philosopher.

After speaking to his heart at high noon, Zarathustra hears the call
of a bird and looks up into the air (27). "And look! An eagle turned in
wide circles through the air, and on him there hung a serpent, not like
booty but like a friend, for she kept herself wrapped round his neck."
The proudest and the wisest of the animals have left the cave to look
for Zarathustra. This is an echo of the scriptural passage about serpents
and doves, except that Zarathustra replaces the dove with an eagle. In
German, "eagle" is masculine and "serpent" feminine. This has two

different senses for Nietzsche. Courage and pride raise the serpent, or intelligence, from the dust of the earth; this is Nietzsche's correction of the doctrine of Genesis and the role of the serpent in the Garden of Eden. It is no criticism on Nietzsche's part to associate intelligence with the temptation of Satan, nor is it a denigration of the female, but a representation of the duality of the wholeness of human nature. The flight of the eagle is an emblem of modern daring; the scriptural heritage of the serpent acknowledges the need to purify rather than simply to repudiate tradition. What recurs eternally cannot be repudiated.

The appearance of the eagle and the serpent is timely, since Zarathustra has just announced his repudiation of the townsfolk. Their circles symbolize the eternal return, and their totemic significance recalls Zarathustra to the Apollonian dimension of his mission. He found it more dangerous among men than among beasts; "let my animals lead me." The German word *Tier* can be translated as "animal," "beast," or "brute." "Animal" distinguishes living from nonliving: *anima*. "Beast" brings out the element of ferociousness, whereas "brute" accentuates lack of speech. I will use "animal" as a neutral term whenever the context does not require one of the stronger senses. "Animal" is also better because it does not immediately exclude the possibility of communication or common activity.

Let us reflect for an additional moment on Zarathustra's animals. The eagle has sharp eyes as well as a powerful beak and talons; it is a superb aviator and is stronger than other birds. Hence it rules the air and can escape from possible enemies on the ground. Furthermore, it is not modified by sympathy or sentiment. The eagle is unmoved by any consideration other than the direct expression of its natural strength and grace. The eagle's very freedom from restrictions on its expression of power makes it an excellent symbol of pride. Pride shades into cruelty, arrogance, lack of sympathy, and mercilessness. What keeps it from deteriorating into these "bestial" or "brutal" qualities? In human beings, it is properly attuned by a standard or table of values, by a sense of the noble; the eagle represents the natural foundation of the rank-ordering of human values. This representation makes sense because the look of the eagle is one that we associate with proud persons, and in the eagle this look is concentrated, much purer or more intense than it is in human beings. The case of the serpent is quite different. Serpents do not look cunning or wise. They do, however, slide silently along the face of the earth, unseen and unheard until they strike their enemy unawares. Serpents are a metaphorical expression of a low wisdom, the wisdom of deceit and poisonous attack. Mythical associations of the serpent with wisdom express a merited fear of the intellect, which enables us to trick the other animals and thereby to overcome their physical advantages, but also to trick our fellow humans.

Tastes vary, but I think it is reasonable to say that serpents do not strike us as noble in their motion, in part because eagles are above us, whereas snakes are for the most part beneath our feet, in the dirt or the grass. "Eagle in the sky" is not a pejorative expression when applied to a human being, as is "snake in the grass." We fear serpents as we do not normally fear eagles. The eagle could attack us, of course, but its natural habitat keeps it for the most part separate from human beings. Even if the same is true of snakes, they are in location closer to us; and we walk in their domain as we cannot do in the air. Finally, the eagle is not only physically higher as a resident of the sky, but it is at a higher stage of evolution, and so closer to us, than is the snake. Pride is more natural to us than the cunning of intelligence: This is certainly implied by Nietzsche's image. It should also be noted that Nietzsche does not give intelligence explicit dominance over spiritedness, as does Socrates' analysis of the soul in the *Republic*. Perhaps we are to assume that the cunning serpent whispers into the ear of the eagle and thereby directs his flight.

More could be said, but I will leave it at this: The phenomenological look of the eagle's behavior is more directly, but not completely, representative of the property which we ascribe to it than is the look of the serpent's behavior. Serpents do not look wise, but they do look cunning. The linking of the serpent with the eagle should not then be straightforwardly understood as an emphasis on pride and intelligence. The pride of the eagle is very close to cruelty; the intelligence of the serpent is not wisdom but cunning.

So much for the significance of the eagle and the serpent in themselves. But there are two other points that require comment. First: The eagle is said to soar in circles, with the serpent wrapped round its neck. This gives us a circle around a circle. The eagle is the eternal return as a natural force: merciless and strong. The serpent is the human interpretation of the eternal return, an interpretation of cunning rather than of wisdom; that is, an interpretation that is required in order to allow us to neutralize the mercilessness and cruel strength of the process itself. From this standpoint the fact that *Schlange* is feminine is again suggestive.

Second: Why does Zarathustra associate with animals? Why not a more straightforward presentation of the properties required by a philosophical prophet who is a destroyer as well as a creator, and so who soars above mankind with the pride of an eagle and the cunning of a serpent? For the time being, the following suggestion is in order.

The animals are a middle region between the inanimate forces of nature and human beings. Zarathustra requires this level of insulation and is himself a resident of that level. He is closer to his animals than he is to the present race of human beings. The animals will lead him safe in the midst of the dangers he faces from human beings.

In the last statement of the Preface, Zarathustra himself brings out the difference between his two animals. "If only I were cleverer (*klüger*). If only I were clever from the ground up (*von Grund aus*), like my serpent! But here I ask for the impossible. So I ask my pride that it always accompany my cleverness." Kaufmann translates *klüger* as "wiser," which I feel is not the right word here, although it is one of the possible meanings of the German term. "Cleverer" is both more literal (*weiser* would be literally "wiser") and better expresses the property represented by the snake. The idiom *von Grund aus,* "thoroughly," also alludes directly to the connection between the ground and the snake.

Zarathustra lacks the cleverness and cunning, and in that sense the wisdom, of the serpent, which is illustrated in the biblical story of the fall of man in the Garden of Eden. His cleverness must be sustained – literally, raised up – by his pride. And when his cleverness deserts him, as it loves to do, "let my pride then fly with my folly." The eagle flies, not the serpent. How will the serpent get away? Only by persuading the eagle to land on a tree branch or the ground. Serpentine cunning is thus both required and insufficient for the task that Zarathustra's pride sets for him. Pride seems to be higher than the wisdom of cleverness. This corresponds to the dominant role of the will in the act of production. But the will is incapable of proper activity without the whispered advice of cunning.

So much for the Preface, which, although it is contained in Part One of *Zarathustra,* in fact anticipates the outcome of the entire work. We are now ready to study the speeches of Zarathustra as he "goes under" (28). This expression has sometimes been taken to refer to the setting of the sun; if this is right, then the speeches of Zarathustra are delivered in the dark, despite their internal temporality. In this sense, the speeches are all "night songs" (to borrow the title of a speech in Part Two). It is both impossible and unnecessary to study each speech exhaustively; we shall have to be selective without omitting anything essential. Nietzsche assists us here because of his repetitiveness; nevertheless, if our view of the whole is not to disappear into endless detail, we must pass by themes of secondary importance as well as passages which repeat in another idiom a point that has already been made more effectively.

ZARATHUSTRA'S SPEECHES: PART ONE

"On the Three Metamorphoses" (Section 1)

The last sentence of the Preface reads: "Thus began Zarathustra's descent." Kaufmann's translation implies that the descent begins with the conclusion of the Preface. In fact, however, Zarathustra's descent began at the start of the Preface, which is a general introduction, whereas the speeches of Part One are an initial stage of the development of the doctrine. In this connection, we have to consider Zarathustra's location. We are told at the end of the first section that he is now sojourning in the city of the Motley Cow. This odd name combines two apparently contrasting characteristics. The cow, like the camel of the first speech, is a cud-chewer, a trait associated by Nietzsche with tradition and the unoriginal repetition of past customs. The diverse coloring conveyed by "motley" is also applied to the costume of the jester in the Preface. Nietzsche may be alluding here to the spiritual emptiness of late-modern democratic diversity, in a way that recalls Socrates' criticism in Books VIII and IX of the *Republic* of the association between variety and license in the Athenian democracy.

To turn now to the first speech (29), Zarathustra introduces three transformations of the spirit. *Geist* refers to mankind as a whole, to its highest aspiration; *Seele* refers to the personal or subjective side of the individual human being. It is the spirit, not the soul, that becomes a camel; the latter is a modification of what one could call the human essence. This is developed in the next two paragraphs of the speech.

The spirit in which reverence (*Ehrfurcht*) dwells is presented with many burdens; *Schwere* can mean heavy things or difficulties; later in the work it will be personified as the spirit of heaviness or gravity that impedes ascent. Here, however, the meaning is different. The strength of the reverent spirit, or human aspiration, "longs for" (*erlangt nach*) what is heavy and for the heaviest; in other words, for what is difficult. This is how we develop, and it is what Nietzsche means by "will to power." But will to power is expressed initially as reverence, namely, as reverence before the gods and so by extension before the tradition that manifests the will of the gods. Reverence means bowing down to what is higher than ourselves. This is the necessary foundation of the distinction between the human and the superhuman, hence between the noble and the base. We master our primitive fear by the transformation of natural forces and heavenly bodies into gods. In so doing, we animate them; this is the basis of personification, which is extended to every aspect of natural being, not only to the stars and the planets, but to mountains, lightning, thunder, trees and bushes, animals, and eventually to human beings.

Reverence is the first stage in the conquest of nature. It is a slavish condition when viewed from above, but it is necessary in itself. And it takes determinate shape as the camel. This transformation into the camel is willed by an external force. "What is heavy? Thus asks the spirit that is able to bear; so it kneels down, like the camel, and wants to be well loaded." Being heavily burdened makes the spirit happy in its strength. This is as true of the superman as it is of the camel. It is not the camel that asks the series of questions addressed initially to "you heroes," but the spirit of reverence.

There follow a series of rhetorical questions about what is heaviest or most difficult to bear. Let us look ahead for a moment; immediately after this list, Zarathustra says: "All these heaviest things the spirit that is capable of bearing takes upon itself, like the camel that, loaded up, hurries into the desert; thus the spirit hurries into its desert." This could mean that the spirit is already like a camel as it asks these questions and then kneels to take on its burden. But such a reading fails to harmonize with the opening phrase "how the spirit became a camel." I think that this opening phrase is decisive; the human spirit is not by nature a camel but is unformed or incomplete. At this point we may remember the doctrine of the eternal return: If the stages of the transformation recur, then the camel was formerly a child. Zarathustra does not tell us in this paragraph that the child will decay into a camel, because in this context the child represents the possibility of a new epoch: the coming of the superman. But we have read the Preface, and we know that the present stage is already the beginning of the last men.

In other words, if we look at our own historical epoch, we are much closer to the camel than to the lion or the child. There is a certain deterioration in the camel's endurance; its reverence is breaking down: "God is dead," although the camel is not yet fully cognizant of this fact. We are still carrying the dead weight of tradition. But if we look at the full cycle of transformations of the spirit, and so at a complete cycle of the eternal return, then we can say that the spirit begins by transforming its aspiration to overcome into reverence, or the bearing of burdens. To overcome is and must be initially to bear the burden, that is, to undergo the process of animating, humanizing, and so eventually assimilating or conquering nature. We cannot begin by ourselves becoming supermen.

On the other hand, as the representation of innocence, rebirth, and potentiality for the new, the child is the precondition for the coming of the superman. Accordingly, the camel must become a lion before becoming a child, and the child can become either a superman or another camel. The superman, then, must be a disruption of the tripartite transformation. Let us keep this general problem in mind and return to the text. What can we make of the series of questions posed by the reverent spirit? The first question reminds us of Christianity by citing humility and folly as the heaviest burden. The second sounds like an inversion of the Christian doctrine of Satan tempting Christ: as if Christ were to part from his cause when it triumphs and climb high mountains to tempt the tempter. In general Zarathustra means that in order to overcome, one must abandon the triumphant cause for a higher triumph. But how could the camel pose this as a possible choice?

We see immediately that the reverent spirit, although it is like the camel in kneeling down to be loaded up, is not as such or at once the same as the camel. It is in the process of justifying the decision to become a camel. Apropos of the third question: If I become a camel, I will have to eat acorns and grass instead of beefsteaks and pastries. But won't this keep me hungry and train me for the task of overcoming? Question four contains an ironic reference to Zarathustra's own present condition. It is harder to make friends with the deaf than to be sick and have sent home the comforters. The sickness is that of one who has been repudiated; the citizens have turned a deaf ear to him, yet Zarathustra takes them as his friends in place of those who, like the holy man in the forest at the beginning of the Preface, would have kept him in isolation. Thus question five alludes to the task that awaits Zarathustra: The waters of truth are filthy because of the frogs and toads that inhabit them. "Cold" refers to unsympathetic and "hot" to foolish disciples who will misunderstand his teaching. Question six

(30) concerns the recommendation to love those who despise us: This is Zarathustra's version of Christianity; he insists on bringing his message to those who despise it. And he will offer a hand to the (holy) ghost who tries to frighten him.

In sum: The three transformations apply to Zarathustra's own career and not simply to the human spirit as such. His persistence in the face of the incomprehension of his auditors, whether hostile or friendly, is a mark of his own reverence for what is highest. The first speech is then appropriately enough quite general and indicates the structural isomorphism between the spirit of Zarathustra and the cycle of human history.

So Zarathustra speeds off into the desert with his burden; and it is in the desert that the second transformation will occur. Again, we have to understand it as applying both to mankind in its historical development and to Zarathustra as he will evolve in the course of the present work. With respect to history, the camel represents the epoch of Egypt. According to Herodotus (book II, 37), the Egyptians are the most pious of men; they have the largest number of gods. In Zarathustra's personal history, the camel represents acquiescence in contemporary decadence. We should not assume that the three stages of spirit are literally or simply chronological; Zarathustra will also behave like a lion and a child. Nevertheless, the overall stance is that of resignation to the fact of decadence; the time is not yet ripe for the understanding, let alone the reception, of Zarathustra's prophecy. And Zarathustra respects this, as his disciples do not. He shows reverence for the tradition in this sense; it has to achieve the precise moment of ripeness in order to decay.

"In the loneliest desert, however, the second transformation occurs: The spirit becomes a lion who wishes to capture freedom and become master in his own desert." The desert stands for Zarathustra's isolation in the midst of decadence. At this point, strength and courage are required. The lion takes his own freedom as booty. As booty from whom? I believe that it is from the camel, that is, from itself as acquiescent, burdened. This experience must be transformed into something positive; exile is transformed into an inner or spiritual kingdom in which the lion is master. The passage continues: "He looks here for his last master"; "here" means "here in the desert." The last master was not some external ruler, but the camel-determination of the spirit. The lion wants to become an enemy to that last master and to his last god; "he wants to struggle with the great dragon for victory." It is unclear whether the last god is identical with the great dragon, but we may take our bearings by Zarathustra's own reference to the dragon: "Thou shalt" ("Du sollst").

As the continuation makes clear, the great dragon is the Western tradition that guards the entrance out of the cave of the decadent city with the accumulated values of the past two millennia. These values are fundamentally Christian. But "thou shalt" certainly reminds us of the Ten Commandments: "Thou shalt not kill," "thou shalt have no other Gods before me," and so on. In addition, the dragon is ferocious, whereas the dove would be a better symbol of Christianity. I suspect that Nietzsche is here indicating that Judaism supplies the muscle to Christianity, but also that the apparent pacifism of Christianity is in fact quite ferocious and weakens our courage to destroy, the courage required for creation. This is why the stage of the lion is needed; more precisely, the lion of Judah. The spirit of the lion says, "I will." It should be remembered that in Nietzsche's fully developed doctrine there is no "I." The ego is an illusory combination of continuously dissolving points of consciousness, which are themselves physiological affects, or at bottom moments of will to power. The lion represents a stage of the spirit, which is the effective manifestation of chaos. The spirit projects the lion as an image or simulacrum of itself as particular persons.

From the standpoint of world history, the lion refers first to particular periods like that of the Greek heroes and the Italian soldier-artists of the Renaissance; second, it refers to an imaginary time that exists only in Zarathustra's (or Nietzsche's) imagination. It is in fact not an epoch but a moment, an *Augenblick* that is, to adapt a Hegelian metaphor, the absolute counterpart to the temporal moment in which Hegel understands the significance of Napoleon at the battle of Jena as "reason on horseback." As we have seen, in *Beyond Good and Evil* Nietzsche identifies the prophet-philosopher or lawgiver as the man who says, "Thus shall it be" ("So soll es sein"). Here he says, "I will" ("Ich will").

Zarathustra then explains to his "brothers" why we need the lion. I postpone the question of the identity of the brothers. Neither the camel nor the lion can create new values. And the camel is also incapable of creating the freedom from old values which is the necessary precondition for the creation of new values. The lion is needed "to create freedom for new creation," hence to say a holy no to the obligations of the whole tradition. This is extremely interesting; the lion is still restricted by the tradition he repudiates. The child starts with a *tabula rasa*. It is once more evident that Nietzsche is talking about the three stages of his own spiritual development. First: He assimilates Western culture, which is primarily Greco-Roman (and in so doing he is immunized against the Judeo-Christian dimension, although this is not completely ignored but rather radically transformed on the pagan basis). Second: He manifests the courage to reject the command "thou shalt" or to obey the values of Western culture. Nietzsche's "reverence" for these values persists even in the midst of decadence. But they are now eroding, and it is time to expose the substructure of illusion, as the preparation for a fresh beginning.

This beginning is represented as the activity of a child. And here an interesting difficulty becomes visible. Zarathustra assumes that children have no memory or that they act spontaneously: "The child is innocence and forgetting, a new beginning, a game, a wheel that rolls out of itself, a first excitation, a holy yea-saying" (31). It is true that children do not act on the basis of a rational reappropriation and application of tradition. But it is also true that they act out of obedience to their elders, from habituation. Accordingly, the children must be separated from their parents, just as Socrates notes in the *Republic;* but they must also be prepared for what is here portrayed as spontaneous production. Without such preparation, their action is unpredictable, haphazard, childish.

A moment's reflection thus shows us that the rhetoric of the child conceals the need for indoctrination. This is the task of the book we are studying. Zarathustra, the hero of the book, is neither a camel, a lion, nor a child. All three are elements or modalities in the growth and cultivation of his spirit. The child stands for a new beginning but not for a truly spontaneous beginning. The prophet-lawgiver must prepare the context from which the work of the child originates and by which it is guided.

Zarathustra's reference to "a wheel that rolls out of itself" is a prefiguring of the eternal return. If the child is a recurrence of what has already occurred, or if the new beginning is neither new nor spontaneous but necessary and predetermined, why is an invocation to revolution required? The answer must be that invocations as a response to decadence, although they appear from the human perspective to be spontaneous acts of the will, are in fact necessary consequences of the shifting configurations of chaos: of the dispersion and accumulation of power.

In other words: From within the illusion, human beings must be persuaded to act spontaneously or freely. But as seen from above downward, outside the illusion, from Nietzsche's own "Hyperborean" stance, the need for persuasion is itself an enactment of fate. Hence philosophy is *amor fati.* This distinction is fundamental for our understanding of the entire book. That is why Zarathustra says that "for the game of creation, a holy yea-saying is required." Creation is a game precisely because of the innocence of Becoming: Becoming is the fluidity of chaos, not the enactment of divine will or a transcendental teleology. The yea-saying is holy, not as an expression of a transcendent deity, but as an assertion of the divinity of the human being who says yes and thereby delivers the rules of the game.

But this is all communicated indirectly in the details of the prophecy, which is externally couched in the rhetoric of an invocation to Zarathustra's "brothers" to act. The invocation is to those whom Zarathustra wishes to persuade that they are spirits akin to himself. I have no doubt that in the next sentence Nietzsche is speaking, through the words of Zarathustra, of himself: "Spirit now wills its own will; he who has been lost to the world wins *his* world." Nietzsche has no place in the world of nineteenth-century Europe; but he is about to set into motion the creation of a world which is his in the sense that he can live in it. But note: As the lawgiver, Nietzsche is also outside this world; he cannot fully live within it except by forgetting the fact that he has created it or that he sees its ultimately illusory status.

"Thus spoke Zarathustra." This phrase recurs at the end of each section of Part One. It continues in Part Two until the section called "The Grave Song," where it is replaced by "Thus sang Zarathustra." In the section "On the Redeemer," no such phrase occurs. The general situation is like that in the Platonic dialogues; attention is drawn away from the deeds of the hero by the emphasis placed on his speeches. It is up to the discerning reader to balance the scales. The broad distinction between speaking and singing corresponds to a difference in the personal intensity of the communication.

"On the Despisers of the Body" (Section 4)

Sections 2 and 3 contain straightforward criticisms of the values and religious beliefs of the academicians of Nietzsche's day. At first glance, Section 4 is a continuation of the same theme. As we look more closely, however, there are some significant shifts in emphasis and doctrine. Perhaps the most important is that Zarathustra will now make explicit his critique of the doctrine of the primacy of the ego. " 'Body am I and soul' – thus speaks the child" (39). But those who are awake and who know say something quite different. This brings out an important qualification of the initial tripartition of the soul into camel, lion, and child. The child is the symbol of rebirth and innocence, hence of the possibility of creation. But we now learn that the child is also the symbol of sleep, dreams, illusion, and ignorance. The child has to wake up and become an adult. To be an adult is to say that one is nothing but body: "Soul is only a word for something about the body."

Previously we distinguished spirit, soul, and heart. Now we are about to reduce the dualism between soul and body, although not between spirit and body on the one hand or heart and body on the other.

Nietzsche is here attacking in the first instance the Christian doctrine of the separation of soul and body, a doctrine which is also to be found in the Platonic dialogues, although with considerable attendant ambiguities. "The body is a great reason (*Vernunft*), a multiplicity with one sense, a war and a peace, a herd and a shepherd." This unites the features of the traditional dualism between soul and body. Body is itself reason, hence both the shepherd and the herd. But it is also a multiplicity with one sense or meaning. There is no war between soul and body, but rather a war of corporeal moments; and this war is also peace, or meaningful integration of moments of force. The meaning is that of the will to power.

In place of the old dualism between body and soul, Zarathustra announces the dualism of the great and the small reason: body and spirit. The spirit is the tool of the body; in other words, just as heaven is a projection of earth, so civilization and *Bildung* are expressions of physiology or desire. Zarathustra inverts the heavenly and the pandemic Eroses introduced by Pausanias in the *Symposium*. Instead of an erotic ascent, there is a descent into the ground, back to the roots of life. And self-consciousness is not the independent master of the body, but its toy. The body *plays* with the spirit. The body, or great reason, is the playing boy, the *pais paizōn*, as Heraclitus calls Zeus. This is a clear expression of Nietzsche's reversed Platonism.

The Platonic ascent to the Ideas is also an ascent from the ego or personal consciousness to a universal perception of the universal. It is thus an ascent from the living to the nonliving; one could express this in genuinely Platonic metaphors as an ascent from life to death by way of the love of the deathless, which, as such, is also lifeless. Zarathustra reverses this, but not in order to reaffirm the ego. The ego is reduced to the self, *das Selbst:* " 'I' thou sayest and art proud of this word, but greater is that in which thou willest not to believe, – thy body and its great reason: This does not say I but does I." The will of the ego, as such, is not the will to power but a mask or an illusion: a simulacrum or a false image of the deeper will. The ego wills its own survival and as a consequence projects the imaginary heaven of Christianity. The body, or great reason, is not an ego, not personal, but also not the lifeless universal of Platonism. Personality, self-consciousness, the ego are all projections or deeds of bodily activity.

This is a pivotal assertion: The ego is not a substance, and it is not primarily *logos*. Speech, including the speeches of Zarathustra, is a kind of action. The ego is activity; here again we hear echoes of German Idealism and Kant: In Kant, the categories and rules are products of the activity of thinking. Thinking *actualizes* as categories and rules; it is not an independent activity of a self-conscious substance that applies eternal and separate categories to objects of perception. Stated with maximum concision and in a way that brings out the preparation for Nietzsche: The world as object of rationality is an artifact of transcendental activity. The world is a work of art produced by the transcendental ego, which is of course not a person and not even a god, but the world-constituting activity of thinking and perceiving.

Nietzsche transforms the world-constituting activity of the transcendental ego into the world-constituting activity of the earth, the body, or, as Zarathustra is about to call it, the self. Underneath thoughts and feelings, or the Kantian *Verstand* and *Empfindung*, is the mighty master and unknown sage called the self that not only lives in, but is, the body (40). The self is not the I or the ego; we should not be confused by the fact that Zarathustra personifies it in his account of what the self says to the ego. The self does not think; hence it cannot think or be conscious of itself. The leaps and flights of thought of the ego are detours to the deeper ends of the self: The ego is the puppet of the self, and its thoughts are all designed by the self in order to feel pleasure and avoid pain.

This is Nietzsche's materialism, or physiologism. The purpose of thinking is not to know the truth but to give pleasure to the body. Note the similarity of Freud's doctrine of the ego as a projection or crystallization of the id. The self is the life force of the body expressed as the pleasure principle. This is the principle of thinking: We are made in such a way as to think in order to acquire pleasure and avoid pain. "The creative self created for itself respect and contempt; it created for itself pleasure and pain. The creative body created spirit for itself as a hand of its will." There is of course no explanation in Nietzsche as to how this act of creation happens. Nietzsche projects the illusion of an explanation of life as will to power. But the reduction of life to physiology, and of physiology to a modification of Becoming, or chaos, does not account for the reverse movement or development from the nonliving to the living.

Today we explain this as a chemical process; although Nietzsche was not a Darwinian, the two accounts are nevertheless not incompatible. But the same argument arises with respect to Darwinian and Nietzschean evolution: How explain the shift from the lifeless to the living? And second: Even if the chemical explanation is accepted as more satisfactory than that of dualism or divine creationism, what has this evolutionary materialism to do with the structure of the intelligible world (including that of the genetic code) and human values? If nobility, to take the decisive Nietzschean example, is manifested by virtue of chemical transformations of primeval matter, that does not make nobility into a chemical transformation. Furthermore, if the spirit is the hand of the will of the body, then civilization is a consequence of the desire for pleasure. Pleasure, however, is also a creation of the body; it is not the ultimate stratum of nature. Zarathustra speaks of pleasure as an artifact of the will to power; more generally, life itself is the accumulation of power.

The section concludes with a condemnation of the despisers of the body. At first glance, it seems that Zarathustra is attacking Platonist and Christian asceticism; many have inferred from this assumption that Zarathustra advocates a celebration of bodily pleasure as part of his repudiation of Christian morality. But this is an impossible interpretation. It is true that for Nietzsche moral asceticism is a consequence of ressentiment, that is, of resentment against one's own low social position, poverty, physical ugliness, sickness, and other defects. But the healthy, noble, brave, and powerful human animal, who, as healthy, is also beautiful, is not one who dissipates his strength on sensuality. The superman is a creator of life-enhancing works of art, a doer of splendid deeds, not a hedonist or a libertine. This will become explicit when we read the section on the chastity of the philosopher.

"On the Pale Criminal" (Section 6)

In *Zarathustra,* Nietzsche both prepares an enlightenment of mankind and signals the "horrible" nature of its antecedent. Exaggeration and frankness go hand in hand in the rhetoric of decadence. The relation between the good or healthy and bad or sick aspects of the Enlightenment is now taken up, following Zarathustra's analysis of suffering as the essence of joy. Otherwise stated, health and sickness are no more sharply separable than joy and suffering. Whereas previously Zarathustra spoke of the relation between the thief and the night watchman, he will now deepen this analysis in terms of the relation between the criminal and the judge. To state the pivotal point of my interpretation at the outset, the pallor of the criminal is Nietzsche's own mask of enlightenment. Nietzsche, the father of Zarathustra, is not only the agent of transfiguration or salvation but also of a radicalization of decadence. In slightly different terms, Nietzsche meditates here on his own guilt as a revolutionary who can teach only by destroying. There is an implicit comparison between himself and Christ, who combines judge and criminal by taking upon himself the sins of mankind.

My discussion of the pale criminal is also directed toward a broader hermeneutical goal. This section contains the most difficult of all the parts of *Zarathustra.* Nietzsche's good friend the classicist Erwin Rohde said of it: "In some sections the figuration strikes me as taken, not out of life, but as from an isolation that is a stranger to this world, a ghostly abstract representation . . ."[1] If "The Pale Criminal" proves to be intelligible, then we can with considerable confidence assume the same to be true of the work as a whole.[2]

Consider first the title "On the Pale Criminal." What image does this communicate? A criminal is of course a lawbreaker. Pallor may remind us of the prison cell, where little, if any, sunlight shines. But it may also remind us that Zarathustra is currently resident in the city of the Motley Cow; "motley" refers to the multicolored gay, vivid dress of the court fool, the jester who entertains the king, whereas "cow" stands for complacency, thoughtlessness, and chewing the cud and so evokes the camel in the speech "On the Three Metamorphoses." The criminal may be pale because the laws he has broken are those of the city of the Motley Cow. Those who give new laws are of course criminals from the standpoint of the laws they transgress or discard.

I will come back to the striking expression "pale criminal" in a moment. Let us turn to the beginning of the section. Zarathustra addresses otherwise unidentified "judges and sacrificers" (45). As the image makes plain, judges are like the pagan priests who sacrifice the criminal in order to expiate his sins, but also like those priests who sacrifice a scapegoat to purify the city of its sins. In this case, the scapegoat is of course innocent of any crime. But scapegoats do not assent to their sacrifice, whereas the judges anticipate or at least expect this from the pale criminal. The judges and sacrificers do not want to kill until the animal has nodded. Assent here means that the criminal not only admits his guilt but is prepared to be destroyed as part of his own sacrifice for the sake of the creation of new values.

This point needs to be developed in some detail. "To nod" [*nicken*] can mean both to nod assent, like Zeus when he grants a request, or to doze off. But if anyone is dozing, it is the judges. That the pale criminal is not dozing is evident from "the great contempt" that speaks from his eyes. And evidently he does nod, since Zarathustra indicates a few lines later that the pale criminal has judged himself; he agrees to his own death penalty. A comment on the expression *Thier*, "brute": The pale criminal is closer to the animals than he is to the human beings who judge and execute him. This is also true of Zarathustra, whose audience symbolically judges and executes him by misunderstanding or ignoring him.

The adjective "pale," about which I have already said something, goes oddly with the expression "the great contempt." This expression was used in the Preface by Zarathustra (15) to designate the proper attitude of human beings toward their own existence, in contrast with that of the superman. In order to prepare for the coming of the superman, we must repudiate as contemptible everything that mankind has accomplished. It is not simply the case that destruction precedes creation; creation, as continuous overcoming, is itself destruction. This point is closely related to Zarathustra's earlier identification of joy as suffering and shows how Nietzsche blends Romanticism with *Sturm und Drang* in a way that underlies recent interest in the doctrines of Sade on the one hand and Freud on the other.

In the present speech, Nietzsche develops with a series of dialectically linked antithetical figures the mirror image of the criminal and his judges. We begin with a simple physiological observation. The eyes must be shining brightly in order to express this great contempt, whereas the skin of the criminal is pale. Zarathustra first explains the great contempt: It is directed against mankind, and so too against the criminal's own ego, or identity as a member of the human race. More precisely: "My ego is to me the great contempt of man." In other words, I myself, as who I am, and so as a man, am the expression of the great contempt, and so of self-contempt. The pale criminal desires to be overcome or to die through the replacement of the species man by the species superman.

The pale criminal thus represents to begin with the previously invoked self-recognition by mankind of its own contemptibleness. This self-contempt is already a desire to overcome and also to be overcome. We see here an example of the principle that extreme forgetfulness is not only motivated by, but is itself a concealed version of, recollection, or clear vision. Even the lowest types who suffer from ressentiment against the world wish to elevate themselves to the level at which they are representatives of the Christian God.

On this basis, we may return once more to the name "pale criminal" and say that its bearer is a criminal because he has repudiated the laws of his own civilization and pale because his crime was an expression of the impossibility of further existence. The pale criminal is decadent; hence his acquiescence in his death sentence. The prophet, or lawgiver, is already too decadent to enter into the promised land; he must sacrifice himself in the act of lawgiving. This helps deepen our understanding of "the great contempt." Enthusiasm for the future is also contempt for the present. The pale criminal is altogether more awake than his judges. He holds them in contempt, whereas they merely pity him (although pity is higher than vengeance, as Zarathustra is about to say). At the same time, however, the judges are a projection of Nietzsche's self-condemnation, which is also represented by the acquiescent nod of the criminal.

I believe it will be helpful at this point to make a brief comparison between the present scene and the trial of Socrates as recounted in Plato's *Apology*. Socrates behaves in such a way as to elicit the death penalty. It has been suggested that he does this in order to show that philosophers will subordinate themselves to the laws (*nomoi*) of the city. His life is coming to its natural close; what better way, the suggestion continues, to complete it than by demonstrating that, despite the private conversation in the Piraeus, the philosopher will not subvert the city? I regard this suggestion as plausible in general, although some questions remain. Does not Socrates' forcing of the death penalty also entail that he is guilty of hubris? Alternatively, if he is unjustly condemned, then why should a philosopher conform to injustice?

In order to show that the philosopher obeys the law, Socrates might very well have accommodated himself to the charges raised against him by requesting a reasonable penalty instead of making the outrageous claim that he is the city's benefactor and deserves public support for the rest of his life, like the victors at the Olympian games. He could also have avoided the trial by living a more circumspect life. The problem he faced was clearly to politicize philosophy in part, and so to come into conflict with the *nomos,* yet to refrain from a full repudiation of its verdict.

Who would be fooled by Socrates' behavior? Certainly not those who are shrewd enough to rule the city, as Protagoras points out in the Platonic dialogue bearing his name. These few are capable of seeing through the disguises worn by the wise men (*sophoi*) who conceal their views concerning politics. Protagoras assumes that he can combine frankness with valuable service to the discerning and powerful few. This service consists in educating the sons of the ruling class in how to govern the city. Socrates' behavior is much closer to that of the pale criminal. He demonstrates his "great contempt" by hubristic behavior, not simply prior to being accused but even during his trial.

Our questions about Socrates resolve into the following query: What does Socrates do to the sons of the ruling class? It is true that by making a show of his obedience to the *nomos,* he implies that he, or philosophy, is not a revolutionary. Yet this is patently falsified by the insolence toward *nomos* that he has exhibited throughout his life, and never more so than when forcing the verdict of death. Nonetheless, the death of Socrates is the mask of his insolence, and the paradigm of the relation between theory and practice that, thanks to the still more revolutionary Plato, he leaves to subsequent ages. The peculiarity of the Platonic analysis is that Socrates expresses the great contempt in the *Apology* as a sign of the superiority of philosophy to political life, whereas his pallor is expressed in the *Crito* as the subordination of philosophy to the *nomos.* Nietzsche presents the inner unity of these two figures in one and the same text. In sum: Plato preserves philoso-phy behind the mask of conformity; Nietzsche condemns the philosophy of the tradition to death, a fate that is a necessary element in the preparation for a new epoch.

The Platonic mask leads directly to the public appearance of philosophy as disguised by demotic justice. How does Nietzsche understand this paradigm of transformation through accommodation to the many? This accommodation has the dangerous consequence of politicizing philosophy. As is evident in the speech "On the Chairs of Virtue," it is Nietzsche's contention that philosophy in late-nineteenth-century Europe is nothing more than political philosophy in the pejorative sense of an apologia for the state and bourgeois society. Socrates' death is the first act in a drama that culminates in the acceptance by the pale criminal of the sentence of his execution.

Nietzsche, in other words, represents his own honesty in this acquiescence. It is he who nods while expressing with his eyes the great contempt. But in his persona as the most decadent, and hence the highest representative of a decadent age,[3] his contempt is directed toward himself. Socrates dies with a clean soul; he is innocent, and no great contempt shines from his eyes. His crime is an act of initiation, and there can be no injustice prior to the founding of the philosophical city. But Nietzsche's soul is unclean; the Socratic experiment is over, and Nietzsche's honesty is the knife that will slit the throat of the scapegoat. Honesty is like the creative frenzy of the Dionysian who struggles to forget because he recollects all too clearly. Nietzsche's creativity is required by the decadence of the age that has produced him.

We can then understand Zarathustra's assertion that the self-judgment by the pale criminal was his highest moment; that is, the peak of decadence, or the self-understanding that is possible only when an age has run its course and is beginning to dissolve. The first step in this dissolution is the mask of forgetfulness, although it will be donned once more as we pass from this stage of the eternal return to the next.

The sentencing of the criminal to death must be an expression of the pity of the judges, not an act of vengeance. As the spokesmen of an age, they would in the latter case be taking vengeance against themselves, that is, against their own highest aspirations. Old age is pitiful; better a quick death. And this also casts light on Nietzsche's self-analysis. As in the case of Socrates, despite all differences, the concealed survival of the noble is, precisely as concealed, an expression of baseness; hence Nietzsche's extraordinary honesty.

It is Nietzsche's view, in other words, that this natural concealment is valid only as the forgetfulness of a virile epoch of civilization: It is the expression of the structure of the difference between the few and the many. When energy begins to dissipate, concealment loses its political but also its aesthetic validity and becomes mere self-indulgence, mannerism, and at last self-deception, or the mistaken view that one is living dangerously and creatively rather than as the solitary actor of an empty ritual.

The invocation to destroy is thus also the nodding by which the pale criminal assents to his own death. In so doing, he exercises a last outburst of courage, and may thus be said to provide the motile power that launches his hope into the future. Nietzsche, as the pale criminal, has nothing to lose: Either he will succeed in clearing the way for an epoch amenable to the happy few, or he will fail, and the inevitable epoch of the last men will institute itself, as would have been the case had he not launched his revolutionary campaign.

To return to the judges, Zarathustra urges them to justify life as they kill the pale criminal. Their sorrow at carrying out the execution shall then be love of the superman. But this assumes that the judges are capable of such a love. If the judges are another aspect of Nietzsche himself, this is possible. But as separate from, and lower than, the pale criminal – in other words, as the priests and rulers of the present age – they are indeed engaging in an act of vengeance against their own higher nature. Zarathustra wishes to persuade them to reach a higher level by regarding their victim as an enemy rather than a villain, as sick rather than a scoundrel, as a fool rather than a sinner.

This triple reinterpretation would transform the verdict from a legal to a military, medical, and pedagogical act. Some dignity would accrue to self-destruction, the same dignity that marks Nietzsche's own readiness to sacrifice everything he holds dear for the sake of the coming of the superman.[4] It would no longer be an empty, self-deluded ceremony, but an act of purification and an expression of health. Zarathustra thus implies that the judges and the criminal are two sides of the same phenomenon. By admitting that their highest aspirations lead to the destruction of their own society, the judges are condemning themselves to death. When we understand this self-condemnation at its deepest level, we see that the judges are also a metaphor for Nietzsche himself.

The next part of our section, beginning with the words "And thou, red judge," is especially difficult to understand. Red stands for blood and also for the scarlet robes of the priestly and judiciary figure. It is a dramatic and powerful color that conceals the thoughts of the judge, which, if they could be known, would be condemned as filthy and poisonous. I take this as a reference to the decadent values of which they are the expression. "But thought is one thing, the deed is another, and the image of the deed still another. The wheel of the ground does not roll between them" (46).

This tripartition refers, I believe, to the three stages of thinking the deed, performing it, and then representing it in a work of art. The deed is the Nietzschean revolution or invocation to the overcoming of mankind. Let us refer to these three stages as thinking, doing or enacting, and portraying. Nietzsche himself exemplifies all three stages. It is his thought that serves as the precondition for the revolution, namely, the Apollonian understanding or circumscription of the whole. And it is his portrayal in writing of this revolution that serves as its initiating deed.

Why then does Zarathustra say that the wheel of the ground does not run between them? What is this wheel? *Grund* means cause and basis, but also purpose or motive. I suggest the following interpretation. The wheel of the ground refers to the sequence of causality or consequence. In this sequence, *A* causes *B*, which in turn results in *C*. But there is no such connective bond that unites the aforementioned three stages. The wheel of the ground does not roll between them, because they are not separate moments but the rotating wheel itself. They are points on the wheel of the eternal return, which is not a wheel of causality and so is not accessible to conceptual understanding, like the circular concept of Hegelian logic.[5]

The wheel of the ground is the groundless ground of chaos, the innocence of Becoming, an ancestor of certain Heideggerian notions, in part attributed by him to Schelling. What this wheel presents in its circuit also "goes to ground," to employ another Hegelian expression, but in a Nietzschean sense. That is, it collapses in order to be reconstituted by the random processes of chaos, which are at once destruction and creation when viewed from a human perspective.

On the other hand, if we consider the three stages as the consequences of Nietzsche's prophetic activity, they are manifested as three different kinds of disciple, each of whom is disconnected from the other two. The thought is the activity of the ideologues; the deed is the work of revolutionary activists, terrorists, soldiers of fortune, and the like. The image of the deed refers to the artist, the valet of morality,[6] who does not think for himself but copies and so popularizes the thoughts of the ideologues: I remind the reader of figures like Thomas Mann, Stefan George, Rainer Maria Rilke, George Bernard Shaw, D. H. Lawrence, André Gide, and T. S. Eliot.

In the next paragraph, Zarathustra shifts to the pale criminal: "An image made this man pale. He was equal to his deed when he did it, but he could not bear its image when it was done." The act of performing the deed modifies the criminal's essential nature by raising him to the level of the deed itself, which expresses the nobility of his nature. But then he looks at the consequences, the image of his deed, which we may identify as representing Nietzsche's disciples; and this he cannot bear.

More generally, I believe that Nietzsche was himself frightened by what he frequently describes as his terrifying doctrines of nihilism and the eternal return, in other words, by the perception of the illusory nature of the interpretations by which human beings both make possible and justify their lives. Nietzsche's Apollonian lucidity led him up to the heights represented in *Beyond Good and Evil* as the esoteric standpoint, and in *The Antichrist* as the land of the Hyperboreans. But Nietzsche was not Apollo; he was a man, a decadent resident of a decadent age, and it was precisely as the exemplification of the best side of this age, its own understanding of its decay, that Nietzsche made his discoveries.

This is of sufficient importance to bear repeating. The peak of decadence comes quite close to what seems initially to be its opposite: the superman. What is decadence but a superfluity of experience, a hyperbolic imagination, excessive refinement of perception with a correlatively exaggerated nervous sensibility, the inability to bear crudeness and baseness, and hence a need for isolation that is protected against boredom only by elaborate experimentation in modes of concealment, an experimentation that sooner or later deteriorates into the manipulation of those whose vulgarity threatens our solitude and so our daydreams of splendor?

In a word, decadence is understanding that one is decadent: The owl of Minerva takes flight only at dusk.[7] And it is this twilit wisdom that mediates between the sunshine of Apollo and the intoxicated darkness of Dionysus. Dissipation of energy is thus the negative form of creative explosion. Closely related to this is the anguish Nietzsche feels as he reflects on the certain consequences of the publication of his books. The books themselves were produced in a synthesis of Apollonian lucidity and Dionysian inspiration. They are Nietzsche's monologue on the inner consequences of decadence, and thus, by explaining these consequences, they negate them, in a way quite close to what Hegel calls the negation of the negation.

Nevertheless, the explanation is not uniform; it speaks differently to the few and to the many, or, more precisely, to the happy few and to the spokesmen for the many, to the deep and to the superficial. Nietzsche warns against publication, which makes truth common and hence base; he implies that the philosopher of the future will say "*my* truth," not "the truth."[8] But in order for *my* truth to be something more than a private reverie, in order for it to be enacted in a historical epoch, it must be published and thus rendered common or at the mercy of disciples.

This is what drove the pale criminal mad: seeing the image or reflection, in other words the consequences of his deed, from which he tried to separate himself by taking responsibility for the deed alone: "Now he always saw himself as the doer of one deed. Madness I call this: The exception was transformed into the essence for him." Once again I have to make an allusion to Hegel. In the *Phenomenology of Spirit*, Hegel uses the word employed here by Zarathustra, *verkehren*, to refer to the "inverted world," or to the result of the process by which rationalist thought attempts to detach the essence of the world from its generated and contingent instantiation.[9]

Hegel refers to the separation of scientific laws, but also of Platonic Ideas or Aristotelian essences, from the instances they explain. To limit myself to the indispensable point, thinking converts the sensuous world into a supersensuous world of essences or laws. But these essences or laws are precisely the inner nature of sensuousness and so are quintessentially sensuous. This is not a fatal contradiction but a crucial step in the unification of essence and appearance, that is, in the process by which essence shows itself *to be* appearance: that which appears or shows itself fully.

I do not mean to suggest that Nietzsche studied or was directly influenced by Hegel. Philosophical influence is in the decisive cases often indirect. However this may be, Nietzsche's very obscure remark about the *sich verkehren* of the deed, taken as an exception to life as it is normally lived, into the essence, has the following meaning. The peak of human existence is philosophical thinking, the exception *par excellence* to life as it is normally lived. But philosophical thought is by its nature productive, not purely theoretical or contemplative. Just as in Hegel, thinking participates in the production of the world. In Hegelian language, the supersensuous, as the essence or defining principle of the sensuous, is sensualized: It is the essence of this sensuous world that appears in the details and as the shape of the sensuous phenomenon.

By denying or repudiating the productive consequences of his thought, the criminal, now grown pale with fear, attempts to reverse or invert the procedure by which temporal existence emerges from the "gateway," or perspective, that is the ancestor of Heidegger's "project." The pale criminal, however, is not what Heidegger calls "authentic" or "genuine." He repudiates his own Eros, or attempts to sublate the results produced by the deed back into the deed, in other words, back into supersensuous thinking. But this is impossible; Zarathustra refers to such an attempt as madness.

We cannot disown the consequences of our thoughts. And thoughts do have consequences; there is, once more, no separation between

Apollo and Dionysus. Exaggerated as it may initially sound, we can say that for Nietzsche there are no unpublished thoughts; certainly this is a historical if not a private truth. Thought makes itself public as the will to power, as the need to spill over, to give and thereby to rule. The essence of the nonlover is the intoxication of love; the essence of love is the clarity of the nonlover.

Zarathustra next draws a further distinction. The criminal attempts to overthrow the established order out of love for the superman; that is, for the sake of overcoming. But the consequences of this deed make him pale with fear and drive him mad; this is what Zarathustra calls madness after the deed. The madness before the deed is the creative, or Dionysian, frenzy of the philosopher.

I turn now to the judges' account of the deed as robbery and murder. "Thus speaks the red judge: 'Why did this criminal commit murder? He wanted to rob.' " To which Zarathustra replies: "But I tell you, his soul wanted blood, not booty; he thirsted after the bliss of the knife" (47). The judge explains the criminal's murder as a consequence of the intention to rob, but this is an error. We rob only if the victim has something that we desire. More fundamentally, the victim must be kept alive so that we can continue to rob him. But the criminal was moved by thirst for the bliss of the knife: by lust for the victim's blood.

The criminal could have continued to support himself by periodically robbing his victim, namely, society. He could have sustained himself on the standards of the age that have in fact formed his own sensibility. Instead he succumbs to a violent desire to destroy, to cut off the hand that feeds him. This is the impulse that we find so often in the highly educated revolutionary decadents of the nineteenth century. Zarathustra goes on to clarify the behavior of the criminal by distinguishing between poor reason and madness. The poor reason does not comprehend the madness. The latter desires blood; it wishes to replace the present decaying order with a world of its own creation. But the poor reason persuades the mad will that this is a desire for vengeance. Why?

Nietzsche's meaning, as I understand it, is this: He who creates as the exemplification of decadence does so in vengeance against his own weakness. One must not, in other words, create for motives or as the direct consequence of a rationalization. Apollo, remember, is a nonlover; he is not spontaneous or productive until he becomes transformed into Dionysus. And Dionysus acts while intoxicated, not rationally. Yet note the irony of the situation: It is the poor reason that persuades the will against mad vengeance. Reason thus contradicts the need for spontaneous creation. And this is Nietzsche's quandary: He must persuade himself to become a partisan of Dionysus, a creator of a new race or breed of human beings; yet creation is a matter of instinct, not of persuasion.

There is, in other words, something wholly lacking in spontaneity and reeking of careful ratiocination in Nietzsche's elaborate destructive critique of Western European civilization, and especially in his invocations to madness and creation. We see through the hyperbolic rhetoric in which this invocation is swathed to the cold calculation of the inner Hyperborean. The perfervid rhetoric of the lawgiver conceals the pallor of the criminal. Pallor is a sign of fear, but fear makes us sober. It is this sobriety that counsels the pale criminal to rob in addition to murdering. But what could the victim possess that is worth stealing?

Nietzsche's text is silent on this point as on so many others; we have to think for ourselves. The only hint is that the robbery takes place so that the criminal will not be ashamed of his madness. I suggest that what the criminal steals is the power of the victim. This is a constant Nietzschean theme; creation is war, and war is the struggle for power. Nietzsche advocates bloodletting and writing in blood, initially in one's own but inevitably in the blood of one's victim. By writing his books in the blood of his victim, the criminal – that is, the revolutionary – steals the manhood of his victim.

As a consequence of listening to the poor reason, which is poor because it contradicts itself or lacks substance, the pale criminal avoids shame by taking vengeance; this is exactly what Zarathustra warned the judges not to do when judging the criminal. The judges are to avoid vengeance by pity; the criminal is to avoid shame by vengeance. By pitying the criminal, who is their own highest self, the judges pity themselves without knowing it. By murdering his victim, the criminal in fact murders the judges, but thereby knowingly commits suicide. He has taken vengeance against himself; hence his shame. Suicide is an act of weakness and despair, not of strength and creative ecstasy.

So "the lead of his guilt lies over" the pale criminal, who is as heavy as lead and pale because of his guilt. But he is also pale because he lacks vigor or virility: He is as good as dead; indeed, as a suicide, he is already a ghost, or at least a heap of diseases, a ball of wild snakes, a sick body, in other words that which is both dissolving and destructive, that which can bite the unwary passerby with the venom of decadence and so transmit to others the shame it feels at its own weakness, a weakness that caused it to strike out as it lay dying, in the effort to create, an effort that has only negative consequences as far as one can see.

Zarathustra says: "Whoever becomes sick now is overcome by the evil that is now evil; he wants to cause pain with what causes him pain." I have now unpacked the content of these cryptic lines. We come at last to the conclusion; and, like the endings of so many Platonic dialogues, there is a descent here from the level of self-revelation to that of the immediate audience. The judges are once more the priests and officials of the city of the Motley Cow. They are too orthodox to listen to the elaborate interpretation of the pale criminal that we, following Nietzsche, have just developed. They want to hear only speeches at their own level of mediocrity, a level that does not harm the "good people," or the citizens of the town.

Zarathustra thus wishes in vain that the people of the city possessed an evil like that of the criminal's madness. In putting the criminal to death, the judges, and so the people for whom they speak, enact their desire to survive rather than to exist at the highest level of intensity. And so Apollo returns, or emerges from the ashes of Dionysus, but as a weakened, vulgar, decadent Apollo. The nonlover returns, fresh from the corpse of the lover, in a further illustration of the reversed world, an illustration of how the dependence of the high upon the low and the noble upon the base inevitably conceals the noble with a mask, not of profundity but of baseness.

My interpretation of the pale criminal may now be summarized in the following terms. The exaltation of Nietzsche's quasi-religious rhetoric of transformation fits like a mask over the features of resignation toward the inevitability of failure. This inevitability can be represented in two fundamental observations. The first is that the production of disciples is a flat contradiction of the doctrine of the superman as radical creator. It is impossible to be a Nietzschean without oneself becoming a slave and thereby exposing Nietzsche's mastery as slavish.

The second observation is that in order to enter into the promised land, the prophet must himself perish. Moses led the Israelites through the desert for forty years so that those who had become decadent through slavery would die before the entrance into Jerusalem. Socrates makes the same point in the *Republic* (VII, 540e5) when he says that in order to found the just city, everyone over the age of ten must be sent off into the countryside. But Socrates, the initiator of political philosophy, does not regard himself as decadent: He is present in his city as its lawgiver. Nietzsche, on the other hand, is the most decadent resident of the most decadent age, who must himself be prevented from entering into the new epoch in his proper historical identity. Otherwise put, Nietzsche praises prophets and lawgivers, but he himself lays down no laws.

Laws bind chaos with an artificial order and thereby prevent the creation of new values. After the lion's liberating slaughter, the child emerges spontaneously, which is to say independently of Nietzsche, whose prophecy is validated only by rejection, or (what comes to the same thing) by the eternal return of the same. What is meant by "the same" in this famous expression? With respect to the figure of the pale criminal, it refers to the perpetual cycle of destructive creations through which chaos organizes itself into illusory and incoherent attempts to overcome destiny. But an overcoming that is at once a loss of identity is not an overcoming at all: It is a momentary perturbation on the surface of chaos.

From this standpoint, the paleness of the pale criminal is the sadness that underlies creative frenzy. What Nietzsche calls the "gay wisdom" is thus finally the happiness of the Hyperboreans and must not be confused with the transient joy of the historical perspective, as represented by the end of Plato's *Symposium,* where a tireless Socrates contends before a half-awake Aristophanes and Agathon that the same man can excel in the writing of comedies and tragedies, a thesis denied by Socrates in the perspective of the ahistorical *Republic.* In the enlightened city, the difference between comedy and tragedy is the reflection of the difference between the Hyperborean philosopher-king and the citizens of silver, bronze, and iron souls. In human history, on the other hand, or in actual cities, the mask of enlightenment is a sign that comedies are nothing more than amusing tragedies.

"On the Tree on the Mountain" (Section 8)

In this section Zarathustra has his first conversation with a resident of the city of the Motley Cow. He notices a youth who is avoiding him (51). The youth has observed something in Zarathustra that makes him uneasy. This is already a mark of kinship. The conversation takes place in the mountains surrounding the city, that is, outside the city. Zarathustra is walking there in the evening and comes upon the youth, who sits leaning against a tree. This setting recalls the *Phaedrus,* an exemplary text for us, which also takes place outside the city, and in which Socrates talks to a youth who is concealing something from him, namely, the scroll containing Lysias's speech on the nonlover. Socrates and Phaedrus stop to enjoy the shade of a tree. But the *Phaedrus* takes place at high noon, a time of concealment via intense illumination, as opposed to the concealing shadows of dusk.

The conversation takes up the first half of the section; the second half consists of a typical Zarathustran monologue, addressed here to the youth rather than to himself or to the citizens in general. Socrates will sometimes end a conversation by telling a myth, as in the *Republic* and the *Phaedo.* Zarathustra begins the conversation by warning the youth that the soul is bent and tormented most by invisible hands: by unheard speeches, as one could also put this; in other words, not simply by a fear of ghosts, or incorporeal beings, but also by doctrines or interpretations that permeate our perceptions without our being fully conscious of them. The youth was thinking of Zarathustra, and now he hears him; this frightens him.

Zarathustra asks why he is frightened and says: "It is with man as with the tree. The more he wishes to rise up into the heights and the clear, all the stronger do his roots strive earthward, downward, into the dark, deep – into evil." Trees mediate between heaven and earth. The spirit cannot overcome without drawing sustenance from the earth understood as the source of creativity; there is no simply heavenly ascent into the heavens. Just as Zarathustra's animals are the eagle and the snake, and as the prince must use both the human and the bestial (Machiavelli), so the effort to transcend outmoded or decadent standards of good and evil, and thus to create a new standard of excellence, is fueled by what is evil in the perspective of the old standards.

This is plain from the youth's subsequent response. He is surprised that Zarathustra has discovered his soul. Zarathustra laughs and says that "one will never discover some souls unless one has first invented them." He has already understood the dilemma faced by the youth, who represents an early and incomplete stage of the awareness by the present generation of the need to take a new turn. The young man is still conditioned by the values of the epoch he wishes to transcend and not yet hardened either to the scorn that is heaped upon the innovator or to the loneliness that he must undergo.

Note also that the discussion is of the soul, not the spirit. The dialogue is intended to bring out the personal anguish of those who are in advance of their contemporaries, who first come to understand what lies ahead and what must be done. It thus tells us something about Nietzsche's own feelings as a youth. "I transform myself too quickly; my Today contradicts my Yesterday" (52). Yesterday is of course convention; this transformation initiates isolation and the suffering induced by loneliness. "My contempt and my longing grow with one another; the higher I climb, the more do I despise him who climbs."

Zarathustra's response refers more to himself than to the youth: It is Zarathustra who has grown higher than man and beast (even higher than the eagle, since the eagle is not a maker of interpretations but an element within an interpretation). If the tree wanted to speak, it would have no one who could understand it. This is Zarathustra's condition, and he knows this from the outset. In other words: He cannot speak openly of what he understands and of what he is doing. His speech is masked by prophecy or poetry: It is masked, or accommodated to the particular condition of his audience. Zarathustra exposes the lower branches but not the top of the tree of his longing. The tree is waiting for the first lightning. This will illuminate the forest and reveal the treetops. But it may also set the trees on fire.

The lightning represents two different illuminations, which are also dangers: The truth is dangerous, not simply salutary. The first danger is that Zarathustra will himself be destroyed when the people understand what he is up to. The second danger is that the youth, in other words the partially emancipated representatives of society, will be destroyed by a fuller understanding of the truth. The lightning was identified in section 4 as the superman. In the present context, the lightning takes the form of the youth's partial emancipation: "What am I now, since thou hast appeared amongst us? It is *envy* of thee that has destroyed me!"

The question now arises: Can Zarathustra enlighten the partially emancipated contemporary, or is such a person too decadent to be preserved? Perhaps partial understanding is worse than complete ignorance. We will get some indication of the answer to this question from the second half of the scene (53–54), which is a monologue delivered by Zarathustra to the weeping youth, whose suffering affects him deeply. He is himself most akin to the sensitive souls who are aware of, but have not succeeded in freeing themselves from, the chains of a decadent epoch. The youth thirsts for freedom, but he is still searching for it. An important point: "But thy bad impulses (*schlimme Triebe*) also thirst for freedom. Thy wild hounds will to be free. They howl with pleasure in their cellar when thy spirit thinks about opening all prisons. To me thou art still a prisoner who is contriving (*ersinnt*) to be free . . ."

This is the fundamental problem of the partially emancipated artist or thinker: The desire for freedom extends to all parts of the soul. Note that it is the spirit that thinks about opening the prisons; the soul is itself a prisoner. The spirit is the force that motivates the soul. But the impulses, or drives, of the soul are not simply imprisoned by it; they imprison the soul. Each is the jailer of the other. The impulses are not fully controllable by the spirit or intellect; they will tear the jailer to pieces if he releases them. In other words, they will destroy the advance guard of the partial revolution. "Even the liberated part of the spirit must purify itself."

It is not enough to be free in the sense of knowing that one wants to be free and so that one is imprisoned. The freedom of the soul through awareness of imprisonment is a partial freedom of the spirit. How can this part be purified? I think that the answer is: Only by being destroyed. The part can be free only if the whole is free. But only the part is capable of positive or healthy freedom; the whole will destroy this part. Otherwise put, the intellect will be destroyed by the spirited and passionate parts of the soul. Phaedrus cannot be raised to the roof of the cosmos. This is to say that the part cannot be freed, cannot be purified. The situation of the youth is insoluble; but Zarathustra does not tell him this openly.

I therefore take Zarathustra's consoling words to the youth to be masked or to possess a double meaning. He asks the youth to preserve his nobility: "By my love and hope I adjure thee: Do not throw away the hero in thy soul. Keep holy thy highest hope!" (54). But the detailed statement that precedes this adjuration indicates the actual situation. The reference to love is also suggestive. In the Preface, Zarathustra claimed to love mankind; when challenged by the holy man, he denied it and said that he was bringing man a gift. Zarathustra also spoke at length in the Preface of those whom he loves. He did so in Section 4, where he referred to himself as the herald of the lightning called *superman* (an expression also applied to the superman in Section 3 in conjunction with "madness"). The present section must be understood in the light of the substitution of "gift" for "love."

Zarathustra "loves" as a destroyer: His love is a gift that is indeed a *Gift*, or *pharmakon*, that poisons in order to produce health. Zarathustra destroys in love, not in hatred or out of vengeance. He recognizes his own kinship with those partially liberated spirits whom he must destroy for the sake of the superman. More precisely, it is Nietzsche who sends Zarathustra as a loving force of illuminating destruction. One could say that by sending Zarathustra, Nietzsche destroys himself or signals that he himself, *qua* decadent soul, must die together with all that he loves in the present epoch.

Note the distinction between noble (*Edel*) and good (*Gut*). "Good" refers to the man who obeys the values of his historical epoch; "noble" refers to the man who wants to create a new virtue, that is, a new epoch. Noble men may also become decadent, or nihilistic. They may become destroyers who do not create.

"Of War and Warriors" (Section 10)

The main addressees of this section are Nietzsche's fellow philosopher-prophets. He speaks through Zarathustra to the great spirits of the past, and in particular to those of the future, in order both to justify his radical break with the former and to provide a standard of conflict with the latter. Secondarily, Nietzsche is speaking to the best of his contemporaries; and these are not the disciples of Zarathustra, but his enemies.

"We do not wish to be spared by our best enemies, and also not by those whom we love from the core. So allow me then to tell the truth to you" (58). Note again the reference to love. This has to be understood in two senses: (1) Zarathustra here expresses Nietzsche's personal longing to meet thinkers or souls at his level of spiritual power, but (2) his love is a gift, and hence it expresses the generosity of enmity, not of love in the conventional sense. The gift is intended to be accepted by the enemies also, and so to triumph over them. In addition, Zarathustra continues to insist that he is speaking the truth to everyone, even to his enemies. But we know that it is a masked or epigrammatic truth that requires deciphering in order to be understood.

Zarathustra goes on to say that he knows the hatred and envy in the hearts of his best enemies because they are persons of his stamp; he knows himself. These are natural passions in the heart of the creator; they become defects only if the creator is ashamed of them. (This point is related to the invocation to violence and the advocacy of mass destruction in the preceding – and here unexamined – section, "On the Preachers of Death.") This is the rhetoric of global war, and not just rhetoric. Zarathustra's enemies are the generals of opposing armies, not university professors or café intellectuals. The hatred is directed against the sick (see the repudiation of pity in a previous section); the envy is directed toward one's rival prophets who have become gods in our place.

"And if you cannot be saints of knowledge, at least be its warriors. These are the companions and forerunners of such holiness." The saint is the spokesman of God, which means here the mouthpiece of the ruling doctrine. The warrior fights to become a saint of triumph; he accompanies this holiness in the sense that he is fighting for its triumph. There is an implicit reference here to Plato's *Republic*. The "saint of knowledge" there is the philosopher-king. The warriors protect the philosopher-king and enforce his rule. But Nietzsche indicates that the warriors have it in their power to prepare for new saints. He does not, however, say that they will themselves become saints. Nietzsche too is a forerunner; his affection for his enemies is rooted in their common destiny.

At a more immediate level, however, Zarathustra is speaking to those who believe themselves to be warriors but are in fact only soldiers. Zarathustra is encouraging the ostensible warriors, or leaders of advanced contemporary thought, to fight for these thoughts. I note that thinking is for Zarathustra already what one could call a second-order activity; it is not as fundamental as the will to power or the spontaneous creative drive of the superman. These thinking warriors are encouraged to fight continuously and to regard defeat as a cause for triumph.

We have to ask ourselves: What does this really mean? If a multiplicity of thinking warriors engage in continuous battle, there will be massive carnage, and the warriors themselves will slaughter each other. As they sink to the ground with triumph in their hearts, Zarathustra is standing in the wings, waiting to take their place. In effect, Zarathustra is saying to his enemies: Try to be just like me by slaughtering each other, so that I can get on with my work. Otherwise put, Zarathustra is not himself engaging in slaughter; he is merely delivering speeches or trying to stir others up to do his preliminary work for him.

One could object to this: Won't these enemies attack Zarathustra himself and kill him as well? Only if he engages in direct "hand-to-hand" or "soul-to-soul" combat with them. But Zarathustra is not promulgating a positive doctrine which he intends to implement after the final military victory. All of his talk about supermen and creativity is part of the rhetoric of justification for the invocation to mass destruction. I don't deny that Nietzsche prefers certain ages to others, or that he regards the archaic Greek warrior and the Renaissance artist-condottiere as superior to Baudelaire and Rimbaud. But these preferences are local or historical exemplifications of the higher positions in the rank-ordering within a complete cycle of the eternal return; they are not specific identifications of what the next epoch will incarnate. Nietzsche is saying at the most: Human beings who resemble the archaic Greeks or the Italian Renaissance heroes are entirely superior to the present decadent types. He is not saying that we are to reinstitute the Greek *polis* or the Italian city-state. This is the doctrine of vulgar political reaction, or of what is sometimes called conservatism. But Nietzsche is not a conservative, because he knows that man is not a crab. We have to go forward, not backward or sideways.[10]

The superman is just a symbol of the promise of the future. It is not a well-developed paradigm for political reconstruction, nor could it be, since the superman is one who overcomes, is healthy rather than sick, life-enhancing rather than diminishing, confident rather than timid, all of which can be actualized in many different ways. There can be no doubt that Nietzsche wants an aristocracy of the spirit and not a democracy or age of egalitarianism. But he provides us with no program of positive action for the implementation of an aristocracy. And there is no such program, because the aristocracy of the spirit must be spontaneously manifested by the creative genius of the human race, not by a group of bureaucrats or professors following a methodically sound procedure.

For this fundamental reason, Nietzsche's "positive" doctrine is the same as his "negative" doctrine. His positive recommendation is to destroy existing sickness on the basis of the hope that health will then emerge.[11] Nietzsche cannot guarantee us that the destruction of modern Europe will be followed by the return of sixteenth-century Florence. This is why the book *Zarathustra* is an allegory or an imitation of the Christian Bible: It is a wish or a dream that substitutes war for peace.

Continuing: "I say unto you, it is the good war that renders each thing holy" (59). In other words: If we fight hard, we enhance life; this is the only healthy sense of "holy." Zarathustra designates bravery as goodness; remember his earlier assertion that it is not good to have too many virtues.

The rest of the section is relatively easy to understand. The brave man has a heart which he is ashamed to show; he is shamed by pity, which he knows to be the true form of heartlessness, because it is soft and decadent; it tolerates sickness and cowardice. The noble is the cloak of ugliness; what look from the Christian perspective like hateful (*hässlich*) or ugly deeds are transformed into beautiful ones by the nobility of the cause. "And when your soul becomes great, it becomes *übermüthig*, and in your sublimity there is malice (*Bosheit*)." Kaufmann translates *übermüthig* as "frolicsome." This is a possible sense of the term, but I think it should be translated here as "insolent" and even perhaps as "hubristic." The *über* in *übermüthig* echoes the *über* in words like *Übergang* and *Übermensch*. *Mut* means courage or spiritedness, almost like the Greek *thumos*. The great soul is the great-spirited soul, which is marked by what Aristotle calls *megalopsuchia*. Furthermore, "sarcasm" is much too weak for *Bosheit*, which contains the root *Bos*, as in *Böse*, "evil."

The next sentence is more difficult: "In malice, the high-spirited meets with the weak. But they misunderstand each other. I know you." The elevated, high-spirited man is malicious toward the weak-spirited, or base, man. It is perhaps plain why the weak-spirited man cannot understand the high-spirited man, but why can't the latter understand the former? The weak man assumes that the elevated man is cruel and therefore seeks to destroy him. He does not understand that a salutary transformation is being effected, one from which he himself will benefit (if only by ceasing to exist, since it is better to be dead than sick).

What does the strong, or elevated, man assume? As a warrior, he assumes precisely what is attributed to him by the weak man; namely, the desire to conquer, to dominate, and so to destroy whatever opposes his will. It is his conception of nobility that might makes right, that he has the right to rule because he is stronger. But this is an incomplete assessment of the meaning of nobility. The warrior does not care about improving the psychic tone of the weakling, but he does this by the very act of imposing a higher set of values, namely, his own. The warrior marked by *Erhabenheit* is "sublime" or "elevated" but not genuinely noble; this will be indicated below when Zarathustra speaks of the "nobility of slaves (*die Vornehmheit am Sclaven*)."

There is, in other words, something self-transcending about the fact of conquest. But this is not true in all cases; there is a crucial qualification. The conquest must be effected by a high-spirited man, not by a vulgar tyrant like Hitler, for example. The base multitude cannot distinguish between the triumph of a base, or low-spirited, tyrant and a noble warrior. But is Nietzsche himself in a position to make this distinction? If conquest is life-enhancing, and if this in turn makes sense at some level other than the mere accumulation or excrescence of power, then we can distinguish between a noble and a base triumph. Otherwise, all triumphs are noble by virtue of being triumphant.[12] Here Nietzsche's values enter into the picture: There is a disjunction between the values internal to the illusion of life, or the anthropomorphic interpretation of chaos, and the random fluctuations of chaos itself. The ontology of chaos does not explain, but is contradicted by, the psychology or politics of the illusion, namely, human life as it is lived.

I would therefore say that Zarathustra is mistaken when he asserts that he knows the high-spirited and the weak men. But to come back to his intended meaning here: The elevated warrior brings more to the triumph than his personal glory or the satisfaction of his own will to power. He is also acting philanthropically, or elevating his victim. And this makes it possible for the weak coward to evolve into a high-spirited warrior in his own right. This is Nietzsche's version of the Hegelian "master–slave" dialectic.

Finally, and equally important: By conquering a weak opponent, the high-spirited man lowers himself. Zarathustra makes this explicit in the next paragraph: "You must have enemies who are hateful but not enemies who are despicable. You must be proud of your enemy; then the successes of your enemy are also your successes." If this is true, it must apply to Nietzsche himself. Who then are his enemies? To the extent that Nietzsche must combat weaklings, or the base multitude, this is necessarily demeaning to his own spirit. I believe this also applies to the various efforts on his part to seduce the many, or, in the first instance, to seduce the leaders of the many. The invention of the prophet Zarathustra is a device intended to preserve the delicacy and refinement of Nietzsche's own soul from contamination by contact with the souls of the many, here represented by the citizens of the city of the Motley Cow. Nietzsche the man of almost decadent refinement hides behind the blustering rhetoric of Zarathustra.

"Resistance (*Auflehnung*) – that is the nobility (*Vornehmheit*) of slaves. Let your nobility be obedience! Let your commanding itself be obeying!" The dialectic of high and low spirits is not the war between genuinely noble enemies. It is true that the weak-spirited man is raised, "elevated," and in that sense made sublime, through submission to a high-spirited conqueror. But at the same time, this battle between the high and the low is demeaning to the high – and therefore it demeans the low as well, by raising them to a lower level than would be attained if they were represented by a champion who is at the same level as the genuinely noble warrior.

But in this passage, Zarathustra is not recommending surrender to the weak- or low-spirited. To the contrary, he is addressing the high-spirited, or the conquerors. The conqueror must not resist the base opposition of the vulgar, or weak-spirited; he must not conquer by military might but by prophecy: "Thou shalt" instead of "I will." The genuinely noble conqueror triumphs by lawgiving, as befits a god among mortals. "And everything that makes you glad, you ought first to allow yourself to be commanded."

What makes the genuinely noble glad? A refined triumph over the refined. But this is impossible, both absolutely and in the present context. The next best thing is to persuade others to obey one, without engaging in a self-demeaning battle. This is the path represented by the prophetic rhetoric of Zarathustra. Let me interject an observation here about Nietzsche's rhetoric, which becomes increasingly strident in later years – in other words, after it is plain that *Zarathustra* has failed, at least initially. Now Nietzsche cannot rest content with masking his refinement beneath a rhetoric of religious sublimity. He has to call attention to his teaching and hence to himself. Nietzsche now requires a rhetoric that will make notorious and so effective the invocation to action contained in the text. He has to call attention to his refinement and superiority, yet in such a way as not to blunt the delicate rhetorical balance of intentions in *Zarathustra*.

I think that this is an impossible task and that Nietzsche failed. By this I mean that the influence he achieved was not the influence he intended. In other words, part of the reason for his failure is that the strident rhetoric canceled out the subtle rhetoric. There is of course a good bit of frank speech in *Zarathustra*, but it is muffled by the purple prose, by the Romanticism and religiosity of the book. People were carried away by Nietzsche's candor as candor, rather than by the content of that candor. This accentuated the revolutionary side to Nietzsche's teaching as revolutionary: revolution for the sake of revolution. And so inevitably the destructive side took precedence over the creative side in the understanding of Nietzsche's books.

To return to our section: At first glance, Zarathustra seems to be saying: Don't ask anyone to do something that you yourself are not glad to do. This would mean here: Be ready to obey the "thou shalts" of your table of laws. But that means in turn that the lawgiver must also be subject to the laws. And that requires the prophet to enter the promised land. In other words, the prophet must cease to be a prophet, or outside history; he must also exist as a human being within the perspective that he has opened or enforced. This advice cannot be directed by Zarathustra to himself. It is not possible to be the source of laws and their subject; even in Kant's doctrine of spontaneity, the rational manifests itself as law, but the laws are manifestations of the transcendental ego, that is, of the rational *qua* rational, and not of the thoughts of some reasonable historical individual. Zarathustra's actual meaning comes out in the next couplet. He is talking to his enemy prophets: "Your highest thought, however, you must receive from me as a command" (60).

Zarathustra's enemies, namely, those whom he as it were loves to hate, who are worthy of his enmity and so of battle with him, must subordinate their own love of life to a highest thought which he himself furnishes: that man shall be overcome. I believe Zarathustra means that he is the first person to have articulated this thought fully; no previous prophecy was a fully explicit or conscious attempt to overcome man in a comprehensive sense. "I do not spare you, I love you *von Grund aus*, my brothers." In other words, I am prepared to destroy you, to arrange for you *zu Grunde zu gehen*. Zarathustra's love is a dangerous gift, as we know now.

"On Chastity" (Section 13)

In the eight sections beginning here, the main theme is one form or another of love, with two sections among them devoted to creation. There follow two sections: one on death and the concluding section, which summarizes the teaching of Part One. This last section has as its explicit theme Zarathustra's gift, which, we remember, replaces his claim to love mankind. As we shall see, giving is identified as creating; this is preceded by the discussion of death, or destruction. More generally: Part One of *Zarathustra* culminates in a discussion of Eros as the ground of creation and destruction, hence of life and death.

The section on chastity may come as a surprise to those who have misunderstood Zarathustra's invocation to return to the body and the earth. This was certainly true of writers like D. H. Lawrence, who spoke of "the blood knowledge," by which he meant sexuality; but when Nietzsche speaks of blood, his primary meaning is violence and destruction, not sexuality or generation. Nietzsche is not a sensualist, nor does he advocate sexual liberation. At the same time, the asceticism he advocates is that of the soul, not of the body. As will shortly become evident, Nietzsche does not mean abstinence by "chastity," and he opposes the enforced chastity of Christianity. The return to the body and the earth must be chaste in the sense that it is a turn to the spiritual production of a new epoch or a new table of values (as will be discussed below in "Of the Thousand and One Goals").

The creator is a divine figure who is detached from human beings by the loftiness of his vision and the refinement of his spirit. He cannot experience the indiscriminate lust of promiscuity, since this is a mark of humanity. On this point, Zarathustra is closer to Christ than he is to the pagan gods. "Mud is at the ground of their souls; and woe if their mud still has spirit!" (69). In other words, the promiscuous entrepreneur, intellectual, or ideologue is much worse than the lusty peasant or worker, who is expressing an animal passion. In the case of the intellectual, lust is transformed into ideology; words and ideas are prostituted to the service of passions and are used to justify the lowest and most perverted desires.

"Would that you were as perfect [or, literally, complete] as the beasts. But innocence belongs to the beast." The beasts are "complete" in the sense that they act from instinct; human beings debase instinct by the artifice of language. In slightly different words, human beings are not complete but open to a wide range of possibilities. They can become corrupt or decadent as the beasts cannot.

Now comes the distinction between Christian asceticism and Nietzschean, or philosophical, chastity. Zarathustra counsels the innocence (*Unschuld*), not the murder, of the senses. Sexual love is the natural basis of reproduction as well as of community (the human version of the herds or packs of the brutes). But Zarathustra does not associate it with spiritual creativity; on this point, he differs from what is at least the explicit statement of Platonic Eros. To stay within the traditional formulation: Plato advocates the sublimation or purification of sexuality in the erotic ascent. For Zarathustra, there is no erotic ascent, but two different levels of Eros, corresponding crudely to the difference between the body and the soul, or the many and the few. His doctrine of Eros is thus distantly related to the previously mentioned distinction made by Pausanias in Plato's *Symposium* between the Uranian and the pandemic Eros.

Zarathustra of course does not deny that the few also have bodies, but here the innocence of the senses obtains. The sexuality of the few is chaste or innocent, and on that point it resembles the animals. To state this point somewhat more precisely: The very few like Nietzsche himself will indeed be chaste in the literal sense ("a married philosopher belongs *to comedy*"),[13] because their energies are devoted to the highest spiritual tasks. But there is a larger sense of chastity that is compatible with an "innocent" sexual love that is in accord with nature as noted above: for reproduction, community, friendship.

By "larger sense" I do not of course mean "universally applicable." "Chastity is a virtue in some, but almost a vice in many." Here Zarathustra is certainly thinking of Christian morality, which conceals, distorts, intensifies, and corrupts the sexual drive by denying it or identifying it with original sin. Sensuality thus infects all aspects of human society, including its virtues or spiritual aspects. Sensuality as it were goes underground, dons the masks of acceptable social practice, and thereby corrupts everything. The net result of Christian puritanism, as one could put this point, is the doctrine of Freudianism. Freud reveals the nasty secret that the Christian soul is in fact a sex maniac! "Is it not merely your lust that has disguised itself and calls itself compassion?" (70).

Zarathustra closes the section by asking: "Do I speak of dirty things? That is not the worst thing I could do. Not when truth is dirty but when it is shallow does the knower step reluctantly into its water." Compare Plato's *Parmenides* 130c5ff., where the old philosopher tells the young Socrates that when he becomes mature he will recognize Ideas of mud, dirt, and other low things. Note too the connection between chastity and laughter; this is the reverse of the Platonic analysis. In *Zarathustra,* laughter indicates a separation from life, like the unquenchable laughter of the Homeric gods.

"On the Friend" (Section 14)

Here Nietzsche speaks of his own loneliness through the words of Zarathustra. We know from his letters that he felt completely isolated and that he had never met a human being of his own rank.[14] His relations with Lou Salome were marked by an initial enthusiasm for her intellectual and spiritual powers, but this enthusiasm eventually paled. The question arises: Who is Zarathustra's friend? But the answer is that Zarathustra is not a human being, not even a superman. He is a personification of natural force; hence he lives with his totemic animals. Zarathustra is the expression of Nietzsche's loneliness purged of its purely subjective or personal elements.

The hermit or solitary talks to himself; he engages in an excessive meditation that sinks him into the depths of detachment. A friend who can share the burden of this thought is like a third to the two of "I" and "me" (71). But a friend of the proper caliber is a potential enemy;

here Nietzsche reverses the perspective of the earlier section in which he spoke of the proper enemy who is a potential friend.

"And often one wants to leap over envy with love." This is the sense in which our longing for a friend is often our betrayer. We admire a potential rival, envy his gifts, and seek to neutralize his advantages by binding them to us with ties of love. In other words, friendship is needed by the most superior persons, yet is at bottom impossible for them. They need it because their superiority detaches them from their humanity; it is impossible for them because the only persons whom they can love are those who are their natural enemies. Aristotle says that friends love the same thing, not each other but something else: justice, honor, wisdom, and the like. For Nietzsche, however, love is an expression of the will to power, the need to overcome and hence to destroy what exists and to create something new. The love we feel for the suitable friend is thus at bottom self-love, or the desire to transform the friend into a projection of ourselves, into an artifact of our will. And the friend reciprocates this need.

It is necessary for friends to approach each other with masks, or, as Zarathustra calls them here, beautiful clothing. Stated with maximum bluntness, this means that the mutual desire to dominate must be concealed as affection and admiration for each other's powers or gifts. Gods could show themselves to one another as they are, because they are like animals in being complete natural forces. In human beings, mutual envy must be transposed into longing for the superman.

The two remarks about viewing the friend asleep (72) make two different points. First: If you see your friend without his masks, you will see yourself. I have just explained this. Second: To see him without his masks is to see his naked ambition and desire, and so too his unlovable, or human, all too human, self. In order for friendship to endure, we must avoid too much intimacy. Instead of seeing our friend when he is asleep and we are awake, the reverse should be the case; we should see our friend's actions in our dreams. The detachment of sleep will insulate us against the anger of direct understanding.

There follows one of Nietzsche's difficult remarks about women. Neither tyrants nor slaves are capable of friendship; both are concealed in woman, who therefore cannot be a friend (72f.). What does this mean? Nietzsche's point is that women, because of their position in the family and society, tyrannize men either through the instrument of sexual desire or through respect for the weaker, for the mother. Or else they are themselves enslaved, domesticated: They are either cats and birds, household pets, or at best cows. Why this preference for cows? Because cows give milk; they nourish and thus fulfill a necessary function. They are not mere ornaments, like pets, which are instruments for the expression of the vanity, cruelty, and love of power of the human master.

"Of a Thousand and One Goals" (Section 15)

The title is obviously an echo of the *Thousand and One Nights*. A woman's life is spared for each night that she can tell a new and entertaining story, full of wonders. So too human beings exist by beguiling themselves with fairy tales, with marvelous fictions of wonderful deeds, of gods and monsters; to which one might add, of supermen. Note again: Zarathustra saw many *Völker*, "peoples." These are the units of the original creation of value: of definitions of good and evil. Human life is perspectival; no *Volk* can live with the values of another. This thesis is deeply Germanic; one finds it already in Luther; it is used as the basis for anti-Semitism by the leading German thinkers of the modern epoch. In Nietzsche, the thesis has nothing to do with anti-Semitism, but it is nevertheless the expression of a German obsession. At the same time, one must grant that this "obsession" is a version, however excessive, of a thesis that goes back to antiquity and that is maintained by the great political thinkers from Plato to Rousseau: In order to be healthy, a polity must be unified by blood and custom. A multiplicity of peoples and customs divides the state.

Custom is the king of all men: This is the thesis not only of Herodotus but of the Sophists, with whom Nietzsche has much in common. Note the formulation: "Never did one neighbor understand another. Each soul was constantly amazed at the neighbor's madness and evil" (74). Not *good* and evil, but *madness* and evil. So Nietzsche also accepts Heracleitus' assertion that war is father of all things; in other words, that human life is fundamentally war, not peace. This is a radicalized version of the view, made fashionable in the nineteenth century by Dilthey, that understanding is *Verstehen* of "lived experience (*Erlebnis*)," which is in turn defined by "values (*Werte*)." Conversely, one can see how nineteenth-century historicism is a softened version of the pagan doctrine of *nomos*.

Zarathustra reinterprets the tablet of the good (e.g., the Ten Commandments) in the light of the radical pagan thesis of the dual primacy of change and hence of war: Change is itself war, a war on what persists. The tablet of the good is thus the voice of the will to power of a given people: their understanding of what it means to overcome. This is the first appearance of the expression "will to power" in *Zarathustra*. The prophet next defines three crucial terms: (1) Praiseworthy is what is held to be difficult; (2) good is the indispensable and difficult; (3) holy is what frees a people, thanks to the highest need; it is the rarest and the hardest. This is self-explanatory. The divine is the personification of our highest need: to overcome. The human being cannot stand still; it must overcome or decline. And the valuable is tied to difficulty, not to ease or softness but to hardness. Again the point is obvious; if life is war, then virtue or excellence is embodied in the warrior ethic.

So the political expression of health, virility, creativity, life enhancement (as opposed to decadence) is what makes a people rule, triumph, and shine, to the horror and envy of its neighbor. This will to power can take on a variety of formulations; Zarathustra summarizes those of the Greeks, Persians, Hebrews, and Germans (75). The German version, "to practice loyalty and for the sake of loyalty to apply honor and blood to evil and dangerous things," is for most of us the least admirable of the four, but Zarathustra draws no hierarchical distinctions here. The Germans are on the same level as the pagans and the Hebrews.

Zarathustra then restates the main point that man is the source of value. Value could not come from the gods, who are a human invention. Nor could it come from nature (*phusis*), which is itself a human artifact; the innocence of Becoming is rooted in the chaotic interior of external order.[15] The most one could say is that power, dominance, and overcoming are the human expressions of the accumulation of energy that overrides even destruction at the heart of chaos. Man is the esteemer or evaluator: To estimate is to create. This is now fully intelligible. There is no distinction between facts and values; what we take to be facts are themselves values and the products of still more fundamental values.[16] This is of course true not merely within a given world order or perspective, but with respect to the totality of perspectives. The highest evaluation is that of the noblest man. And this raises the fundamental question of who is higher, the one who sees, or understands, whom we may designate as the Apollonian, or the one who creates and acts, the Dionysian?

Nietzsche's reply is that these two are the same at the peak of humanity.[17] Comprehensive or synoptic understanding is necessarily action, or creation. But this is not at all obvious. For Nietzsche there is no difference between understanding and evaluating. What then do we understand? First: We understand that chaos is at the heart of things. How is this an evaluation? Chaos is higher than stability, or eternal order, because it permits us to create, to overcome, to evaluate. Death and destruction are therefore superior to immortality, not alone or in themselves but as the inner core of life and creation.

Second: We understand the finite number of fundamental tablets of the good, that is, the perspective-defining values. And these are better or worse, nobler or baser, depending on how they add to or diminish our power to overcome. But let us make a distinction between those who dwell within one perspective or another, and those few who, like Nietzsche, are not simply residents of one perspective but also, because of the freedom permitted by the extreme decadence of their time, beyond all perspectives. In other words: Within a perspective, there are the rulers and the ruled. The ruled obey the tablets in a literal sense; the rulers do not obey, but enforce. So they are closer to the transperspectival man, because they incarnate the principle of evaluation, namely, the will to power. The transperspectival, or Hyperborean, philosopher evaluates all perspectives from the standpoint of the will to power. But in order for the philosopher himself to instantiate the will to power, he cannot simply understand all this; he must also act, and thereby he must dominate.

For this reason, the Hyperborean is driven to descend from his mountaintop in order to enact his knowledge by creating a new epoch of world history. The key premise here is that knowledge of chaos, that is, of destruction and creation, at the highest or most comprehensive level dissolves the split between *theoria* and practico-production and moves the philosopher to action. Nietzsche implicitly denies the superiority of the purely theoretical or contemplative life. One could perhaps say that his enemy is not Plato but Aristotle.

There follows one of the most important passages in *Zarathustra.* "Change of values – that is a change of creators. He who must be a creator always destroys." The transformation of values is also a destruction of the antecedent civilization; this is why, as noted previously, Socrates tells Glaucon in the *Republic* that in order to found the just city they must send everyone over the age of ten into the countryside and retain the children for indoctrination. Socrates does not allude to the fact that violence will be required in order to detach the children from their families; Nietzsche is considerably franker.

"The creators were first peoples and only later individuals; truly, the individual is himself only the most recent creation." In antiquity, the *Volk,* or the *polis,* is prior to the person or citizen; the priority of the individual is the result of the secularizing and politicizing of Christianity, which frees the individual person from subordination to the law and brings him into direct contact with God. In modernity, God disappears, and the *ego cogitans* is in direct contact with itself. Late-modern nationalism reinstitutes the priority of the community over the individual, but in the form of the priority of the state or empire, not the divine. The modern bourgeois state is the hypostasis of the bourgeois individual "I," who is selfish, materialist, and a utilitarian.

"There have been a thousand goals thus far, because there have been a thousand people. Only the yoke of the thousand necks is still missing; the one goal is missing. Mankind still has no goal" (76). This cycle of the eternal return is not yet completed by the thousand and first goal; therefore mankind has no goal. In other words, Nietzsche's teaching is the thousand-and-first goal; by revealing the doctrine of the eternal return, Zarathustra shows that history is cyclic, or closed, and so that it is not only comprehensible but that, since it endlessly repeats itself, it has no goal or value beyond that of facticity. Once this is understood, mankind is free to give itself value and so to organize chaos. Goals and values have a fabulous status; they are stories told to keep ourselves from perishing.

"On Old and Young Little Women" (Section 18)

This section contains Zarathustra's analysis of the feminine nature from the standpoint of sexual Eros. It casts further light on why Zarathustra regards love (as opposed to desire) as impossible. The teaching is presented as general rather than as restricted to the superior few, but I believe that Zarathustra is concerned primarily with the latter. The German word *Weiblein* (84) is a diminutive of *Weib*, "woman" or "wife." It could be a term of affection, but even as such it carries a faintly patronizing tone. The "old" is plain enough; it designates the prerequisite for the experience of life and freedom from the distractions of Eros possessed by Zarathustra's interlocutress. The "young" is not plain: It could refer to "a little truth (*eine kleine Wahrheit*)," namely, Zarathustra's truth about woman in general, which he carries around under his coat.

In the *Symposium*, Socrates recounts to an audience of men his youthful instruction by an exalted woman in the mysteries of Eros: His teacher was the priestess Diotima. Zarathustra recounts to an unnamed man ("brother") the confirmation of his own teaching about woman by an unnamed – hence anonymous and therefore not exalted – woman. Socrates has no doctrines, but merely asks questions; Zarathustra may ask questions, but he has a doctrine or prophecy, and he delivers monologues as well as engaging in conversations.

As we are about to see, Zarathustra's analysis of the feminine nature is not only irritating to the contemporary taste, but it seems to be quite shallow by any standards of sophisticated interpretation. Zarathustra speaks in the stereotypes of male dominance and the mystery of woman. I do not wish to endorse these stereotypes but only to understand Nietzsche. In that spirit, I note that the stereotypes serve as metaphors for the presentation of an analysis of the male and female elements in the sexual Eros. They need not be understood simply as Nietzsche's psychological assessment of actual men and women.

With this in mind, let us turn to the details of the section. Zarathustra is presented as sneaking through the twilight with a little truth concealed beneath his coat, like a young child over whose mouth he must hold his hand, lest she cry too loudly. There is evidently something especially dangerous about this little truth. Why is it more dangerous than those truths stated explicitly and in loud, ringing tones to the assembled crowd? Because it exposes what Nietzsche takes to be the blunt truth underlying the most intimate of human relationships. This exposé is somehow peripheral to the inspirational side of Zarathustra's teaching: to that side which exalts mankind to overcome itself and to produce a new epoch of the superman. Nevertheless, Nietzsche wants us to know this truth. Hence the confrontation by the solitary man, rather than a monologue delivered in public.

"It is a treasure that has been given to me." This description of the little truth suggests that the child is not Zarathustra's own. Of course the locution could refer simply to the fact that, like all of his "truths," this one is the gift of divine revelation. But Zarathustra does not refer to all of his truths as gifts to himself; his general description is of his teaching altogether as a gift to mankind. So again there is something indirect about the truth concerning woman. Note that although Zarathustra recites his understanding of woman to the little old woman, she confirms and restates the truth of this teaching (86). In a sense she has "given" something to him, and in particular she gives him some advice about how to approach a woman, as we shall see below. In addition to this, the "brother" to whom Zarathustra recounts the conversation addresses him as "thou friend of the evil." This adds to the atmosphere of danger surrounding the little truth.

The conversation recounted by Zarathustra took place quite recently, today at sunset. He met a little old woman who spoke to his soul: not to his heart, the organ of personal emotion and love. She complained that Zarathustra has spoken much to women but never about women. He replied: "About women one should speak only to men" (84). This is a delicate subject; there is usually no frankness or honesty in conversations between men and women. Note that we are not given a portrait of women speaking to women about men. The old woman points out that her age insulates her from indelicacy; she is, to repeat an earlier observation, neither desirable nor fertile. She is old and partly senile and will immediately forget what Zarathustra says to her.

This whole scene is connected to the section on chastity. Zarathustra does not seek after young women. And when he needs to speak about woman, he does so under cover of twilight, to an audience of one, to a man rather than to a woman, and about a discussion with an old woman, not a young one, an old woman who confirms the soundness of his analysis. So Zarathustra has this teaching in common with the old woman; he is himself, so to speak, an old woman, not a "real man," or an erotic agent.

"Everything about woman is a riddle, and everything about woman has one solution: It is called pregnancy." Our first inclination, I suspect, is to reject this as a platitude. But let us not be so hasty. Why do men attribute to women the status of a riddle? From the male standpoint, woman is desirable but also something to be courted, something that is not immediately accessible. Partly because of the difference in the psychology of the two sexes, partly because of socially imposed differences, men pursue and women retreat; this is the stereotype. Even if the woman pursues, she is supposed to do this under cover of modesty and so with guile, not directly like a man. At a somewhat deeper level, however, the "mystery" of woman has to do with the fact that she is the source of origination. The child is conceived within, and emerges from, her body. Woman is thus the symbol of the origin and hence of chaos. It is true that the seed comes from the man. But this is a physiological truth that is compatible with the symbolic significance of the separation of the man from the physical appearance of the child. Thus the mystery or riddle of woman is pregnancy.

Of course, there is another sense to this ostensible riddle. Zarathustra means to say that whatever women may offer as a reason or explanation for their conduct, the actual reason is to become pregnant. In particular: Women do not love men; they love motherhood, or the bearing of children. "Man is for woman a means; the purpose is always the child" (85). This raises the next question. Is the underlying motivation of masculine Eros also the child? "But what is woman for man?" Let me restate this: Grant that woman is for man a riddle. Presumably Zarathustra does not mean that women are a riddle for other women; each woman must understand the motivation of her own sex. Is the function of being a riddle not the same as that of being a mother?

Zarathustra immediately clarifies this point: "A genuine man wants two things: danger and play." Before I comment on these two desires, let me note immediately that just as woman does not want man as man, but only as a means, so too man does not want woman as woman. Zarathustra is contending that men and women do not desire each other for what they are, as persons of the opposite and so complementary sex; there is no mutual love. This is really quite similar to the Socratic story: Lovers desire something beyond the immediate object of love.

To return now to danger and play: As the lover of danger, man is a warrior. As the lover of play, he needs to relax from war, to regain his strength so that he may fight again. But how does it follow from this that he wants woman as the most dangerous plaything? Think of the warrior-prince who relaxes from the rigors of a tough military campaign by passing the night in his harem or in a bordello or with his mistress or wife. What is dangerous about this relaxation? Zarathustra contends that the safeness or peacefulness of this relaxation is spurious. Why? The answer is suggested in the following passage: "All too sweet fruit – the warrior does not like this. Therefore he likes woman; even the sweetest woman is bitter. Woman understands children better than does man; but man is more childish than woman."

Once more we proceed one step at a time. The sweetest woman has a bitter taste because she is not in love with the warrior; she eludes his need for conquest even while playing. But this elusiveness spurs him on; it is a challenge to his masculinity. In pursuing this challenge, however, he behaves childishly, because he is himself conquered by the woman in serving as the means to her own end. Man is dissolved by the chaos of woman. Something like this is what Zarathustra seems to have in mind.

But this can hardly be the whole story. Remember that the ultimate goal of Zarathustra's teaching is the production of the new race of supermen. We have to consider the image of playfulness from this angle; and here we must remember Heraclitus's assertion that Zeus is a *pais paizōn,* a playing child or youth – a statement cited elsewhere by Nietzsche. "In a genuine man a child is hidden that wants to play." It is the task of woman to uncover this child by assisting in the transformation of the old epoch into the new and thus to complete or activate the creative dimension of playfulness. Life is a game, as we say; but this is for Zarathustra not a condemnation or statement of the futility and meaninglessness of existence. On the contrary, it is the very innocence of Becoming, like a child playing, that allows us to project meanings into life.

Zarathustra develops this point by encouraging woman to hope that she will give birth to the superman. He adds: "Let there be courage in your love. With your love shall you approach him who fills you with fear." We should not forget that this apparent invocation to love is in fact the expression of what was previously referred to as the riddle of woman. A love motivated by courage guides the woman to that warrior who because of his very frightening powers may be the father of the superman. This is of course not romantic love, whether Christian or secular. It is courageous love, the courage to love that which is not lovable in ordinary human terms.

The next commandment is harder to understand. "Let your honor be in your love. Woman understands little of honor otherwise. But let this be your honor, always to love more than you are loved, and never to be the second." The first part of the command seems straightforward enough: Honor is primarily the virtue of warriors, hence of men. For the sake of honor, the warrior risks his life. But honor is also applied to women; they too must risk their lives to preserve their honor if their chastity is attacked by warriors. So in both cases the love of honor means the readiness to die. This interpretation of female honor, however, does not make sense in the present context, since Zarathustra is enjoining women to seek out the warrior; the honor to which he is referring here has nothing to do with chastity.

So Zarathustra is revising the female sense of honor. It is now a corollary of courage, that is, of the acceptance of the warrior as the potential father of the superman. The warrior "loves" the woman as a plaything; the woman "loves" the warrior as the father of her child. But what she loves most, or most genuinely, is the child. And perhaps not even the child as child so much as pregnancy itself. Pregnancy is the feminine expression of the will to power.

Note next the following distinction: "Man is at the ground of his soul only evil; woman, however, is there bad." This means that the soul of woman is worse than that of man. Why should this be so? Zarathustra attributes it to jealousy; woman hates man because he attracts her but cannot raise her to his level. Woman is forced to subordinate her will to that of man. The woman must act through the surrogate of the man. What is called in our century "women's liberation" began as the attempt to make women not merely equal to, but equivalent with, or the same as, men; to do men's work. It is very interesting to note the shift in emphasis more recently from equivalence to distinctness. In the first stage, the sexual difference is said to be irrelevant. In the second stage, it is decisive for the differentiation of psychic attributes.

The upshot of all this is that men and women are for Zarathustra enemies rather than lovers. Nor can there be any doubt that he regards men as superior, as deeper and stronger than women: "Surface is the *Gemüth* of woman; an excited stormy skin over shallow water. The *Gemüth* of man, however, is deep; his stream rushes in caves beneath the earth" (86). *Gemüth* means mind, soul, mood, or disposition. I believe that Zarathustra distinguishes between *Gemüth* and the reproductive instinct. From the latter standpoint, woman represents the source, or chaos; from the former standpoint, namely, with respect to the creative or inseminative power of the mind, man is the stronger manifestation of the will to power and in that sense of the forces of chaos.

The little old woman's reply is not without ambiguity. "Many nice things has Zarathustra said, and especially for those who are young enough for them." In other words, she is not young enough for them; she is thus somehow outside the perimeter of the feminine nature, in a way just as Zarathustra is outside the perimeter of the content of his own prophecy. Age brings freedom from erotic passion, and with it the distance of understanding. "It is strange; Zarathustra knows women little, and yet he is right about them. Does this result because with woman nothing is impossible?" Zarathustra has very little personal experience with women. This is not simply because he is a prophet or an ascetic rather than a Don Juan. The chastity of Zarathustra is that of the philosopher, who by virtue of his superior understanding is detached from sexual Eros and directed toward the creation of vast schemes to transform the human race. The *Gemüth* of Zarathustra (and so too of Nietzsche) cannot be explained by the analysis Zarathustra presents in this section.

The woman also suggests that with women nothing is impossible. This leaves room for the creation of the superwoman, or the woman with the *Gemüth* of a man. But this apart, why should the omnipossibility of woman make Zarathustra's analysis correct? The old woman seems to be hinting that it is even possible for women to conform to Zarathustra's understanding of them, which thus falls short of the truth about the feminine nature. She then offers Zarathustra a gift of gratitude for his little truth: a little truth of her own. "You are going to women? Do not forget the whip!" This is a much-quoted passage. In *Conversations with Nietzsche*, we read of a man named Sebastian Hausmann, who is recounting a conversation he once had with Nietzsche about the "whip" passage. Nietzsche "looked at me in astonishment: 'But I beg you, surely that cannot cause you any difficulty! I mean, it is clear and understandable that this is only a joke, an exaggerated, symbolic mode of expression. If you go to woman do not let yourself be subjugated by her sensuality, do not forget that you are the master, that it is a woman's truly not slight task to serve the man as a friendly companion who beautifies his life.' "[18]

We may exculpate Nietzsche from the accusation that he advises us to beat women with whips. But he certainly intends to keep them in a subordinate position, as an ornament to men. Feminine sensuality is a weapon used by women to subordinate the man's will to power to her own, as expressed fundamentally in the desire for pregnancy.

"On the Bite of the Adder" (Section 19)

One day Zarathustra is asleep under a fig tree with his face covered to protect it against the heat (87). An adder bites him on the neck; when the snake recognizes Zarathustra's eyes, it turns awkwardly and wants to depart. Animals attack Zarathustra by mistake only; and, as he claims, the adder's poison cannot kill him, because he is a dragon. Zarathustra persuades the snake to wrap itself around his neck again and to lick clean the wound. The snake, Zarathustra says, is not rich enough to give him its poison. Zarathustra later explains this story as an illustration of the significance of his destiny: "My *Geschichte* is nonmoral." He means by this not only that he annihilates the values of good and evil as they are understood by modern European morality, but that his response to his enemies is not to be understood in the language of morality of any kind. Zarathustra's significance is both historical and fabulous (the two senses of *Geschichte*). Morality is invented in order to regulate the actions of members of a community toward one another. But Zarathustra is a dragon even to the snakes of the community. We recall again the snake of the Garden of Eden, who is responsible for the knowledge of good and evil. From Zarathustra's standpoint, the snake's trickery of Eve is a poisonous bite that eventually brings mankind down into decadence. But dragons have armor and breathe fire; they can trample on snakes. Zarathustra, however, does not do this; instead he "hypnotizes" the snake into removing its poison from him. Differently stated: Zarathustra neutralizes the snake's venom by refusing to take vengeance on it.

"If you have an enemy, do not repay his evil with good, for that would shame him. Rather prove that he has done you some good." The repayment of evil with evil is Old Testament morality; the repayment of evil with good is New Testament morality. Zarathustra rejects both here. Although in other contexts Zarathustra prefers the Hebrews to the Christians, here he is repudiating the Judeo-Christian conception of morality because it shames or lowers the enemy instead of raising him up or making him better. At the same time, to punish is to take vengeance, which is to accept the standards of the enemy, and thus constitutes self-abasement. The desire for vengeance prevents us from rising beyond good and evil.

Note that Zarathustra does not insist upon complete freedom from anger against the enemy. Anger is better than shame, and a little cursing is better than blessing. Zarathustra is not advocating Christ's doctrine of turning the other cheek. "A little revenge is more human than no revenge" (88). But this revenge cannot take the form of punishment in the usual sense; it comes from honoring the transgressor as one who has honored us by attacking us. Punishment, that is, opposition, is acceptable if it is dispensed as honor of the prowess of the enemy.

Cold justice is angry justice; Zarathustra rejects this angry justice of the executioner and asks for the justice that loves with seeing eyes, that is, with eyes that are not hardened and prevented from clear vision by anger. But clear vision is not in itself anger or love; Zarathustra advocates clear-sighted love. This refers to the raising of the enemy to the status of a friend, namely, someone who has benefited us with his ostensible injustice or injury. Zarathustra desires the justice that acquits everyone except the judge. The judge is the lawgiver; he judges everyone, but not himself, because he is above the law which expresses his will. On the other hand, no one can be held responsible for the judgments of the law except the judge or lawgiver; so he is the only one who is guilty. He takes on himself the responsibility for the moral code, the judgments, of all human beings under his jurisdiction.

There is an interesting comment about justice and lying toward the end of the section. "In him who would be just from the ground up, lies are also *Menschen-Freundlichkeit*," that is, philanthropic. In order to give each person his due, lies are needed, because people do not want what they deserve: They want more. Conventional morality is filled with lying because it must persuade everyone to restrict his desires. Therefore, to give each his own would be to make each person judge or lawgiver; it would be to acknowledge the desires expressed by each person as a manifestation of the will to power. Zarathustra, however, neither gives conventional or duplicitous morality, nor does he emancipate each person by making everyone a superman. He gives to each person his own laws, his own will.

"On Free Death" (Section 21)

This section is of special importance for the prehistory of Heidegger's *Being and Time*. Zarathustra teaches that one must choose one's death on the basis of the value of one's life. One should not simply live out one's life as a form of waiting to die. But Zarathustra goes further than this. He also teaches that the accomplishment of a creative life requires the consummation of death. The accumulation of energy is an expression of the will to power. But the expression of will to power is also the dispersal of energy, or death. If creation is necessarily preceded by destruction, the creator too must die. The prophet, who is tainted with the decadence of his own time, cannot enter into the promised land. To say this in another way, Zarathustra teaches us to burn with a hard, gemlike flame (Walter Pater), or that a short life, if lived to full intensity, is the highest form of human existence. If we live too long, we outstay our welcome, we begin to decline; we become an impediment to the fulfillment of our highest aspirations. Note incidentally the distinction between the heart and the soul; these may age at different rates.

The less obvious teaching of the section centers on a discussion of "the Hebrew Jesus." "Jesus" is the only proper name other than "Zarathustra" to be mentioned in the entire work. This occurs in the thematic discussion of death. Note also that Zarathustra insists upon Jesus's Hebraic origin. (I will come back to this detail.) Let me first introduce the main theme of Nietzsche's analysis of death. Life is to be lived not merely in such a way as to give significance to "my death," but this significance is precisely the overcoming of "me" as an ego or subject. We may approach this theme from the normal human attitude toward death as something terrifying: the extinction of self-consciousness, of *me*. It is plain from simple reflection, and it is confirmed by the philosophical wisdom of our race, that fear of death is demeaning and also enslaving. Stated as briefly as possible: If we live in such a way as to avoid dying, we live in vain, as cowards who avoid taking chances and so will never accomplish anything bold or dangerous. We will not live in such a way as is required by the readiness to die for that which is higher than we are. The fear of death thus leads us to lower our sights, to become base and decadent.

In order to live the life of the highest individual, which Zarathustra represents by the expression "superman," I must not simply be a noble, creative, courageous person; my personality must itself be overcome in its self-expression as the release of energy toward a higher goal. This release of energy is my extinction as a personality. The doctrine of the eternal return is intended among its various functions to recompense me for my loss of personality, to render me secure against the fear of death. If life eternally recurs, I do not in fact die. My death at each appointed moment is the price I pay to live forever. Note that in order to benefit from this indemnification against fear of death, I must first overcome the nausea of the idea of perpetually repeating every aspect of my life, painful or pleasant. But this is no worse than the idea of enduring forever in a static heaven.

Nietzsche, in other words, realizes that he cannot "conquer" death in the sense of rendering it a pleasant prospect. He also rejects the standard philosophical remedies, all of which direct us toward an impossible temporal contemplation of eternity. In general, the traditional wisdom, exemplified by Socrates, is self-contradictory. On the one hand, Socrates tells us to forget about death by immersion in the pure noetic vision of Ideas. On the other hand, he describes the philosophic life as a preparation for dying. Nietzsche replaces the temporal contemplation of eternity with the temporal *experience* of eternity; we experience the circle of time over and over again. Life is also for Nietzsche a preparation for dying, but not as a jettisoning of life on behalf of pure *theoria*. Instead we prepare for death by living to the full.

This full life, or self-consuming, is in a sense suicide. Instead of sitting around waiting for death, or reading books to avoid thinking about it, we are directed to go forward resolutely toward death: to choose it, to extinguish our energies in its festival-like consummation of our lives.[19] "I praise to you my death, the free death that comes to me because *I* will" (94). This is the background for Heidegger's *Sein zum Tode* in *Being and Time*.[20] On the other hand, it should not be assumed that Zarathustra is advocating a quick death in the sense that we are to die as soon as possible. We have to die at the right time; and of course Heidegger would say the same thing (as would Plato and Socrates). For example, Zarathustra says: "One must stop permitting oneself to be eaten when one tastes best." This means not that we should try to live to a ripe old age, when we are withered and tasteless, but that we should not be willing to die until our work is done, until our energy has been used up.

Nietzsche prepares the way for the Heideggerian doctrine that death is the replacement for the Platonic Idea of the human being. I pass by the seldom-noted fact that there is no Idea of the individual soul in Plato. For our present purposes the key point is that human nature is defined in Nietzsche and Heidegger by a void or absence that serves as a boundary or definition of finitude, and not by a transcendent formal structure. The void of death also renders contingent the space of one's actual existence, the content of which must not simply be accumulated but rather produced by one's own resolved choice.

In Nietzsche, as in Marx, choice is the precondition for productive labor. The free death is the sign of the transformation of the transcendence of form into the immanence of activity; German Idealism is thus transformed in Nietzsche into the basis for the subsequent connection between historicity on the one hand and celebrations of creativity and difference on the other. Stated in another way, the monads of Spinoza and Leibniz, that is, the finite egos, are assimilated into the surrogate for substance or formal totality, and so too for the various versions of the absolute ego in post-Leibnizian German thought. Death is now the Absolute, death understood not simply as a void or absence but as chaos, the origin of creation.

Heidegger's early doctrine of resolve (*Entschlossenheit*) is thus a mixture of the Aristotelian virtue of courage and the German doctrine of the will. He retains the higher evaluation given by Nietzsche to courage; and despite his criticism of the key role played by the will in Western philosophy, that role is visible in his own ontology of existence. For Heidegger as well as for Nietzsche, the shift from an ostensibly universal form to that of individual production and the identification of death or chaos as the origin of significance make it impossible to order the lives of individual human beings by rank. What is apparently in Nietzsche an oversight becomes in Heidegger an explicit doctrine, namely, of "authenticity" (*Eigentlichkeit*). Authenticity, or genuineness, is now a structural term that derives its significance from resoluteness and the still less determinate choice of conscience. The anthropology of *Being and Time* provides no basis for a hierarchy of human types. Whereas this is presumably not for Heidegger a deficiency, the same situation obtains in Nietzsche, and with disastrous results.

To return to the text, Zarathustra wishes for preachers of the quick death who will shake the tree of life like a storm. Cowards attempt to extend their lives in idleness, and so they wither and decay. The storm shakes off the fruit before it can grow rotten. This point is applied almost immediately to Christianity, which preaches patience with everything "earthly" (95), that is, not a return to the earth in the Nietzschean sense but a bearing of one's lot and obedience to earthly rulers, and so a return to tradition, for which we are to be rewarded in the next life; in plain language, never.

It is important to note that although some of the first Christians sought an early death in an effort to get to heaven as soon as possible, when Christianity became a political power it was forced to repeat the Platonic teaching that we are the property of the gods and must remain alive until God chooses to gather us to him. Both Socratic philosophy and the Judeo-Christian tradition oppose suicide. Nietzsche does not advocate suicide in any literal way; but he does advocate living in such a way that one uses oneself up rather than waiting for God to bring us death.

We come now to the reference to Christ: "Truly, that Hebrew died too soon, whom the preachers of a slow death honor; and for many it has become a calamity that he died too soon." This sounds at first as though Zarathustra is repudiating his condemnation of a slow or delayed death. But this is not so; instead, he is repudiating both quick and slow deaths if they come at the wrong time. Zarathustra means to say that Jesus died too soon, namely, before he could experience enough of life to be led to repudiate his melancholy interpretation of it. Compare here D. H. Lawrence's *The Man Who Died Too Soon*. Jesus was noble but immature. As a result, his hasty march toward death was the cause of the extension of millions of lives beyond their prime. Jesus himself did not endure; but he preached endurance to his followers.

Jesus lived and died as a Hebrew, not as a Christian. Normally Nietzsche prefers the warrior Jews of the Old Testament to Christianity. Here the reference is mixed. Zarathustra speaks of the tears and the melancholy of the Hebrews as responsible for Jesus's hatred of the good and the righteous, by which latter he means, as the context shows, "man and the earth," the values of the community. Jesus should have remained in the wilderness until he matured; he brought his teaching to mankind too soon. "The tears and the melancholy" refers to the prophetic spirit of the Hebrews, which prevents them from enjoying life and is at odds with the warrior spirit. Sadness detaches us from existence; it can be overcome by the Dionysian frenzy that Nietzsche recommends elsewhere.

Note the distinction between *Jüngling* and *Kind,* "youth" and "child." The youth, or adolescent, is melancholy because he has just enough experience to disabuse him of his illusions; he is still too innocent and idealistic to cope with unrighteousness. The child has no experience and no illusions but only the will to survive. This is the "better understanding" of life and death.

In concluding this discussion of a free death, I want to make a general point about the doctrine of the eternal return. Two objections have commonly been raised against this doctrine. The first objection is that the eternal recurrence of life robs it of freedom; in the particular case, it makes a free death impossible. The second objection is that if everything eternally recurs in the same order and detail, then we cannot possibly distinguish one manifestation of the same life from another; to all intents and purposes, we live just one life. In fact, there is no freedom for the Hyperborean other than the Spinozist *amor fati,* for whom the doctrine of the eternal return is a prophetic commandment, not a discursive analysis of human temporality.

For those who cannot achieve the cosmological level of the Hyperborean, it is an advantage to believe in the uniqueness of one's life: In other words, the truth about the eternal return is stultifying for life. This is the most important example of what Nietzsche means when he says that art is worth more than the truth for life. This point will play a key role in my discussion of the eternal return in the complex economy of Nietzsche's double rhetoric.

"On the Gift-Giving Virtue" (Section 22)

In a graduate seminar on *Zarathustra* given many years ago at the University of Chicago, Leo Strauss pointed out that this section is a parody of the New Testament and the Christian doctrine of the Trinity. This is the only section in the first part of *Zarathustra* that is divided into subsections: It has three parts, which are devoted, very generally, to the Father, the Son, and the Holy Ghost. The Father is here Zarathustra as gift-giver. The Son is the gift of the future; the Holy Ghost is the solitude of one's own spirit. The will to power manifests itself within individual creativity as the ability to shape the *nihil* of a free death into a table of values for the next epoch of human history. To accept Zarathustra's doctrine, however, is to reject him personally, in contradistinction to the acceptance of Christ.

Subsection 1   Zarathustra departs from the city of the Motley Cow, to which his heart was close or attached – his heart, not his spirit (97). This indicates Nietzsche's attachment to European culture, which must be overcome for the sake of his prophetic gift in the persona of Zarathustra. The prophet's followers call themselves his disciples; he delays this appellation. This is the first stage of Zarathustra's influence, as represented by those who are attracted to his teaching and who refer to themselves as his disciples. His vision is directed beyond them to the genuine superman. In the second stage Zarathustra will begin by invoking his disciples to bestow a meaning upon earthly existence, thereby inverting Christ's assertion that "my kingdom is not of this world." In the third stage, there will no longer be disciples but only supermen or individual incarnations of the "Holy Ghost."

In this closing section of Part One, Zarathustra also indicates that whereas Christ came twice to mankind, he himself will undergo a third coming. In the first coming, Christ was crucified; Zarathustra departs voluntarily from the city of the Motley Cow to return to his cave. He asks those who accompany him to the outskirts of the city to leave him, as he wishes to walk alone. Whereas Christ is initially rejected by mankind, Zarathustra rejects those who would follow him.

The disciples present him with a staff "on whose golden handle a snake coiled round the sun." We recall the snake coiled around the neck of an eagle. The eagle may be replaced by the sun, but the snake remains: Pride is replaced by a natural symbol of recurrence. Nature continues to require interpretation by cunning. Zarathustra is delighted with the staff and leans on it. Just as the sun's happiness was said in the Preface to require those upon whom it shines, so the Father cannot bestow his gift without recipients. The sun is the symbol here of the will to power that leads Zarathustra initially to overlook the inferior nature of those who receive his gift; correlatively, the absence of the eagle suggests that pride is the interpretation of natural force insinuated by cunning.

Otherwise put, Zarathustra's pride cannot be sustained by the actual nature of his disciples, as will become evident in the next subsection. At the end of the previous speech on free death, Zarathustra says that he has thrown a golden ball to his friends and heirs and that he wishes most of all to see them throwing the golden ball themselves. At the end of the first coming, the friends and heirs are absent; Zarathustra's disciples cannot throw the golden ball but instead give him a staff with a golden handle to support him on his journey into isolation.

The staff is the expression of the disciples' understanding of Zarathustra's teaching; it both supports him and shows his debility. But why is he delighted? Instead of referring to the figures on the handle, Zarathustra praises the gold of which they are made: "uncommon, useless, gleaming, mild in its splendor." These are in general aristocratic virtues and belong to the golden ball mentioned above. The eyes of the giver gleam like gold: It is a sign of nobility to give rather than to receive. But the gift of the golden ball is bestowed in play. The eyes of the player gleam with the pride of victory. The eyes of the Christian who obeys Jesus's maxim that it is more blessed to give than to receive gleam with pity and humility.

The gleam of gold, as Zarathustra goes on to say, reconciles the light of the sun and the moon. Night and day now draw their meaning from the new teaching, or the new table of values. Zarathustra identifies the gift-giving virtue as selfishness (*Selbstsucht*). For Zarathustra the self is more fundamental than the ego or subject: It brings us closer to the physiological expression of the chaotic will to power. This selfishness is that of the healthy, not of the sick, who steal rather than give. Strictly speaking, disciples do not give their own gift; they steal that of the master and thereby disfigure it.

It is evident that Zarathustra's delight stems not from the attributes of his companions as these are reflected in the staff they have given him, but in the inference of the future that he draws from the golden substance of the handle. Zarathustra infers future success from initial failure. The dialectical nature of the institution of philosophical revolution is represented by the need for three comings. Once more, without suggesting any reliance by Nietzsche on the doctrines of Hegel, I note that the intrinsic similarity to Hegel's description of Christian history is striking. The two comings of Christ, however, are a subdivision of his single role as Son. Zarathustra incorporates Father, Son, and Holy Ghost; he therefore requires a third coming.

The first coming, as the Father, is more fundamentally destructive than creative; in order to prepare for the advent of the Son, it is necessary to destroy the city of the Motley Cow. Let us playfully designate this coming as the first negation. The second coming, as the Son, is intended as the negation of negation, or in other words as the advent of the new epoch with its new table of values. The actual result, however, thanks to the inevitable misunderstanding and intrinsic impossibility of Nietzsche's doctrine, is a race of disciples. Hence the need for the third coming, in which the negation of the negation (consider here the role attributed to the proletariat by Marx) results in a sublation, or overcoming, of the limitations of discipleship. In Hegel, however, there is a historical mechanism, the dialectic of master and slave, to which may be assigned the role of effecting this sublation. There is no such mechanism in Nietzsche; the struggle for recognition, or his own surrogate for the dialectic of master and slave, leads to perpetual war; that is, to a perpetual production of masters who, by virtue of their identity as masters, are revealed as slaves.

I infer from this playful comparison the serious truth that whereas Nietzsche constructed with great care the general outlines of his teaching as well as its written communication, he was lacking in the conceptual or dialectical attention to detail that marks thinkers like Kant and Hegel. Nietzsche's attention to detail is that of the poet; it is therefore too frequently seduced by the power of symbols. But this in no way mitigates our own obligation to submit those symbols to careful analysis. There is no other way in which to understand Nietzsche's thought in its brilliance and in its limitations.

To continue with that task, we return to the text. Zarathustra praises his companions, whom he now identifies as his disciples, because they strive for the gift-giving virtue; in other words, they have not yet attained to it. "What would you have in common with cats and wolves? This is your thirst, to become sacrifices and gifts yourselves" (97–98). The selfishness of the gift-giving virtue is to impose oneself on the will of others: to dominate by raising them to a higher level through one's own force, but thereby to be transformed and so to perish in one's original identity. This is not the case with cats and wolves. Cats are household pets, yet famous for their haughtiness, or indifference to the humans who care for them. Wolves prey on the sheep of the flock; they are hunters or predators who take from humans but give nothing in return. Apparently Zarathustra links cats and wolves as creatures who are parasitic on mankind. Possibly cats refer to those who rule others while concealed in the form of subservience.

In this passage, Zarathustra shifts almost imperceptibly from speaking of the desire of his disciples for the gift-giving virtue to addressing them as though they actually possess it. He exhibits a kind of generous disdain toward their inadequacies which is no doubt motivated in part by the intention to raise them beyond themselves. The main point here is that the genuine gift-giver is a robber who drains old values of their strength in the selfish desire to impose his own will: The virtue of giving is that of strength, not generosity or disinterested philanthropy.

What does Christ give us? Himself as God. But what of the remission of sins and eternal life? Christ redefines virtue as love (*agapē*) and sin or vice as unbelief, or a rejection of his divinity. As to eternal life, it is that of the perpetual disciple, slave, or thief. We can now state the central defect of Christianity from Zarathustra's viewpoint. Christ not only rules us forever but forces us to acknowledge that we are his humble servants or worshipers. Zarathustra rules us in the disguised form of one who persuades us that we are independent supermen, virtual gods among mortals. Whereas both doctrines are illusions, the Christian doctrine abases the human spirit, and the Zarathustran doctrine elevates it.

Gift-giving is normally associated with the soul, as in Christianity. Thus we normally speak of degeneration (*Entartung*) as the absence of the gift-giving soul (*Seele*), or the absence of charity. But Zarathustra does not invoke the return of the gift-giving soul. Instead he reinterprets the upward-bound path of "regeneration," or transformation from one nature or species (*Art*) to another, as an activity of the body. The soul is replaced by the spirit (*Geist*), which is the herald or echo of the triumphs of the body. This coincides exactly with the interpretation of the gift-giving virtue as selfishness. The body is the root of the self; virtues are the parables of the body's desires: Virtue is a parable of physiology. "Thus the body goes through history, a thing that becomes and that fights." Life is war; art, science, and philosophy, or the *paideia* of the spirit: These are the announcement of battles, the echoes of the clashing bodies, and the claims to victory.

In the final series of speeches corresponding to the first coming, or to the Father, Zarathustra spells out the origin of virtue. There is nothing fundamentally new in these rhetorical assertions. We might note two references to love, in both cases interpreted as domination over the whole, not as a personal sentiment toward an individual person (99). The last speech explicitly defines the new virtue, that is, the new interpretation of virtue as power (*Macht*): "A dominant thought is she and around her a clever soul: a golden sun and around her the serpent of knowledge." The sun is power, natural force rather than the pride of the individual, just as I suggested at the beginning of my comments on this section. And nature requires to be interpreted by a clever soul or person, not by *Geist*. So much for subsection 1: Zarathustra has spoken here as the Father who prepares the gift of the future (the Son) by the explanation of the gift-giving virtue as selfishness, the human pseudonym for the will to power.

Subsection 2 Zarathustra punctuates the preceding set of speeches with a period of silence, during which he looks at his disciples with love (99). At the beginning of subsection 1 there was no mention of love for them, but rather of joy at the staff. Zarathustra there leaned on the symbol of his disciples' submission to him. Without disciples, there can be no masters. But the staff also contained a symbolic representation of the peak of Zarathustra's teaching. There is no evidence that the disciples understood this teaching prior to Zarathustra's explanation, which is not complete, to be sure, but which is sufficiently frank and detailed. In sum, Zarathustra the Father explains the underlying principle of his dominance over his disciples; he applies this explanation as the doctrine of selfishness, the gift-giving virtue. Zarathustra selfishly gives to his disciples the future, the epoch of the superman.

But now, in subsection 2, Zarathustra has shifted identities; "the tone of his voice had changed." He is now the analogue of Jesus. He looks at his disciples with love. His doctrine, however, is the reverse of the Christian doctrine: "Remain true to the earth for me, my brothers, with the power of your virtue. Let your donating love and your knowledge serve as the meaning of the earth!" This is a famous passage and takes us back to the section "On the Despisers of the Body." Zarathustra teaches the destruction of heaven (here represented as "eternal walls") and a new sense of bodily "ascension" that proceeds by a return to, and fidelity toward, the earth. Back to the earth, back to the body.

Zarathustra tells his disciples to remain true to the earth "for me" and then asserts that the earth must be given a human meaning. This is an indication that Nietzsche is furnishing the earth with meaning through his proxy, Zarathustra. Within the illusion, the meaning is made by mankind: "ein Menschen-Sinn" (100); the superman is a superior man, not literally a new species of animal. The reader may recall here my earlier contention that the superman, in order to be intelligible to human ears, must somehow be derived by intensification from the highest and hence the most decadent attributes of Nietzsche's contemporaries.

The invocation of fidelity to the earth is Zarathustra's positive expression of the negative doctrine of the destruction of transcendence; we may (playfully) refer to it as the negation of the negation. In the Platonist or Christian tradition, the meaning of individual existence is acquired through participation or residence in the Absolute. Thanks to Zarathustra's second coming, or manifestation as the Son, the transcendent Absolute is replaced by the earth. But this is still too substantial; the earth must itself be made volatile by the power of the negative labor of spirit, which draws its definition from the *nihil* of a free death. The third coming will accordingly transform the Holy Ghost of Christian doctrine into the profane spirit of the radically finite superman, for whom the Absolute is chaos.

The rest of subsection 2 reverberates with earlier themes, so expressed as to inspire Zarathustra's disciples to action. Note the verse "We still fight step by step with the giant accident; and senselessness, without sense, still rules over all of mankind." What is accident inside the illusion of human existence is fate when viewed from outside or above. It is by means of this distinction between "inside" and "outside," or exoteric and esoteric, that Nietzsche attempts to reconcile the apparent contradiction between free creation and determinism.

That this attempt is an experiment may be sustained by citing the following passage: "As knower, the body purifies itself; raise yourself by experimenting with knowledge." Nietzsche often refers to himself as one who experiments with values and modes of life. His laboratory is history; he is seeking to cultivate a new race of mankind through the imposition of his will, rather than by a doctrine of nature or God. From this standpoint, *amor fati* is not so much an acknowledgment of classical determinism as the acceptance of the consequences of one's experiments.

I will restrict myself to commenting on two further passages from this part. The first: "Physician, help thyself; thus thou helpest thy patient too." This echoes Jesus in Luke 4:23: "Ye will surely say unto me this proverb, Physician, heal thyself." Jesus attributes this to the Nazarenes who ask him to perform miracles like those he has accomplished elsewhere. Jesus replies that no prophet is welcome in his own country. Zarathustra is Jesus; he cannot transform his disciples into supermen. They must help themselves by ceasing to be mere disciples. At a deeper level, whereas Jesus heals the lame, the halt, and the blind, it is in the very nature of his prophetic mission that he cannot heal himself, since the mission is itself his spiritual disfigurement. Exactly the same is true of Zarathustra. The invocation of the superman is inevitably fulfilled, and thereby betrayed, through the creation of the disciple.

Second: "There are a thousand paths that have not yet been taken." Again, we hear the echo of the thousand and one nights, as well as emphasis on the future: "From the future come winds with secret windbeats." And here Zarathustra blends elements of the Hebrew and Christian doctrines to preach the coming of a chosen *Volk*. The lonely ones are the outcast "Hebrews" in the sense that they are detached from the majority, not because they obey the old law but because they wish to create a new one. And most important of all: Out of the chosen people comes a superman. There cannot be a tribe of supermen. The disciples must be transformed into the chosen people from whose midst the superman emerges.

Subsection 3   Zarathustra is once more silent; then he announces that he is about to enter into solitude and invokes his disciples to renounce him (101). In order to enact his teaching, the disciples must cease to be disciples. They are united with him only by duplicating his solitude. In the terms of an earlier comparison with German Idealism, the spiritual significance of personal existence comes from the interiorizing of chaos, the Nietzschean surrogate for the Absolute, which as the principle of individuation, or what is today called "difference," sustains the superman in the absence of all external limitations to his self-formation.

The disciple must accordingly hate Zarathustra and not love or worship him as the Christians worship Jesus. Worship is slavery. Zarathustra does not want slaves as disciples; this is the significance of the reference to himself in the following warning: "Perhaps he deceived you." And also: "One repays a teacher badly if one remains always only a student." The unification of the Father and the Son in the Holy Ghost is therefore a phantom or chaotic universal that liberates each of its intended members even as it encompasses them.

In more concrete terms, the historical representation of the universal is initially the *Volk,* consisting of individuals who are united by their status as outcasts. Nietzsche is thinking here in the first instance of the Hebrews, united by the terrifying willingness to act of Abraham, and in the second of the Christians, who are the outcasts of "the Hebrew Jesus." In fact there are three stages here: (1) purificatory isolation of the outcast; (2) union of purified outcasts into a *Volk;* (3) emergence of the superman from the *Volk.* Stage (1) requires the adoption of Zarathustra's teaching; but in order to adopt this teaching, the disciple must reject Zarathustra himself.

"Now I order you to lose me and to find yourselves; and only when you have all denied me will I come to you again." The resurrection is the inverse of Christ's resurrection: It depends upon universal rejection, not universal conversion. Nietzsche improves on the New Testament here: Christ comes only twice, but Zarathustra promises to come three times. In addition to what has been said previously, this refers to the three stages just noted. The third coming is the Holy Ghost, or the *Geist* of the superman. Zarathustra refers to it as the great noon, the moment of maximum clarity, not midnight or the moment of maximum darkness and intoxication.

At the great noon, man is midway between beast and superman. This was prefigured in the Preface by the rope-dancer, who, however, gets only halfway across the rope. *"Dead are all gods; now we want the superman to live"* (102). The precondition for the emergence of the superman is the death of all gods, not just of the Christian God. Only those who believe in nothing, and in this sense are nihilists, can overcome. This is Nietzsche's version of Hegel's double negation. Whether there can be a genuine sublation is more than dubious, as is evident from Nietzsche's subsequent composition of Part Four, in which the main event is the festival of the jackass.

3

ZARATHUSTRA'S SPEECHES: PART TWO

Part Two takes as its motto the passage from the last section in Part One, in which Zarathustra says: "Only when you have all denied me will I come to you again" and love you with a different love. This is an echo of Matthew 10:33 and Mark 8:38. Jesus warns those who will deny him or be ashamed of him that he will deny or be ashamed of them. One could say that the love of Jesus remains the same during his first and his second coming; correlatively, he demands constancy from his disciples. Not so with Zarathustra. The love with which he delivers his first prophecy differs from that which will mark his second prophecy, or coming.

Otherwise put, Zarathustra initially loves (or wishes to present a gift to) his disciples, but after speaking to them he sends them away with the invocation to resist and be ashamed of him, for perhaps he has deceived them. "One repays a teacher badly if one remains always only a student" (101). If those who receive his gift remain simply his disciples, they have misunderstood him and transformed the gift into poison. And in fact, the message has deceived them by turning them into slaves rather than freeing them. Accordingly, Zarathustra must revise his teaching, or at least the rhetorical presentation of that teaching. "Now I bid you lose me and find yourselves; and only when you have all denied me will I return to you. Verily, my brothers, with different eyes shall I then seek my lost ones; with a different love shall I then love you."

These last words of the preceding section are especially important.

134

The first coming of Zarathustra issues in the initial revelation of the death of God and the doctrine of the superman. Zarathustra wins disciples, but rejects them for the very reason that they are disciples and, as such, incapable of enacting his teaching. The second coming will occur only after Zarathustra has been denied by all of his disciples; the situation here is quite contrary to the second coming of Jesus. Zarathustra's second coming will bring with it a different love, which is not the same as a different teaching. But the second coming will also prove to be unsatisfactory. Zarathustra does not explain here why this is so, but he says that there will follow a third coming: "Then shall I be with you a third time, that I may celebrate the great noon with you. And that is the great noon when man stands in the middle of his way between the beast and the superman" (102).

These three comings undoubtedly correspond to the first three parts of *Zarathustra*. It was only after completing these that Nietzsche decided to write Part Four. This part does not represent a fourth coming but is rather a recapitulation of the first three from a peculiarly ambiguous standpoint that blends cynicism and exaltation.

"The Child and the Mirror" (Section 1)

Zarathustra has returned to his mountaintop cave and waits like a sower who has sown his seed (105). But his soul is impatient and desires those whom he loves, namely, those to whom he has more to give. There is an obvious sexual image here of the spilling of seed, and so, despite the agricultural image, more than a hint of a lack of fruition, followed by a return of fullness and desire. As always in this work, one has to balance expressions of love with expressions of instinct or natural, physiological processes. The filling up of the soul and the concomitant desire to overflow are modeled on the process of sexual appetite and generation. This is not simply to be understood in the image of altruistic love. Also striking is the reference to Zarathustra's self-imposed abstinence; the spirit rules over the body and decides when to gratify the physiological need for fulfillment.

Some years pass in this manner; we are not told how many. Zarathustra's "wisdom" grows within him and causes pain: This is not simply the wisdom of the body or Lawrence's "blood knowledge"; it is something more complex. The sexual desire of the body is transformed into a spiritual need for the gift of creation, which is at the same time domination over the spirits of other human beings. Zarathustra's wisdom is not conceptual or discursive but existential, a version of the will to power.

At last Zarathustra awakens one day before dawn, and after some reflection he speaks to his heart. So the emphasis is on Zarathustra as a quasi-person. Zarathustra tells his heart about his dream. He needs to express the wisdom of his spirit in the terms of his human persona, that is, of the stages on his way toward prophetic transfiguration. It is important always to consider the difference between Zarathustra and Nietzsche. Nevertheless, there are times when the impression is very strong that Nietzsche is writing of himself. It is, after all, he who has experienced in his own life the transformation of his human heart into the spirit of the epoch, and in this way has penetrated, or (in keeping with the image of the mountain cave) ascended to, the transfiguration of the Greek understanding of nature by which Christianity is overcome.

In the dream, a child carrying a mirror comes up to Zarathustra and tells him to look into it. A child is a symbol of innocence; we recall here the three metamorphoses. But the mirror directs Zarathustra away from historical actuality into the world of images. Note the double symbolism at this point. A dream is already an image, or the experience of images. Inside this dream, Zarathustra looks into a mirror, which is an entrance into images within an entrance into images. The situation is somehow reminiscent of, but not quite the same as, seeing a mirror reflected in a mirror. I think it is better to regard the dream as an exercise of Zarathustra's prophetic power. Zarathustra has a revelation about himself which is an image of the future. Inside this image, he is shown an image of his past.

On looking into the mirror, Zarathustra cries out, and his heart is shaken: "For I did not see myself therein, but the grimace and sneering laughter of a devil." Zarathustra did not see his customary face, but what he sees is defined by opposition to the child. The devil is the incarnation of the failure of Zarathustra's teaching as delivered in Part One, that is, during his first coming. "My *teaching* is in danger; weeds pass for wheat! My enemies have grown powerful and have deformed the face [*Bildnis:* "portrait," "likeness"] of my teaching" (105–106).

Zarathustra is incarnated in his teaching, which is designed to procreate as his own children a new race of supermen. The seed has gone bad, but this is a direct expression of Zarathustra's personal failure, and this explains why he sees a sneering devil in the mirror. The child represents the need for renewal, and in this way for purification. Zarathustra does not say that his friends have been defaced but rather that they are lost and that he must find them. Stated as simply as possible, Zarathustra's teaching has strengthened his enemies, from whom he withheld his teaching, and made his friends, to whom he gave it, both ashamed and lost to him.

How can we reconcile the admonition of the ending of Part One with the results as depicted at the beginning of Part Two? Zarathustra rejects his disciples precisely because they are disciples. This is the continuing paradox of Zarathustra's teaching. It cannot be accepted without being contradicted. Those who accept the doctrine of the superman and become his disciples are thereby disqualified from becoming supermen. By persuading them, Zarathustra has in fact deceived them. Zarathustra's enemies here are not those who misunderstand his doctrine but those who understand it better than his disciples. They recognize that in order to become supermen they must repudiate not simply Zarathustra's personal authority but the doctrine of the superman itself.

The attempt to become a superman is self-contradictory: Zarathustra's teaching thus looks out at him from the child's mirror with the sneering face of a devil (the opposite, or inverted, image of a saint or prophet). Ironically enough, by loving his enemies, Zarathustra retains too much of Jesus. What he intended was to encourage those at his own level to strike out on a radically independent path, for a superman requires other supermen, not disciples or slaves, as his friends. But those who strike out on their own can no longer be his friends; they cannot share his doctrine. It remains possible for Zarathustra to express his superiority by being always alone, that is, by going through an unending cycle (the eternal return of the same) in which he produces friends who negate his teaching by their own servitude to him, and enemies who become his friends by repudiating that teaching, yet who, in repudiating the teaching, are again transformed into enemies, and so on *ad infinitum*.

Still more sharply put: Zarathustra must preach as the activity of his own fulfillment. But the doctrine that he preaches deceives those who accept it, and this in turn prevents his own fulfillment. Zarathustra is his own devil, his own damnation. He cannot have friends; he can have only disciples and enemies. This is why, strictly speaking, *Zarathustra* has no beginning and no end; it is itself a manifestation of one cycle of the eternal return. Nietzsche certainly denies the doctrine of progress toward salvation, as in Judeo-Christianity; but he also denies the doctrine that ostensibly stems from his own teaching, namely, salvation through radical finitude and resolution to define one's life by a free choice. If the work as a whole culminates in exultation, this is an illusion, or an essential component in Zarathustra's exoteric teaching, designed to conceal from human beings the pointlessness of their existence.

Nietzsche is thus a practitioner of esotericism who is also strikingly honest and outspoken. It is the lack of sense or meaning in life, the chaos at the heart of things, that provides us with the freedom to create and thereby to transcend previous levels of accomplishment, and in particular to overcome decadence. But it is the same chaos that negates the significance of our overcoming. One sees this in the psychological or emotional aura that emanates from Nietzsche's writings, which are both intensely personal and strangely transhuman. Nietzsche exults in the knowledge of the doctrine of despair. And so, in the last analysis, despite the differences with Plato on every crucial detail, Nietzsche is a Platonist for whom salvation or fulfillment lies in knowledge of the truth.

Perhaps he is unlike Plato in that he speaks this truth fully and frankly, often in the same passage in which he is disguising the truth. The resultant contradiction is the truth, just as human existence, and indeed all of temporality, is a self-contradictory genesis and destruction, all in the same moment. As we shall see later, Zarathustra's highest teaching turns on the structure of the moment or instant. And this structure is self-contradictory, since it ceases to be and is about to be, precisely as what it is.

After this speech, Zarathustra leaps up like a seer and singer whose *Geist* has been affected (106). Note the shift from the personal "heart" to the general "spirit." His animals, the eagle and the serpent, who are watching him, marvel: "For like the dawn there lay on his face an approaching happiness." These totems represent Zarathustra's affiliation with nature, understood neither as points of force (modern physics) nor as the superhuman deities of Greek mythology, but as expressions of the link between human consciousness and the chaotic perturbations that Nietzsche symbolizes by the title "will to power." There is no morality in the eagle and the serpent, but the combination of pride and cunning by which mankind may overcome, if only temporarily, the dissolution of chaos. Note: Pride is cruel, or merciless. This is the dark side of the Greek *megalopsuchia*.

Zarathustra is not afraid of what has happened but is made happy by it, exhilarated by the need to preach again. The next several stanzas reiterate that he has once more stored up energy, that it is time to overflow, and that this overflowing is an expression of his love: Zarathustra's gift is also an expression of his need or will to create. It is not the love of Christ, of the dove and the lamb. But one could not say that it is the love of the eagle and the serpent, since these are never portrayed as loving, but as intermediate between natural force and Zarathustra's discursive will.

Zarathustra must explain to his animals what his needs are and how he plans to fulfill them. Whereas his love is also a will to power, this does not reduce to simple desire for domination. As we have seen, domination is defeat, not triumph, for what Zarathustra desires. The peculiar dialectic of friend and enemy may be taken as representative of the misunderstanding of Nietzsche's teaching by many of his disciples, a word that I extend to some who believe themselves to have surpassed or corrected him.

We should note carefully that Zarathustra expresses his desire to speak again, and to find a new mode of speech, with an impatience toward speech. "I have become a mouth altogether," but this mouth is an orifice through which will flow not only the stream of Zarathustra's discourse but also his love, which is here linked to the violence of a storm as well as to the natural torrents of flowing water. "All speech goes too slowly for me – into thy wagon I leap, storm; and even thee will I whip with my malice" (107). Zarathustra is not simply impatient to deliver a prophecy; impatience is part of the prophecy itself. The violence of his spirit is part of the prophecy, if not all of it. This can be related to the previous erotic imagery: Creation is something that overcomes us.

It is very odd that Nietzsche never refers in *Zarathustra* to Dionysus, who seems to embody exactly what is being described here. My own suspicion is that this is because Zarathustra is not intoxicated at all but remains a son of Apollo (his strength comes from the sun). The rhetoric of intoxication is employed by a sober person to transform himself into a creative force. I mean by this that Nietzsche had to overcome his own lucidity, or to intensify his inner rage and exuberance in the power of his own spirit, in order to reach the level of eloquence that would be necessary for the transmission of his teaching. "Truly, like a storm comes my happiness and my freedom!"

The rest of the section is self-explanatory. Zarathustra states that he must combine the shepherd's flute, that is, the music of lambs, with the wisdom of a lioness – not a lion – or a maternal version of royal strength. He must persuade in order to nurture. Persuasion is genesis, a procreating by Zarathustra's wild wisdom on the turf of the hearts of his auditors. The one ambiguous point comes at the end of the section: Zarathustra's wild wisdom is female, not male – a lioness, not a lion. She had already become pregnant on lonely mountains and given birth on rough stones. No mention is made of the identity of the father lion. Similarly, Zarathustra closes this section by saying that his wild wisdom wishes to bed her "most beloved" on the turf represented by the hearts of his friends. Who is her beloved? I suspect that it is Zarathustra's enemies.

"On the Blessed Isles" (Section 2)

The *makarōn nēsoi* are mentioned in Hesiod and discussed at some length in Pindar, *Olympian*, II, 7off. Certain outstanding dead souls are taken here instead of being sent to Hades. There is no death here, no ugliness of scene or violence of nature, nothing but enjoyment in perpetuity. The blessed isles are associated with the golden age, ruled by Kronos, a myth that figures in Plato's *Statesman* as one of the sources for the Eleatic Stranger's myth of the reversed cosmos. This is the background for the dramatic setting of Part Two.

The main features of the original myth are that the residents of the blessed isles are the fortunate few who upon their death have been separated from the normal journey to Hades or to Tartarus and carried away to a land of milk and honey, of freedom from unhappiness and work, and also from Eros and philosophy. They are outside history, that is, as resident in the isles, exempt from the ordinary and mostly harsh circumstances of everyday human existence. On this point they remind us of the previously mentioned Hyperboreans.

In Plato's version of the myth, the residents of the age of Kronos are not exempt from reincarnation, or participation in the normal cycle of human existence, but as governed by Kronos, they grow younger rather than older and eventually disappear into the earth, from which they rise again as old men and women, to live their reversed lives in the next subcycle of this reversed epoch. In addition to an existence free from work and care, they seem to live a herd life very close to that of the brutes. The Eleatic Stranger, who has invented this version of the myth, says that this will be the golden age if and only if its residents philosophize with each other and with the brutes, a condition that the details of the myth almost certainly make impossible of fulfillment.

The residents of the original blessed isles are thus the souls of superior Greeks. But the residents of Nietzsche's blessed isles are on the whole friends and disciples of Zarathustra. In Part One, he approaches the city of the Motley Cow for the first time and is initially unknown there, although he eventually creates a circle of disciples. In Part Two, he descends once more from his mountaintop, not to the city but to the blessed isles and hence to those who have already received his teaching and (in general) have been persuaded by it. This must be related to Zarathustra's assertion in the opening section of Part Two, which takes place not in the blessed isles but in his cave, that he requires a new way of speaking, that is, a new rhetoric or a new accommodation of his teaching for a different audience or a different set of circumstances.

The first two stanzas of the section give crucial details about the dramatic setting. The figs (shortly to be identified as the fruit of Zarathustra's teaching) are ripe to the point of bursting and are falling from the trees with no effort on the part of those who are about to eat them, but blown to the ground by Zarathustra himself: "I am a north wind to ripe figs" (109). The season is autumn; the time of the speech is afternoon. Bursting ripeness, autumn, afternoon, fruit falling into one's hands, nourishment without effort; these details suggest that we are at a crisis or turning point – and even more, that we have already taken the turn. Ripe fruit signifies that the time is also ripe to act on Zarathustra's teaching; overripeness, or ripeness to the point of bursting, suggests that decadence has already begun. The moment has been missed (109).

In the last section of Part Two, Zarathustra's "stillest hour" tells him that "thy fruits are ripe but thou art not ripe for thy fruits! So must thou return to solitude; for thou must become mellow" (189–90). The fault lies not in Zarathustra's friends and disciples nor in his teachings, to the extent that they can be separated from himself. Zarathustra is not yet ripe for the fulfillment of his own teaching. It is much too soon to conjecture on the meaning of this assertion. One might be tempted to say that we see here the reverse of the situation in Part One, in which the disciples proved to be inadequate. But this inference is subordinate to a deeper question. Can we distinguish between Zarathustra and his friends and disciples? Is not their own inadequacy due to the prophet and his teaching, in other words, to the inadequate formulation of the teaching that prepares unripe disciples? If Zarathustra had spoken more judiciously, could he not have produced the ancestors of the superman from the residents of the city of the Motley Cow? Or was a preliminary dieresis needed, a "carrying away" of the friends and disciples to the isles of the blessed, where they might ripen properly for the task that has been set them?

We will not be able to answer these questions simply by a literal reading of the text. The details that we have just inspected suggest that we must distinguish between the exuberance with which Zarathustra announces the need for a new mode of speech and the mode of speech itself, which may be keyed to overripe fruit, an autumnal afternoon, and Elysium. There may be some difference between the way in which Zarathustra speaks to himself and the ways in which he speaks to his various audiences, including the manner in which he recounts to them what he ostensibly said to himself.

Despite the voice of Zarathustra's stillest hour at the end of Part Two, he begins his autumnal speech by introducing the topic of God and the need to abolish all gods in order to create the superman, a work of which he states that his friends are incapable (109). From the blessed isles, one looks out on the beauty of distant seas. "Once one said God when one looked upon distant seas; but now I taught you to say: superman." The sentence is grammatically interesting; Nietzsche combines the temporal "now" with the past tense. *Nun* is probably a conjunction here indicating cause. The blessed islanders no longer say

"God," because Zarathustra taught them in the past to say "superman." He taught them this in some previous incarnation, and no doubt it is just this knowledge that has brought them to the blessed isles. By knowing that God "is a conjecture," we somehow escape from the eternal return, that is, from the endless recurrence of historical existence. Zarathustra's stay on the blessed isles, and thus Part Two, is a kind of intermezzo. In Part One he descends from his mountaintop cave to the city of the Motley Cow. In Part Three he sails away from the blessed isles, no doubt because of what his stillest hour told him at the end of Part Two, back to the city of the Motley Cow on his way home to the mountaintop, which he eventually reaches. Part Four takes place in a variety of settings in the vicinity of Zarathustra's cave.

Let us say as a preliminary observation that there are three main dramatic settings for *Zarathustra:* the mountaintop and the adjacent woods, the city of the Motley Cow, and the blessed isles. There are other locales, for example on board the ship that transports Zarathustra from the blessed isles back to the city and thence to his mountaintop cave. Once more only as a preliminary hypothesis, I shall suggest that there are two poles to *Zarathustra,* or, otherwise put, two "homes" for the prophet: his mountaintop cave and the city of the Motley Cow, which we are told that he loves ("On the Apostates," p. 230). The speeches in the city, I suggest, are Zarathustra's accommodation to the concrete historical situation of his time. When Zarathustra is talking to himself and to his animals on the mountaintop, we are presented with a more direct (but not necessarily candid) statement of his fundamental teaching.

Conversations with visitors to the mountaintop or in the adjacent woods are somehow mediations of these two modes of discourse. The speeches on the blessed isles and on the ship that carries Zarathustra away from those isles have a distinct dramatic setting: Zarathustra is not at home in either sense of the term, neither by himself nor in the midst of those whom he has come to transform. He is neither outside history, looking down from above, nor immersed in history, in his own epoch; instead he is in a phantom domain, associated with ships and distant seas, somehow talking to ghosts.

"God is a conjecture, but I will that your conjectures reach no farther than your creative will. Could you *create* (*denken*) a god? Then be silent to me about all gods! But you could indeed create the superman!" (109f.). The residents of the blessed isles have been detached by Zarathustra's teaching from ordinary historical existence, but they lack the strength to enact his teaching. It is interesting to contrast Zarathustra's treatment of this point with that of his eventual student, Heidegger. Zarathustra invokes the creation of a new form of human existence: The superman is still a man. But Heidegger rejects humanism entirely, including "superhumanism." In so doing, he also rejects the creation of new gods. Unlike Zarathustra, however, he awaits the coming of a new god. Heidegger rejects the thesis that man is the creator of the cosmos. The Kantian doctrine of the projection of significance by *Dasein* is replaced in his later teachings by the anticipation of the gift of a new revelation. Regardless of the details of Heidegger's teaching, it is plain that it falls within the ambience of the Christian tradition in this decisive respect: Human existence is a gift from a transhuman source. Perhaps the most striking difference between Heidegger and Christianity is that the savior god whose coming we are to facilitate is an "ontological" but not a "personal" savior.

However this may be, there is no reference to a *Schick des Seins* in Zarathustra's prophecy to the islanders. The prophecy is a message of activism, not of anticipation, or *Gelassenheit*. This message is not compatible on the face of things with the invocation to *amor fati*, or the eternal return. But this is not the place to attempt to reconcile these two aspects of Zarathustra's teaching. We note instead that the action recommended by Zarathustra is suitable to "afternoon men" who live in a land of already ripened fruit, a land in which the maximum effort of spiritual intensity is neither possible nor necessary. The best creation of which the islanders are capable is to recreate themselves into fathers and forefathers of the superman.

"God is a conjecture; but I will that your conjectures be limited by the thinkable." Human beings expend their spiritual strength in the vain effort to conjure into existence that which is beyond their power. Zarathustra does not mean by this merely that the "concept" of a God is unthinkable or unintelligible. In a sense one could say that the "concepts" of the will to power and the eternal return are also unthinkable, except as conjectures. But the notion of a god or a transhuman limitation to the human will is a contradiction of the will: "But this is what will to truth shall mean to you, that everything be transformed into the humanly thinkable, the humanly seeable, the humanly feelable. You ought to think your own senses to their last consequences!" (109–10).

"And what you called world, that shall first be created by you; your reason, your image, your will, your love shall themselves become the world" (110). What will subsequently be referred to as *Auslegung* is already prefigured here. The cosmos, or order of human life, is a product of human spiritual activity: of thinking as defined by feeling and sensation, in other words, as defined not by religious or metaphysical speculation but by the expression of one's own nature. The world is a projection of the human spirit, not a creation of a transhuman god. One can also say that the projected world is a function of the strength of the will of the individual human being. But there is a hierarchy of worlds that corresponds to the degrees of power exhibited by individual wills. Nietzsche is not a "relativist" in the vulgar sense; the world projected by the strongest will is the best world. This best world is represented by the doctrine of the superman.

I do not mean by this that Nietzsche has defined the contents and limits of a definite number of worlds and graded them in the order in which they manifest the will to power. He does of course have his historical paradigms, such as the Italian Renaissance or archaic Greece. But these are examples of his "values" and represent only two of the many possible configurations of historical existence by which the values may be embodied in human existence. These values cannot themselves be defined with precision or deduced from a transcendental principle. But they are also not entirely amorphous, nor is the list endless. Over and over again, Nietzsche makes it explicit that he places a premium on strength, health, virility, fecundity, continuous self-overcoming, and in general the political and aesthetic values of a spiritual aristocracy that possesses the physical strength and courage to flourish and to dominate.

Nietzsche's popular expression for his table of values is "will to power." It is plain from the details of his later teaching as well as from explicit passages in his notebooks that the will to power, if understood as anything other than the accumulating points of force of chaotic flux, is an exoteric notion. Since Being, or the heart of all things, is chaos, there are no wills, and consequently there is no will to power. This follows directly from Nietzsche's denial of the coherence of subjectivity. In preaching to his disciples, however, Zarathustra does not inform them that their subjectivity is an illusion. To the contrary, by invoking them to self-transformation, and so to participate in a radical revolution, he speaks directly to their subjectivity as individual persons or agents of intentionality. We can therefore say that the deepest mystery of *Zarathustra* is that its hero is preaching to phantoms or to illusions, and that he who preaches is also a phantom or illusion. This is not because the worlds of Zarathustra and of his respective auditors are each private perspectives or interpretations of chaos. It is rather because the world as world is an illusion: The world is not a subject's interpretation of the object "chaos," but an interpretation that is produced by chaos.

It is therefore not possible to understand *Zarathustra* simply as a revolutionary handbook, that is, as an explicit invocation to individual residents of the late-modern epoch to transform themselves by the strength of their own wills into supermen. We do not have to restrict ourselves to the writings, published and unpublished, of the post-*Zarathustra* period in order to find the contradiction between what can be called Nietzsche's activism and his doctrine of chaos and fatality. In fact, we do not even have to go outside the text of *Zarathustra* in order to find this contradiction. In its most explicit form, it is visible in the doctrine of the eternal return.

But it is also visible indirectly, in the dramatic structure of *Zarathustra*. In the fundamental sense, nothing happens in this work. The prophecy is a failure. Zarathustra repudiates throughout the work the very people whom he has apparently persuaded: his friends and disciples. It looks very much as though Zarathustra has two different intentions. One is to modify the behavior of his audience. But the other is somehow to modify himself, thanks in part to the recognition or to the assimilation of his inability to modify his audience in accord with the doctrine of the superman. Remember: If we become disciples of Zarathustra, then we are not supermen. If we become supermen, then we repudiate Zarathustra or become his enemies. And a society of friendly enemies, of supermen, each of whom is unremitting in the desire to dominate the others, is surely unthinkable. It barely rises to the level of a conjecture.

The balance of the section is a paean to the will to create as that which liberates Zarathustra from the imprisonment of his feelings within suffering. It is this will to liberation that underlies the rejection of gods and the affirmation of impermanence. Zarathustra reveals his heart to the blessed islanders: "If gods existed, how could I bear not to be a god! *Therefore* there are no gods" (110). By underlining the word "therefore," Nietzsche indicates the irrelevance of efforts to demonstrate rationally the existence or nonexistence of God. The conception of God is rooted in the need to create; but the need to create requires the primacy of Becoming: "What? Should time disappear and everything transient be a lie? . . . Everything permanent – that is only an image! And the poets lie too much" (110).

Two points need to be made about this passage. The first has to do with the connection between the doctrine of interpretation, according to which the world shall be created in one's own image, and the intrinsic impossibility of Zarathustra's teaching. If it had been Nietzsche's intention, as so many of his disciples believe, to unleash an epoch of radically free creative individuals, each of whom is a loosely assembled collection of continuously dissolving perspectives, then the world would be nothing more than a simulacrum of chaos – a simulacrum, not an image or likeness, since the illusion of cosmic order is in fact an erroneous accommodation of chaos to human faculties of apprehension.

In other words, by bending his audience to his will, Zarathustra must create a world in his own likeness that is also the likeness of his auditors. But this leads either to a universal homogeneous world state, as Alexandre Kojève refers to his "Hegelian" revision of Hobbes, or else to chaos. On the former alternative, the eternal return is transformed into the "turning" of eternal permanence, or what Zarathustra calls "the turning sickness" (110). Continuous overcoming requires a fluidity of form and order; if the worlds of mankind are all images of Zarathustra's will, they cannot change their shape without deviating from his will unless these changes are in obedience to that will. In short, Zarathustra is not a radical innovator but only the latest in a long line of prophets of permanence. On the second alternative, the attempt to create a world by the will is equivalent to the dissolution of all worlds; and, more fundamentally, self-assertion is equivalent to self-negation.

The second point has to do with the claim that poets lie too much. Zarathustra does not subscribe to a straightforward and simple-minded interpretation of the adage, formulated in subsequent texts by Nietzsche, that art is worth more than the truth for life. The value of art derives from its service to truth, or to its construction and employment of what Socrates calls "noble" or "medicinal" lies, without which public life is impossible.[1] The identification of falsehoods is possible only by means of a standard of truth. The poets lie too much, and Zarathustra, or in other words Nietzsche, is a poet, exactly like Socrates, or in other words Plato.

We are told nothing of the response of the blessed islanders to Zarathustra's invocation to create and his repudiation of the conjecture of God. In the Preface, the crowd in the marketplace of the city of the Motley Cow mistook the introduction of the tightrope walker for Zarathustra's announcement of the superman. Zarathustra's disciples, even his animals, respond in various ways to his speeches. But often there is either no explicit reference to an audience, or it is explicit in the context that Zarathustra is speaking to himself. In the present section, we have a silent audience. The residents of the blessed isles, as blessed, are apparently immune to further prophecies.

"On the Compassionate" (Section 3)

The next three sections contain a series of attacks on Christianity and present no major problems of interpretation in themselves. A more difficult question has to do with the dramatic structure. Why is it necessary to denounce Christianity to the phantom residents of the blessed isles? Nietzsche's principal objection to Christianity is that it enervates the human spirit and dissolves the rank-ordering of types. The metaphor of the overripe fruit of autumn, together with Zarathustra's assessment of his audience's limited capacity for change, suggests a link between "blessedness" and the diminution of energy.

The main topic of Section 3 is the denunciation of compassion and of "petty thoughts" (114), to which evil deeds are preferable. The former are like a disease that debilitates the spirit, whereas the latter provide a pathway to greatness (115). Zarathustra reports on a conversation with the devil, whereas he never talks to God. The devil tells Zarathustra that God died out of compassion for mankind (115). This is connected to Zarathustra's earlier assertion that, "to one who knows, man is the animal with red cheeks" (113). Man is the animal who blushes with shame at his own weakness: but this shame is misdirected toward sins, whereas it should be directed toward the ignobility of petty thoughts. This is a message that applies to the islanders as well as to the citizens of the Motley Cow.

It is worth emphasizing the fact that the devil survives the death of God. Satan is closely connected to the cunning of the serpent that is required for continuous overcoming. In cosmogonic terms, war is the father of all things; in psychological terms, evil is more interesting than good. There are no great portraits of God in Western literature, whereas Satan is immortalized in Milton's *Paradise Lost.* God is beyond the possibility of our imagination; Satan is our darkest self.

"On the Priests" (Section 4)

This section is more complicated than its predecessor. "And once Zarathustra gave to his disciples a sign and spoke these words to them: 'Here are priests, and though they are also my enemies, I go silently past them and with sleeping sword' " (117). This may mean that Zarathustra invokes the apparition of priests by means of his sign; it is more likely, however, that they exist already on the island, albeit as phantoms among phantoms. The priests "are evil enemies; nothing is more vengeful than their humility. And one who attacks them easily soils himself. But my blood is related to theirs, and I want my blood to be honored even in theirs."

Zarathustra has stated previously that his enemies are his true friends, and as a prophet he is both related to and a rival of the priestly class. Despite his previous statement against compassion, Zarathustra now asserts that he pities the priests ("Es jammert mich dieser Priester": 117), who have been imprisoned by the one whom they call their savior within bonds of false values and verbal delusions. "They believed themselves once to have landed upon an island as the sea tossed them about; but look! It was a sleeping monster!" I take this to refer to the blessed isles, the blessedness of which is an illusion. The island surrounded by tossing seas is the phantom of detachment from history by adherence to a doctrine of eternal salvation. Thus Zarathustra's own disciples have themselves been imprisoned in true values and words that accurately describe the illusory character of human existence. As disciples of the doctrine of the superman, they worship a genuine savior; but as disciples, they are detached from salvation. The most they can hope for is to be recreated as the fathers and forefathers of the superman. They are, in other words, transient and in that sense insubstantial ghosts who lack any but instrumental status. From this standpoint, the difference between the disciples of the genuine and those of the false savior is minimal.

In the balance of this section, Zarathustra restates his criticism of religion and the restriction of human freedom and knowledge by the worship of deities (118–19). The rhetoric must, however, be regarded as itself a delusion. The freedom that is required in order to become a superman depends on the knowledge of the illusory character of human life; but this knowledge is identical with decadence, not with creativity. Those who create do so out of ignorance and the innocence of becoming, not out of knowledge. In other words, those who require speeches to free them from the doctrines of false saviors are the already dead consequences of those doctrines.

"On the Virtuous" (Section 5)

The central image is that of God as paymaster. Zarathustra denounces those who want a reward for their virtue, namely, heaven or immortality. His own teaching, that there is no reward and no paymaster, is conventional enough. But he does not teach that virtue is its own reward: "That your virtue be yourself and not a stranger, a skin, a cloak: That is the truth out of the ground of your soul, your virtues!" (121). Zarathustra means to say that the virtuous express themselves as virtuous, but for no other reason; not for "revenge, punishment, reward, retribution." This point is connected with the "innocence of Becoming." There is no teleology in the expression of excellence, but only natural force, like the light of a dying star that lives on after the star is extinguished. We use ourselves up in the expression of virtuous activity. Note that the soul is the ground; there is no ground in nature or in heaven, but this does not mean that man is groundless. On the contrary, each of us is his own ground; life is the ground for the expression of excellence, or overcoming.

Zarathustra goes on to denounce various forms of error about virtue, all summed up in his prohibition against revenge. He then concludes with the command "O my friends! That your self be in your act, as the mother is in the child; let that be *your* word for me of virtue!" (123). By comparing the mother/child to the dying star and its starlight, Zarathustra assimilates the human to the natural expression of energy. Motherly love is self-love, and self-love is act, self-expression. That this equation is not entirely satisfactory as a rhetorical device is made clear by Zarathustra's final words: The children, or those whom he persuades, lose their toys (conventional views about virtue). But they will receive new toys. This is not the same as growing up or becoming enlightened. Human beings require toys, not the doctrine that they are dying stars.

"On the Rabble" (Section 6)

This section and its sequel ("On the Tarantulas") are entirely explicit denunciations of the *demos,* or the many, and of those who seek for power over them. Zarathustra finds the source of his pleasure (*Lust*) high above the rabble, in the domain of eagles. He was nauseated by the question "Does life *require* the rabble?" (125). This nausea arises from the recognition that universal enlightenment is impossible. The distinction between the few and the many is a necessary consequence of the will to power. Otherwise put, if the virtues of the few are too pure for the rabble, will it not be necessary to accommodate to them, and so to produce a race of those who seek power through domination of the rabble? Does this not affect the character of the very rhetoric by which the few attempt to transform the rabble? This is the same problem as that of the pale criminal.

Still more specifically: In order to change the rabble, Zarathustra must prepare intermediaries, those who transmit an accommodated version of his doctrine. But the accommodated version is no longer the doctrine; it is now a doctrine for the rabble. If Zarathustra stays in his nest and is fed by eagles while drinking from his pure mountain well – if in other words he remains in the land of the Hyperboreans – then he cannot carry out his transformation of the human race. But if he attempts to descend, even through surrogates, then it is he, or his doctrine, that is transformed downward into a rabble doctrine, and the revolution is aborted or has spawned a monstrous form.

Zarathustra wants to become a wind and to blow through the rabble so that he can take their spirit with his. He warns them not to spit against the wind (127). But all this means is that those who spit against the wind, or in other words resist his doctrine, will be covered with their own spittle even as the wind blows over them. It does not follow that the wind will cleanse them. There is nothing here or anywhere else in Nietzsche's writings to sustain the inference that the distinction between the few and the many will be overcome. On the contrary, Zarathustra's prophecy contains "no food which the unclean may share" with the few. The most one can say is that the distinction between the few and the many is preserved at a higher level. There are no masters without slaves, and Zarathustra's revelation is one of mastery.

"On the Tarantulas" (Section 7)

The previous point is reinforced by a shift in imagery to the tarantulas, whose bite is the teaching of equality, itself a product of the desire for vengeance (128). "For thus righteousness (*Gerechtigkeit*) speaks *to me:* 'Human beings are not equal,' " (130). *Gerechtigkeit* is a key term in Heidegger's interpretation of Nietzsche; he gives it an ontological or metaphysical significance that it will not bear.[2] The correct interpretation is to distinguish the word from political justice; the distinction corresponds to that in Greek between *dikē* and *dikaiosunē*. Zarathustra insists that he be distinguished from the preachers of equality, a request that has been ignored by contemporary Nietzscheans of the left. He then envisions the future as an epoch of warfare instituted by the preachers of equality, a warfare in which the effort is made to populate the heights by means of images and ghosts, that is, to ascend to the domain of the eagle by means of a false doctrine that imitates upward flight in the attempt to dominate, but that is in fact a descent. More specifically, there are various versions of the preaching of equality, and these will be at war with one another for dominance. So the struggle for equality is a ghostly image of the natural inequality of human beings.

Again Zarathustra indicates indirectly what I have stated directly. The tarantula bites his finger (131). Zarathustra must seek revenge; to fight this need, he asks his friends to bind him to a column as Odysseus was bound to the mast of his ship. But Odysseus did this so that he could hear the song of the sirens without succumbing to it. Zarathustra hears the song of the sirens *before* being bound to the mast. The need for revenge is intrinsic to the repudiation of the preachers of equality. In fighting the tarantulas, one is bitten by them. What then does it mean to be tied to a column in order to avoid the consequences of this bite?

Nietzsche is making a double point. (1) To seek vengeance is to lower oneself to the level of the enemy, to grant his importance. But (2) to resist the desire for revenge is not to rise above the enemy.

Zarathustra grants that this desire, and so his enmity, is intrinsic to his enterprise. This point enables us to make a distinction that invalidates Nietzsche's claim that Christianity is Platonism for the masses. Everyone can become a Christian, but only the few can aspire to genuine Platonism. There is no Platonism for the masses, as is indicated in the *Republic* by the fact that the life of the workers and farmers in the beautiful city remains intrinsically the same as it is in historical cities, although it is of course regulated externally by the guardians.

With these points in mind, we can now return to what is the central assertion of this section: "For *that man be delivered from revenge,* that is for me the bridge to the highest hope" (128). Nietzsche's revolutionary project is itself inseparable from a desire for revenge against the multitude, and in particular against their corrupt surrogates among the class of artists, academicians, and intellectuals. The application to the contemporary status of Nietzsche interpretation should be self-evident. In political terms, freedom from vengeance is thus dependent upon the exercise of vengeance. At the same time, we are required to embrace human existence in its totality and thereby to assert the innocence of Becoming by an *amor fati.* These steps are not consecutive but simultaneous, because both the exaction of vengeance and the total embrace are the necessary conditions of revolutionary activity. The desire for vengeance is not an exoteric version of *amor fati* but a genuine expression of the revulsion of the higher man for everything that restricts his will to power. To the extent that human life is itself an illusion, so too are the desire for vengeance and *amor fati.*

One might wish to remove the inconsistency by interpreting struggle as divine play and citing in support the following passage: "Let us also securely and beautifully be enemies, my friends! We shall struggle against one another like gods!" (131). As we have already seen, however, gods oppose one another by the creation of alternative worlds or the revelation of conflicting commandments. The invocation of the Heraclitian image of the *pais paizōn* is a poetical mask for the reduction of creativity to chaos. Wherever we look in *Zarathustra* and after, the problem is always the same. The presuppositions of creative play vitiate creativity and playfulness.

I want to add a final word on the confusion disseminated into Nietzsche studies by books like Deleuze's previously cited *Nietzsche and Philosophy.* The emphasis on difference to the neglect of rank-ordering, and on the multiplicity of perspectives to the neglect of Nietzsche's classification of these perspectives under a finite number of types,[3] has led to a vulgarization of his teaching that is unfortunately typical of our time. Democracy and egalitarianism are not well served by the attempt to assimilate all doctrines of emancipation into the celebration of chaos; Nietzsche does not make that mistake at the human or political level. The value of democracy itself depends on a rank-ordering of distinct regimes and therefore upon the coordination of identity and difference. Without identity, there is no difference between democracy and aristocracy, not to mention tyranny.

"On the Famous Wise Men" (Section 8)

In this section Zarathustra condemns the wise men who have accommodated service to the truth to "the folk and the superstition of the folk" (132). This is a continuation of the theme of the last two sections, but now with emphasis on the radical separation of the genuine philosopher from prudential speech. Note that Zarathustra takes for granted the "Unglauben," or lack of belief, of the wise men. He refers here not merely to religious belief but also to the doctrines that have been promulgated in accordance with popular superstition. Zarathustra claims that the people have understood and tolerated the unbelief that underlies this accommodation, but I think he goes too far here. What he should perhaps have said is that the leaders of the people have understood this and tolerated it because it assists them in their own domination over the many; compare the previously mentioned long speech of Protagoras in the Platonic dialogue that bears his name about the inability of his own predecessors among the "wise" to delude the few who rule in the city. In short: The traditional wise man has been an ideologue for the ruling class; this is essentially Marx's analysis.

More narrowly understood, Zarathustra is probably referring to the figures of the Enlightenment, not merely to the French atheists who identified scientific progress with universal enlightenment, but in particular to Rousseau and Kant, for whom morality is associated with the universal will. From Nietzsche's standpoint, this is still accommodation to the people: a kind of egalitarianism and denial of rank-ordering, but therefore a kind of traditionalist conservatism and suppression of the truth on behalf of public order. Those whose power stems from the people make use of the wise man like a little ass harnessed to lead the horses that draw the carriage of the rulers. At the same time, the ass is partly concealed by the lion's skin; that is, the wise claim to love the truth above all else. Zarathustra wishes to expose the ass entirely and so to reveal the identity of the genuine wise man as a beast of prey who lacks the "reverential will" and who both investigates or seeks and conquers (133).

The lion is now represented as a creature of the desert, who avoids even oases because one finds there idols. Zarathustra shifts between the persona of the lion as destroyer and as a solitary. This apparent contradiction is in essence the same as the apparent contradiction between the Hyperborean who sees all of human history and the resident of the historical perspective. The philosopher, as a genuine lover of truth, must be free of, and so beyond, every historical perspective. But as prophet and lawgiver, as breeder of a new race of mankind, the philosopher must destroy the old laws and the old race; and this requires an entrance into the perspective of one's own historical time.

On the one hand, the lion/will decrees itself to be "hungry, violent, lonely, and godless," a solitary who rules in the desert, not in the city of the Motley Cow. On the other hand, "the happiness of the spirit is this: to be anointed and to be consecrated by tears as a victim" (134); compare *Opfertier* with the opening lines of "The Pale Criminal" (45). There too the lawbreaker is described as a sacrificial beast, or scapegoat, but one who agrees to his own execution. Here self-sacrifice is associated with the destruction of tradition; it is a consequence of the loneliness and solitude of the lion. Again note the shift within the image from one sense to another. The lion must himself die as a resident of tradition. But this death is not merely one of isolation in the desert; it is a destruction of the tradition of wisdom, a slaying of the ass of tradition that precedes creation.

Zarathustra thus shifts from self-sacrifice to creation: "Let the knower learn how to *build* with mountains," that is (as the sequel shows), to build something new rather than to preserve the old with the faith that moves mountains (Christianity). And at once the connection between building and destroying is indicated: "You know only the sparks of the spirit, but you do not see the anvil that it is, nor the cruelty of its hammer!" (134).

In the balance of the section, Zarathustra emphasizes the extremes of the genuinely philosophical nature: burning hot and ice cold, eagle as well as lion. In a memorable image, he compares his wisdom to a sail skimming across the sea, trembling to the wind of the spirit: "my wild wisdom" (135). In this way the section ends as it began, with emphasis on solitude, searching, and wildness, that is, on liberation from traditional restrictions. The wildness of Zarathustra's wisdom is initially radically dissimilar to the urbanity of its Socratic counterpart. The dissimilarity narrows if we reflect on the Socratic doctrine of Eros, but it does not vanish. The public expression of wildness is the epitome of the difference between ancients and moderns, but also between the eighteenth and nineteenth centuries. Kant's *sapere aude* (dare to know) is constricted to *aude*.

"The Night Song" (Section 9)

In the next three sections, Nietzsche changes style and presents us with three songs to follow the three more or less explicit sections about the split between the few and the many, or, more precisely, between the solitary individual who is a genuine philosopher, or destroying creator, and the rest of the human race. These songs are all associated with darkness: night, evening, the tomb. But they are not simply night songs, as we are about to see. There is light in the darkness.

The first song begins with the assertion that night has come. Fountains speak louder at night, and Zarathustra's soul is a fountain. At night the sounds of the city are stilled; hence the plash of the fountain is more distinct. This seems to mean that Zarathustra is within the city and that his voice is more distinct at night, when we are relatively (but not completely) detached from everyday activity. It quickly becomes apparent that this song repeats the theme of love as a giving of gifts, like the overflowing of the sun's light, a theme that is introduced early in the Preface as Zarathustra recounts his speech to the sun and prepares to descend from the mountaintop.

In the present song, Zarathustra makes especially evident the connection in his doctrine of creativity between pleasure and pain; again one may discern here the basis for the subsequent assimilation by some of Nietzsche's admirers between his views and those of Sade: "They receive from me, but do I touch their souls? There is a cleft between giving and receiving, and the narrowest cleft is the last to be bridged. A hunger grows out of my beauty; I should like to hurt those for whom I shine; I should like to rob those to whom I give; thus do I hunger for malice" (137). To undergo receptive enjoyment is thus to suffer enslavement to the malice of the creator. But conversely, complete domination brings no satisfaction that is not itself slavish; the corollary to sadism is loneliness: "Oh the loneliness of all giving! Oh the silence of all shining!" To which one may add: Oh the loneliness of a Satan who has outlived the death of God.

"The Dance Song" (Section 10)

This song is delivered in the evening, in the company of Zarathustra's disciples, out of town and next to a well where girls are dancing. One should expect something less personal and perhaps less frank in this song than in the previous one. The girls stop dancing when they recognize Zarathustra; he tells them to continue. He is no enemy of girls, but God's intercessor or spokesman before the devil, who is the

spirit of gravity (139). Note the two differing strains of imagery running through the work, one of which connects Zarathustra with flying,
dancing, mountaintops, and isolation; the other with a return to the
earth, a desire to touch the souls of those who receive his gifts, and (as
he is about to sing) a love of life.

Zarathustra invokes the girls to dance with Cupid, who is lying
beside the well with his eyes closed, while Zarathustra himself sings a
dancing and satirical song about the spirit of gravity, of whom they say
that he is the master of the world (140). Zarathustra identifies himself
as a forest; the entire scene is a projection of the obscurity of his
spiritual interior. He must compete with the spirit of gravity, not
merely for world mastery, but initially for self-mastery. This illuminates
the sharp fluctuations in mood shown by Zarathustra even within the
same speech.

As we are about to learn, there is a conflict between Zarathustra's
love of life and his "wild wisdom," a phrase introduced in the preceding song and about to be repeated here. One has to bear in mind
throughout that prophets never enter into the promised land, and
that, as Nietzsche writes in his notebooks, he is himself prepared to die
as a decadent resident of a decadent age, in the destructive attempt to
create a new breed of mankind.[4] Otherwise put, immersion in life is
not the same as solitary song, nor is it the same as the founding act of
the prophet and lawgiver. These are three distinct roles. Within the
work itself, Zarathustra regularly fails in the first and third roles.

We turn now to the song itself. Zarathustra recounts how he once
looked into the eyes of life. Life is personified as a woman. Zarathustra
seemed to be sinking into the *unergründliche* eyes of life: unfathomable,
without a ground or bottom, like a deep river; but she pulled him out
with a golden fishing rod. Zarathustra does not refer to himself as a
fish; it is life who calls him that. Fish do not sink; they swim. But
Zarathustra is rescued from disappearing into the deep by life itself.
Life tells Zarathustra that he speaks like all fish: "What *they* do not
fathom is unfathomable. But I am merely changeable and wild and a
woman in everything, and not a virtuous woman" (140). Life thus
claims that these attributes are themselves the "ground" that fish, that
is, human beings who look for the meaning of life, cannot find. Life
attributes wildness to herself; this is the basis for the subsequent comparison by Zarathustra between life and his wisdom.

In the song, men are represented as serious and at the same time as
attributing to the feminine life their own virtues. Woman here represents not the stability of hearth and family but the boundlessness of
fertility. Life laughs, and Zarathustra says that he never believes her

when she speaks ill of herself, but it is not at all evident that life regards her self-portrait as a criticism. In this exchange, Zarathustra is the serious man who is looking for an ideal of virtue.

Zarathustra then tells how he discussed this exchange privately with his "wild wisdom," which is clearly separate from life and takes us back to his solitude of the night song. Wisdom speaks angrily to Zarathustra: "You will, you desire, you love – that alone is why you praise life!" Wild wisdom is also a woman; the underlying tone is one of jealousy, as though wild wisdom is competing with life for Zarathustra's praise. But the love of wisdom cannot be the same as the love of life; the latter is connected with will and desire, whereas this is not true of wisdom. So there is a distinction between love, here identified as love of life, and wildness, which is possessed by both life and wisdom.

Now Zarathustra himself comments on this difference. He almost answered wisdom wickedly and told her the truth. First let us note the participants in this exchange. Zarathustra loves one woman, life (most of all when he hates her), and he likes another, wisdom, sometimes too much because she reminds him of life. This is extremely important. Wisdom is like, but not the same as, life. This is connected to the distinction between the Hyperborean and the historical. The likeness between life and wisdom is that both are wild. When Zarathustra describes wisdom to life, she says that he is speaking of her; the description is that of ambiguity, variability, elusiveness, deception, and female seductiveness (141). Life cannot be captured, regulated, subjected to laws: It has no eternal or enduring structure. But neither does wisdom, because wisdom can only be an understanding of life; there is no metaphysical or transcendental dimension, no Being, but only life as Becoming. Hence the pursuit of wisdom is almost the same as the pursuit of life. The difference, not explained here or even indicated by life herself, is the one between being immersed in life and observing or understanding it.

What about Nietzsche's own revolutionary enterprise, or Zarathustra's prophetic mission? It is the unification of wisdom and life, the attempt to produce a "lived wisdom," or to transform life by wisdom. In traditional terms, it is the unification of theory and practice, but for the philosopher only, not for the many. The limitation of the enterprise, and Zarathustra's regular failure, is prefigured by the lack of identity between life and wisdom. This difference is granted by life, who then asks Zarathustra to speak of his wisdom. In so doing, however, she opens her eyes, which were presumably closed during the actual conversation. This also indicates the difference between life and wisdom. And when life opens her eyes, it is not to see the truth but to reveal the unfathomable. Zarathustra is unable to speak, but sinks into the unfathomable eyes of life. The song ends; the dance concludes, and the girls depart.

Zarathustra now grows sad and chilled. He is enveloped by the unknown and asks himself a series of short questions about life. Is he still alive? Why? For what? And so on. In other words, he poses the typical questions of the lover of wisdom. "Is it not foolishness to continue living?" "Ah my friends, it is the evening that asks through me. Forgive me my sadness" (141). Zarathustra asks forgiveness for the coming of evening. Sadness begins with evening, and as evening deepens into night, sadness deepens into loneliness (in the night song, no friends are present). Joy is associated with dawn. But the day is always followed by evening and night, and these turn once more into day. Life at each day is an emblem of the eternal return. Wisdom concerning life thus also detaches us from her by depriving her of permanence or individual significance. From this standpoint, life is perpetual dying; life is a tomb. And that is the next song, in which Nietzsche tells us how the hopes of his youth for a higher culture were destroyed by his enemy friends, the most prominent of whom was of course Wagner.

One can summarize the teaching of this song as follows: The unfathomableness of life turns certain wild individuals toward the revolutionary or emancipatory effort to create a world of order and value. But the very wildness of revolution conflicts with the intended order and value. The net result of the attempt to overcome the split between theory and practice in the act of world creation is the reinstitution of the split between theory and practice. There is no genuinely philosophical overcoming of the loneliness of wild wisdom.

"The Tomb Song" (Section 11)

The themes of the preceding song are transposed into a lament for Zarathustra's youth: "There is the isle of tombs, the quiet one, there are also the tombs of my youth. I want to take there an evergreen crown of life. Resolving thus in my heart, I traveled across the sea" (142). I take the isle of tombs to be one of the blessed isles which, as we saw previously, are populated with ghosts. Zarathustra wishes to bring these ghosts of his youth back to life. The ghosts are those of the songbirds of his youth, the visions and wonders that were his playmates, murdered by his enemies (143).

The song is perhaps best understood as Nietzsche's own lament for the old dreams of a comprehensive aesthetic, personified by Wagner, a "gay wisdom" (*fröhliche Weisheit*) that was transformed into putrid boils by the sight of a ghastly owl, which we may identify as the Owl of Minerva (144). "And when I did what was hardest for me and celebrated the triumph of my overcomings, then you made those who loved me scream that I was causing them the greatest pain." And again: "And once I wanted to dance as I had never yet danced. I wanted to dance away beyond every heaven. Then you persuaded my dearest singer. And he struck up a horrible dull tune. Ah, it hurt my ears like a gloomy horn!"

This seems to me to correspond reasonably well with Nietzsche's break with Wagner, once allowance is made for the hyperbolic language. But the general point holds good for all of Nietzsche's initial efforts to establish collaborative friendships, with the exception of his relations with Peter Gast. On the whole, Nietzsche was doomed to continual disappointment and loneliness, as we have already had occasion to observe. Zarathustra insists that his will cannot be overcome or restrained in the tomb; he utters the mysterious words that he is invulnerable "only in my heel" (145) as clarification of the previous assertion that his will walks on his feet.

Zarathustra is the inverse of Achilles, who is of course vulnerable only in the heel. One has to take a risk in commenting upon passages like this; I suspect that Nietzsche is distinguishing his own philosophical heroism from that of the tragic hero of the poets. Zarathustra, alias Nietzsche, is closer to Odysseus, the paradigm for the philosopher, who can walk among the dead and survive the experience. The last couplet is of importance as a preparation for the later episode of the night watchman: "Yea, thou art for me still the demolisher of all tombs. Hail to thee, my will! And only where there are tombs are there resurrections."

The three songs thus traverse the distinction between life and wisdom and the intimate tie between life and art. The resurrection of the will to which Zarathustra refers is no doubt intended to presage a radical revision of Wagnerian *Gesamtkunst* in the creation of the world of the Odyssean superman. The link between the will and wisdom will be deepened and discursively articulated as we shift from song to speech.

"On Self-Overcoming" (Section 12)

Zarathustra begins with a regular theme of Nietzsche's thought: The philosophers speak of the love of truth, but in fact they are marked by a will to truth, a will to make all things thinkable. Zarathustra calls this the will to power (146). He passes directly and without justification from thinkability to good and evil. In other words, he recognizes no split between theory and practico-production in the history of philosophy. Being is an evaluation, not an essence or a formal structure. Since this is so, the will is its own greatest enemy; each evaluation will be overthrown in its turn by the next evaluation. The boat carrying the values on the river of Becoming is hardly more substantial than the river itself.

Zarathustra is addressing the creators of previous evaluations. He will explain his sense of good and evil by saying something about life and the manner of all living things (147). This explanation consists in three points. But let us note first that Zarathustra learned the nature of life by observing the look in life's eyes as reflected in a hundredfold mirror; life is silent as this look is caught in the mirror. I believe this means that Zarathustra has learned nothing from the philosophical speeches uttered by the spokesmen for life. At the same time Zarathustra does not say that he looked at actions directly, like a natural scientist or even an observer of human behavior. He looks at a reflection or image of the look in the eyes of life; in other words, like Socrates in the *Phaedo,* he does not look directly at the sun, or at beings, but neither does he look into *logoi,* as does Socrates.

What do we see when we look into someone's eyes? This depends upon whether that look is itself a mask. But I think the contrast to which Zarathustra is pointing here is between external and therefore accommodated manifestations of speech and deed on the one hand, and the inner, unmediated expression of the spirit on the other. The mirror plays two roles. First, it protects us from the intensity of the direct gaze, which, like the view of the Medusa, can kill us. Second, we can see around corners and behind our backs with mirrors, that is, see without being seen, and so see what occurs without the obstruction of artifices designed to mislead us.

Now to the three points. First: "Every living thing is obedient." Since Nietzsche regularly identifies life with the will to power, obedience must be compatible with the expression of this will. In other words, the will to power contains an inner limitation, or a structure of command and obedience. It is not simply an undisciplined and chaotic outpouring of force. Chaos is at the heart of all things, but domination requires organization and rank-ordering.

Thus the second point: "He who cannot obey himself will be commanded." I have now explained this. The expression of will to power contains an inner structure of commanding and obeying. The third point: Commanding is harder than obeying, because the commander is responsible for, carries the burden of, the obedient. This is almost self-explanatory, but I can add a word of clarification. The commander is not simply responsible for the welfare of those who obey him. More fundamentally, he is responsible for the rank-ordering or particular structure that transforms his expression of force into a "political" entity. And as we have already seen, the task of enforcing such a structure leads to its inner deformation: The commander does not rule absolutely; he must accommodate the regime, or rank-ordering, to those who obey. So the commander is threatened with destruction by the act of commanding itself. "It must become judge and avenger, and sacrifice [or "victim"] to its own law." Again this is the message of the section on the pale criminal.

Zarathustra then spells out the central thesis that life is will to power, or self-overcoming. This is familiar ground, and I note only the repetition of the important connection between creation and destruction: In order to create new values, we must annihilate old ones; but the whole process of life is one of the overcoming or annihilating of *our* values as well. Creation is possible only because of the prevasiveness of the transitory (149).

"On the Exalted" (Section 13)

Zarathustra criticizes the "penitent of the spirit" who has not learned "laughter and beauty" (151). He refers obliquely to the Christian covered with ugly truths, torn garments, and many thorns but "not a single rose." Such a person is distorted by tension arising from a self-conscious and hence repressive relation to his own sublimity. He is a creature of shadow, namely, the shadow of his own immobility. Action must be spontaneous; Zarathustra's meaning is conveyed by a striking image: The exalted one must forget his exaltation, jump over his own shadow, and become a roaring white bull with the eye of an angel.

In other words, he must become part beast and part daimon and thereby cease to be human.[5] And this requires not simply the expression of will to power but a transformation of the merely human will: "He must also forget his hero will; he must be for me uplifted and not merely exalted: – the ether itself must lift him up, the will-less one" (151). Differently stated, the expression of the will to power is not intentional; the attempt to act in a sublime manner leads only to rejection of the world, with a consequent diminution of the power to act. But the willed or conscious attempt to be a white bull leads only to bestiality.

"But the *beautiful* is the most difficult of all things precisely for the hero. The beautiful is unachievable for all violent wills" (152). The will must be released, not by an act of tension but by relaxed muscles. And very important: "When power becomes gracious and descends into the visible, I call such descent beauty." This section supplies a necessary corrective to the rhetoric of violence that is so often associated by Nietzsche with the doctrine of the will to power. It also reminds us that human beings cannot be transformed into "superheroes" by conscious indoctrination. The "secret" of the soul is that only when the hero has abandoned her does she approach him in a dream. And he is then no longer the hero but the superhero.

"On the Land of *Bildung*" (Section 14)

Bildung should not be translated by the single term "education." It contains the notion of formation as well as of construction. A *gebildeter Mensch* is beautiful and cultivated, not simply well trained or learned. The "educated" man of Nietzsche's own time is "Buntgesprenkeltes," a motley of colors or paints, in other words, a resident of the city of the Motley Cow and thus one who has accumulated the colors of the past or concealed his own identity with historical knowledge (153).

Zarathustra addresses these paint-bespattered persons as follows: "Truly, you could hardly wear a better mask, you contemporaries, than that of your own face. Who could recognize you!" This is another version of the mask of enlightenment. As Nietzsche argued in the essay on the "use and abuse of history," knowledge of all ages and an appreciation of all points of view makes one incapable of taking seriously one's own time; it renders impossible the creation of a vital civilization. The creation of form is replaced by the deformation of erudition. *Bildung* thus becomes a pejorative term. This is connected to the separation between genuine, or spontaneous, and intentional, or self-conscious, sublimity discussed in the preceding section.

"You are sterile; therefore you lack belief. But he who was compelled to create had also always his truth from dreams and his guiding star – and believed in belief! You are half-opened doors, within which gravediggers wait. And that is your actuality: 'The value of everything is that it dies'" (*zu Grunde geht*), sinks back into the grave (154). This is Zarathustra's criticism of historicism; knowledge embodied in perspectivism is destructive but correct: Truth is dangerous for life; art is worth more than the truth for life. Those who learn and are persuaded by the doctrine of perspectivism will then be immobilized or become effectively like the *Gebildete* of the city of the Motley Cow. It is only those who emerge from the rubble of the Motley Cow, and so whose faces are free of paint but, more fundamentally, who lack the distortion and paralysis of historical *Bildung*, who will be able to create.

This same problem must obviously face Zarathustra as well. "Nowhere did I find a home; I have no place in any city and am a departure at all gates . . . So I love only the *land of my children*, the undiscovered, in the farthest sea: For it I set my sails in constant search" (*in suchen und suchen*: 155). The prophet cannot enter the promised land because he too is a *Gebildeter,* or a resident of the Motley Cow. He knows too much to create; he can only destroy on behalf of a promise or dream of future creation.

"On the Poets" (Section 17)

The sections (12–16) following the three songs are devoted to criticism of the traditional European conception of philosophical formation: a will-less sublimity; *Bildung,* or a well-rounded formation that frees one from loyalty to any one set of values; a Platonist surrender to pure perception that is detached from life; and scholarship. Nietzsche denounces the academic ideal of what the Germans call *Heiterkeit,* literally, serenity, but used to characterize a kind of lofty distance in which arrogance is masked by the pose of indifference to the human, all too human.

The pivotal accusation occurs in "Of Unspotted Knowledge" (wittily translated by Kaufmann as "Of Immaculate Perception"), in which Zarathustra interprets what is today (or rather what was the day before yesterday) called "phenomenology" as a lecherous perversion (156). I take this accusation as an ironic reference to the Platonic doctrine of Eros, according to which the philosopher transcends the love of beautiful bodies in a vision of beauty itself, or, more generally, of pure Platonic Ideas. I will not analyze these sections in detail, since they repeat previously studied themes. I note only the closing assertion from "Of the Learned": "For men are *not* equal; thus speaks justice" (162).

"On the Poets" requires a closer look, since Nietzsche is often mistaken as an aesthete or philosopher of art, in particular by those who fail to notice that his praise of art as superior to truth refers to its political or existential function. This is an extremely important section. The disciple asks Zarathustra why he once said that the poets lie too much. The reply makes two points. First: "I am not one of those of whom one may ask for their why" (163). This assertion tells us something of the poetic nature as contrasted with the discursive philosopher. In reading Nietzsche, one has to know when to ask "Why?" and when this is inappropriate. Second: " 'But what did Zarathustra once say to you? That the poets lie too much? – but Zarathustra is also a poet. Do you believe now that he is here speaking the truth? Why do you believe that?' The disciple replied: 'I believe in Zarathustra.' But Zarathustra shook his head and smiled."

The general meaning of this section is as follows. Nietzsche is a poet rather than an academic philosopher, but this must be understood to characterize his spirit, or perceptual style, on the one hand and his rhetorical skills on the other. Thanks to his intuitive understanding, it is not only unnecessary for him to engage in discursive argumentation, but also the effort to do so would be vulgar and painful. Furthermore, the discursive argumentation favored by professors of philosophy is worthless as a tool of political revolution; for this purpose, prophetic poetry is required. And prophets, as poets, are liars.

The following pejorative description of poets is given from the standpoint of the genuine philosopher; as usual, Nietzsche combines extreme frankness with ironic evasion. The poets must lie because they are bad learners and know too little. This angers the disciple, but he remains silent. Zarathustra is also silent for a time and then speaks of his weariness with the poets on account of their superficiality and lack of cleanliness. In other words, they are too immersed in life, and especially in Eros, as Zarathustra makes clear with references to their interest in girls. Even though the poets have invented the gods, they cannot themselves rise to the divine level.

Zarathustra introduces this criticism of the poets with one of his famous lines: "I am from today and before . . . but there is something within me that is from tomorrow and the day after tomorrow and someday" (165). Zarathustra is both resident and product of the civilization he has come to destroy, but his vision is of the future, and the time has not yet arrived for his teaching to be efficacious.

He then hints that the poets will evolve into a higher type; the last line of the speech reads: "I saw penitents of the spirit arriving; they grew out of the poets" (166). The poets must lose, in addition to superficiality and uncleanness, their vanity and desire for an audience. They must rise to the level of the divine creator of the world, and for the sake of creation, not for applause. So Nietzsche does not here nor does he elsewhere advocate a simple return to the earth or immersion in "blood knowledge." Zarathustra wants a mixture of purity, dancing, creativity, and innocence: These provide the inner structure or form to the will to power.

In sum, Nietzsche, and through him Zarathustra, is and is not a poet. As one could explain this, the nature of the genuine philosopher is closer to that of the poet than to anyone else, but it is nevertheless more comprehensive and therefore different. The philosopher possesses the poet's perceptiveness and prophetic powers as well as his rhetorical skills, but he combines these gifts with a synoptic or Hyperborean vision of the human being. Without the poetic element, the ostensible philosopher deteriorates into the erotic pervert of detached perception and an accumulation of facts. Without the philosophical context, the poetic element deteriorates into the unmitigated loneliness of the songs of night and the tomb.

"On Great Events" (Section 18)

The scene is another island, not far from the blessed isles, that contains the entrance to hell. It is unclear how Zarathustra arrives at this island, and there is a suggestion of the supernatural. The crew of a ship at anchor see a man coming toward them through the air, saying, "It is time! It is the highest time!" They recognize the man as Zarathustra, whose disciples they are (167), and take him to be descending into hell. After five days, Zarathustra reappears and recounts to his disciples from the ship his conversation with the firehound. The firehound seems initially to stand for Satan, who is reduced to the status of the expectoration and upheaval devils of whom human beings ("not only old women") are afraid (168). Zarathustra has traveled across the sea to find out the truth about the firehound. So it cannot be learned on the blessed isles nor in the city of the Motley Cow.

Human beings "spit out" devils; these latter are the expression of something that chokes us or irritates our digestion. I take this in connection with the theme of *ressentiment.* The devil is a personification of that which is disgusting in us. But this is to say that the human race is disgusting; mankind is a disease of the earth, as is the firehound. The image of the firehound represents those fantasies of "great events" or institutions that preach revolution to the masses. Firehounds are sputum; they stir up the mud by preaching revolution and freedom (169). Weichelt is probably correct to refer to socialism in this context.[6] Why could this not be learned in the city? The island setting seems to be a symbolic way of focusing our attention on the actual nature of what is concealed by the frenzy of political mass movements.

Despite the reference to the church and the dramatic connection with hell, this section has its climax in a denunciation of the state. The church is a kind of state; in other words, religion is assimilated downward into politics, which is in turn a type of firehound or devil that arises from the expectoration of the masses. But now we learn that not all firehounds can be explained in this way. There is one who speaks truly out of the heart of the earth, and whose breath is gold and golden rain (170). This firehound is distinguished from the mud, ashes, intestinal disturbances, and so on, of the firehounds who are a disease of the earth's skin. He comes from the golden core of the earth, and therefore he cannot come from human beings, who are also creatures of the earth's skin.

I take this to mean that the heart of the earth is identical to the sun, from which Zarathustra draws his inspiration when he steps out of his mountaintop cave in the morning. Human existence is intermediate, a disease of the earth's skin, or surface, the boundary between heaven and hell. Heaven and hell are themselves products of the surface, or skin, of the earth, whereas the sun and the golden core of the earth are the natural force that both produces and dissolves this skin. The force is chaos, also known as will to power.

Zarathustra's disciples are scarcely listening to his account; they are eager to tell him about the members of the crew, their hunting for rabbits on the island, and the flying man they saw five days ago. In other words, they are absorbed in the external signs of the message, not in its content. Zarathustra alludes to the wanderer and his shadow, the title of another work by Nietzsche. The flying man was the shadow of the wanderer; in other words, not Zarathustra himself but the insubstantial understanding of his teaching. This scene may be compared with the passage in the Preface in which the townsfolk listen to the announcement of the superman and take it to refer to the rope-dancer.

"The Soothsayer" (Section 19)

I shall restrict myself to the essential points in this crucial passage; for an elaboration and supplementary detail, see the commentary in my book *The Limits of Analysis*.[7] Although Nietzsche is much given to the use of dashes, expostulations, and fragmentary sentences, this is the only section in *Zarathustra* that begins with a dash and an incomplete sentence. Three sections in Part Four (including the first) begin with dashes that suggest discontinuity with what precedes; each is followed by a complete sentence. In the present unique case, the abrupt beginning indicates that Zarathustra does not report the entire speech of the soothsayer. It also heightens the mood of mystery and fragmentation that pervades the entire episode.

Zarathustra hears a soothsayer who compares human life to existence in tombs. This is a generalization on the previous comparison by Zarathustra of his youth to a graveyard of tombs. He is himself affected by this message of the sadness and emptiness of life (as in the tomb song) and raises the question of how to save his light through the long twilight (172–73). His doctrine is not for the present but for the future. Yet how can it survive the present? How can it survive his disciples, who are creatures of the twilight (or in the metaphor of the previous section, of the earth's skin)?

Zarathustra fasts for three days and then falls into a deep sleep that lasts an unspecified time. In the preceding section there was a disappearance of five days. These intervals give weight to the sequel and also underline Zarathustra's separation from his disciples. They cannot accompany him on his visions but can only hear, and misunderstand, his subsequent accounts. When Zarathustra awakens and speaks to them, they hear his voice "as from far away" (173).

Zarathustra's dream is still a riddle to him; he asks his friends to help him decipher its meaning. The structure of the dream is an extension of the soothsayer's analogy between life and tomb existence. In the dream, Zarathustra had given up life and become a night watchman of graves in the lonely mountain citadel of death. This corresponds to the passage in the tomb song in which the dead hopes of Zarathustra's youth have broken out of their tombs and sit on top of them. One hears Nietzsche's own voice in this passage: It is his youth, dead in himself, that lives on in Zarathustra, who is the resurrection of Nietzsche's youth.

Now, however, Zarathustra himself dreams that he is a night watchman of the dead. "Life that had been overcome looked out at me from glass coffins" (173). Apparently Zarathustra's own youthful hopes have undergone the same fate as did Nietzsche's. He sits with loneliness and silence in the brightness of midnight: The entire passage is a powerful evocation of the sharp perception of isolation amidst the dusty rubble of the graveyard. There is no sense of time here; it is always midnight. This is an inversion of the moment of high noon in which Zarathustra discovers the gateway into the eternal return of the same. Here the bright midnight is the gateway into the eternal continuation of the same. In other words, becoming and life are replaced by death.

Zarathustra has rusty keys which he knows how to use to open the rustiest of gates: The reference is to the gate into the graveyard. The keys may be Zarathustra's teaching, which in the dream open the door to nihilism and despair as the consequences of the doctrine of eternal return. The dream exhibits Nietzsche's worst fears about the terrifying aspects of his "liberating" doctrine.

After a long interval, Zarathustra is awakened (so he sleeps within the dream) by three strokes of thunderlike noise and their echoes. He asks who is carrying his ashes to the mountain. We recall that Zarathustra himself lived on a mountain prior to his descent into the city of the Motley Cow. There he would converse with the sun. In the dream, the cave on the mountain is replaced by the graveyard and citadel of death. I believe that the black coffin contains Zarathustra's teaching, coming back up the mountain from the failure of his mission to mankind. In other words, Zarathustra the watchman of the dead is also brought face-to-face with the black coffin of his prophetic mission.

The coffin springs open and releases shrill noises and thousandfold laughter, as well as a thousand grimaces of children, angels, owls, fools, and butterflies as big as children. This is a satirical description of Zarathustra's own teaching: in brief, of the innocence of Becoming.

Zarathustra is terrified and cries in horror, the greatest cry of his life, which awakens him: the shock of recognition. But the recognition is unconscious, since Zarathustra purports not to understand his dream.

Zarathustra's most beloved disciple provides a positive interpretation: Zarathustra is the wind that tears open the gates of death, and he is also the black coffin full of "motley malice and the child's grimace of life" (175). The word "motley" indicates that, contrary to the disciple's positive interpretation, the doctrines of Zarathustra are accommodations to the city of the Motley Cow. But not for the disciple: He takes these doctrines to be the overcoming of death – namely, Zarathustra's enemies – by the laughter of children. Zarathustra's response to this interpretation is plain. He has been deeply disturbed by the dream and is initially distant from his disciples. When he looks at them at last, he fails to recognize them. And then he speaks reassuringly to them, but follows this with a long period of silence during which he regards the face of the disciple who gave the positive interpretation, "all the while shaking his head" (176).

"On Redemption" (Section 20)

Zarathustra crosses over a great bridge (presumably back on the blessed isles) and is approached by cripples and beggars. Their spokesman is a hunchback; he says that the people are beginning to believe in Zarathustra but that before they will do so entirely, the prophet must first persuade the cripples. The initial sense is obviously that of an allusion to Christianity. The crippled and blind may be Zarathustra's disciples; on the other hand, the crossing of the bridge may indicate that Zarathustra is passing over from his disciples proper to the people. But how could they live on the blessed isle? There is no explicit reference to the geographical location of this section. But it is quite important; there may be an incoherence here.

The hunchback says that Zarathustra must heal the blind and the lame (177). But Zarathustra declines to do so. In so declining, he cites the teaching of the people as his authority: To cure the crippled is to harm them rather than to help them; in returning to the normal condition, they also fall victim to despair at the sight of evil and immersion in vice. In other words, the people's version of Christianity attributes merit to the halt, the lame, and the blind, because Christianity is a doctrine of *ressentiment*. But why should Zarathustra accept this doctrine here? His willingness to learn from the people is clearly ironic.

He then explains his deeper meaning. All human beings are maimed, and some are marked by an absence of all attributes but one;

they are dominated by one characteristic which is represented here in physical terms. Zarathustra calls these "reversed cripples" (178). They may appear as great men or geniuses, but they are not whole human beings. The notion of totality or completeness is not rejected by Nietzsche despite his celebration of Becoming and creativity. There is a difference between excellence in one domain and total excellence. A healthy life is like a work of art: harmonious and complete. It must therefore be open to the wholeness of existence; this is the practical counterpart to the synoptic vision of the philosopher or Hyperborean. Zarathustra is preaching here to the people, not to the philosophers; to the many, not to the few. The deeper problem is how to unify synoptic vision and a harmonious historical existence in the life of the extraordinary individual. Otherwise put, it is how to avoid the false totality of conventional Western European *Bildung* with the comprehensive totality of the Hyperborean philosopher.

Zarathustra finds mankind in ruins, maimed by excessive specialization and division of labor, which has taken on an extreme form in late modernity. His own life among these fragments of humanity would be unbearable if he were not himself a prophet of the future. "A seer, a willer, a creator, a future himself and a bridge to the future – and ah! also at the same time a cripple on this bridge: Zarathustra is all this" (179). Here he expresses Nietzsche's acknowledgment of his own decadence; as a historical person, he too is crippled by his epoch. But as a seer, he conceives of the present moment as a bridge to future health. This is the highest example of how defects can be transformed into virtues by the proper context.

"And this is all my *Dichten und Trachten*": my poeticizing thinking, as I would translate this. Compare with this expression *die dichtende Vernunft* in *Twilight of the Idols*.[8] Zarathustra is the expression of Nietzsche's will to create a harmonious and complete "superhuman" animal out of the fragments of late-modern humanity. Zarathustra's poeticizing thinking makes the One by combining "what is fragment and riddle and cruel accident" (179). This is of course not the Eleatic One but the aforementioned wholeness or totality of existence.

"To redeem the past and to transform all 'it was' into a 'thus I willed it!' – this I should now call redemption!" Here Zarathustra refers to the doctrine of the eternal return, which he identifies not as a metaphysical or ontological doctrine but as an expression of *personal* redemption via an act of the will. Zarathustra's own salvation depends on his ability to transform the fragments of modern life into a vision of the future. But he must do so freely, not in a spirit of *ressentiment* or vengeance against the past, or else he will himself be crippled by this distorting emotion.

Why is this so? Why must Zarathustra affirm the past, and hence the present? Is it because Becoming cannot be judged by some standard outside itself, since there is no place outside Becoming? Then how explain the violent judgment leveled against modernity, the judgment of *Rangordnung*? Zarathustra and Nietzsche must condemn the actual course of European history without rejecting it as a manifestation of Becoming. Becoming is innocent in the sense that it produces this history to no purpose and for no end. But that does not alter our own existence or the terrible price we pay for this "innocence."

Nietzsche wants human beings to create spontaneously, as a manifestation of the will to power, or as an expression of the innocence of Becoming. This implies that creation is so to speak operationally distinct from destruction. The need to destroy and then to create is evident to the person of synoptic vision, who prepares a program of destruction in the name of future creativity. But the precise nature of the future creation can of course not be foreseen, since it would then no longer be spontaneous. Plans are made in the light of what one already knows; but this is a function of what has been, and is therefore tainted with the decadence of the past. When all is said and done, there is still a contradiction between the acceptance of the past and the condemnation of the present. These two parts of Nietzsche's program do not cohere. There is a contradiction between the innocence of Becoming and the eternal return of the same. Innocence is compatible with freedom or slavery; but the eternal return is synonymous with slavery, which Nietzsche conceals beneath the mask of *amor fati*.

To come back to the text, Zarathustra addresses the point I have just been examining. The will remains a prisoner until such time as it can free itself from the past. Even worse, this powerlessness makes the will an angry and malicious witness of the past (180). "The will cannot will backwards." But it attempts to do so, or to free itself from the prison of the past, and this in turn transforms the will into a fool. Even worse, it makes the will angry and vengeful; the will becomes an enemy of the past.

This is represented in the "spirit of revenge," or the desire for punishment. Zarathustra's exposition is not explicit here. Consider the modern scientific Enlightenment. This is a kind of condemnation of the past, but is it a frustrated anger that leads humanity to suffer, or is it an assertion of freedom and the pursuit of happiness? Zarathustra silently condemns the Enlightenment here as the spirit of vengeance that leads to the crippling or fragmenting of mankind. But this line of criticism suggests that mankind cannot free itself from nature or, in Nietzsche's terminology, from the past, from history, from what was. This shift, incidentally, is of considerable importance. For Nietzsche, it is not nature that is our master, but history. Strictly speaking, man has no nature, except in the sense of the will to power, or the expression of a rank-ordering based on power, health, and overcoming. The apparent inconsistency with which Nietzsche fluctuates between the affirmation and repudiation of nature is removed only when we understand the equivocal sense of the term in his writings. Nature is affirmed as will to power and repudiated as transhistorical *telos*. The two senses coincide in the figure of the eternal return, which elevates the contingent expression of power into the *telos* of the circularity of human time.

But whether we refer to nature or to history, Zarathustra's message is the same. Human happiness is rooted in free creation, or the unfettered expression of the will. But this is impossible. The attempt to achieve freedom leads to a spirit of revenge against the past (or the present), and this in turn leads us to "punish" the past in the only way that is available to us. We try to empty it of significance. As Zarathustra puts it, we say that everything passes away because it deserves to do so. Temporality is then identified as righteousness: *Gerechtigkeit* (180). Again compare Heidegger's interpretation of this term, which he bases on the late fragments of the *Nachlass*, while putting *Zarathustra* to one side as a *Vorhalle* into Nietzsche's major period. But the present passage in fact supports his interpretation better than the passages he cites. Righteousness is the *dikē* of Anaximander: namely, the removal of one thing in order to make a place for another.[9] But the point is that Zarathustra *rejects* this interpretation of *Gerechtigkeit* because it is also a punishing of the future. And this is a preaching of madness, as Zarathustra says.

There can be no redemption if there is eternal righteousness; this would be the condemnation of time altogether, of the eternal return, or the perpetual contingent expression of will to power. Or rather, to redeem an act would be to condemn it in the name of an atemporal eternity. We should rather consider that a deed is not annihilated by our attempt to punish it through condemnation. It could also be argued, even by those who reject an atemporal eternity, that existence is itself punishment; we must continuously punish what has happened by suppressing it in the emergence of the future; but what will happen must itself become what was and so exist, thanks to human power, and therefore be something to be punished (181).

Zarathustra now repudiates this entire line of reflection because it empties historical existence of all value. Otherwise put, in order for mankind to be able to create value, it must deny the guilt of the past and, by extension, of the present and the future. Time must be judged to be innocent. We must therefore accept the past, or say, "Thus I willed it!" This cannot be taken literally; it is a statement of our independence or indifference to the past, a rejection of the past as a hindrance to free action toward the future. In saying "Thus I willed it," the creative will says, "Thus shall I will it" (181).

Does this make any sense? How can we free ourselves from the past by willing it? Is freedom from the spirit of vengeance not compatible with a repudiation of the past? By willing the past, we also will the present and the future. This is to say that we will time or history (the eternal return). But this is to will fate, not to assert our freedom or to transform love of fate into creation. There is no reason for the future to be anything other than a potential past, or that from which a still more distant future must in turn liberate itself. As soon as we see this, we understand that our "creation" is just another historical episode, "a fragment, a riddle, a terrifying accident." Zarathustra anticipates a teaching of reconciliation with time (a willing of the past that is also a willing of the future) that is higher than any reconciliation. This is the willing of the will to power; but this in turn is neither willing nor condemning but simply an accumulation and discharge of points of force.

That Nietzsche understands the inadequacy of this teaching is now made quite clear. Zarathustra breaks off his speech in shock and then laughs; he acknowledges his garrulity. The hunchback had been covering his face while listening to Zarathustra's speech (compare Socrates' behavior in the *Phaedrus* as he delivers the defense of the nonlover), but he looks up in curiosity at Zarathustra when he hears him laugh. He asks why Zarathustra speaks differently to the cripples than he does to his disciples. The prophet replies that this is not surprising; "With hunchbacks, one may well speak in a hunchbacked way" (182). The hunchback says, "Good. One may chatter with students outside of school. But why does Zarathustra speak otherwise to his students – than to himself?" (182). No commentary is required.

"The Stillest Hour" (Section 22)

Zarathustra announces to his friends (the residents of the blessed isles) that he must leave them and return once more to solitude, like a bear to his cave (187). It is time for him to hibernate, to regain his strength for another season. In so doing, he is following the orders of the stillest hour, his most frightening mistress (commander, not lover). The stillest hour is the "gateway" back to solitude; it is an exit from history. The moment (*Augenblick*), as we shall see in Part Three, is the gateway into history.

Zarathustra recounts a dream in which he has a silent conversation with an unnamed interlocutor, presumably the stillest hour. The silent voice rebukes him for not yet being sufficiently humble. This is explained as follows. Zarathustra states that he has not yet moved mountains, by which he means that his words have not yet reached mankind. The voice replies: "This is most unpardonable in you: You have the power, and you do not will to rule" (189). The entire exchange indicates that Zarathustra has not yet been able, despite his immediately previous claims to prudence, to accommodate himself to the valleys and hollows, that is, to the lowness of mankind.

To this Zarathustra replies: "I lack the lion's voice for commanding everyone" (189). This corresponds to the previous remark by the stillest hour that a commander of great things is most needed "by all." Zarathustra cannot command "all," that is, the many. On this point, there is a certain resemblance to Socrates, who is the paradigm of the philosopher. But Nietzsche was more successful than Plato in devising a rhetoric for the many.

Zarathustra says: "I am ashamed." But this is not the same as to be humble. His shame prevents him from commanding, whereas humility would lead him to command for the sake of the many rather than for himself, that is, rather than to gratify his aesthetic sensibility. The stillest hour makes clear that Zarathustra's shame is another name for pride and is thus a mark of youth. Zarathustra must overcome his youth and so his pride in order to lead mankind. After some reflection, he replies: "Ich will nicht" ("I do not will it").

The stillest hour surrounds Zarathustra with lacerating laughter. It says that his fruit is ripe but that he himself is not. Compare with this the opening paragraphs of "On the Blessed Isles," which takes place when the fruit is ripe and falling from the trees. Zarathustra weeps aloud; note the difference between him and Socrates on this point. Zarathustra expresses passion through weeping and laughing. This goes with his purple rhetoric. That night he leaves his friends and returns to his cave.

I remind the reader that Part Two of *Zarathustra*, which we have now traversed, is said by Nietzsche to express the corporealizing of experience, or, as I have suggested, that it takes place at a lower level than Part One, a level at which death presents an insuperable obstacle to overcoming. The residents of the blessed isles are phantoms, impervious to revolutionary doctrine. This lack of response is the silent background to the turn from the city of the Motley Cow to the songs of night and their pervasive themes of solitude and failure. The same point is conveyed by the central concern in this part with the problem of vengeance and innocence. To exist is to take vengeance upon the future by converting it into the past through the aperture of the present; at the same time, the future is the symbol of innocence, spontaneity, and creation. There is a contradiction at the core of human life that we can also express as the dependence of recollection on forgetfulness. Without periodic infusions of the latter, the former is drained of vitality. And yet forgetfulness is the human mask of death.

ZARATHUSTRA'S SPEECHES: PART THREE

This will be the shortest part of my commentary. Part Three of *Zara-thustra* is the most intensely poetic, the part that gives the greatest support to those for whom the work is one of inspiration rather than discursive forethought. The reader will recall Nietzsche's previously cited assertion that this "is the most interior of all that I have thus far written; it hovers over the heavens: 'of the last happiness of the solitary.'" Since I am concerned with Nietzsche's thought rather than with his poetic diction, I shall provide an analysis of his metaphors only when this contributes to our grasp of the inner teaching. Despite this caveat, it is my intention to omit nothing that is essential for such a grasp. In particular, it should be noted that Nietzsche presents his fullest statement of the doctrine of the eternal return in Part Three. This doctrine may or may not express the last happiness of the solitary; its consequences for collective human existence are correspondingly equivocal. How we assess these consequences will be closely dependent upon our interpretation of Part Four.

"The Wanderer" (Section 1)

Zarathustra is leaving the blessed isles to return to his mountaintop cave. He has to cross a mountain in order to reach the harbor by morning. En route, he engages in a reflection about himself as wanderer and mountain-climber. This reflection takes place at night as he is climbing a mountain, and it turns into a speech delivered by the personified hour of his final and hardest task: Zarathustra is about to climb his final peak. This shows that Nietzsche thinks of Part Three as the culmination of the entire work; as has already been indicated, the status of Part Four is ambiguous. The nucleus of the work as originally conceived may thus be expressed as follows. Parts One through Three describe the failure of the revelation to the city-dwellers, the accommodation to this failure by recourse to solitary recuperation in various settings, and now the attempt to achieve an *Aufhebung* of the universal and the particular by a sea voyage that is to culminate once more in Zarathustra's mountain dwelling and that takes him to the city as well as to the peak of solitude, upon which he contemplates the gateway into the circle of the eternal return.

In the preface to the conversation with his culminating hour, Zarathustra makes the important point that "man erlebt endlich nur noch sich selber" (193). "One experiences finally only oneself." *Erlebt* does not mean simply "lives" or even "experiences," but "lives through" and hence "comes to see" or understand. The adventures of Zarathustra have all been interior; his conversations are all monologues. This is true not simply because Zarathustra is an invention of Nietzsche's imagination, but because within the drama, the external events of Zarathustra's life are not meaningful in themselves but must be regarded as stimuli for internal comprehension and growth. Zarathustra cannot, strictly speaking, learn from, or even converse with, others. Knowledge is personal; Zarathustra can understand the world only by understanding himself. "What *could* now still happen to me that was not already my own?"

Zarathustra gives a voice to the hour of his hardest and final task: self-overcoming. He is on his way to greatness; he has effaced the path behind him: There is no retreat. By the same token, no one can follow him. The path is erased by his steps, and over this disappearing path is written the word "impossibility" (194). Furthermore, Zarathustra lacks all ladders for the trip upward. He must climb on his own head and over his own heart: "Now must the gentlest in you become the hardest." This takes up the theme of the stillest hour in Part Two. Zarathustra has been too soft, too reluctant to command. He has not yet inured himself to the deformities of the human race, that is, not yet transcended them or overcome his repugnance for ugliness, hence also his pity and his shame.

The denunciation of ugliness, deformity, and evil is a form of bondage to it, masked as isolation. Genuine solitude is no longer prevented from commanding by aesthetic disgust. Hence the invocation to climb by his head, not by his heart. In slightly different terms, the hour says: Zarathustra has spared himself too much; this is the softness of the heart. He must learn to ignore himself: "To learn to look away from oneself is necessary in order to see much." This is the vision of the mountain-climber or the Hyperborean who is beyond good and evil. Zarathustra wishes to see the ground and beneath the ground of all things; he wishes to achieve the synoptic vision of the philosopher and must therefore see even himself from above.

Is this compatible with Zarathustra's initial remark that in the end he has experienced or understood only himself by living through or internalizing outward events? In one sense, no. And this is why Zarathustra is chastised by the hour of his final ascent. In another sense, yes. Zarathustra himself arrives at the hour by an internal meditation as he engages in a solitary climb up the mountain that separates him from the harbor and the journey away from the blessed isles.

"Thus spoke Zarathustra to himself as he climbed . . ." This makes the point just noted. Zarathustra is himself the hour of decision, as one could call the hour of the final and hardest ascent. The shift from the ascent of the heart to the ascent of the head cannot be made by the head; hence there is a dramatic personification of the need to decide. In other words, Zarathustra must persuade himself by his own rhetoric. It is his spiritedness (*thumos*) that initiates the shift.

At last Zarathustra stands on the mountaintop and looks out over "the other sea" (195). Why "other"? This is the sea between the blessed isles and the land of the Motley Cow, the forest, and the mountaintop of the Preface and Part One. I take this to mean that the island containing the entrance to hell lies on the other side of the blessed isles. In any event, there are two seas, corresponding to the two paths stretching away from the gateway of the moment, which we shall encounter shortly. Thus the blessed isles correspond symbolically to the gateway itself. But corresp ' dence is here polarity rather than identity; we can either remain on the blessed isles speaking to phantoms, or we can embrace the entrance into history. This latter alternative is what Heidegger calls *Entschlossenheit*.

It is of the highest importance for us to understand that philosophy and situated or resolved historical existence are irreconcilable. Nietzsche is very close to the Socratic association of philosophy and death, which is to say that his affirmation of life is a gesture of self-sacrifice. After a period of silence, Zarathustra states in sorrow that he understands his fate. "Well, I am ready. My last loneliness has just begun." This is another indication that Part Three is intended as the culmination of the work. It should contain the shift from the ascent of the heart to that of the head. Note that this ascent is preceded by a descent. The ascent of the heart has to be reconstituted, not simply repeated. In the affirmative dimension of Nietzsche's double rhetoric, he implies that the ascent of the heart and the head will be united in the appearance of the superman. If, however, this appearance is impossible, then Nietzsche's genuine teaching amounts to the classical Platonist juxtaposition of philosophy and politics, or in other words to the concealment of the noble lie beneath the mask of enlightenment.

The paragraph closes with an indication that Zarathustra has not yet overcome his faults. He tries to comfort the sea, and this is an expression of the heart, not the head. As soon as he recognizes this, he denounces himself and laughs at his excessive trust, his foolishness, and his modesty in love (196). Modest love must be replaced by the Eros of the head, to put the point in Platonic language. Zarathustra, of course, is not a Platonist *tout court:* He laughs and weeps.

"On the Vision and the Riddle" (Section 2)

This is the classic statement of the doctrine of the eternal return, the central theme of *Zarathustra* according to Nietzsche himself. My interpretation will consist of two parts, of which the first is a reconsideration of Section 20 in Part Two, "On Redemption." Nietzsche offers the teaching of the eternal return as a replacement for the Christian doctrine of redemption. Since Nietzsche regarded Christianity as Platonism for the masses, it will be necessary to say something about Plato as well as Christ; at the same time, there can be no doubt that Christ is the primary rival to Zarathustra. For our purposes I can unite the role of Plato and Christ in the background of *Zarathustra* as follows. The anti-Christian character of the book takes the form of an alternative doctrine for the masses, whereas the anti-Platonist doctrine is reserved for the connoisseur, or "the happy few." A genuinely Nietzschean hermeneutics requires the separation of these two dimensions. Whether the happy few are actually happy is another question.

In "On the Vision and the Riddle," Zarathustra is about to depart from the blessed isles on a sea voyage back to the city of the Motley Cow and from thence to his mountaintop cave. As he said in the immediately preceding section, "Well, I am ready. My last loneliness has just begun" (195). The vision of the eternal return is thus intended as a culmination to the work as originally conceived. The episodes in Part Three that follow this vision are intended to portray Zarathustra's behavior in response to the passive reception of the revelation by the crew of his ship. That Nietzsche soon came to regard this behavior as inadequate is shown by the composition of Part Four.

Once on board ship, Zarathustra is recognized by the crew. He is silent for two days and speaks on the third day, just as Christ rises on the third day. The revelation of the eternal return is in the first instance a substitute for the Christian gift of eternal life. The crew correspond in the first instance to the apostles, or immediate disciples, of Christ. Zarathustra says that he is their friend, as he is to all "who make far journeys and do not like to live without danger" (197). Unlike the Christian apostles, Zarathustra's friends seek a dangerous salvation rather than tranquillity in the bosom of the Lord. They are seekers who would rather guess than infer, friends rather than disciples, voyagers rather than residents of the city of the Motley Cow or the blessed isles, the main dramatic settings for Parts One and Two respectively.

The difference between the voyagers and the residents of the blessed isles corresponds to the difference between Nietzschean and Platonic Hyperboreanism. The Platonist regards the differing human perspectives from a standpoint outside time, as is represented by the Ideas or in the *Statesman* by the lookout point (*skopos*) from which the divine artificer regards the cosmos during its independent cycle. Nietzsche, on the other hand, is required to identify the viewpoint on the nature of time, and so the totality of Becoming, with Becoming itself. The grasp of time is itself temporal; hence the restless daring of the sea-voyagers.

Zarathustra and his friends are wanderers with no fixed abode or perspective. The price of continuous discovery is detachment from life; the sailors cannot be faithful to the earth, because they are immersed in the sea of Becoming. They do not wish even to remain forever on the blessed isles. Like the Platonic philosopher on his erotic ascent, they leave behind the cities of mankind; unlike him, they do not ascend to the Hyperuranian Ideas but continuously circle the globe. Both devote themselves to seeing the sights; but their relation to time is not the same. Finally, the islanders are detached from life, whereas the sailors continue to explore it.

The central image of time in Zarathustra's revelation is the gateway of the moment (*Augenblick*). It cannot, however, be true that we first enter into time by passing through the gateway. As we shall see, this passage represents, among other things, a choice, an act of the will. Accordingly, we must be able to consider the gateway from a standpoint outside it, and thus to deliberate on whether or not to enter. This standpoint cannot be that of eternity in the Platonic sense; Being is for Nietzsche Becoming. One can speak of eternity in Nietzsche's thought only in the sense that Becoming is intrinsically chaotic, and, strictly speaking, chaos is atemporal. The standpoint for considering the gateway must be a kind of immanent temporal transcendence. I shall refer to this transcendence as occurring in cosmological time, as contrasted with the historical time of passage through the gateway that is also an affirmation of life.

The sailors to whom Zarathustra recounts his image are wanderers like himself. They belong properly to no city and to no historical epoch, but as residents of cosmological time they are prepared to consider all interpretations of historical time, including that of the eternal return. What keeps them from sinking into the sea of chaos is their courage, the ship that keeps them afloat. They thus differ from those personages who are in transit from one historical perspective to another. Nietzsche often represents transitions of this sort by the image of a bridge or a tightrope. But these are rigid links, whereas the sea is fluid and carries the rigid ship from one point to another.

The bridge is the central figure in the previously mentioned section on redemption. Both Christ and Zarathustra offer to redeem us from our sins, but with differing results. If we accept the doctrine of the eternal return, we gain an eternal or perpetual temporality, whereas the consequence of the Christian redemption is a temporalized eternity. In the first case, we remain historical creatures who repeat forever their transient existence. In the second case, there is an eternal continuum of life everlasting. At first glance, Zarathustra's doctrine may seem more reasonable than the Christian version. The eternal return is connected, however loosely, to an argument supplied by modern physics: If time is endless and the quantity of matter is finite, then all possible combinations of matter, and with them all possible events, must recur endlessly.

Whatever may have been Nietzsche's reliance on this argument (presumably derived from Boscovitch), and regardless of its inner deficiencies,[1] there is a more serious difficulty in Zarathustra's doctrine of redemption. This can be shown by a brief reflection on the human implications of both doctrines. Zarathustra refuses to heal the cripples in order to win the belief of the people, as Christ did before him. If he were to do so, Zarathustra would repudiate the significance of the human history that has produced the lame and the halt as well as those whose spiritual distortions make them resemble a giant ear, mouth, eye, or some other organ. In order for this life to be the unique source of value, as it must if it is to avoid the danger of devaluation by contrast to transcendent sources, it must be affirmed in its totality. We cannot take vengeance against the past or submit to ressentiment against the fortunate few without transferring our allegiance to imaginary principalities.

On Nietzsche's interpretation, the Christian doctrine of redemption attributes value to suffering only through the mediation of faith in heaven. The sole value of this life is as a bridge to the next world. Christianity thus teaches both the worthlessness of historical existence – or the hope of escape to the next world – and submission to religious authorities in this world – or acceptance of one's low and crippled condition. We are urged simultaneously to become other and to remain the same as we are.

The parallel difficulty in Nietzsche's doctrine is of even greater magnitude. The Christian can reply to Nietzsche that his doctrine assigns each of the conflicting orders to a separate world. But Zarathustra is restricted to one world in which to reconcile the acceptance of what we are with the invocation to continuous self-overcoming. There are no miraculous cures in Zarathustra's vision of historical time. The crippled are not transformed into the healthy; everything is left as it is. Yet at the same time, and literally within the same time, by remaining – or, as Zarathustra expresses this, by becoming what we are – we are supposed to be transformed into creators of new values, and perhaps even into supermen.

Zarathustra states the true meaning of his own creation in grandiose language that muffles by its very extravagance. "I wander among men as among the fragments of the future; that future which I see. And this is all my creating and striving, that I create and draw together into One what is fragment and riddle and cruel chance." And again: "To redeem the past and to transform every 'it was' into a 'thus I willed it!' – this is what I first call redemption" (179). Redemption, in other words, is not the healing of cripples but their integration into a totality to be reiterated forever. If it is true that Christ takes vengeance against history, "against time and its 'it was' " (180), Zarathustra does not transform but simply affirms "it was" as "so shall it be."

With this statement of the problem, we can now return to the vision and the riddle as recounted on shipboard by Zarathustra. This vision is of the loneliest (197), namely, Zarathustra himself. In it, he is walking sadly at twilight on a stony and difficult path up the side of a mountain (198). His progress is impeded by the spirit of heaviness or gravity (*Schwere*) that sits on him and pulls him down. The spirit is half-dwarf, half-mole; in other words, a deformed creature of the earth. It is lame and makes others lame by dripping leaden thoughts via the ear into the brain. There is obviously a connection between the lame dwarf and the cripples who demand to be healed by Zarathustra; in plain words, human life demands Zarathustra's pity, with the ambiguous consequences that we have just noted.

The dwarf says that Zarathustra has thrown himself up high, like a philosopher's stone shot from a slingshot, and now, like everything that rises up, he must fall. Zarathustra has attempted to transform humanity into the superman, just as the philosopher's stone was used to transmute the elements; both enterprises are failures. But Zarathustra climbs on resolutely, sustained by what he calls *Mut,* courage or spiritedness. This is his equivalent of the Greek *thumos,* which, in Socrates' account of the soul, is regulated by the intellect. Zarathustra, on the contrary, gives precedence to *thumos.* Also unlike Socrates' philosopher-kings, he is, as we have had previous occasion to notice, much given to laughing and weeping.

Zarathustra's courage at last responds to his suffering from the weight of the dwarf by bringing him to a stop; again, it is his *Mut,* not his intellect, that confronts the dwarf (the *Geist* of gravity) with these words: "Dwarf! Thou! Or I!" (198).[2] The immediate sense of the image is as follows. Zarathustra can rise no higher until he overcomes the pity for humanity that still pulls him back to the earth below. But one emotion or spiritual determination can be counteracted only by another; discursive argumentation is useless here. At a somewhat deeper level, we are about to see the gateway of the moment, thanks to the intervention of courage, which connects Zarathustra to the sailors on shipboard to whom he is actually speaking. Zarathustra must go no higher, lest the gateway pass from his sight. In view of the terrifying nature of the doctrine of the eternal return, it takes courage for Zarathustra to remain where he is.

"Courage is the best *Todtschläger* – courage that attacks: For in every attack there is resounding play" (*klingendes Spiel:* 199). A *Todtschläger* is a weapon for beating someone to death, but there is also a pun here on the notion of striking down death through courage in the presence of the eternal return. At the same time, the assault on death is resounding play, which I take to refer to the illusion of rhetoric. The eternal return, as will emerge shortly, is itself an illusion, the most important instance of what Nietzsche means when he writes in *Twilight of the Idols* that "art is the greatest stimulus to life."[3]

That the attack on death is rhetorical rather than conceptual is indicated immediately. Courage strikes death dead with the assertion: "Was *that* life? Very well! Once again!" Courage rejuvenates by the rhetorical recollection and reaffirmation of life. This is a double repudiation of Platonism, in which the philosopher conquers death by the recollection of noetic vision, whereas in the myth told by the Eleatic Stranger in the *Statesman,* the human race, except for those who are carried away to the blessed isles, is rejuvenated by the forgetfulness induced by a divinely imposed reversal of cosmic motion, including the chronology of human existence. Zarathustra's courage neither recollects the Ideas nor forgets the pains and sorrows of quotidian existence.

Stated with perhaps excessive concision, life is transformed by courage into its own quasi-Platonic Idea by the conquest of pity. We are sustained in the present by our recollection of ourselves in the past, which is also an anticipation of our future existence. Courage by itself is of course insufficient; there is, as I have just indicated, a kind of Platonic Idea toward which it is directed and to which Zarathustra refers when he tells the dwarf, in the second half of his vision, that he is the stronger of the two: "Thou knowest not my abysmal thought; that thou couldst not bear!" (199).

The German word for "abysmal" is *abgründlich*. The abyss is groundless, but also the ground itself, namely, the thought of the eternal return. This is the groundless ground of Nietzsche's teaching. By this expression I do not mean to imply that Nietzsche is what we call today an antifoundationalist thinker. On the contrary, the abysmal thought is the foundation. But as a thought, it is also a manifestation of the will; I repeat that for Nietzsche, *nous* is an instrument of *thumos*. There is, however, a crucial qualification that must be made at this point. We have to distinguish between the act of the will by which Zarathustra poses the doctrine of the eternal return, as represented here by the gateway of the moment, and the act by which we pass through the gateway and into historical time as willed or interpreted by Zarathustra.

In one sense, of course, we are all continuously passing through the gateway, namely, if it is considered as an image of the structure of temporal flow. All those who, like Zarathustra and the ship's crew, sail the sea of Becoming in pursuit of danger and distant sights are also marked by that structure. But they have not necessarily accepted the doctrine of the circularity of time, or the eternal return. As will shortly become clear, this is a special interpretation of the gateway. Previously I referred to the two senses of time as cosmological and historical. In fact, however, there are three temporal modalities implicit in Zarathustra's adventures. There is a difference between considering alternative interpretations of human life and accepting the doctrine of the eternal return. But there is also a difference between accepting that doctrine and the affirmation of life in the form of what one believes to be a creation of new values but is actually the reiteration of a moment on the great wheel of time.

This accounts for the fundamental difficulty in Nietzsche's teaching. In cosmological time, we philosophize, as it were, or investigate the various interpretations of human time. Once we accept the abysmal thought of Zarathustra's will, we become who we are, or affirm our lives by remembering past and future. We assert in accord with the *Todtschläger* of Zarathustra's courage: "Was *that* life? Very well! Once again!" It follows that life is not creation but repetition. From a cosmological standpoint, life is valueless until we impose an interpretation on it. But the interpretation of the eternal return deprives our acts of generative value; overcoming is replaced by *amor fati.*

The function of the doctrine of the eternal return cannot be to enhance historical existence but rather to validate the repudiation of Platonism and Christianity. Life enhancement depends on our forgetting the doctrine of the eternal return by stepping through the gateway out of cosmological and into historical time, in which we create, as it seems to us, spontaneously, so that we rather than fate are the source of value. Love of fate is just a Spinozistic version of Platonism; it is a shift into cosmological time. And since this shift has been induced in us by Nietzsche, we are his disciples: followers of Zarathustra, not supermen. The promise of the superman was a *klingendes Spiel,* a resounding play, or, more bluntly, Nietzsche's version of the noble lie. The continuous invocations to create new values are nothing but rhetorical devices to conceal from us that we remain exactly who we are under the illusion that we have been transformed into something "beautiful and new," as Plato says in the *Second Letter* (314c1-4) of the Socrates of his dialogues.

We have, however, anticipated the flow of the story. After the celebration of courage, the dwarf jumps down from Zarathustra's shoulders and sits on a nearby stone, curious as to what will follow. We are at a crossroads in our understanding of the human situation. The forces of ascent and descent balance each other out for a moment. This is another level in the significance of the image of the gateway. The moment on the stony path is the moment of decision about the doctrine of the eternal return. The stony path is the horizon from within which we attempt to explain time. An enormous effort is required to take this path; we are hindered by the spirit of gravity, by pity, by time itself.

In particular, we are hindered by the prosaic common sense of the spirit of gravity that pulls us down from our lofty thoughts and mocks the extravagant rhetoric of Zarathustra. First let us summarize Zarathustra's exposition of the gateway. The gateway has two faces (*Gesichter*) – a word that brings out its peculiarly human significance. "Two ways come together here. No one has yet taken them to their end. This long road back continues for an eternity. And that long road outward – that is another eternity" (199). Zarathustra says that these roads, which come together at the gateway named "moment," contradict one another, an assertion which he then transforms into a question: "And who goes farther along one of them, ever farther and more distantly; dost thou believe, dwarf, that these ways forever contradict one another?" (200).

Let us note that in one sense Zarathustra and the dwarf have been moving along the road leading up to the gateway; in another, however, they are apart from and above the gateway as they pause on the stony mountain path. In the first sense, the two are governed by the same temporal structure that regulates all living beings. In the second sense, they are, as about to consider whether to pass through the gateway, separate from it, and so they stand still on the stony path of decision.

Zarathustra says nothing as yet about the circularity of time, that is, about the union of the roads at the far side of the moment. His initial description is of a temporal structure that applies to cosmological as well as to historical time. The structure is obscure, but there seems to be no contradiction here. We enter the gateway at the moment, which corresponds to the present. Having so entered, we must walk simultaneously forward into the future and backward into the past. And in so doing, we remain continuously within the gateway, or what is for us the present moment. At the moment of death, we can no longer walk forward but are as it were conveyed ever farther backward into the past.

The dwarf replies to Zarathustra's question in a contemptuous murmur: "Whatever is straight is a lie . . . All truth is crooked; time itself is a circle." His contempt is directed toward the prophet's portentous rhetoric and his failure to make explicit the crucial premise of his own revelation. Zarathustra is outraged; the dwarf has made truth too easy and has forgotten that he would not have reached this height without the prophet. Nietzsche indicates here the difference between discursive accounts that trivialize and the persuasiveness of inflated rhetoric.

Zarathustra continues with the exalted account. He notes first that "a long eternal road runs backward from the gateway of the moment." He then asks the following questions of the dwarf. Must not everything that moves have already traveled on this road? And if so, must not everything that can happen have occurred already, including the existence of the gateway before us? Finally, are not all things knotted together in such a way that this moment draws after it all future events? These rhetorical questions convey the crucial additions to the initial description of the gateway and the two roads. They thus constitute the particular interpretation of the structure of time as the eternal return.

The image of the gateway plays a dual role. As the structure of time, it applies to all human beings, including Zarathustra and the sailors. Zarathustra indicates this universal function of the image by asserting as obvious the existence of the gateway and the two eternal roads extending in opposite directions. He indicates the hypothetical status of the special interpretation of the gateway as the eternal return by shifting from assertion to rhetorical questions.

The events in what I have called cosmological time, including the entire account of Zarathustra's voyage away from the blessed isles and the vision he recounts to the ship's crew, constitute Nietzsche's alternative to Platonism. In this alternative, Nietzsche explains to us how he proposes to replace Christianity – Platonism for the masses – with a more salutary myth, or what one could call a nobler lie. In order for the nobler lie to take effect, the masses cannot remember the doctrine of the eternal return but must instead forget it. For them, passage through the gateway is an entrance into historical time in the sense of the affirmation of an illusion about creativity and the uniqueness of one's life.

The peculiar complexity and allusiveness of Nietzsche's rhetoric in *Zarathustra* arise from his attempt to convert Platonists and Christians in the same book. I myself believe that this was an error on Nietzsche's part, but it is an error to which he was led by Plato, who also conveys two teachings, one for the few and one for the many, in the same dialogue. This is in my opinion what Nietzsche was referring to when he wrote to his friend Overbeck, in a previously cited letter: "In reading Teichmüller I am ever more transfixed with amazement at how little I know Plato and *how much* Zarathustra *platonizei.*"[4]

Zarathustra's Platonism consists in his politico-prophetic intentions and his employment of a rhetoric of indirection, not in his understanding of time or (as Heidegger contends) Being. For Zarathustra or Nietzsche, both cosmological and historical time are intrinsically chaotic; both owe their respective order to the will of the human beings who inhabit them. Nietzsche thus anticipates the Heidegger of *Being and Time* in his interpretation of human being as the aperture through which time is secreted. Apart from human intentional activity, there is no time. The quality of time depends, however, on the degree of lucidity with which it is secreted.

Whereas previously the dwarf responded to Zarathustra with contempt, he is silenced by the announcement of the eternal return, and in particular by Zarathustra's contention that the order of return is always the same, down to the last detail, such as that of a spider crawling in the moonlight (201). The knot of necessity deprives life of significance. And Zarathustra himself speaks ever more softly as he continues with his explanation. He is himself afraid of his thoughts and of his *Hintergedanken,* the thoughts concealed by his thoughts.

The doctrine of the creation of new values is an illusion, because the openness of the future, on which it depends, would be a source of vengeance against the past. The future is therefore closed, or made identical with the past, by Zarathustra's doctrine of the eternal return. Let us not fail to note that this applies to historical but not to cosmological time. The eternal return is only one possibility within cosmological time; we are as free to reject Zarathustra's vision as he is to assert it. I suspect that this is the thought behind Zarathustra's thought. Frightening as the eternal return may be, equally frightening is the prospect of its rejection. The acceptance of the doctrine leads to the temporalization of eternity, which is a necessary condition for the attribution of all value to historical existence. Unfortunately, it is not a sufficient condition; in fact, it may itself lead to the same nihilism it is intended to combat.

Life responds at first with contempt and then with silence to the vision of the circularity of time. At this point the dwarf disappears, and life is now represented by a howling dog that frightens Zarathustra and reminds him of a similar occurrence in his youth. In an earlier image, Nietzsche represents his doctrine as an eagle flying through the heavens with a serpent coiled around its neck; wisdom, in other words, is sustained by pride and courage: by *Mut*. In the present passage, there is no eagle; Zarathustra's spiritedness, like life, has been terrified by the abysmal thought.

A young shepherd now comes into view, writhing in fear on the ground, with a heavy black serpent fixed in his throat, choking him to death. Zarathustra tries in vain to pull the serpent out of the shepherd's throat, into which it must have crawled while the youth was sleeping. The prophet cries out to the shepherd to bite off the head of the serpent. He says nothing about the transition from one image to the next, but the general meaning is clear.

The serpent represents Zarathustra's teaching of the eternal return. This teaching must be insinuated into the spirit of mankind by an indirect rhetoric. Once so insinuated, it will destroy its unwilling host unless it is overcome by an act of the will, which must in turn be evoked by Nietzsche's exalted rhetoric. Zarathustra is the instrument of persuasion, but only the shepherd can save himself by direct action. He bites off the serpent's head in response to Zarathustra's instruction. And Zarathustra can himself utter the persuasive command only if he conquers the terror and nausea induced in him by the abysmal thought. By destroying and expelling the serpent, the shepherd passes through the gateway of the moment, or forgets the doctrine of the eternal return. The shift from shepherd to superman, however, expresses Zarathustra's vision of what he represents in a much earlier section as the transformation of the lion into a child. This shift neither is guaranteed by the doctrine of the eternal return, nor could it be implemented through its recollection. It is Zarathustra's (or Nietzsche's) substitute for Christian prayer: "Thus shall it be!"

A moment before the shift to the shepherd, the howling of his dog moved Zarathustra to ask: "Where now was the dwarf? And the gateway? And the spider? And all whispering? Did I dream it? Have I awakened?" The whispering in question is the conversation between Zarathustra and the dwarf as they stand in the gateway, through which they have not yet passed. Nor is the image of the gateway sufficient to persuade the dwarf, who must be replaced by a dream possessing greater rhetorical power. Zarathustra urges the sailors to guess the identity of the loneliest: "What did I see in the image? And *who* is it who must still come one day?" (202).

I regard it as crucial to our understanding of Nietzsche's intentions that Zarathustra does not persuade the dwarf to pass through the gateway. The dwarf must be replaced by a shepherd into whose throat the doctrine of the eternal return crawls while he is asleep. The circle of time is replaced by a murderous serpent; the doctrine of the eternal return is now revealed as destructive rather than creative. "Change of values – that is a change of creators. Whoever must be a creator always annihilates."[5] We can apply these words in the present context; the interpretation that frees us from Platonism must now be destroyed in order to make way for the interpretation that replaces Christianity: The coming of the superman replaces the coming of the Messiah.

Zarathustra, the teller of the vision, is the loneliest of all because he can neither cross through the gateway nor be reborn as the superman. The prophet is always excluded from the promised land. The transformation of the shepherd is a vision of the superman: "No more shepherd, no more human, one who is transformed, illuminated, who laughs. Never before on earth did a man laugh as he laughed!" In a later section, Zarathustra will identify himself as the shepherd; the loneliness of the terrified thinker of the abysmal thought is replaced in the vision of the future by the uniqueness of the new species. But as witness to the vision, Zarathustra is consumed by a thirst for the laughter of the superman, a thirst that eats at his throat as the serpent gnaws at the throat of the shepherd.

Let us distinguish three stages in the career of Zarathustra. In the first and present stage, Zarathustra is recounting his vision to the sailors on board the ship that takes him away from the blessed isles. In the second and past stage, he experienced the vision. In the third and future stage, he will be transformed from the spirit of courage into the spirit of the superman. These stages correspond to the gateway and the two roads that stretch out from either face. As we read *Zarathustra,* we are ourselves in the position of the dwarf who whispers with Zarathustra in the gateway. The conversation is intended to free us from Platonism by means of the vision of time that appropriates the sense of the past. But the hardest step of all is to enter into the future, not simply by going forward, but by retracing the history of Western Europe with steps that erase its original trajectory by raising it to a higher level. This move into the future by way of the past is what Heidegger and Derrida refer to as deconstructive reappropriation.

At each stage of Zarathustra's career, Nietzsche employs a slightly different rhetoric that is intended to seduce us to his will. The doctrine of the superman is as much an interpretation or act of the will as is the doctrine of the eternal return. Nietzsche is at his most discursive with respect to the past, namely, in his criticism of previous philosophers and his analyses of works of art and pivotal historical events. To say this in another way, Nietzsche's critique of modern European culture and politics is original only in the sharpness of his perceptions and the power of his language.

When Nietzsche turns to the present stage of decadence and the future destiny of nihilism, his prose sharpens, and the level of rhetorical exaggeration heightens. The peak of Nietzsche's rhetoric of extravagance is reached in *Zarathustra,* which contains his proposed remedies for Platonism and Christianity. That this is not simply a mark of Nietzsche's intoxicated inspiration should be evident from the previously mentioned fact that the name Dionysus never appears in the book. Nietzsche's Bacchic frenzy, or the rhetoric he employs in order to whip his readers into a stage of Bacchic frenzy, is Apollonian at the core.

I must, however, qualify this judgment in one important respect. The pathos of Nietzsche's personal loneliness and the fervor of his longing for a future epoch in which the laughter of the Homeric gods will be transferred to the cities of mankind is certainly genuine. At the end of the account of the vision to the sailors, Zarathustra says with unforgettable intensity: "Oh how do I bear to go on living? And how could I bear to die now?" With respect to the internal economy of the book, these words show us that Zarathustra has not yet freed himself from pity for humanity and, most important, for himself. But the words also apply to the author of *Zarathustra.*

Whereas Christ dies once for the sins of humanity and thereby opens for us the bridge to redemption, there is no conclusion of earthly or historical time for Zarathustra. His work is never done, because, as he claims, time recurs eternally. His life is perpetual death, and his death is perpetual life. The puzzle for the reader of Nietzsche's work is how one can both recollect and forget the doctrine of the eternal return. One could of course deny that forgetting is at issue here and insist that the question is one of recollection or acceptance only. In this case, the serpent is not the doctrine, but only the fear that it engenders. As such, it is false wisdom, just like the serpent in the Bible.

But this interpretation is unacceptable. The serpent is the condition of our historical existence, which is grounded in disobedience to God. As such, it is both courage and terror. Zarathustra invokes us to conquer our terror with courage; in so doing, the great opponent of utopian transcendence invites us to commit an ungrounded act of utopian transcendence – ungrounded, that is, in anything but the will. The solution implied by Nietzsche to the riddle of Zarathustra's vision is to accept the eternal return as the ground of perpetual laughter, even while forgetting its terrifying consequences. Can one will not to be terrified by the truth that truth is an illusion? And if it is an illusion, what are we to understand by *amor fati*?

On my reading of this text, the one who wills or remembers is distinct from the one who, having forgotten, creates. In other words, Nietzsche's version of or replacement for Platonism is addressed to those who are able to enact his philosophical revolution. If there is any version of salvation for persons of this type, it is identical with that offered by Plato to his philosophical readers, the aforementioned "happy few." To these few, Nietzsche, through the rhetoric of Zarathustra, holds out the hope of rejuvenation, not in their own persons but in the creative acts of the future for which a space is opened by the acceleration of nihilism and the destruction of the current epoch of historical time. Salvation for these "supermen" depends upon their ignorance of the truth about cosmological time, namely, that it is an eternal recurrence in the sense of a continuous contraction and expansion of the lines of chaotic force.

Some have seen here an anticipation of what is today called the pulsation theory of the expansion and contraction of the universe. But this does nothing to make more palatable the final truth of Nietzsche's teaching: To say that art is worth more than the truth for life is to say that life is an illusion. Creation, as understood by Nietzsche, although not by the creator, is enthusiastic lying. On this point, Nietzsche's doctrine is in full accord with the modern science of the European Enlightenment.

"Before Sunrise" (Section 4)

The two sections following the revelation of the eternal return, 3 and 4, emphasize Zarathustra's loneliness in the afternoon of his life that is at the same time mysteriously also "this morning light of my highest hope" (203). "Of Involuntary Bliss," Section 3, is an inconclusive mélange of imagery from previous episodes; perhaps the most striking assertion in this section is Zarathustra's statement that "at bottom (*von Grund aus*) one loves only one's child and work" (204). These are for Zarathustra one and the same.

In Section 4, the beginning of the sun's declension, which one may associate with the onset of decadence, contains within itself an anticipation of the visibility of the heavens prior to sunrise. Zarathustra calls this a time of "happiness against one's will," because it pursues him even while he awaits his unhappiness (206). One can no more capture happiness by intentional activity than one can deliberately become a genuine prophet or creator. What Nietzsche referred to in his letter to Köselitz as the extreme sadness of Part Three must also be understood as the earliest light of the not yet visible sun. This boundary between night and day, during which no "gods," or solar bodies, are visible, represents the isolation in which the thinker as yet lacks the courage to summon "the abysmal thought that is *my thought*" (205).

This statement (from Section 3) is puzzling, coming as it does after the vision and the riddle of the eternal return. Zarathustra offers an explanation in Section 4. In the first part of his explanation, he repeats the doctrine of affirmation: "I have arrived at blessing and yea-saying" (209), or in other words *amor fati*. To this he adds the important statement of what I have been calling the Hyperborean nature of the philosopher: "This, however, is my blessing, to stand over each thing as its own heaven, its round roof, its azure bell and eternal security; and blessed is he who thus blesses. For all things are baptized in the well of eternity and beyond good and evil" (209). These words refer not only to the doctrine of eternal return, and the attendant affirmation of each temporal occurrence, but also to the exalted position of him who "blesses" each occurrence, that is, who understands the totality of temporal existence and thereby repudiates all longing for some other destiny.

In the very next breath, however, Zarathustra identifies the eternal return with the rule of chance. "Truly it is a blessing and no blasphemy when I teach: 'Over all things stands the heaven chance (*Zufall*), the heaven innocence, the heaven accident, the heaven wantonness.' 'By chance' (*von Ohngefähr*) – that is the oldest nobility in the world, that I returned to all things; I freed them from the slavery of purposes." Necessity and chance are one and the same. The empty light of heaven just before sunrise represents the openness of time; events "*dance* on the feet of chance . . . there is no eternal spider of reason, or spider web." And what of the spider that spins its web in the revelation of the eternal return? Its perpetual occurrence is without purpose: a chance event in the sense that no god has intended or foreordained it. Nothing but the random play of chaos has produced the spider, but, once produced, the spider is a necessary and purposeless event.

Chance does not convey the sense of freedom, of an open space for unpredictable alternatives. It designates instead the chaotic origins of necessity. The invocation to create is accordingly a noble lie, as empty of inner weight as is the heaven of gods before sunrise.

"On Passing By" (Section 7)

In Section 6 ("On the Mount of Olives"), Zarathustra explains his loneliness as imposed by the distance between himself and human beings; he is forced to conceal himself in order to avoid the crucifixion that befell Christ. The entire description of his isolation and conceal-ment is expressed in a long metaphor of winter and ice: an echo of the Hyperboreans (218–21).

After visiting various peoples (*Volk*) and towns, Zarathustra sets out for his mountaintop cave. He is taking detours rather than the main road, and so arrives unexpectedly at the gate to "the *great city*" (itali-cized in the original). It is never identified further; that it is not the city of the Motley Cow is clear from the next section. In front of the gate, "a foaming fool with outstretched hands leaped out before him and stood in his way. This was the same fool whom the people called 'Zarathustra's ape' " (222). The fool is a caricature of Zarathustra, a false prophet. He is a more violent version of the old holy man whom Zarathustra encountered in the woods on his way down to the city in the Preface.

The fool warns Zarathustra against entering the city, and employs vulgarized versions of the prophet's rhetoric in so doing. In particular, we note that he denounces the virtue of servitude (223). The entire speech is like a cascade of Zarathustran themes taken out of their context and expressed without order in a series of adjectives and metaphors that echo his rhetoric, but in a cheap and hysterical man-ner. No doubt the fool is a grotesque caricature of Zarathustra, but the caricature has some bite; Zarathustra's own rhetoric is sufficiently perfervid to give rise to this sort of imitation. And this is no doubt why Zarathustra is so furious with the foaming fool. In particular he denounces the fool's anger toward the defects of the citizens; the fool's denunciation rises up out of the swamp, whereas his own despising and warning bird will fly up "out of love alone" (224). I think that Zarathus-tra is a bit too self-righteous here; the satire has obviously irritated him because it is not entirely without a point.

In my opinion, Nietzsche has anticipated here objections that will be made to the excesses of Zarathustra's rhetoric, which is completely different from Nietzsche's previous and subsequent prose style. There are at least two connected points underlying the figure of the foaming fool. Nietzsche indicates the susceptibility of Zarathustra to satire, but he also denounces in advance those who would slavishly imitate him. This form of foolish imitation includes those who take Zarathustra's rhetoric for nothing more than a sign of inspiration, or alternatively as a rhapsodic mask of truths too deep to be stated discursively. "But your fool's words harm me, even when you are right" (225). Zarathustra himself shows his anger when he says that he wishes he could see the city destroyed by pillars of fire. This sounds dangerously like a desire for vengeance. So much for his despising that rises out of love like a bird. Instead, he makes it clear that he can love nothing in this city. He gives the fool a parting doctrine: "Where one can no more love, there ought one – to pass by." Which he does. If the fool is the emblem of the great city, then its citizens have been made worse by false under-standing of Zarathustra's doctrines. Is this not a necessary consequence of the doctrines themselves? Is Zarathustra not responsible for the foaming fool?

"On the Apostates" (Section 8)

In this section Zarathustra continues the theme of its predecessor; the term *Abtrünnigen* shows the religious motif, like the previous reference to the Mount of Olives and the foaming fool: These are all echoes of the New Testament. But now Zarathustra is in the city of the Motley Cow, which he loves (see the end of the section, p.230). There is a certain correspondence between the apostates and the foaming fool. Both are misunderstandings and misrepresentations of Zarathustra's teaching; the fool is of course not personally connected to him, but stands for his indirect influence. The apostates are Zarathustra's direct responsibility. They spring from his love (226).

The general distinction drawn by Zarathustra with respect to his initial followers in the Motley Cow is the one between cowards and the brave. Courage is required to remain faithful to Zarathustra's teaching, to be a playful and courageous dancer. This is reserved for the few; most human beings, and thus most of Zarathustra's initial converts, are cowards. This distinction between the few and the many is not itself a product of Zarathustra's teaching, nor could it be called conventional or even be said to occur by chance, despite Zarathustra's rejection of teleology and a natural cosmic order. It is the expression of a natural rank-ordering of wills or centers of power, a rank-ordering that must be explained, if it can be explained at all, by the doctrine of will to power; more precisely, by the perturbations of chaos (226–27).

"Whoever is of my kind (*Art*) must also encounter experiences (*Erlebnisse*) of my kind; therefore, his first companions must be corpses and buffoons. His second companions, however, these will call themselves his *believers . . .*" (227). His kind of man should not tie his heart to the believers, whom Zarathustra characterizes as "springtimes and motley meadows" ("Lenze und bunte Wiese"). The first companions refer to the holy man; the people in the marketplace awaiting the tightrope dancer; the dancer himself, first as alive and then as a corpse; and the gravediggers of the Preface. This sets the scene for Zarathustra's acquisition of disciples in the city of the Motley Cow. The characters of the Preface are not themselves disciples but various aspects of Zarathustra's initial contact with mankind on his descent. The main personages are the buffoons of varying types (holy man, citizens, rope-dancer as living performer) and the corpses (the dead rope-dancer, the corpses buried by the gravediggers). The preliminary situation is one of extreme decadence, disorientation, superficiality: Life has become a satire (*Possenspiel*) in which the more sensible spirits are reduced to playing the roles of buffoons for an audience of corpses.

The second companions are the believers, the "true believers," or original disciples of the revolutionary teaching. The majority of these are cowards; they have not the spirit for genuine "conversion," putting to one side the question whether such a conversion is even possible (i.e., whether conversion in the sense of discipleship can ever be a genuine expression of Zarathustra's teaching).

In the second half of the section, Zarathustra engages in a soliloquy on apostates. These state that they have become pious once more, or have succumbed to the voice of a cowardly inner devil who asserts that "there is a God" (228). The symbolism (cross, fishing) is certainly Christian, and yet it seems odd to say that Zarathustra's disciples deteriorate back into Christians. It would make more sense to say that they transform his teaching into a surrogate for Christianity. Some of these apostates turn to music, some to scholarship, and some to madness that turns to the wind rather than to a discursive doctrine. This is not a renewal of Christian faith but a fall back into decadence (229).

Some of the apostates have become night watchmen; remember the previous appearance of the night watchman in "The Soothsayer." The night watchmen in this paragraph are deteriorated or caricatural versions of Zarathustra's own fear of the dangerous nature of the teaching of the eternal return. Zarathustra overhears the two night watchmen discussing whether "he" (identified afterwards by Zarathustra as God) cares about, or even has, any children. This conversation may refer to the status of Christianity in late-nineteenth-century Europe, but it could also refer at another level to Zarathustra himself and his attitude toward his disciples. Especially interesting is the agreement by the night watchman that "he" has never proved anything and is himself blessed by faith.

Zarathustra virtually explodes with laughter upon overhearing this conversation: "Truly, this will be the death of me, that I choke from laughter when I see drunken asses and hear night watchmen thus doubting God" (229). I find his stated response a bit exaggerated, as though he must have recourse to bravado in order to protect himself against the genuinely tragic implications of this conversation. Zarathustra then says that the old (or pagan) gods laughed themselves to death at the claim of the Hebraic God to be the only deity (230). Before expiring, however, they say: "Is that not precisely divinity, that there are gods, but not God?" Zarathustra adds in his own voice: "He who has ears, let him hear." There are as many gods as there are revelations or radically comprehensive tables of values.

This is the end of Zarathustra's stay in the city of the Motley Cow, from which it is a journey of two days to reach his mountain home. The terminus of his voyage is the dialectical synthesis of solitary self-understanding and the attempt to apply this self-understanding to the cities of mankind, and mankind itself, by the force of his dreams.

"The Homecoming" (Section 9)

We are now back in Zarathustra's mountaintop cave; the first soliloquy is devoted to solitude, which the prophet identifies as his home (231) and which he portrays as both chastising him for the misunderstanding that led to his absence and reaffirming the advantages of his return. Zarathustra has presumably learned the difference between two forms of solitude: being forsaken and being alone from the outset. The regular pulse beat of the entire book is one of enthusiastic departure from loneliness into the companionship of mankind, which proves to be disappointing and leads to a return into solitude. "And that thou wilt always be wild and strange among men: – wild and strange even when they love thee: For above all else they wish to be spared."

Kaufmann translates this last expression as "they want consideration," but the English is too weak here. The voice of solitude brings out the deeper point that human beings are as much isolated from the truth in their community as Zarathustra is separated from his truth by attempting to mingle with them. Human beings wish to be spared the truth; the words of T. S. Eliot come to mind here: "Go, go, go, said the bird. Humankind cannot bear very much reality." Zarathustra can speak freely in the domicile of loneliness; he can pour out the grounds of all things; more sharply yet, he can talk directly and truly to the things themselves without the obfuscating mediation of human beings.

Why is abandonment different from loneliness (232)? By attempting to bring a gift to mankind, Zarathustra has redefined his own nature as a social creature. The prophet is joined inexorably to his people by his prophecy. The forsaken prophet is stamped by a failure of will. One could of course level the same accusation against someone who does not will at all but who remains alone. On this point the words of Zarathustra's solitude are ambiguous and cannot be taken without a pinch of salt. He who restricts his speech to the things themselves is similar to the Platonist of immaculate perception whose inverted lechery keeps him from the erotic existence he desires.

One should therefore suspect the following denunciation of human existence, and in particular of human speech (233). It culminates in Zarathustra's assertion that sparing and pitying have always been his greatest danger. As Part Four will make evident, Zarathustra must overcome his pity for the higher men. He must refuse to spare the human race the destruction that is the necessary prerequisite of the superman. As we shall see, it is one of the central ambiguities of Part Four that the need to overcome sparing and pitying is presented as though it were the same as yet another return to the solitude of the mountaintop cave. And just as Part Four will culminate in satire and carnival, so the present paragraph ends with a sneeze: "At last my nose is freed from the smell of everything human! Tickled by the sharp breezes as by foaming wine, my soul sneezes – sneezes and jubilates to itself: *Gesundheit!*" (234).

So much for the unmitigated seriousness of the ontological interpretations of Nietzsche.

"On the Three Evils" (Section 10)

Zarathustra recounts a morning dream in which he stood in the hills "beyond the world, held a scale, and weighed the world" (235). The imagery is of height and lucidity; in other words, of the Hyperborean stance outside history, from which the philosopher sees the world as a whole and so as finite. Thus Zarathustra's "laughing, wakeful day wisdom mocks at all 'infinite worlds' " (ibid.). He then says: "Where there is force, there *number* will also become mistress; she has more force." This is extremely striking and apparently different from Nietzsche's later thesis that logic, mathematics, and form are all products of the will to power. The attribution of finitude to the world is a necessary corollary of the doctrine of eternal return. The vision of the weighing or measuring of the world is an expression of its human intelligibility, however, and not a statement of scientific precision: "Thus the world offered itself to me today: – not enough of a riddle to frighten away human love, not enough of a solution to put human wisdom to sleep" (236).

In general, Zarathustra's meaning seems to be this: In the Hyperborean vision beyond the world, number and measure triumph over force because force is quantitative. Even rank-ordering is measurement of degrees of force. But note that number has force. One force encompasses another; one magnitude is extended and another assimilated. But the numbers by which we weigh or measure these magnitudes are not changed by the assimilative process. The number of a given magnitude is replaced by the number of the new magnitude: It does not become the new number. Numbers are stable. Zarathustra is not interested in the scientific or theoretical consequences of this rule of force by number. His point is that the ensuing order is human, "a humanly good thing," as he says of his dream. And he uses his ability to weigh the world in order to weigh the three greatest evils "humanly well": lust, thirst for power, selfishness (*Wollust, Herrschsucht, Selbstsucht:* 236).

In Plato's *Statesman,* the Eleatic Stranger distinguishes between two kinds of measurement: arithmetical and that of the fitting (283c8ff.). Zarathustra is concerned with the weighing of the world that corresponds to the second type of measurement. Although it can be applied only to a finite world that is articulated by number, this second type of weighing takes place in a dream by means of a "divine nutcracker" (235), thanks to which the world appears as "a humanly good thing" (236). Arithmetical weighing and measuring is also dreamlike in the sense that mathematics is an interpretation of chaos, but numbers correspond to quanta of force or nature in the modern, Newtonian sense of the term. The mathematical interpretation of nature is the ground of the human interpretation, yet it is radically discontinuous from good and evil. The human interpretation must be imposed upon the mathematical interpretation that makes it possible.

It is therefore not entirely clear that Zarathustra is right to say that wherever there is force, number will become mistress. In Nietzsche's own terms, the significance of number depends on the predominant system of values and so on the human distinction between good and evil. Technical subtleties (such as nonstandard integers) apart, number *qua* number will not change in a revaluation of human goods; but the human value of number is rooted in the will, that is, in the attribution of fitness to enumeration or, still more generally, in the subordination of quanta to estimations of good and evil.

In the sequel, Zarathustra presents a transvaluation of values by reweighing the three best-cursed things, or greatest evils. There is nothing radically new in this section, but we should notice one or two points. The discussion of lust makes it clear that Zarathustra both repudiates what is today called "liberated" sexuality and distinguishes between the passions of the rabble and those of free and innocent hearts (237). These last, incidentally, are apparently not the same as the "lion-hearted." The lust of the latter stands to that of the former as does the wine of wines to the garden happiness of the earth.

Especially relevant to our assessment of those who see in Nietzsche a rejection of domination is his reevaluation of the thirst for power. Zarathustra deprecates the lust for power as it is manifested among the cruel and the vain, but he makes it clear that this thirst ascends up to "the pure and the lonely." "*Herrschsucht:* But who would call it *Sucht* [mania, greed] when the high lusts downward for power?" The lonely high ought not to remain solitary and self-sufficient; Zarathustra calls this longing for power the "gift-giving virtue" (238). By the same token, the revaluation of selfishness separates it from the selflessness of Platonists and priests and is vindicated by the sword of judgment called "the great noon" as the expression of a powerful soul and an equally powerful body (238–40).

This section should be taken in close connection with our previous analysis of the homecoming, or return to solitude. There is a constant tension in *Zarathustra* between the need to give, and hence to go down among mankind, and the need to remain alone and high above good and evil in a Hyperborean lookout on the mountaintop. This corresponds to the tension in Nietzsche between the philosophical Eros that isolates him not only from human companionship but from passage through the gateway of the eternal return into the resolution of a historical perspective, and from the desire to live in an epoch defined by the generous dimensions of his own genius. One of the most confusing aspects of *Zarathustra* is that, entirely apart from the intentional ambiguity enforced by Nietzsche's double rhetoric, the book also mirrors the conflict in his own soul between the need for solitude and the need to be loved.

Otherwise stated, Nietzsche fluctuates throughout his entire active life between two forms of domination: over things and over human beings. His writings exhibit in a peculiarly vivid and excessively candid manner the fluctuations of the Platonic Eros, or the dialectical struggles of the philosophical soul. Plato himself disguises these fluctuations by the masks of his dialogues, but Nietzsche, the first honest philosopher, makes them the founding theme of his writings, published and unpublished. In this sense, Nietzsche's excessive frankness can be characterized as the mask of enlightenment and constitutes the peculiar difficulty in grasping his complex teaching, which is complex because it attempts to identify philosophy with the psychology of the philosopher.

"On Old and New Tablets" (Section 12)

Section 11 ("On the Spirit of Heaviness," or "Gravity") develops the theme of the transformation of selfishness into the proper form of self-love. The main point here is that there are no transcendent sources of value; those who think otherwise are like camels who burden themselves with self-created obstacles (243). Despite the elaborate language and intricate imagery, there is nothing fundamentally new here, and I pass directly to Section 12.

This is the longest section in the entire book other than the Preface. The title refers to tables of values, such as the Ten Commandments, engraved on tablets of stone. Zarathustra is now in an interim period; the old tablets, or sets of values, have been broken, but the new ones are only half inscribed (246). The prophet awaits the sign that his time has come: the laughing lion with the flock of doves. The lion must lie down, not with the lambs, as in the Bible, but with doves: The symbol of peace and reconciliation is a bird, not a terrestrial. The lion rules the earth and is reconciled with the gentle doves. Why not the eagles? Because the eagle is the counterpart to the lion; Zarathustra wants a reconciliation of opposites, like "Caesar with the soul of Christ."

Zarathustra awakened man from his slumber with his teaching that no one yet knows what is good and evil, except perhaps he who creates it. There is nothing intrinsically good and evil, except, of course, the values associated with strength, creativity, and overcoming. These are the foundation of Zarathustra's teaching and the basis for personal and public evaluations, which must be contingent expressions of the foundation, or inner essence (247).

We should note in particular that Zarathustra must still speak in images and limp and stammer like poets: "And truly, I am ashamed that I must still be a poet" (247). Compare the earlier assertion that poets lie too much and that Zarathustra is a poet. Poetry stands here for the rhetoric of accommodation. The balance of the second subsection repeats previous themes. This is true of the entire section, which contains a review of Zarathustra's career and teaching, a kind of retrospective of the entire work, as though it is coming to an end. This is in keeping with Nietzsche's initial intention that Part Three be the final book. I will therefore not discuss the balance of the section in detail, but will summarize the main theme in each case.

The third subsection reviews the notion of "superman" as the symbol of redemption or salvation, that is, as the Nietzschean substitute for Jesus as savior (248–49). Zarathustra notes that he wants to go down to man one last time. He refers to the sun, but the sun "goes under" forever, whereas Zarathustra will die during his final descent. In subsection 4, the superman is expressed as a new tablet or value, a commandment: *"Do not spare your neighbor!* Man is something that must be overcome" (249).

In 5, Zarathustra connects joy to innocence; it cannot be achieved intentionally (250). Subsection 6 reminds us that prophets cannot enter into the promised land; going under is for the prophet a perishing (251). Subsection 7 condemns conventionally good men, who never speak the truth. What they call "good" is "a disease of the spirit," or decadence (251). In 8, traditional values are compared to planks or bridges over the water; those who accept them believe that everything is firm or stands still, in other words that the values are permanent. This is a winter doctrine, one of frozen ice, when one can walk on water and it is too cold to create. But the thaw wind is blowing, which means that revolution is in the offing (252). In 9, 10, and 11, Zarathustra examines various aspects of tradition and exposes them as illusory (253–54).

In subsection 11, Zarathustra turns to the future. He once more repudiates the rabble and announces the need for a new nobility, which he defines in 12 as "creators and cultivators and sowers of the future" (254). In 11, he criticizes the rabble for not looking far enough into the past, whereas in 12 he instructs the new nobility to look not backward but forward to the land of their children, "the undiscovered land in the farthest sea" (255) – again an allusion to the Hyperboreans. According to the eternal return, past and future must be the same. But creativity is associated with the future. In 13–15, Zarathustra inveighs against those who turn away from the world; this attack against world weariness is expanded in subsection 16.

Zarathustra begins there by rejecting the separation of learning (and by implication, theory) from strong desire (or practico-production: 257). This is a new tablet; Zarathustra is thinking here of late-modern decadence and passive or reactive nihilism, according to which "nothing pays" or is worth doing, and which paralyzes the will. Note the strong metaphor: "For truly, my brothers, the spirit *is* a stomach" (258). This is one of Nietzsche's recurring images. The same theme is pursued in 17 and 18, in the latter of which Zarathustra distinguishes between the values of weariness (*Ermüdung*) and those of laziness (*Faulheit:* 259). The weary lack strength for further action; the lazy do not act at all.

Subsection 12 gave the impression that there are to be many members of the new nobility. In 19, Zarathustra makes it clear that the number of those who accompany him on his ascent becomes ever smaller (260). There is a fundamental difference between understanding Zarathustra, or in other words Nietzsche's teaching, and being a product of that teaching. Zarathustra warns in particular against the *Schmarotzer*, the parasites who dwell in the weak spots of the strong and noble; these are the imitators of the superman, the false disciples, the popularizers, the journalists who in our own time accommodate Nietzsche's teaching to egalitarianism and the tastes of the rabble.

In subsection 20, Zarathustra is explicit about his intention to destroy contemporary society: "O my brothers, am I not then cruel? But I say, that which falls, one ought also to push! Everything contemporary – it falls, it decays: Who would wish to stop it! But I – I even want to push it!" (262). Whoever cannot be taught to fly should be taught to fall faster. In 21, we learn that this advice entails saving one's strength for the right enemies. Zarathustra warns against entering into the struggle of the people for justice, because it will vitiate one's energy and bring one down to the level of those who are already corrupt.

In subsection 22, Zarathustra says that the very rapaciousness of the people for their daily sustenance can be intensified in such a way as to make them beasts of prey. This has vaguely Marxist overtones: a dialectical transformation of brutality into the superman, whereas Marx speaks of the dialectical transformation of the negativity of the proletariat into free self-overcoming (263). Subsections 23 and 24 speak of the sexes – man fit for war, woman fit for giving birth (264) – and of marriage, the primary goal of which is to produce something higher, not simply to reproduce. Note that Zarathustra speaks on behalf of marriage and against adultery. Fidelity and chastity are important to him, a point on which he has been misunderstood by many of his admirers.

Subsections 25–28 speak of the destruction of the old society and the consequent creation of new peoples and hence of the danger of Zarathustra's teaching for the contemporary audience (264–68). Note: "Human society is an experiment (*Versuch*: trial or attempt, but also experiment), thus I teach – a long search: It searches, however, for the commander!–" (265). In 26, Zarathustra identifies the good as the Pharisees and the just as those who hate the creators of new values: Goodness and justice are here what Socrates calls "demotic virtues" in the *Republic* (266). In 29, Zarathustra says that in order to be noble, one must be hard as a diamond: "Only the noblest is entirely hard" (268). Note the difference between the diamond and its relative, the kitchen coal. The section concludes in subsection 30 with an invocation by Zarathustra to his will: "*My* necessity! Keep me from all small victories!" (268).

Despite the apparently equal weight given by the title of this section to old and new values, Zarathustra speaks for the most part of the new as an inference from a shift in attitude toward the old. Given the doctrine of the eternal return, there is no genuine creation of new values. One could say that Nietzsche's teaching is concerned not so much with the creation of new values as with a particular reevaluation of the human soul. The rank-ordering of values is a trivial consequence of the rank-ordering of human types; and the number of these types is finite, regardless of the apparently endless diversity of individual and communal values.

"The Convalescent" (Section 13)

One morning Zarathustra emerges from his cave full of enthusiasm, awakens all of his animals, and then experiences an attack of nausea that causes him to lose consciousness. His convalescence takes seven days, during which time his animals gather food, including two lambs stolen by his eagle (270–71). When he has recovered, the animals ask if some new knowledge has come to him. His reply is quite striking. Words and sounds are an illusory bridge of things that are separated by an eternity (272). I take this to refer to the eternal return; we experience the external world as independent yet present, whereas in fact each element of our world is eternally distant because it eternally recurs. "To every soul belongs another soul," namely, one's recurring self.

But this has another consequence: "For me – how could there be an outside-me? There is no outside." To begin with, Zarathustra makes it clear that the entire work is to be understood as a monologue. As he said elsewhere, "In the end, one experiences only oneself." But how is this compatible with the remarks of the present episode? The answer seems to be that things have no independent existence, but are created by our speech; as one might put this, naming is creating. If we did not speak, there would be no things, but simply the circle of Becoming, that is, the accumulation and discharge of points of force, or in other words chaos. This is the point of contact between Nietzsche and analytical philosophies of language.

The experience of eternity thus functions as a double separation from immediate experience. (1) It separates us from immediacy, which is now experienced as eternity; yet each of us as a conscious individual is trapped in the presently experienced cycle, namely, in the historical time of a particular perspective. Eternity is from this standpoint inaccessible to us. (2) The perception of eternity reveals the illusory nature of immediacy, that is, of the stability of the things that constitute our immediate experience. It reveals that chaos lies at the heart of all things.

This does not explain why chaos perpetually recurs as a world made up of definite things. It does not explain why those things are created by our speech. The animals are clearly unable to understand Zarathustra's remarks and repeat phrases from the speech by which he introduced the gateway of the moment and the doctrine of the eternal return. In other words, when they are presented with problematic consequences of the doctrine, they simply repeat the doctrine itself. As the animals put it, "The same house of Being builds itself eternally" (272).

Zarathustra replies scornfully: "O you buffoons and barrel organs!" In this speech he identifies himself as the shepherd who bit off the head of the snake that was choking him (273). This is not entirely compatible with the original image; perhaps one could say that in watching the shepherd undergo his transformation into the superman, Zarathustra represents Nietzsche watching a fantasy of his own hopes, hopes that can never be realized. To come back to the present passage, the animals have made a barrel-organ song, or a farce, out of Zarathustra's doctrine. Zarathustra himself was rendered violently ill by his revelation and forced to convalesce; his animals have no such difficulty. They are not actually touched or transformed from within by the doctrine. They watch, but do not experience, his great pain "as human beings do. For man is the cruelest animal" (273).

This is again extremely obscure. First, who are the animals? What do they represent? In one sense, obviously, they indicate lack of comprehension on the part of Zarathustra's disciples, who have not given birth to his doctrine but simply listened to it. But the animals are closer to nature than human beings; I suggest that they represent the testimony of Becoming but not the subjective appropriation of that testimony by a human prophet and lawgiver. They are part of Zarathustra's illusion whereby he gives meaning to things by speech. The animals personify forces of nature and attributes of the human spirit. They are not human, although their silent eavesdropping is an imitation of human cruelty. Man is the cruelest animal because he creates values; he lacks the innocence of Becoming that the animals exemplify. The silence in question here refers to an absence of genuine communication, as witnessed by Zarathustra's scornful characterization of the animals' repetition of his doctrines. By watching Zarathustra's pain mutely, the animals reverted to their natural, or nondiscursive, state, and hence offered him no genuine compassion or understanding. But by mimicking his teaching, they show him that nature, even when invested with speech, can give him no comfort.

Zarathustra then shifts to a pejorative description of human beings and a discussion of their cruelty. Once again we note the "dialectical" thesis that human cruelty, or, more generally, what is most evil in man, is actually best for him; evil and cruelty (as Machiavelli taught) can be transformed into goodness in the sense of will to power (274). In the persona of the shepherd, Zarathustra gagged on the thought that humans are "small" and so that the doctrine of eternal return guarantees the perpetual recurrence of small men. Again the animals provide a thoughtless imitation of his own doctrines; they ask him to stop this speech about his nausea and to go out into the garden of the world to sing. And again Zarathustra characterizes them as buffoons and barrel organs who have anticipated his thought. This is because they are personifications of nature and spirit, that is, the basis for that thought.

The animals are unaffected by Zarathustra's scornful words; they repeat that he is the teacher of the eternal return and reiterate its main points (275–76). When they are done speaking, they wait for Zarathustra's reply, but he does not know that they have ceased to speak. He lies silent, conversing with his soul. As personifications of natural forces (including the human spirit), the animals do not represent Zarathustra's personal subjectivity. He can converse only with himself (276–77). This inner conversation is a silence to the animals, a silence that is honored by the serpent and the eagle, the two most important of Zarathustra's animals (277). The animals depart when he speaks to his innermost self.

"The Other Dance Song" (Section 15)

In Section 14 ("Of the Great Longing"), Zarathustra delivers an elegy to his soul in which he says that he cleansed it of sin and returned its freedom; in particular, freedom over the created and uncreated (279). But he also gave the soul the name of destiny. If the soul is the destiny of the chance (*Zufall*) of the cosmos, Nietzsche comes quite close here to a kind of transcendental doctrine. The soul is then the ultimate intention, or goal, of the randomly self-configuring cosmos. Underlying this imagery is a deep ambiguity in Nietzsche's doctrine. On the one hand, the cosmos produces the soul as a consequence of the chance accumulations of quanta of force. On the other hand, the cosmos is itself a creation or interpretation of the human soul.

This ambiguity can be partially removed by holding that the soul is indeed a chance event of the process by which the world gives birth to itself, but that the previously discussed "weighing" or interpreting of the value of the world, that is, the assigning by the soul of a particular rank-ordering or table of values to the chance event of the cosmos, provides it with its destiny. The cosmos, so to speak, is a text in search of an interpretation. But this approach is obviously metaphorical and does nothing to mitigate the contingency of destiny.

In general, the section reads like an expression of attempted self-exhilaration. The last three sections of this part give it a positive, even ecstatic, ending which seems to have been initially planned as the conclusion of the entire work. The emphasis is on songs of the future. Having himself sung the praises of his soul, Zarathustra ends Section 14 with a request that is his final gift to it: He bids it to sing. The soul complies in Section 15. The title of this section refers us back to Section 10 of Part Two, "The Dance Song," which is one of three songs sung by Zarathustra about the sadness and unfathomableness of life.

The first line of the present section repeats the first line of the original dance song: "Into thine eye I looked recently, O life!" (140, 282). In the first dance song, Zarathustra contrasts the wild wisdom of solitude with immersion in life; life is associated with sadness and death. Zarathustra initially finds life unfathomable and is sinking into its eye when life rescues him with a golden fishing-rod. In the present, or other, dance song, Zarathustra looks into the eye of life and sees a golden boat; the vision stimulates him to dance toward life, but life runs away from his grasp. When he leaps away from life, however, it stops and turns toward him, "eyes full of desire" (282).

Life is personified as a cruel temptress who both eludes and encourages Zarathustra's dancing courtship. This is compatible with the first song, in which life and wisdom are represented as women who are similar but distinct. Zarathustra loves life and likes wisdom; the attempt to unify the two leads him to sink once more into the unfathomable eye of life, this time without being rescued. One more detail: In the earlier episode, the song is preceded by an encounter with dancing girls. In the second, or other, dance song, it is Zarathustra himself who attempts to dance, not with complete success.

"With crooked looks – you teach me crooked paths; on crooked paths my foot learns – tricks!" Despite the constant asseverations of frankness and the apparently confessional tone of the rhetoric, Zarathustra indicates in this image that life can be mastered only by duplicity and indirection. Note the reference to the whip with which he will mark time, to which life will dance and cry (284).

In the second subsection, life speaks to Zarathustra and says that they do not love each other from the heart but can nevertheless be on good terms. This is presumably a rebuke addressed to Zarathustra's claim in the initial dance song that he loves life; I suspect that life has correctly discerned in him the partial detachment of the philosopher. Life then accuses Zarathustra of being insufficiently faithful to her; she says that he is planning on leaving her soon. He replies hesitantly, "yes," but then whispers something into life's ear. To which life replies: "You know that, O Zarathustra? No one knows that –" (285). Life and Zarathustra then look at one another and weep together. I take this as a sign that life is fundamentally tragic, but that this tragedy is, as Zarathustra says next of life, dearer to him than all his wisdom. It is the source of his wisdom: of the desire to mitigate and even to disguise the tragedy with music and dance. Hence "art is worth more than the truth" for life.

The third subsection is a lyric in twelve parts, the last of which is silence, a silence introduced by the assertion that all pleasure (*Lust*) wills eternity (286). The tragedy of life is its transience; this is transformed by Zarathustra into the delight of eternity, in the form of the doctrine of the eternal return, the conclusion of which is silence, not discursive reason.

"The Seven Seals (or: The Yes and Amen Song)" (Section 16)

The ultimate mystery is sealed with seven seals, and this is the originally planned conclusion of *Zarathustra*. The section is divided into seven subsections, each of which ends with the assertion "For I love you, O eternity!" In each, this assertion is introduced with the claim that Zarathustra has never found a woman with whom he would wish to have children, except for eternity. Zarathustra abandons his human heritage in order to procreate a new race of human beings, symbolized by the figure of the superman. Remember Nietzsche's epigram that "a married philosopher belongs to comedy." The section does not require detailed analysis; it is a song of self-explanation and resumes the main themes of the work to this point. The original conclusion of the work affirms the doctrine of the eternal return as the source of prophetic generation. That this cannot be satisfactory is evident from the fact that the doctrine is itself Zarathustra's child. It looks as though Zarathustra's actual bride is the eternity of Platonism. But Nietzsche cannot accept this without repudiating his allegiance to Homer's army. For if the doctrine of eternal return is eternally true, then the structure of temporality is not an interpretation, and we are led to understand the vision of eternal return as *theoria*.

In the work to this point, Zarathustra has identified three women to whom he is strongly attracted either by love or by friendship: wisdom, life, and eternity. The first, wisdom, is similar to but other than life;

Zarathustra says that he likes but not that he loves her. Life is more humanly attractive than wisdom; one wishes to sink into her depths, but unfortunately she is unfathomable. A genuine love of life is therefore impossible. This is why Zarathustra turns to eternity in his desire to procreate. Eternity is neither life nor wisdom. Wisdom is Apollonian, or Hyperborean; as such, it is too similar to the immaculate perception of Platonism to allow us to engender children with her. Eternity is the great womb of chaos, the confluence of creation and destruction. It is not life but the mother of life, and hence too of death.

5

ZARATHUSTRA'S SPEECHES: PART FOUR

Part Four has a motto taken from Part Two, Section 2 ("On the Blessed Isles"). The passage warns against the folly of loving from a height that is not above pity, and quotes the devil as saying that God died of his pity for mankind. So presumably this will be the theme of the last part. Nietzsche does not explain in his Notebooks or correspondence what led him to add this part, which was apparently intended as an intermezzo between Part Three and a subsequent addition. It is therefore not clear how many parts Nietzsche intended to add to the book as we have it.

This being so, it is obviously impossible to arrive at a final interpretation of the work as a whole. I do not myself believe, however, that the situation necessitates an entirely open-ended approach to the significance of *Zarathustra*. On the contrary, one could say with hermeneutical justice that the indeterminate nature of the ending is the doctrinally correct form of the text. Given the doctrine of the eternal return, there is a dramatic beginning but no ending. We meet Zarathustra when he is thirty years old because this is the point in the perpetually recurring cycle at which he detaches himself from mankind in order to prepare the revelation of the superman. There follows a sequence of arrivals among and departures from mankind which could be continued as chronological events without adding or subtracting anything from the teaching as we have it. Zarathustra will never die, because he is himself the paradigm of the eternal return.

The dramatic beginning is thus for the convenience of the

nineteenth-century reader only; it renders accessible the starting point of the unending story that Nietzsche wishes to tell. At the same time, we are not freed of our responsibility to grasp the necessity for the addition of Part Four to the kernel, or essential unit of meaning, of that story. We shall have to infer the reason from the text. Apparently Nietzsche felt it necessary to develop at greater length the leave-taking from life described in the last section of Part Three. That we do possess what is more or less the kernel is at least suggested by the fact that in Part Four Zarathustra is an old man.

"The Honey Sacrifice" (Section 1)

Years have passed, and Zarathustra is now white-haired. His animals approach him as he is sitting in front of his cave and gazing out at the sea. They ask if he is looking out for his happiness. He replies: "I do not think any more about happiness; I think about my work" (295). This is a strikingly Hegelian – perhaps one should say Lutheran – statement. I am thinking of Hegel's association in the *Phenomenology of Spirit* of the unhappy consciousness with the knowledge that God is dead, as well as of his description of *Geist* as the *Werkmeister*.[1] Zarathustra's statement reminds us of his assertion in the preceding part that happiness follows him who does not pursue her. But it is more likely that he now intends to place his work beyond happiness and sorrow, both of which are the constant companions of human existence. The animals attribute this statement to Zarathustra's great happiness. Throughout the work they are unable to perceive his darker side or to view him as anything but successful. Once more he calls them buffoons.

In discussing a previous section, I suggested that the animals represent the testimony of Becoming, Nietzsche's version of nature. This testimony is rendered articulate by Zarathustra himself: The natural order is an expression of his own will. Nietzsche represents this testimony in the form of animals to indicate that it is neither simply chaos nor entirely human. The animals are proto-human; they are the basic stratum of the interaction between human subjectivity and the innocence of Becoming. They verify Zarathustra's teaching but do not grasp the tragic implications of that teaching for human beings. Otherwise stated, innocence is compatible with happiness but not with sorrow.

Zarathustra does not deny that he is happy, but only that he is thinking about or is concerned with happiness. The calm discerned by the animals comes not from enjoyment but from ripeness: "It is the *honey* in my veins that makes my blood thicker and my soul calmer"

(296). The animals suggest a mountain ascent, and Zarathustra agrees. He requests that honey be found at the destination, as he intends to make a honey sacrifice. When they arrive at their destination, Zarathustra sends the animals away and talks to himself. The animals cannot be present at crucial revelations of Zarathustra's understanding of human existence, or else they cannot grasp the implications of his denunciations of their buffoonery. This suggests that at such moments Zarathustra transcends the merely animal or arrives at the characteristically human level of his thought. On the other hand, the animals can succor Zarathustra when he is suffering because they are close to nature, that is, precisely because they do not understand his suffering. Zarathustra is regularly healed by returning to nature: to his solitude, to the mountain cave, to his animals.

Zarathustra sends the animals away and speaks frankly. Talk of honey and sacrifice was a subterfuge: "At this height I may speak more freely than before hermit caves and hermit pet animals" (296). Why then did he speak at all to the animals? Why did he ask them to accompany him to the mountaintop? This must have something to do with their misperception of his calmness. Zarathustra told the animals that he is a ripe fruit who must sacrifice honey. This honey is thickening his blood and so is inside his body. But the honey to be sacrificed must be gathered by the animals and stored at the mountaintop site of the proposed sacrifice; it is external to Zarathustra.

The one secure point is that Zarathustra wishes his animals to believe that a sacrifice will occur in their absence. The sacrifice has to do with the body, namely, with honey in the blood, and of course with nature or actual honey. Honey is associated with bees, and bees with work. Zarathustra said initially that he no longer thinks of happiness but of work. Honey represents sweetness or happiness; but honey is produced or gathered by work. It is the work, not the sweetness, that interests Zarathustra. The animals work, but it is the sweetness that interests them, not the work. This is the difference between the animal and the human (and it indicates the curative function of the animal). Zarathustra makes this explicit in the opening remarks of his monologue; honey is bait for animals.

To sacrifice honey is to exalt it, to incorporate it into a religious ritual. But Zarathustra now reveals that talk of honey sacrifice was a trick and a useful folly (like a noble lie). What the animals might regard as sacrifice is to Zarathustra prodigal waste or squandering of his riches. He lavishes honey on others; he offers humanity the happiness of overcoming as a free act of his own extravagant nature that overflows with riches. And the honey is also like the sugar-coating of the bitter pill prescribed by physicians (see Lucretius).

Zarathustra compares himself to a fisherman who uses honey as bait and casts a golden fishing rod: "My happiness itself I cast out wide and far," like Christ, who fishes for souls. Zarathustra's happiness is the bait intended to raise human beings up to his level, namely, to enable them to withstand the terrifying consequences of the teaching of the eternal return. This dark side is to be concealed with honey: "Become who you are!" (297). The honey is the promise of happiness arising from the work of overcoming. It is the link between Zarathustra's golden fishing rod and the same implement as employed by life to rescue the drowning Zarathustra in the first dance song.

Zarathustra indicates that he has changed his strategy. Instead of descending to mankind, he waits for men to rise up to him. But of course he does not simply wait; he also fishes. I believe he means that he has cast his honey-baited doctrine and is now waiting for the fish to rise. This fishing takes place in the human world, the human abyss, the human sea, and not among the animals. They cannot overcome; they are what they are, whereas human beings must become who they are. Note again that Zarathustra omits *mathōn* from this cryptic citation of Pindar, who says that we become who we are "by understanding." There is an implied substitution by Zarathustra of the will for the intellect. Zarathustra's fish will become who they are by taking his bait, not by understanding. They will be caught by sweetness, or happiness, not by work. That is, they will overcome not through the philosopher's work of understanding and prophecy but through an activation of that prophecy.

In the balance of the section, Zarathustra consoles and stimulates himself by predicting the coming of his kingdom of a thousand years; but he cannot say when the kingdom will come. Once more there is an echo here of Christ ("Thy kingdom come": 297–99).

"The Cry of Distress" (Section 2)

On the following day, Zarathustra is again sitting in front of his cave, and the animals are looking for more honey, as he has used up the previous supply. The honey, or sweetness of happy life, comes from nature, from the innocence of Becoming. Suddenly Zarathustra notices a second shadow next to his own: It is the soothsayer of Part Two, who sang there of the sameness and meaninglessness of everything and of how knowledge strangles (300). In Part Two, this led to the vision of the night watchman and the theme of the impossibility of overcoming death as well as of the dangerous implications of Zarathustra's doctrine. The reference to strangulation reminds us of the shepherd with the serpent fixed in his throat. Whereas Zarathustra sees the release of the shepherd from the serpent, the soothsayer represents a darker alternative. The proximity of their two shadows suggests this relationship of two possible outcomes of Nietzsche's teaching.

The two acknowledge one another by a respective wiping of the face, as though to wipe it away, after which they shake hands. Each manifestation of Nietzsche's own spirit is attempting to wipe away the fear of what it represents. The soothsayer tells Zarathustra that the waves of great need and sadness are rising higher and higher around his mountain and that he will soon be swept away. The reference is to the disaster effected upon European civilization by the doctrine of the eternal return, or the intensification of nihilism. Zarathustra hears a noise echoing from peak to peak which he explains to the soothsayer as originating with mankind; it is man's cry of need (*Notschrei:* 301). In reply to Zarathustra's question, the soothsayer tells him that his final sin is pity, and says that he, the soothsayer, has come to seduce Zarathustra to that sin. When taken with the motto, this indicates the main function of Part Four. Zarathustra is not yet entirely free of the danger of pity for mankind. One must surmise that Nietzsche is struggling with the final attempt to overcome the tragedy of his existence as a person by immersion in the vision of his prophetic teaching. But the soothsayer also identifies the *Notschrei* as the cry of the higher man for Zarathustra. In other words, Zarathustra can respond with pity to human suffering, but then he will abandon his teaching, which requires a ruthless destruction of the present breed of mankind. The correct response is to overcome pity, since the present suffering of the human race is the basis for its self-overcoming.

The soothsayer says: "It is time, it is the highest time!" This is an intensification of the cry "It is time" that all things called out to Zarathustra in Part Three ("Of Involuntary Bliss"), but prematurely. Zarathustra had not yet dared to summon his most abysmal thought (205). But now the time has come to face up to the implications of the doctrine of the eternal return for those who are called in Part Four "the higher man." It is toward him, and, as we shall see, toward himself, that Zarathustra must overcome his pity and thereby complete his mission. The higher man stands at the crossroads before which Nietzsche's doctrine has brought him. His cry of need has two senses; on the one hand, as understood in terms of Zarathustra's hopeful vision, the higher man requires that Nietzsche sacrifice him for the sake of the superman, to which he is nothing more than a transitional figure. On the other hand, as understood by the soothsayer, the higher man represents those superior few who have been doomed by their comprehension of the eternal return.

It is important to note that Zarathustra asks the soothsayer to identify the cry that summons him to the highest time, and that Zarathustra shudders and sweats with terror (*Angst:* 302) when he hears this identification and demands to know why the higher man is approaching. What I referred to in the previous section as the crossroads is another image for the gateway of the moment. This conversation between Zarathustra and the soothsayer is a kind of mirror image of the previous conversation between Zarathustra and the spirit of gravity, except that here the soothsayer takes the leading role. The higher man approaches like "a black sea" (301) to sweep Zarathustra through the gateway that opens into the abyss of a meaningless temporal flux.

The dwarflike spirit of gravity stripped Zarathustra's doctrine of eternal return of its affirmative vision of renewal. Now the soothsayer adds to the dwarf's neutral restatement the emotional intensity of despair. After a moment of silence he comments on Zarathustra's lack of "dizzying" happiness and urges him to dance lest he collapse before him (302). Dancing is a key form of the playful attempt to avoid responsibility, referred to by the soothsayer as pity, for the human race. In his role as an incarnation of the *pais paizōn,* or innocence of Becoming, Zarathustra has in fact deprived mankind of its innocence. The soothsayer reiterates his denial that Zarathustra is happy, a denial linked to his own version of Zarathustra's teaching: "Everything is the same, nothing is worthwhile, searching does not help, there are no more blessed isles" (302).

This assertion moves Zarathustra to emerge from his terror and to reaffirm his doctrine: "No! No! Three times no!" The three noes correspond to the third day, on which Zarathustra broke his silence while sailing on the ship away from the blessed isles. He now contradicts the soothsayer: "The blessed isles still exist!" (303). This echoes Zarathustra's previous repudiation of the spirit of gravity. He says that he will search for the higher man in the woods, where he may be threatened by evil brutes. This suggests the ambiguity of nature. On the one hand, Zarathustra wishes to return humanity to nature in the sense of the innocence of Becoming; on the other hand, the will to the eternal return is also a detachment from nature, or an interpretation, and so an expression of the comprehensive philological art.

The soothsayer dismisses Zarathustra with the assurance that this outburst of confidence is to no avail. When the prophet returns after his search in the woods, he will find the soothsayer waiting for him in his cave. Zarathustra agrees and urges the soothsayer to share whatever he finds in the cave, in particular honey. This will sweeten his soul; the soothsayer will dance to Zarathustra's songs like his dancing bear. As we saw previously, honey stands for the sweetness of natural labor. The image here is a kind of harmony of nature and art. A dancing bear is a trained beast, a circus performer. Zarathustra will receive a variety of visitors in Part Four, all of whom become characters in a carnival of ironic reiteration of the crucial stages in his mission. If Zarathustra can transform the soothsayer into a dancing bear, he will have conquered death by play; that is, by art as the stimulus to life.

"Conversation with the Kings" (Section 3)

Two kings with one laden ass approach Zarathustra's cave. The kings are united by a common burden, which is articulated by the king on the right. Note the explicit distinction between right and left; the king on the right denounces contemporary society and manners as marked by the people, the mob, the rabble (*Gesindel*): "The best and dearest to me today is a healthy peasant [or farmer: *Bauer*]: coarse, cunning, obstinate, long enduring; that is today the noblest species" (305). There is an amusing anticipation of Heidegger here. Nietzsche's point is not so much to endorse that thesis as to indicate that the denunciation of late-modern bourgeois decadence follows from right-wing as well as left-wing criticism of the historical epoch and the political situation. The Enlightenment has destroyed the old aristocratic society and replaced it with a vulgar rabble; but this rabble is the proletariat of liberal, industrial, and technological reform.

The king on the left of the ass sympathizes with the king on the right, but says that no one is listening to them; he does not join in the outburst; he is far less articulate than the king on the right. Both kings say in unison that they are searching for the higher man: "We are leading this ass to him. The highest man namely shall also be the highest master on earth" (306). The kings are united in denouncing the rule of the mob or rabble (*Pöbel*) and the mob virtue that says, "Look, I alone am virtue!"

It is possible to infer that the king on the left is not a revolutionary radical but one who has been disillusioned by the modern liberal intention, stemming from the aristocracy, to enlighten the multitude by the deeds and speeches of the few. He is the passive member of the duo. In the second subsection the king on the right again takes the lead and tells how Zarathustra's reputation and rhetoric of war have finally persuaded them to seek him out. The rage of the right assimilates the disillusionment of the left; as one could say, the result is the left-wing tyranny of the twentieth century, whose intention is to purify the people, to transform the peasant into the virtuous proletariat.

This is of course a mere conjecture based on a small textual detail. I find it plausible, but I cannot prove it and do not insist on it. A safer approach simply takes the kings as reactionary spokesmen who represent a partial and distorted reflection of Nietzsche's critique of modernity. Zarathustra welcomes the kings and tells them to wait: This is the sole virtue remaining for kings (308).

Why do the kings bring a laden ass to the higher man? They wish to transfer their burden to him. The kings, or rulers of contemporary Europe, have been degraded into representatives of a mob (305). But release from their burden is not the same as transformation to a new epoch; if he accepts the ass, the higher man will himself become an instrument of the mob. The burden carried by the ass is thus the political counterpart to the spirit of gravity who sat on Zarathustra's shoulders, and to the message of hopelessness delivered by the sooth-sayer.

Zarathustra tells the kings that he is called away by a cry of distress and invites them into his cave to await his return that evening (308). The *Notschrei* of the higher man is the common thread in Part Four of *Zarathustra*. The soothsayer has informed him of this distress and moved him on his journey of salvation. In his search for the higher man, Zarathustra encounters the various symbols of the distress of contemporary European civilization. These symbolic figures are also seeking for the higher man, but in a way that will lower him to their level. Zarathustra assembles them in his cave for a satirical epiphany in which the last vestiges of his pity are overcome. This permits him to reaffirm the doctrine of the eternal return and to experience the joy of that affirmation. It remains to be seen whether the higher man is found in the woods and rescued from the evil beasts that reside there.

"The Leech" (Section 4)

Zarathustra inadvertently steps on a man lying on the ground next to a swamp in which his arm is immersed. The man is allowing himself to be bitten by leeches. This image reminds us of the shepherd who is strangling on a serpent that entered his throat while he slept. But this man submits himself voluntarily to the leeches. At first he is angered by Zarathustra's intervention, but when he learn Zarathustra's name, he is delighted and calls him a leech more beautiful than those who have been drinking his blood. The man identifies himself as the consci-entious in spirit; the two things that matter most to him are Zarathustra and the leech (309–11). He knows just one thing and concentrates all of his energy (his "blood") on it; that is, he is the master of and expert on the leech's brain. The conscientious man makes clear that he is a follower of modern science; he is a specialist and is consumed by his specialty, which is, however, on a par with any other scientific activity:

"In genuine scientific knowledge there is nothing great and nothing small" (311).

What is the connection for this man between Zarathustra and the leech? The doctrine of the eternal return is a rival to science for the loyalty of modern man. Dedication to a single cause that defines one's life is akin to Zarathustra; the difference here is that science sucks out the life blood, whereas Zarathustra restores it. The hero of this episode cannot distinguish between conscientiousness and the will to affirmation. Otherwise put, the bloodless conscientiousness of the *Wissenschaftler* is entirely diluted by its narrowness and detachment from rank-ordering. Instead of engaging in science for the sake of life, the man drains his life away in his specialized domain. He is a false master. Zarathustra invites him to come to his cave that night and then says that he must go because he hears a cry of distress.

Nietzsche assigns destructive as well as supportive functions to animals; we have already encountered the adder, the serpent in the shepherd's throat, tarantulas, and now leeches. This dual symbolism should be taken together with Nietzsche's denunciation of the Stoic invocation to live in accord with nature.[2] Nature is indifferent to human beings. To express this indifference in human terms, nature is both friend and enemy; it is divided against itself. Since nature is a human interpretation, in the last analysis one must say that humanity is divided against itself. The creative or life-enhancing consequences of the will to power are balanced by the destructive or decadent consequences. At a deeper level, of course, the will to power is not will, but mere accumulation and discharge of energy. Creation and destruction are euphemisms for a cosmic process.

"The Magician" (Section 5)

Zarathustra comes upon someone who is thrashing about like a madman and who finally falls flat on his stomach. The prophet says that this must be the higher man, whom he can perhaps help. This reminds us of the mistake made by the crowd in the Preface, who took the rope-dancer for the superman (313). But upon approaching closer, Zarathustra finds a trembling old man with staring eyes who will subsequently identify himself as "the penitent of the spirit" (318). The man seems not to know who is helping him and delivers a long lamentation (which is found in the *Nachlass* of 1888 entitled "Dionysus Dithyrambs" and described as a song sung by Zarathustra to endure his loneliness).

The burden of the lamentation is that the singer is being tortured by "the unknown – God" (314), who is trying to climb into his heart.

The singer says that the god has fled, and prays to him to return, "with all your tortures." "Oh, come back, my unknown God! My pain! My last – happiness!" (316–17). As the continuation will make clear, the singer is imitating, and also satirizing or playing with, Zarathustra. His lament describes in mocking terms how Zarathustra is tortured by his prophetic mission yet cannot exist without it. From one standpoint, then, the penitent of the spirit is related to the foaming fool.

Zarathustra interrupts angrily and asserts that he recognizes the singer, whom he calls an actor and a magician, among other things. The magician admits that he was playing, or, more precisely, acting: He was trying out for Zarathustra the part of the penitent of the spirit, "the poet and magician who finally turns his spirit against himself, the changed or converted man who freezes to death from his evil knowledge and conscience" (318). This is a satire on Zarathustra's loneliness, induced by his mission and his fear of the consequences of his doctrine. If this aspect of Zarathustra's spiritual experience is allowed to dominate, it will destroy him. The unknown god is destruction, not salvation.

At the same time the magician represents the fate of those who seek greatness in the age of the mob (319–20). He says that he seeks Zarathustra, who invites him to his cave and tells him to ask his animals, in particular the eagle and the serpent, for advice (320). The road to greatness, that is, away from the mob, lies in detaching oneself from contemporary society and passing through the curative dimension represented by the animals. Zarathustra's guests are fragments of his own nature who have to be purified and in that way reunited into his own destiny ("Become who you are").

In Section 6, Zarathustra encounters the last pope and invites him to his cave. The pope shares with Zarathustra a piety, in the one case for a dead God, in the other for the deification of what is highest in mankind. This is why the pope refers to Zarathustra as the most pious of those who do not believe in God (322). I pass directly to Section 7.

"The Ugliest Man" (Section 7)

Zarathustra enters a valley that stands for the kingdom of death and is called by the local shepherds "serpent death" because "a species of ugly thick green serpents came here to die when they had grown old" (327). In the vision of the gateway, a serpent representing the terrible doctrine of the eternal return was strangling a shepherd, who bit its head off in response to Zarathustra's invocation. The death of the serpent initiated a transformation of the shepherd into the superman. In the present section, the serpents die of old age; they stand for discarded interpretations of human existence. This is the setting for Zarathustra's encounter with the murderer of God.

Upon entering the valley, Zarathustra closes his eyes and sinks into a dark recollection; it seems to him that he has stood here before. He is surrounded by high-rising black and red cliffs; I believe that these are the same "wild cliffs" (201) that surrounded him upon the disappearance of the gateway and the sudden shift to the vision of the shepherd and the serpent fastened in his throat. But there is a crucial difference between this passage and its predecessor. The breaking of a table of values, or the destruction of a comprehensive interpretation of human existence, can be viewed either as an act of liberation – as the destruction that precedes creation – or as the desecration of what was once sacred and the source of vitality. On the second alternative, the murderer is the spirit of the civilization that once drew its vitality from that source; the murder is in other words a self-desecration.

This explains why the murderer of God is represented as the ugliest man, "shaped like a man and scarcely like a man, something unspeakable. And instantly Zarathustra was overcome by the great shame that he had seen something like this with his eyes; he blushed right up to his white hair, looked away and raised his foot so that he could leave this bad place" (328). This shame is the counterpart to the thirst Zarathustra felt for the laughter of the superman. He wishes to turn away with averted eyes from the terrible sight of the necessary preliminary to the longing for salvation.

As he is about to depart, however, a noise "gushed up gurgling and rattling from the ground, as water gurgles and rattles at night through stopped-up waterpipes." The ugliest man is attempting to speak; his voice comes from the ground because he is himself almost a corpse, belonging neither to the surface nor to the interior of the earth but to a desolate intermediate zone inhabited by the decaying remains of dying epochs. The entire scene must therefore be understood as a moment on the great circle of time. More concretely, it is Zarathustra's vision of the complement to the transfiguration of the shepherd into the superman.

The gurgling and rattling becomes a human voice that addresses Zarathustra: "Solve my riddle! Speak, speak! What is *vengeance against the witness*?" This corresponds to the riddle Zarathustra posed to the sailors, which he referred to as "the vision of the loneliest" (197). Zarathustra was the witness to the vision of the gateway, the shepherd, and the serpent. Now the ugliest man returns Zarathustra to the scene of his vision in order to take vengeance against him for his own participation in the death of God. This is not to contradict my earlier assertion that it is European mankind that has murdered God by an act of suicide or self-desecration. But Zarathustra is the murderer of God, and indeed of all gods, at the higher level of the witness to the doctrine of the eternal return. It is Zarathustra who identifies the ugliest man (namely, humanity) as the murderer of God.

The vengeance taken is the infliction of pity upon the Zarathustra who prides himself on his wisdom, as the ugliest man asserts. "As soon as Zarathustra had heard these words, – what do you think happened to his soul? *Pity overcame him,* and he sank down at once like an oak tree that has long withstood many woodcutters – heavily, immediately, terrifying even those who had wanted him to fall." In the motto for Part Four, taken from the earlier section "On the Blessed Isles," Zarathustra quotes the devil as saying, "God also has his hell; that is his love for mankind," and again, "God is dead; he died from his pity for mankind." The immediate reference is to Christ; the implied contrast to Christ is, however, not Dionysus, who never appears in *Zarathustra,* but the prophet himself, and behind him Nietzsche. Between the destruction of one table of values and the creation of another is the intermediate stage, represented in two different but complementary ways by "On the Vision and the Riddle" and "The Ugliest Man."

Each of the encounters in Part Four is with some aspect of himself that Nietzsche must overcome if he is to achieve his own salvation as the prophet of the eternal return and the superman. The final overcoming will take place in Zarathustra's cave, to which the prophet invites those whom he meets in his search for the higher man. Let me emphasize that Zarathustra is not simply a literary mask for Nietzsche; Nietzsche encompasses all of his dramatic characters, just as Plato encompasses all of the persons in his dialogues. Zarathustra is the highest and purest aspect of Nietzsche's spirit; he stands for what Nietzsche would wish himself to be but cannot become until he has integrated the disparate elements in his own nature. Otherwise stated, Nietzsche is still bound to the domain of decadence and death by the feeling of pity.

Zarathustra overcomes his momentary panic and rises to his feet with a hard look and a voice of bronze to identify the ugliest man: "*Thou art the murderer of God!* Let me go." The pity has not yet been overcome; it has only hardened into anger, which is a form of vengeance. He thus remains tied to the ugliest man and cannot leave, despite his wish to do so. The vengeance enacted against himself is like the bite of a dying serpent that infects him with the desire for vengeance in return. The ugliest man takes hold of Zarathustra's garment and bids him stay. He has solved (*errieth*) the riddle of the nature of the ax that struck down the prophet: Zarathustra guesses (*erriethest*) the *Mut,* the courage or spirit of him who has murdered God (329).

The emphasis on guessing, or solving riddles, underlines the connection between this section and the section on the gateway, the shepherd, and the serpent doctrine of the eternal return. We are in the domain of symbols, not of discursive arguments. Both Zarathustra and the ugliest man are riddles and solvers of riddles – riddles that we must ourselves decipher. Part of this riddle is the reference to the *Mut* of the ugliest man. Hitherto his ugliness has designated the pitiful face of self-desecration. But there is a kind of ugly courage or spiritedness implicit in the murder of God. This is brought out by his animated speech in response to Zarathustra's hard look and bronze words of accusation.

The *Mut* of the ugliest man is overwrought at the pity of his persecutors, which he seeks to escape by fleeing to Zarathustra. This is initially puzzling, since Zarathustra himself was felled by pity for the murderer of God, a pity that is still visible in the hardness and anger that ostensibly replaces it. This is brought out more clearly by the fact that Zarathustra was overcome with shame at the sight of something so ugly. It is precisely this shame that the ugliest man prefers to the pity of his persecutors. I understand this complex passage as follows. Zarathustra's shame arises first from the degradation of his vision by the sight of the ugliest man, but second from his solution to the riddle of the man's identity. In this second instance, the shame is directed against himself as contributor to the self-desecration of humanity. The murder of God, like any destruction of a table of values, is a desecration of the human spirit, however necessary an act of destruction as the precondition for the creation of new values.

Zarathustra is felled by pity when the ugliest man says that he has lured the prophet back into the valley as "vengeance against the witness." Zarathustra is the most articulate witness to the murder of God; as such, he shares in the responsibility for the crime, and in particular for the acceleration of its consequences. He pities the human generation that must undergo a lingering death, and in so pitying, he is pulled down to the level of the suffering of what must be overcome. Zarathustra is raised immediately by hardness, but this is not so much freedom from pity as its transformation into the desire for vengeance against the avenger. By denouncing the ugliest man and demanding to be released from his sight, Zarathustra indicates that he is still bound to him. The ugliest man clings to the shame that underlies these subtle transformations of spirit, because Zarathustra's tie to him is his own salvation.

It is of course true that the ugliest man denounces the pity of his persecutors and turns instead to Zarathustra's shame. But shame is more fundamental than pity. It plays an essential role in the very act of overcoming and so in the act of overcoming pity of a more superficial type. By this I refer to the difference between the pity for suffering and ugliness that binds us to the object of pity by our need to comfort it, and the pity that prevents us from remaining in the presence of something so shameful, thereby driving us to overcome or be free of it. We must remember that the production of a new race of higher men does nothing to mitigate the ugliness and suffering of the present race, except in the sense that destruction is salvation from that ugliness and suffering. By appealing to Zarathustra's shame, the ugliest man calls on what is deepest in the prophet rather than on what is more superficial. In so doing, however, he hopes to be rescued from the superficial condemnation of his ugliness by a recognition of the spiritedness of his act. This is connected to the figure of the tightrope-dancer in the Preface, who represents the highest manifestation of spiritedness in a decadent age, and whom Zarathustra honors accordingly.

The ugliest man thus says to Zarathustra: "Everyone else tossed me his alms, his pity, with looks and words. But for this – I am not beggar enough, thou hast guessed (*erriethest*) it – For this I am too rich, rich in what is great, frightening, ugliest, most inexpressible! Thy shame, O Zarathustra, honors me!" The ugliest man is the *Mut,* or spirit, of mankind in its most frightening and inexpressible form of the murder of what is highest in its own nature. This ugliness is the dark human side of the destructiveness of what Nietzsche calls elsewhere will to power but which is referred to in *Zarathustra* as overcoming and salvation. As the murderer of God, the ugliest man will die in one sense, namely, as the spirit of the present epoch of mankind. But as spiritedness, the ugliest man will himself be resurrected through the overcoming that is initiated by shame for "the little people" (330) of the present epoch. "Pity contradicts shame." It prevents overcoming through the very need to make good for the shameful. Pity for the ugliest man is finally Christian; it is like the healing of cripples, except that the ugliness is preserved rather than removed.

All this is made more or less explicit by the ugliest man's next speeches, which are a denunciation of Christ, "that wonderful holy man and spokesman for the little people." More interesting is what follows. After testifying to Zarathustra's repudiation of Christian pity and his shame before the shame of "the great sufferer" (Christ), as well as to his thesis that "all creators are hard, all great love transcends (*ist über*) its pity" (330–31), the ugliest man warns him, "Warn thyself against *thy* pity!" Zarathustra must guard against pity for the various figures whom he has invited to his cave; in particular, the ugliest man warns Zarathustra against himself. The ugliest man understands that the ax that felled Zarathustra was pity; by giving this warning, he implies that Zarathustra, despite his hardness, has not yet overcome that pity.

The final speech of the ugliest man is a justification of the murder of God, or alternatively of Christ. This God saw into the depths of human ugliness; nothing was concealed from him. "His pity knew no shame: He crawled into my dirtiest corner . . . He always saw me; on such a witness I willed to have vengeance – or myself not to live. The God who saw everything, *even human beings:* This God had to die! Mankind cannot *bear* it that such a witness live" (331). At a first reading, one could easily conclude that the ugliest man gives an exalted interpretation of his murder as an act of vengeance against the shamelessness of God. In other words, one could say that Nietzsche does not here represent the self-interpretation of the human spirit as that of self-satisfaction in the spirit of progress and material enlightenment. To the contrary, the ugliest man admits his own ugliness and shamefulness; what he repudiates is the right of a god to witness and pity it. On further reflection, however, I believe that this reading is inadequate.

The shamefulness and ugliness of human existence is itself a consequence of the Platonist and Christian interpretations of genesis and historical existence as a fallen domain. In order to restore the innocence of Becoming, eternity must be temporalized. In order to free humanity of its debasement, a reconciliation with life is required; this is one of the most important meanings of the doctrine of the eternal return. In the terms of an earlier discussion, the cripples must not be healed, because this implies a repudiation of their lameness as shameful and ugly or, equivalently, as pitiful. The ugliest man in effect attributes the murder of God to his own shame at being perceived as ugly. In so doing, he demonstrates that this murder is an act of desperation rather than of overcoming or transformation. The ugliest man continues to be ashamed of himself; what he requires is not forgiveness, but the purification of acceptance.

This must somehow be accomplished in the final scene. Zarathustra's response to the cry of distress of the higher man brings him into contact with the symbols of the pitiable residue of the present stage of mankind. We can now see the magnitude of the problem that Zarathustra faces. On the one hand, he must accept this residue or free it of sin and guilt and thereby integrate all aspects of human existence into an affirmation of the eternal return. On the other hand, the residue is ugly and shameful, thanks to the distortions intrinsic to Platonism and Christianity, distortions that have been exacerbated by late-modern decadence. As such, it cannot be used as the raw material for a transformation of humanity. He who would create must first destroy. It is of course easy to say that what must be destroyed is the table of values, not the persons who mistakenly submit to it. But this evades the point: The human spirit is defined by its values. Just as the prophet cannot himself enter into the promised land, neither can the generation that receives his prophecy.

Upon hearing the speech of the ugliest man, Zarathustra shivers down into his intestines, but prepares to depart. He invites the ugliest man to his cave. "Thou hast warned me from thy way. In thanks for that, I praise mine to thee." This praise is not simply verbal but consists in the adoption of a new way of life. The ugliest man has expelled himself from the human society that formed him by his murder of God. "Thou dost not will to live amongst men and human pity?[3] Very well! Do as I do! Thus learnest thou also from me; only the doer learns." This is the key to Nietzsche's rhetorical style in *Zarathustra*. Its goal is action, not theoretical persuasion. It remains to be seen what action Zarathustra has in mind for the ugliest man. But the first step will be to speak with Zarathustra's animals (332), or in other words to return to nature in order to purge the hideous distortions of contemporary European life.

In departing, Zarathustra muses to himself about the contradictory nature of the ugliest man, who both loves and despises himself. "I have found no one else who has despised himself more deeply; that too is height. Woe! Was *he* perhaps the higher man whose cry I heard? I love the great despisers. Man, however, is something that must be overcome." This confirms my interpretation of the ugliest man as analogous to the tightrope-dancer; both are expressions of the heights reached by a dying and trivial, or ugly, society.

"The Voluntary Beggar" (Section 8)

Zarathustra next encounters "the voluntary beggar," whom he refers to as "Berg-Prediger," "mountain preacher" (334), an obvious reference to the Sermon on the Mount. The beggar has fled the mob, the contemporary representation of the poor, who have rejected him. "It is no longer true that the poor are blessed. The kingdom of heaven is rather among the cows" (335), from whom human beings may learn how to overcome the great nausea by chewing the cud. The voluntary beggar represents in the first instance the fate of Christ in the nineteenth century. But as the next section will indicate, he is also a satire on the implications of Zarathustra's own teaching for the rabble (*Pöbel*). They must in some sense "chew the cud" if they are to be spared the great nausea instilled by the doctrine of the eternal return.

The beggar praises Zarathustra as "good, and better even than a cow" (337). The cows are a caricature of Zarathustra's own animals. Instead of pride and cunning, the beggar praises the "eternal return" of the cud, that is, of the life of the herd, which is a reinstitution of the cycle of nature understood as the suppression of continuous overcoming.

"The Shadow" (Section 9)

Shortly after having chased away the voluntary beggar, whom he has also invited to his cave, Zarathustra is accosted by another voice that identifies itself as his shadow (338). The prophet is annoyed by the rush of the crowd to his mountains and speaks to his heart: "Where has my solitude gone? . . . My kingdom is no longer of this world; I need new mountains." He then runs away from his shadow, which follows him, and is followed in turn by the voluntary beggar, who thus acquires the symbolic status of the shadow of Zarathustra's shadow. The mountains stand for the domain of Zarathustra's spirit or, in slightly different terms, the destiny of his mission; it is within this domain that he speaks to his heart of his personal destiny.

The shadow duplicates Zarathustra's steps but not his substance. He is the dark side of the prophetic mission who frightens and displeases Zarathustra by his ghostly appearance, "so thin, so dark, so hollow and used-up (*überlebt*)" (339). He is related to the spirit of heaviness, the dwarf who sat on Zarathustra's shoulders just prior to the vision of the gateway. Each of these figures asserts an essential thesis of Zarathustra's doctrine, but without his rhetoric of affirmation. The dwarf asserted the circularity of time; the shadow states the principle of nihilism: "Nothing is true; everything is permitted" (340). He has lost "the innocence of the good and their noble lies," that is, the salutary dimension of the Platonic rhetoric which Nietzsche himself employs in order to present Zarathustra as a teacher of salvation and overcoming.

The doctrine of the eternal return may be considered either a noble lie or a revelation of the insubstantial and dreamlike character of human existence: a shadow on the surface of chaos. Either it acquires eternity for mankind or replaces that acquisition with perpetual wandering. The shadow is the perpetual wanderer, the eternal Jew who is neither eternal nor a Jew (339): "Where is – my home? . . . O eternal everywhere, O eternal nowhere, O eternal – in vain!" (341). Zarathustra acknowledges the shadow as his own and warns it against succumbing to its restlessness by seeking security in the prison of a narrow belief, a doctrine that is a "harder, stronger madness" than Zarathustra's own teaching. In place of this prison of sleep, which corresponds to the chewing of the cud praised by the voluntary beggar, Zarathustra invites his shadow to join the other guests in his cave for an evening dance that will complete his solitary pursuit of the higher man.

The shadow and the beggar represent two possible consequences of Zarathustra's teaching. The affirmation of the eternal return may dissolve into nihilism; or else one may escape from nihilism into the cowlike tranquillity that itself caricatures the salutary effects of Zarathustra's animals. The herd of cows is the prison against which Zarathustra warns his shadow. The alternative to the prison cell is Zarathustra's cave, in which are gathered the various fragments of his own psyche that collectively constitute the higher man to whose cry of distress Zarathustra is attempting to respond. Once they have all been gathered, the fragments of the higher man will be cured of their various ailments by song and dance, not of course by doctrines or arguments, but by music, the greatest of the arts and so the greatest stimulus to life. This is the sense of Nietzsche's personal salvation and overcoming: What is in fragmentary form a cry of distress is unified by an act of the will into a harmony of affirmation.

"At Noon" (Section 10)

Zarathustra lies down at high noon under an old tree that is obscured by a grapevine; he is asleep, but his eyes are open and continue to regard and praise the tree and the "love of the grapevine," which embraces the tree (342). High noon is the moment of choice; the sleep of high noon stretches out Zarathustra's "strange" soul, makes it "long and weary." As we are about to see, Zarathustra must choose between remaining asleep or waking up to face the balance of his mission. Zarathustra's soul has been exhausted by its encounters with fragments of itself. But now the contraction of self-confrontation is over. He is alone with nature, resting from his dangerous journeys and contacts with human beings. In his sleep he asks himself whether he has not fallen into eternity (343). Again one thinks of the *Phaedrus*, in which Socrates and his companion also rest in the shade of a tree at high noon as they are about to stretch out their souls toward the hyperuranian realm of the Ideas.

In Socrates' myth of the soul as charioteer of two winged horses, the soul does not speak at all during its ascent to the eternity of hyperuranian beings. Zarathustra, on the other hand, talks continuously to his soul as he sleeps in the "stillness and secrecy" of the grass by the tree. Platonic Eros comes from outside and above the soul to raise it upward independent of the will of the lover. In the present text, it is sleep that comes from outside Zarathustra's soul and that must be overcome by the will to awaken. This decision is preceded by speech about silence; the speech indicates Zarathustra's weariness by equating happiness and eternity with silence. " 'How little suffices for happiness!' So I spoke once, and thought myself clever. But it was a blasphemy; I have learned *this* now. Clever fools speak better" (344).

Zarathustra asks himself whether his own prophetic teaching is not rather a blasphemy; note the reference to an *Augen-Blick,* a moment that is a look of the eye rather than a gateway into historical time,[4] and so not a doctrine of eternal return but an individual occurrence like the rustling of a lizard or a passing breeze. Perhaps eternity is accessible only through the silent acceptance of these moments. At this point in his soliloquy, Zarathustra is confused. It is not clear whether he refers to the past or to the present moment. "Quiet. What happened to me? Listen! Did time fly away? Do I not fall? Did I not fall? – listen! – into the well of eternity? – What is happening to me?"

We recall that Zarathustra is speaking here to his soul; he goes on to say that he has been stung in the heart: "Oh break to bits, break to bits, heart, after such happiness, after such a sting!" The image is violent and peculiar; there may be here an echo of the early image in the Preface of bees and the happiness of natural as distinct from creative labor. The breaking to bits of the heart would then signify a dissolution of personal mood analogous to the triumph of sleep over speech. The series of questions culminates in a virtually explicit reference to the eternal return: "What? Did the world not become indeed complete? Round and ripe?" This question also begins the soliloquy, which is devoted to the question of the mood or spirit in which to respond to the eternal return. "O golden round ripeness – where is it flying away? Shall I run after it? Hurry!"

The question is whether the solitary silence of immersion in the flow of time from moment to moment is not the only happiness and experience of eternity that is accessible to humanity. Otherwise stated, Zarathustra must decide whether to pursue the circle of time from within or outside its perimeter. If from within, then he can no longer preach the doctrine of the eternal return, which is fully intelligible only to those who are themselves outside the circle, on the mountain path looking down at the gateway of the moment.

Zarathustra's decision is to waken himself as soon as he realizes that he is asleep; in other words, to free himself by an act of will from the immobilism of merely natural mobility. He rouses himself to continue the journey. "Thou midday sleeper ... there is still a good piece of road ahead of thee – now how long hast thou slept out? Half an eternity!" The balance of the road will take Zarathustra back to his cave for the final overcoming of pity through reconciliation with the fragments of his soul, a reconciliation that will also bind together the fragments of his heart that were scattered by the sting of happiness. In an important sense, already introduced and to be repeated near the end of the book, Zarathustra affirms his work, not happiness, which is associated with sleep rather than with waking speech.

Zarathustra falls asleep again, and his soul alternates between attempting to awaken him and lying down herself. Again the question of the sleeper is posed: "Did not the world become complete?" This alternation will not be resolved until after the reconciliation in the cave. He is awakened decisively by a ray of sunshine that reminds us again of the Preface, in which Zarathustra talks to the morning sun of their common overripeness and need to give of their surplus to mankind. As one could express this, the need is Apollonian rather than Dionysian, because it requires Zarathustra to retain full self-consciousness.

He speaks to the heavens above him: "When will you drink this strange soul?" When will Zarathustra be assimilated into the completed eternity? He rises to continue, and notes that it is still high noon. The sleeping soliloquy was a kind of simulacrum of the *Augenblick*, a mirror image. Instead of entering into historical time, the dream is an entrance into eternity, an exit from human existence, a return to nature and solitude (like Rousseau's reveries of a solitary promenader). But Zarathustra rejects this and forces himself to awaken (345). Eternity is accessible to him not as a salvation but as a vantage point from which to understand his doctrine of salvation.

"The Greeting" (Section 11)

It is late afternoon, and Zarathustra returns to his cave without having found what he was looking for. Suddenly he hears "the great cry of need" coming from his own cave (346). This is where Zarathustra must overcome the last danger: pity, which has fatigued his soul and left him open to the temptation of rest, that is, of accepting half an eternity rather than striving for it in its entirety. The cry of need is in fact not one voice, but is composed of the voices of those whom Zarathustra encountered earlier in the day: (1) the king at the right and the king at the left, (2) the old magician, (3) the last pope, (4) the voluntary beggar, (5) the shadow, (6) the conscientious in spirit, (7) the sad soothsayer, (8) the ass, and (9) the ugliest man, who has adorned himself with a crown and two crimson belts to pretend that he is beautiful. Note that the ass has been separated from the two kings who led it in the original encounter with Zarathustra.

"In the midst of this grieving company stood Zarathustra's eagle, ruffled and restless, for he had been required to answer too many questions for which his pride had no answer. The clever serpent hung round his neck" (347). There is an indication here that the guests form a circle around the eagle, who is in turn encircled by the serpent. On the one hand, the guests represent the higher members of contemporary society, who have been pulled down to the earth by the dominance of the rabble. Their questions keep the eagle on the ground by counterbalancing his pride. On the other hand, the guests are fragments of Zarathustra's spirit, and as such are not only objects but manifestations of pity for those who must be canceled by the eternal return. The original order of Zarathustra's encounter with his guests was as follows: (1) the sad soothsayer, (2) two kings and the ass, (3) the conscientious in spirit (whose blood is sucked by leeches), (4) the magician, (5) the last pope, (6) the ugliest man (who killed God), (7) the voluntary beggar, (8) the shadow. The rearrangement seems arbitrary; there is no intrinsic order to the cluster surrounding the eagle because the guests have not yet been transformed by reconciliation.

Zarathustra had advised his guests (except for the shadow) to speak to the animals. Apparently they addressed themselves to the eagle; the serpent in any case is silent. This is very striking. The guests ask pride for a cure to their various ailments, but do not receive satisfactory answers. Perhaps pride is the precondition for the speech of the serpent rather than a discursive function of the eagle. The animals are able to console Zarathustra because the conflicts within his spirit are aspects of the pride that is intrinsic to his prophetic mission. By the same token, they do not genuinely understand that mission, even when they know the formulas from which its message is composed. What counts is not the assertion of propositions but the strength of will and integrity of spirit with which they are asserted.

Zarathustra examines the souls of his visitors and determines that they are in fact the higher man. To repeat, this has two meanings. First, the best specimens amongst Zarathustra's contemporaries are too decadent to serve as initiators of the epoch of the superman. Second, Zarathustra himself encompasses in his own soul all types of the higher man; but he himself suffers thereby from their defects. He goes on to say that someone must come to make them laugh again, "a good gay clown, a dancer and wind and wildcat, some old fool" (347). This is an ambiguous list; it recalls the contents of the coffins in the vision of the night watchman. The overall effect of the image is that of movement, playful and yet savage. We note that, having spoken, Zarathustra laughs from love and wickedness.

Zarathustra says that he speaks so playfully because he has been made brave by viewing the despair of his guests. In exchange for this gift, he urges them to take his hospitality and the protection of his wild animals for the night. He offers them first security and then his little finger. "And once you have *that,* take next the whole hand; go ahead! And the heart besides!" (348). The guests must proceed slowly, step by step, in their recuperation, which culminates in Zarathustra's heart (the organ of pity). The animals have not been of use in Zarathustra's absence. So the return to nature was of no avail, at least not in itself (just as Zarathustra could not sleep through all of eternity). Why then did he recommend that his guests consult his animals? For one thing, when he did so he did not yet understand that these persons were the higher men.

The first guest to speak is the king at the right. He praises Zarathustra's pride and compares him to a pine tree that grows up high in silence, hardness, and solitude. More precisely, Zarathustra has delighted the king by knowing how to humble himself with pride ("mit solchem Stolze zu erniedrigen": 348). The eagle does not know how to do this; he cannot lower himself. To the contrary, he raises the serpent up to the sky. But he was lowered by the despairing questions of the visitors to Zarathustra's cave. Zarathustra, on the contrary, has a heart that is lacking in comparison with the cold-blooded eagle. He combines humility and pride, at least in the king's account. Zarathustra is softer than the eagle. But what looks to the king like humility is a rhetorical concealment of Zarathustra's reaffirmation of his will to destroy as a precondition of creation. He will employ the rhetoric of the clown and the graceful motion of the dancer to beguile with laughter those whom he must destroy by a purgation of pity. The king failed to understand the inner truth of his initial comparison of Zarathustra to a pine tree.

The king goes on to say that those who have been filled with Zarathustra's honey cannot live without him. He refers to Zarathustra's absence by means of the image of death; Zarathustra must emerge from his solitude like a corpse leaving a broken tomb (again see the vision of the night watchman and the tomb song). He must be resurrected; he is the last remnant of God among men, their great hope (349–50). This explains why the eagle could not answer the questions of the guests. They are still Christians, still looking for a God to raise them from the baseness of their lives. The eagle was too harsh for them. It remains to be seen whether Zarathustra's playfulness is not the velvet glove hiding an iron fist.

Zarathustra will not allow the king to kiss his hand, but steps back and says that he will speak to them "deutsch und deutlich," in plain German. "It was not for you that I waited here in these mountains!"

(350). Note the left-hand king's aside on the German language; Nietzsche once said that the two best writers of German were himself and Heine[5] – the latter a Jew, the former a self-styled Pole. The "liberal" king approves of coarse German.

Zarathustra goes on with his speech. He makes clear that these visitors are, even if higher men, not high or strong enough for him. "Whoever himself stands on sick and tender bones, like you, wants above everything, whether he knows it or hides it from himself, that he be *spared.* But I do not spare my arms and my feet. *I do not spare warriors*" (350). As already noted, Zarathustra must have fresh, uncorrupted material with which to breed a new race. But the point goes deeper. Since the guests are all aspects of himself, he is himself too sick and too soft to be a superman. "I need a pure, smooth mirror for my teaching; on your surface, my own image is distorted." The guests contain the mob within themselves; this is why the ass is given a separate position in the list of guests.

In sum, these higher men are only bridges to still higher men for whom Zarathustra waits and for whom he will go down to the city for the last time: "*Laughing lions* must come" (351). Zarathustra longs for his children; but his children are not his contemporaries, even the best of whom have been poisoned by the great longing and nausea of Christianity. And he is in a crucial sense not his own contemporary; when Nietzsche speaks of himself as a man of tomorrow and the day after tomorrow, or as a posthumous man, he means that he cannot himself participate in the triumph of his doctrine.

"The Holy Communion" (Section 12)

Kaufmann translates this "The Last Supper." When Zarathustra has finished the speech to the visitors, the soothsayer demands supper, and in particular wine. The king at the left says that he and his brother have a whole assload of wine. All that is lacking is bread (353). The ass stands for the mob. Its load is wine; this is the vulgar version of Dionysian intoxication, namely, intoxication with or surrender to the mob. Note that the animals run away in fright when they hear the soothsayer; they realize that they have not gathered enough refreshment for the visitors. In other words, they cannot cure them of their ailments. Zarathustra has no bread: Man does not live by bread alone. This is of course a satire on the New Testament. Zarathustra adds the flesh of lambs to bread; the bread and wine of the holy sacrament is, as it were, replaced by meat and water (354: "Grind thy corn; drink thy water"); the cruelty and sobriety of nature replace the pity and intoxication of religion for the masses.

Exactly as in Plato's *Republic*, Zarathustra makes clear the link between meat-eating and war[6] that marks his own kind: "I am a law only
for those who are mine; I am not a law for all." "Wars and festivals,"
but not philosophy. The artist-soldier who dances and feasts at festivals
when he is not fighting is Nietzsche's replacement for the guardian of
Plato's *Republic*. Although this side of the guardian's nature is not
overlooked by Plato, it is emphasized to the exclusion of mathematics
and philosophy by Nietzsche. "The best belongs to me and mine; and
if one does not give it to us, we take it: – the best food, the purest sky,
the strongest thoughts, the most beautiful women!" (355).

The king at the right approves of Zarathustra's assertion of strength,
but the ass says "with wicked will, Eee–aah" (in German, *I–A*). The
braying of the ass underlines the fact that the king on the right has
misunderstood Zarathustra's description of his law by taking it literally.
It is not impossible that the initials "I–A" are intended to stand for *ich
auch*, "I also." More probably, the sound is an echo of "Ja" ("yes"). In
any case, the melodramatic bravado of Zarathustra's rhetoric is given a
counterpoint of absurdity by the braying of the ass. The satire on
the Last Supper is not an ontological transformation or reversal of
Christianity but an important indication by Nietzsche that irony and
foolishness are coordinate elements in the overcoming of pity for the
"higher" men of the present epoch. The braying of the ass is one
melodic line in the polyphony of salvation. Thus begins the long
supper "that is called 'the holy communion' in the history-books."

"On the Higher Men" (Section 13)

In this long section, Zarathustra takes the first step toward reconciliation with the higher men of the present epoch and so toward release
from pity. It is important to understand the inner dialectic of this
process. One might suppose that pity is an essential component of the
process of reconciliation with life. On the contrary; it is in fact the
repudiation of the innocence of the pitied, by an attribution to them
of negative value. At the same time, the affirmation of the totality of
temporal existence is intended by Nietzsche to serve as the liberation
of mankind from the vengeance against human suffering that is for
him implicit in Platonism and its vulgar counterpart, Christianity. But
this liberation is not intended as the justification of suffering; it is not
intended as the basis for a doctrine of equality, a doctrine that levels
all human beings and thereby makes all suffer through the absence of
rank-ordering, by the suppression of standards of nobility to which all
must be held accountable.

In short, the pitiful must be accepted as a natural consequence of human existence; but it must also be destroyed in order to make way for the creation of higher values that will themselves exclude or minimize pity by the imposition of a natural hardness that looks like cruelty and even savagery to the resident of the late-Christian epoch, but is for Nietzsche the indispensable complement to the birth of a race of warrior-artists. The key to what look like incompatible goals is the recognition that Nietzsche's task differs with respect to the past and the future. Zarathustra speaks to us from outside the gateway of the present moment, or what comes to the same thing, as standing in the gateway without having yet passed through. The present moment is not yet defined, except in its role as element in the structure of temporality and thereby as the moment of decision. The concrete historical future in which we arrive by passing through the moment of the present will be determined by our decision. But this decision will itself be determined by the success or failure of the prophetic mission of Zarathustra, and in that sense by what we may call, using Nietzsche's exoteric metaphor, his will to power.

To repeat, the teaching of the eternal return is necessary in order to liberate mankind from a life-diminishing eternity. But this is in turn necessary in order to make possible the self-assertion of humanity in an act of self-overcoming by way of the creation of new values: new in the sense that they repudiate the decadence of the past, not in the sense that they are unique. This is obvious from Nietzsche's praise of aristocratic values as they were manifested in previous epochs. The eternal return guarantees the finitude of values – the *oldness* of the new, as one could put it. But the teaching of the eternal return is also an obstacle to the invocation to self-transformation through a creative decision concerning the future. It supports instead Nietzsche's invocation to *amor fati*, whether in the Spinozistic sense of the love of divine necessity or in the Heideggerian sense of *Gelassenheit* (letting be) to the gifts of Being. Nietzsche can be understood as attempting to combine in one step the *Entschlossenheit* (resoluteness) and *Gelassenheit* that constitute two successive and mutually incompatible periods in Heidegger's development.

Two paths face the interpreter of Nietzsche. The first is to assume that Nietzsche either did not see, or could not eliminate, the contradiction between creative overcoming and the eternal return. The second is to distinguish between the different functions of the two doctrines. In the first case, Nietzsche is regarded as an incoherent thinker who is the prisoner of his own undisciplined rhetoric as epigrammatist in his other works and as pseudo-prophet in *Zarathustra*. In the second case, one follows the explicit indications in the Nietzschean corpus that he was engaged in an entirely self-conscious attempt to redefine the course of human history, an attempt that required him to alter his rhetoric in accord with the different segments of his audience, and the interpreter to identify the stages of this attempt as well as the rhetoric and doctrines that are appropriate to each stage.

In this book, as elsewhere, I have taken the second path. The reader will have to decide whether the evidence I present is convincing or not. But I need to make one point explicit. Whereas I believe that my assessment of Nietzsche's intentions is sound, this is a matter of secondary importance for my own intentions. The more interesting, and in fact the only philosophical, question is whether Nietzsche's enterprise is susceptible to the interpretation I have given it. Is there a teaching in Nietzsche that can be formulated in such a way as to rise above its inner incoherences and that deserves our closest attention and highest respect, a respect that includes the exercise of detailed textual interpretation and ruthless criticism? I answer in the affirmative. But I do not mean by this that the eternal return is at bottom compatible with the command of the philosophical prophet, *So soll es sein.*

We can see the coherence of Nietzsche's teaching if and only if we see that the love of fate and the will to create are embedded in two distinct rhetorics, each addressed to a different aspect of his audience. I do not mean by this simply that Nietzsche had one doctrine for the few and another for the many, although he made it quite clear that this was indeed the case: "Everything rare for the rare." The two different aspects to which I refer here are aspects of each of us and so of the souls of those who constitute the happy few – foremost among them, Nietzsche himself. Human happiness depends upon two distinct stages, one of them an act of understanding and the other an act of will. The act of understanding coincides with remembering; the act of will coincides with forgetting. We must understand the eternal return as the doctrine that liberates us from God and the Greek nature for the act of forgetfulness toward the past that is identical with the creation of a healthy and dynamic future.

In short, Nietzsche possesses a coherent overall intention which is rendered ambiguous by the inner contradiction between fate and chance, that is, between the eternal return and will, or, in one last formulation, between remembering and forgetting. In my opinion, the ambiguity deepens into theoretical incoherence: Chaos is not a satisfactory ground for rank-ordering. Nietzsche's doctrine is from this standpoint a kind of aristocratic or pagan version of secularized Christianity in which humanity replaces God and the will replaces the intellect. But Christianity rests upon a miracle, not a discursive account of the whole. Nietzsche presents us with the strange spectacle of a self-professed philosopher who seems to mask his philosophy by the founding of a new religion. As a prophet, he possesses the further peculiarity that his revelation contains multiple expressions of doubt, not merely with respect to the fallibility of mankind, but concerning the truth of his own teaching.

All this is by way of summary and preface to the concluding events of *Zarathustra*. My remarks were necessary in order for us to make sense out of the apparently disorganized and episodic, even incoherent, scenes that follow, with their strange blending of pathos and exultation, vulgar satire and dignified exhortation, and the ostensible vision of happiness even as Zarathustra is rejecting happiness on behalf of his work. It looks almost as though Nietzsche is attempting to hypnotize the reader into accepting the affirmation of Zarathustra by immersing us in a carnival of the absurd. Instead of succumbing, let us do Nietzsche the higher honor of keeping our wits about us.

In the first of twenty numbered subsections, Zarathustra sets the stage for the entire speech. He draws a sharp contrast between his behavior in the marketplace as described in the Preface and the present soliloquy. Originally Zarathustra spoke to the citizenry of the town called Motley Cow, who mistook his description of the superman for an account of the rope-dancer. Now he repudiates the public, or mob, and speaks directly to the representatives of the higher men (356). The difference between the two scenes is not so much in the content of the prophecy as in Zarathustra's own attitude. In the earlier scene, Zarathustra learns very quickly that the public is not prepared for his message of overcoming. At first glance it might seem that in the present scene Zarathustra speaks to the higher men in the belief that they will understand him and enact his teaching. If this is true, then Zarathustra must be unusually naive; Nietzsche could have no such anticipation, as he makes clear from the general carnival nature of the episode and the comical, even grotesque, forms he gives to the personages representing the higher men.

At no point in *Zarathustra* could one say that the prophet is correctly understood by any of his interlocutors, whether singly or in groups. The inner dynamic of the work is one of frank revelation, received with incomprehension or, what is even worse, miscomprehension, followed by Zarathustra's repudiation of his attempt to be understood and a return to solitude. Among the most powerful of the individual sections in the work are those that make clear the extraordinary obstacles faced by Nietzsche in the attempt to carry out his philosophico-prophetic revolution, obstacles that include the terrifying nature of the key elements of the prophetic doctrine itself. It is highly unlikely that Zarathustra, after all these experiences and repudiations of his own disciples, should at the present moment seriously believe that he will accomplish his purpose in addressing the higher men, if by "purpose" one means the effective communication of the inner truth of human existence. And the opposite can be demonstrated from the text.

The speech to the higher men is in principle a request that they transform their contempt for mankind into reverence, not for the higher man, but for the superman (357). Zarathustra is asking the higher men to destroy themselves for the sake of the superman. They are to be the apostles of salvation for the next generation, not for themselves; the last supper is truly to be the last for them. Zarathustra delivers this message of self-destruction in so many words; but he partially camouflages it by also praising the nature of the genuinely higher men in order to raise the possibility for his audience that he is speaking about them. The praise of the higher men is sincere as directed toward beings who do not yet exist and whom Nietzsche symbolizes with the expression "superman." It could not possibly apply to the various figures assembled in Zarathustra's cave, as is very appropriately indicated by the leitmotif of the braying ass.

Zarathustra's speech rehearses the radical corruption of contemporary society by doctrines of egalitarianism that are easily understood as secularizations of Christianity, but hardly, it is important to note, of Platonism. Zarathustra's denunciation of the mob, together with the present rulers of the mob, is not only Platonic in spirit (analogous passages may be found in the *Republic* and the *Statesman*) but is also addressed to the higher men themselves. When Zarathustra repudiates "long mob ears" (356) and asserts that "this is not said for long ears; not every word belongs in every mouth" (359), he is certainly alluding to the ears of the jackass that belong symbolically to each of his interlocutors. The inner truth of Zarathustra's words is addressed to a future that will itself come about only on condition that the leaders of the mob cease to exist. This is what Zarathustra means when he says, "And truly, I love ye for not knowing how to live today, ye higher men" (358). In asking these "higher men" to overcome the leaders of the mob, Zarathustra is asking them to destroy themselves.

If it were not for the preposterous misrepresentations of the contemporary Nietzscheans of the left, it would scarcely be necessary to point out the radically Platonist nature of Zarathustra's aristocratic politics. Of course, Zarathustra's Platonism is inflected by what one might call a tincture of Machiavellianism. In order for the human race to overcome, it must first grow still more evil. I take this in two senses. First, the more radical the decline, the more rapid the destruction of contemporary society. Second and more profoundly, one cannot rise beyond good and evil by doing good, but only by doing evil. We do evil by freeing ourselves from current standards of good and evil; by doing good, we simply adhere to those standards.

One could object to this that there is a higher sense of "good" that exists beyond good and evil, and I would agree. But the point is that one cannot reach that higher sense in a single affirmative step. It is always necessary to prepare the ground for the ascent beyond good and evil by a radical step of destruction, namely, the destruction of the leaders of the mob. Zarathustra must overcome pity in order to sanction this radical destruction which, as I have already had occasion to note, is also an act of self-destruction. Apropos the warning about long ears, it is worth noting again Zarathustra's very striking use of extreme frankness in the midst of concealing rhetoric. Thus Zarathustra quite explicitly refers to the need for the higher men, whom he is ostensibly praising, to perish. They radically misunderstand him if they believe that he has come to set right what they have done wrong, to free them from suffering and to set them on new paths. "Ever more, ever better members of your species must be destroyed" (*sollen zu Grunde gehen:* 359).

Zarathustra goes on to state that he wants the members of his immediate audience to be blinded by the lightning of his wisdom. He then warns them to restrict their will to their capacity (*Vermögen:* 360). There should be no doubt here that he is condemning rather than praising the higher men; but to the ears of a jackass, anything is possible. Zarathustra speaks past them to genuinely higher men, and in particular he discusses honesty. He first praises honesty, but in a strange way: "Be prudent, you higher men, for nothing is today more priceless and rare than *Redlichkeit*"; sincerity, integrity as well as honesty. But today *Redlichkeit* is clearly impossible, because "today" belongs to the mob (360). In the very next section, Zarathustra says: "Have today a good mistrust, you higher men, you stout-hearted ones! You open-hearted ones! And keep your *Gründe* secret! This today belongs to the people!" *Gründe* means principles, but also the foundations or grounds of one's being. The same word was used in the singular on the preceding page to refer to the necessary destruction of members of the same species.

In this subsection (9), there is a slight but significant shift in Zarathustra's rhetoric which makes it difficult to distinguish between the higher men of the future and those whom he is now addressing. The intention is to muffle the frankness with which Zarathustra has just condemned his audience. We must not forget that he wishes to drive these higher men to their destruction by intensifying their evil actions while at the same time indicating their baseness and vulgarity. This is a striking, and at the same time confusing, instance of Nietzsche's version of traditional esotericism, which he discusses in Sections 25–30 of *Beyond Good and Evil.* Nietzsche conceals, not by indirection alone, but also by shouting the truth at the top of his voice. One could easily receive the impression that Nietzsche is not himself always in control of his two different voices. My own impression is that the rapid shift from one register to the other is part of the conscious intention to project an atmosphere of carnival, of rapid motions to and fro, of dancing and singing as opposed to sober argument. The atmosphere of forced absurdity and satire is directed to the ears of the jackass; it carries quite another message to the Hyperborean.

The courageous and open-hearted higher man must keep secret the inner ground of Zarathustra's speech. This is in no way a restriction on *Redlichkeit,* as Zarathustra makes clear with respect to the scholars, who hate the higher men because of their own sterility: "Such men boast that they do not lie, but an inability to lie is far from the love of truth. Watch your step!" (361). In other words, frankness and bombastic rhetoric are not simple expressions of honesty. Nietzsche keeps his *Gründe* secret, not by never mentioning them, but by concealing them beneath diverse rhetorical masks. In the present instance, it is difficult for the audience to distinguish between what Zarathustra is saying about them (they must be overcome) and about the genuinely higher men. But we must remember this at all times when reading Nietzsche: "He who cannot lie does not know what truth is."

Subsections 10 and 11 emphasize the independence of the creator; one gives birth only to one's own child and not "for" anyone. Subsection 12 is more interesting: "Who must give birth is sick; who, however, has given birth is unclean" (362). This is tacitly connected with the discussion of lying. The newborn child has to be washed clean of the filth that accumulates in the process of birth. These three parts continue Zarathustra's frankness about the need to destroy in order to create. In 13, the tone shifts to caution. Zarathustra recommends that the creators walk in the footprints of their fathers' virtues and says that they cannot ascend without carrying the will of their fathers (363). I take him to be saying that not every superior person is capable of rising to the height of the superman; that of which we are capable is a function of our tradition. This sounds like an anticipation of Heidegger's *Entschlossenheit* within the possibilities accessible to one's own tradition. The genuine creator, on the other hand, has no father but is born *ex nihilo* in the wake of radical decadence.

Subsection 14 is a transitional section in Zarathustra's speech from denunciation of the mob to an invocation of laughter and dancing. Life is compared to a perpetual game of chance in which one must play and mock (364); what is from the cosmological standpoint chaos can be interpreted by human beings in two different ways: as fate or chance. These are for us the same because, even though everything eternally recurs, we who sit at the gaming table do not know how the dice will fall in the next throw. Since life is for us a game, we must both wager and mock at ourselves for wagering in what is, after all, a rigged game. After this blunt assessment, Zarathustra shifts immediately into the rhetoric of exaltation; the failure of the higher men is a half-success because it expresses itself as an inner pressure toward the future of humanity. What Nietzsche elsewhere calls will to power is here presented as the self-deprecatory and ironical urge of the gambler.

Zarathustra's praise of laughter deviates from both Platonism and Christianity. Plato's Socrates laughs only twice, on the day of his death (*Phaedo*); he is never presented as weeping. Christ, on the other hand, never laughs and weeps thrice. There is then a closer relationship between Zarathustra and Plato on this point, as subsection 16 makes especially clear with its critical allusion to Christ's denunciation of laughter as the greatest sin to have appeared on earth (365). On the other hand, Zarathustra deviates from Plato in his excessive reliance upon laughter as the purgation of failure. From this standpoint, Christianity could perhaps be called Nietzscheanism for the masses, since it evokes pity for what Nietzsche mocks. Both constitute a repudiation of the seriousness of human existence; both offer a higher stage of existence as retribution for earthly failure.

I want to underline the following remark in 16: "All great love does not *want* (*will*) love: – it wants more" (365). This is important for the assessment of Zarathustra's frequent invocations of love and giving. The "more" means "more power," that is, the acceptance by others of one's "gift." In general, the creator is motivated by the desire to transform humanity, but not by love of this or that human being. Hence there is no personal tragedy in failure, and so one may laugh at it. Laughter as it were transforms walking into running and dancing (365–66). Zarathustra the dancer is crowned with a rose wreath of laughter; again, he is a replacement for the weeping prophet who wears a crown of thorns. The sad clowns (367) of contemporary humanity must be repudiated by Zarathustra himself, the wind that rushes out of mountain caves to sweep away his audience in dance. The concluding subsection 20 raises the pitch of the rhetoric of enthusiasm as Zarathustra urges the higher men to laugh away the failure of their lives.

"The Song of Melancholy" (Section 14)

After delivering the "sermon" (as we may call it) to the higher men, Zarathustra must leave his cave for fresh air; he calls his animals to him: The higher men smelled bad, but the animals smell good: "Now I know and I feel for the first time how I love you, my animals" (369). Again the animals are connected with healing or purification. They could not fulfill this function for the defective higher men, and they can do so only to a certain extent for Zarathustra. They can refresh him after his contact with human beings, but they cannot truly understand him or enact his teaching.

In Zarathustra's absence, the old magician speaks. He is the penitent of the spirit who copies and satirizes Zarathustra's prophetic poetry, and in particular his loneliness. The magician sang previously of his longing for an unknown God (Section 5). Now he attributes "the great nausea" to himself and the other guests (370). The magician claims to love Zarathustra, who fills him with melancholy. He represents the darker side of Zarathustra's laughter; his melancholy reveals what is concealed within the self-mockery recommended by the prophet as the purgation of failure. The balance of the section contains a song of melancholy sung by the magician in Zarathustra's absence.

The most interesting theme in this poem is the expression of mistrust for the poet, who is not a seeker after truth, but a liar. This reminds us of Zarathustra's earlier assertions that poets lie too much and that he is a poet. The poet is a fool who wears a mask and lyingly pretends to be a seeker after truth (371–72).

"On Science" (Section 15)

The magician is disputed by the conscientious in spirit, who previously defended the narrow but secure foundation of a scientific specialization, a foundation that gives security by sucking the blood of its devotee; that is, leaving him with no strength for anything else. The conscientious man turns to Zarathustra as a source of still greater security (376); the scientific need for certitude is like that of the religious man, except that science seeks security in the mastery of nature, whereas religion seeks security in the master of nature. The magician, on the contrary, seeks insecurity or danger; this is because he believes in nothing, neither in science nor in religion, and seeks an unknown God.

Zarathustra enters and denounces the celebration of fear just presented by the conscientious man; he attributes man's ascent to courage

(377). Once again the visitors praise Zarathustra and seem to effect a reconciliation with him; but he once more feels the need to leave the cave for fresh air and the company of his animals (378). Zarathustra is not having much success in the purification or healing of his disparate selves, namely, the corrupt higher men of the day.

"Among Daughters of the Wilderness" (Section 16)

Zarathustra's shadow persuades him to remain in the cave. The shadow finds the air in the cave better than anywhere else in the world, with the exception of the vicinity of the daughters of the wilderness, to whom he once composed a song which he now sings (379–80). I remind the reader that the shadow is the only guest whom Zarathustra did not advise to consult with his animals. The shadow seems to be a caricature of Nietzsche's persona as cultivated philologist. The daughters of the wilderness, whom the shadow says that he loved, are not European, but Oriental (380): They are distinct from Nietzsche's own cultural and *wissenschaftliche* formation. As exotic creatures, they represent something fresh and unfamiliar and are therefore invigorating.

African animals figure in the initial stanza, to be followed by reference to an oasis. The exact continent is not important: Asia or Africa; the song is directed beyond Europe. The reference to the animals is probably a satire on Zarathustra's own animals. The image of the oasis that turns into a whale reminds us of the Book of Jonah in the Old Testament. Jonah declines to follow God's orders and flees on a ship, but is cast overboard during a storm and swallowed by a whale. After praying to God, Jonah is released. Note the shadow's remark: "You understand my learned allusion?" (381). Here the whale is an oasis that unites the shadow with the attractive and exotic girls.

Disobedience to God means here repudiation of the prophetic mission, or decadence. In slightly different terms, the repudiation of the doubt-ridden Europe is also a surrender to mere aesthetic play, that is, a repudiation of the will to overcome. After some playful stanzas that it would be obtuse of us to analyze (even if there are some concealed references in the images), the shadow admits that he cannot escape his European heritage: the howling of dignity, virtue, and morality: "European ardor, European voraciousness" (385). The howling of a moral lion (again a caricature of the lion in Zarathustra's own imagery) is the European response to the exotic daughters of the wilderness. European decadence cannot free itself from the excessive seriousness and restlessness of the modern Western soul; it cannot attain even to a satirical version of Zarathustra's Asiatic dancing.

"The Awakening" (Section 17)

Zarathustra's guests begin to talk and laugh all at once; even the ass is moved to join its braying to the confusion. This pleases the prophet by its gaiety, which he takes as a sign of the guests' convalescence, but which nevertheless instills "a small aversion and derision" toward them (386). He leaves the cave in order to converse with his animals. The transition corresponds to a shift in Zarathustra's soul from the residue of spiritual decadence to the natural powers of pride and cunning. The eagle and the serpent are offended by the air in the cave during the visit of the higher men, whose questions they cannot answer. Zarathustra must interpret the behavior of the higher men to the animals, who cannot themselves cure the visitors of their ailment. The visitors have no direct access to the natural powers of the soul.

Once outside the cave, Zarathustra is freed from his "small disgust" and explains to the animals that the higher men have "unlearned" from him the cry of distress, if not crying. This is probably a reference to the shift from the original perception of despair to the carnival mood of the absurd that will culminate in the Ass Festival. The repeated braying of the ass is a sign of inverted or masked distress, not genuine convalescence. As Zarathustra puts this initially to his animals, even if his guests have learned to laugh from him, "It is yet not *my* laughing that they learned" (386). The most they can do is to imitate or satirize his doctrines. In this they resemble the animals, except that the animals do not laugh, but only talk or mimic Zarathustra.

Zarathustra goes on to say that the spirits of heaviness and nausea are retreating from his guests. He claims this as his triumph, but he uses ambiguous language to describe its results. "They are biting; my bait works" (387). This is an echo of Jesus the fisher of souls; that the reference is not one of enlightenment is made clear by Zarathustra's subsequent remark: "They celebrate and chew the cud; they become *thankful*. In a short time they will think up festivals and put up memorial stones to their old friends." The convalescence of the higher men is a loss of self-understanding, represented by the shift from the cry of distress to the celebration of the absurd. The Ass Festival is a caricature of Zarathustra's dancing and singing.

Suddenly the laughter and talk cease, and Zarathustra smells incense. He sneaks back to the entrance to observe the behavior of his guests. "They have all become *pious*, they *pray*, they are mad!" (388). This confirms my previous remark; the higher men are worshiping the ass. We are reminded of Moses watching the fall of the Hebrews back into idolatry. The cud-chewers worship the ass, the beast of burden who is loaded with wine, in other words, the mob or the burden of tradition that makes the higher men forget the will to overcome. But the cud chewed by the higher men in their convalescence is no longer that of the Christian tradition. It is a caricature of Zarathustra's joy at the overcoming of humanity. The convalescence of the higher men is in fact death, if a death masked by carnival.

It is quite significant that the ugliest man, namely, the murderer of God, is the one who delivers the eulogy to the ass. This is like the myth of Er in Plato's *Republic;* the soul of the most just citizen in the previous incarnation chooses the life of the tyrant for the next cycle of existence. The liturgy requires no analysis; it is a caricature, but makes the serious point that the ass has created the world in his own image, "namely, [to be] as stupid as possible" (389).

"The Ass Festival" (Section 18)

Zarathustra is unable to master himself and breaks into the litany with a cry of "Eee-Aah" (390). His guests have gone mad; in order to attract their attention, Zarathustra must imitate the sound of their idol. He asks his guests in turn how they could have succumbed to ass worship. The pope says that he is more enlightened than Zarathustra with respect to gods: "Better to worship God in this form than in no form" (*Gestalt:* 390). By *Gestalt* he clearly means corporeal appearance; the claim that God is *Geist* was the biggest possible leap to disbelief. In an age of materialism, there cannot be spirit worship except of the "spirit" of modern progress, the spirit of the mob, which is represented by the ass.

The shadow blames his piety on the ugliest man, the murderer of God, who he says has awakened God once more. "Death is with respect to gods always a prejudice" (391). This may mean that man is by nature a religious animal and that the destruction of one god is always the creation of another. The ugliest man is the modern nihilist; in place of the old god, he substitutes the deity of absurdism. The conscientious in spirit (the narrow scientific specialist) finds something pleasing to his conscience in the spectacle of ass worship. God is said to be eternal; whoever has that much time takes his time "as slowly and as stupidly as possible." The ass is the conscientious man's surrogate for the eternal return: for a "stupid" or purposeless iteration of random patterns of motion.

The ugliest man says that he has learned from Zarathustra that laughter, not anger, is the best means of murder. Perhaps the Ass Festival is a necessary part of the process of enforcing the death of God, namely, by transforming religion into absurdity (392). At this point Zarathustra breaks off the interrogation of his guests and denounces them collectively as children, with an allusion to the New Testament. Children enter *that* heaven, but men are required to inherit the earth (393). But then, apparently quite inconsistently, Zarathustra says how much he likes the higher men since they have become gay again. He says that they require new festivals as part of their convalescence and urges them to remember him when they repeat their Ass Festival (393–94).

The general sense seems to be as follows. The consequence of decadence is nihilism. This is initially marked by solemnity and even desperation. In order to purify this desperation, one must undergo the intermediate stage of the celebration of absurdity; one must see the absurdity, not merely of the dying age, but of one's excessively violent responses to it. For these responses are reactive and thus marked by the defects of the age rather than by the spirit of overcoming. But the transitional stage of absurdity is a very dangerous one if we remain in it too long; witness the worst excesses of twentieth-century efforts to transform despair into creation simply by the instruments of absurdity. The carnival is one step removed from the madhouse.

"The Sleepwalker Song" (Section 19)

In the Schlechta edition of Nietzsche's works, this episode is entitled "The Drunken Song" (*Das trunkne Lied*) and is translated accordingly by Kaufmann. In the Colli-Montinari edition, the title is *Das Nachtwandler-Lied,* which I translate. I have found no explanation for this change in title in Montinari's philological notes.[7] The earlier title could give rise to misinterpretation of the fact that Zarathustra is said to be "like a drunkard" (396). But he is not said to be drunk or even to have taken any wine. The speech he gives is that of a sleepwalker, and as such it is more like a prophecy than an illusion or drunken hallucination. This is not a genuinely Dionysian speech.

Zarathustra again tells himself how much he likes the higher men; they are outside the cave and wrapped in the "secrecy" (395) of the night. Then the most amazing event of the amazing day occurs. The ugliest man begins to gurgle and snort, and all at once his voice sounds deep and clear with a question. He asks the others what they think of the fact that "for the sake of this day, I am for the first time glad that I have lived my entire life" (395). He repeats Zarathustra's earlier statement from "The Vision and the Riddle": " 'Was that – life?' I want to say to death, 'Very well, then! Once more!' " (396). This assertion initiates the outburst of drinking and reveling among the higher men, and their surge of affection and gratitude for Zarathustra.

The whole scene is not and cannot be a genuine transfiguration. It is part of the Ass Festival; the affirmation of life is part of the caricature of Zarathustra's doctrine. At the very least, the entire episode indicates that the transfiguration of mankind rests upon the interchangeability of Zarathustra's teaching with the cry of the ass, which the prophet imitated in order to attract the attention of his maddened guests. Happiness and reconciliation with the earth are as much delusions as were Christianity and the longing for heaven. Man is the cud-chewing animal; the deepest secret of Zarathustra's doctrine is that the same holds true of the superman. Note the closing lines of subsection 1 of this section. The ass may have danced, but if not, "as Zarathustra's proverb has it, 'What does it matter!' "

Now Zarathustra stands like a drunken man, in response to the ugliest man's words; his spirit flies off to a remote distance, "between past and future wandering like a heavy cloud" (397). Zarathustra is about to have a vision. He is himself in an unstable present, not in the gateway of the moment, but in a dreamlike condition that imitates it. He speaks as if in a trance: "Come! Come! We are approaching midnight!" Zarathustra invokes his companions to wander in the night. This is the reverse of resting beneath a shade tree at high noon. The speech to follow is not illuminated by the sun but disguised by the refracted light of the moon. The atmosphere of madness has not abated.

Zarathustra's speech evokes the eternal return and echoes the language of "The Vision and the Riddle." This is a dream, a prophecy rather than a perception, and a fantasy rather than a prophecy. Zarathustra whispers into the ears of his audience "as secretly, as terrifyingly, as heartily as that midnight bell spoke to me" (398). His lucidity is demonstrated by his recognition that the higher men are marked by a leg, not a wing; they cannot fly high enough (398–99). In the balance of the song, there are rapid fluctuations between joy and sorrow. Zarathustra repudiates the day in favor of the night; he prefers solitude to action: "Leave me! Leave me! I am too pure for you," he says to the day (400). Just before, he spoke of the drunken joy of dying at midnight; just after, he says that he is no god; his happiness and sorrow are deep, but not as deep as those of a god (401).

Zarathustra goes on to say that he has not been understood by the higher men. He asserts his will to life and expresses this with the cry of woe: "I want heirs, so speaks everything that suffers; I want children, I do not want myself." But this is immediately followed by the counterassertion of *Lust;* Kaufmann is right not to translate this as "pleasure." "Joy" is better, or "delight." "Joy, however, does not want heirs or children. Joy wants itself, eternity, return, everything eternally the same" (402). In the next two sections, Zarathustra harmonizes, or reconciles, these two opposites. All joy wants eternity (402); but even further, it wants *all* things, and therefore suffering as well as joy. This is what it means to say, "Once more" to life (403). The last section expresses in verse the fundamental thought of the dream/vision. In the affirmation of the eternal return, joy overcomes woe (*Weh:* 404).

"The Sign" (Section 20)

It is the following morning; Zarathustra is refreshed and comes out of his cave like a glowing sun. As a sun, he speaks to the sun above his cave, repeating words spoken in the opening scene of the work. The sun's happiness depends upon those whom it illuminates (405). Zarathustra has still not found the proper recipients for his gift; he states explicitly that the higher men, who continue to sleep in the cave, are not those recipients. In other words, despite the events and speeches recorded in the entire work, everything lies ahead.

Zarathustra affirms that he has the right animals, mentioning the eagle in particular. "But I still lack my right humans" (406). Suddenly he receives a sign: He is surrounded by a flock of birds and finds himself next to a lion. The lion and the doves lie down together: Compare "Caesar with the soul of Christ" (406–407). Zarathustra takes the sign to mean that his children are near.

Next the higher men emerge from the cave and are frightened away by the lion; in fact, the former disappear (407: "im Nu verschwinden"). Zarathustra makes explicit the significance of this episode. He has been cured of pity for the higher men of his own time. He is now entirely free from the imperfections of the contemporary age. And there follows a repetition of the earlier "Hegelian" assertion: "My suffering and my pity – what does that matter! Do I think about *happiness*? I think about my *Work!*" (408). This is in a way an expression of anti-Platonism and an affirmation of the fundamental modern principle of production.

"Rise now, you great noon!" Zarathustra is referring to the immediate future as the time in which his work will be fulfilled. He goes forth glowing like a sun. As for ourselves, the last residents of the modern age, we are left with the braying of the ass.

CONCLUSION

From the very beginning of the European tradition, both poets and philosophers have spoken of the illusory, dreamlike character of human life. In general, the poets have lamented the insubstantiality of this dream, whereas the philosophers have taken it as the necessary, even trivial, consequence of a higher or deeper truth. Modern science, which begins with a synthesis of classical atomism, experimentation, and mathematical modeling, brings a new note of exaltation to the reductive analysis of the myth of the given. Recognition that life is a dream is obliterated by the apparent access to ultimate mastery of nature. Not much attention is directed by enthusiasts of science to the fact that the dream of mastery is itself a dream within a dream, and so an image of an image, or what postmodernists call a simulacrum.

Nietzsche derives both his originality and his depth from the combination of the poetic vision of the tragedy of the dream and the scientific exaltation of the mastery to which it is a gateway. In a decisive exercise of what he himself calls the transvaluation of values, however, Nietzsche associates science with despair and poetry with exaltation. Stated more precisely, the despair or nihilism that is the necessary consequence of the scientific world view, together with its technological, industrial, and political implications, is to be transformed through the interpretation of science as a species of poetry. But Nietzsche vitiates the sense or (in his key term) value of artistic creation by a radical intensification of the scientific thesis that life in general, and so consciousness in particular, is nothing but a random accumulation and discharge of points of force. Science reduces secondary attributes to the primary attributes of extension, figure, and motion. Nietzsche takes the next step and reduces extension, figure, and motion to chaos.

The doctrine of primeval chaos is in itself compatible with a variety of postulates about the status of human creativity; it could be argued (and Nietzsche makes use of this argument from time to time) that human creativity depends on primeval chaos, or freedom from the order of the supernatural on the one hand and the natural on the other. Something like this argument is to be found in Kant's celebration of the spontaneity of reason, although it is not creativity so much as transcendental constitution that Kant wishes to establish. Otherwise stated, Kant distinguishes between the phenomena of human experience and the noumena, or things in themselves, not between phenomena and intrinsic chaos.

The deconstruction of the noumena, whether these be understood as things in themselves or the ultimate particles of matter, leaves open the understanding of chaos as necessity or chance. Scientifically grounded determinism is predicated upon the independence of mathematics from chaos. Nietzsche rejects this independence by reducing mathematics to the status of interpretation or, in my previous formulation, poetry. It is thus open to him to assert the primacy of chance as the source of human freedom and hence of the creation of values. Instead, Nietzsche once more engages in a transvaluation of values and applies the *amor fati*, or the strict determinism of mathematical rationalism, to the consequences of his poetic prophecy of contingency and illusion.

We can approach the resulting problem most expeditiously by noting that the doctrine of the eternal return is incompatible with the doctrine of free choice. In addition, very far from serving as the basis for the validation of human creations, it vitiates, even negates, that validation. The same contradiction is contained in the doctrine of the will to power. What is intended to express the impulse of creation, and so to underlie the distinction between the noble and the base, proves to be incapable of sustaining that distinction. The noble is the expression of power, but power is itself employed either nobly or basely. If one reserves the affirmative sense of power for noble creations, but glosses nobility as power, one has argued in a circle, a circle as vitiating of human freedom as the circle of the eternal return.

We thus find two fundamental doctrines at the bottom of Nietzsche's thought. The first doctrine tells us that life is an illusion, along with the philosophical and scientific interpretations of genuine order and intelligibility. According to this doctrine, chance is a mask for necessity; we and our interpretations are random fluctuations of chaos, but random fluctuations that recur forever in a unique and fated manner. The second doctrine tells us that humanity cannot exist on the basis of the truth and so must be persuaded of a noble lie, namely, the lie that the identity of chance and necessity on the one hand and the accumulation and discharge of force on the other can serve as the basis for a creative transvaluation of values: for the overcoming of decadent nineteenth-century humanity and the advent of the superman.

These two doctrines are not mutually contradictory. They become so only when we ourselves succumb to the rhetoric of Nietzsche's noble lie and attempt to derive freedom and the creation of noble rank-ordering from the eternal return and the will to power. Nietzsche's teaching is obscure and often seems to be incoherent, because he takes the drastic step of announcing both these doctrines publicly and in such a way as to encourage us to draw what is an incoherent inference of the one from the other. One may justify Nietzsche's confusing procedure by attributing to him the conviction that the frightening truth is required in order to free humanity from the decadent and stultifying remains of a dying civilization, whereas the noble lie is required in order to conceal the deeper nihilism intrinsic in the destructive or purificatory doctrine. I have argued that this was indeed Nietzsche's intention, but I have also attempted to demonstrate in considerable detail the instability and even the extreme danger inherent in his complicated enterprise.

In order to carry out his intention, namely, to speak simultaneously to the few and the many, Nietzsche is forced to employ a double rhetoric, a rhetoric that juxtaposes the registers of despair and exaltation, or of what Leibniz called pessimism and optimism. In *Beyond Good and Evil*, Nietzsche discusses at length and in detail the distinction between the esoteric and the exoteric, which he connects with a doctrine of masks. In *Lectures on the History of Philosophy*, Hegel denies the ancient contention that Plato practiced esotericism with the assertion that philosophers cannot keep their ideas concealed in their pockets. In the same paragraph, however, he goes on to say that philosophy is by its nature esoteric;[1] as Nietzsche might put this, "Everything rare for the rare."

Nietzsche's practice of esotericism is in one sense Platonic; in another, Hegelian. As he himself makes explicit on numerous occasions, Nietzsche's enterprise is Platonic in that he wishes to create by legislation a new race of human beings. In order to accomplish this, he must destroy the already existing race; he who would create must first destroy. But the existing race, even if it is partially immobilized by the death wish of decadence, is not yet prepared to destroy itself; or rather, self-destruction in this case is identical with a lingering death. Hence Nietzsche must have recourse to the noble lie. On the other hand, Nietzsche's esotericism is Hegelian; he is convinced that he cannot keep his ideas in his pocket if he is to accomplish the destructive act upon which creation depends.

In no sense would I deny that for Nietzsche there are deep truths, perceptions, and experiences that are by their nature reserved for the rare or the few. But Nietzsche is the first major thinker to employ what others have preserved for the rare in a teaching directed to the many or, perhaps more accurately, to the spokesmen for the many. Nietzsche is the first to transform esotericism into an exoteric doctrine. The immediate justification for this step is that it is necessary in order to persuade the representatives of the many that they are in fact the few, or in other words putative supermen. The danger of this step, regularly indicated by Nietzsche in *Zarathustra,* is that the transformation of esotericism into exotericism leads to the debasement of the first by the second. Otherwise put, Nietzsche's disciples are caricatures of the superman. The nobility of the noble lie is thus transformed, contrary to Nietzsche's intentions, into baseness, or what is synonymous with baseness: the inability to distinguish it from nobility.

One way to bring out the radical difference between Plato and Nietzsche is by reflecting on the expression "noble lie." If a lie is noble, then there is a difference between nobility and baseness that cannot be reduced to chaos or derived from the expression of accumulated power. Nietzsche's perception of nobility suffers from two internal flaws that render it unstable. On the one hand, he combines a classical elegance and *Heiterkeit,* or serene distance, with the sensibility of late-modern skepticism. On the other hand, his perception of human existence is decisively colored by the ideology of nineteenth-century materialism, which is incapable of encompassing the concept of nobility, even when it attempts to apply that concept to itself.

Once we have penetrated Nietzsche's double rhetoric and become accustomed to the mask behind the mask, we are startled by the absence of a stable human visage; Nietzsche's most profound insights are sustained by nothing more than the reverberations of chaos. To say this is not to repudiate Nietzsche's profundity but to come once more into contact with the pervasive emptiness of a radical skepticism for which we are such stuff as dreams are made on. The exquisite subtlety of the deconstructive analysis of human illusion can neither explain nor justify the nobility of the character that endures the truth while dwelling beyond good and evil in the land of the Hyperboreans. If philosophy is possible, or in other words if Nietzsche's teaching may speak some part of the truth, then part of what it says is a lie. The noble cannot be reduced to power. The attempt so to reduce it is a sufficient explanation for the failure of Nietzsche's revolution.

There is, however, a more general problem raised by the Nietzschean enterprise. I have already referred to it as the explicit transformation of the esoteric into the exoteric. Nietzsche attempts not so much to effect an exoteric safeguard for the esoteric practice of philosophy as to identify the esoteric and the exoteric. The clarion call to a self-overcoming of human beings, whether with reference to the superman or to the philosophers of the future, is virtually indistinguishable in essence from the Marxist attempt to free humanity from history and class consciousness and so to transform every person into a philosopher of the future who, in the famous expression, will hunt in the morning, fish in the afternoon, and read Kant in the evening.

Nietzsche is both more elegant and more skeptical than Marx, and his doctrines, although blatantly, even explicitly, political, are more amenable to the distortions imposed by the aesthetics of the individual than are those of his prophetic competitor. Life is not a dream for the robust Marx, who continues to be sustained in the exigencies of human existence by the divine afflatus of Hegelian dialectic, whether authentic or inverted. In my opinion, however, Nietzsche's doctrines are at least as dangerous politically as those of Marx, and in a post-Marxist epoch, obviously even more so. Once the Marxist dream of wakefulness is punctured, the temptation intensifies to turn to the Nietzschean effort to derive individual significance from chaos. In this parlous epoch, one quickly forgets that it is impossible to pull a rabbit out of an empty hat. That Nietzsche himself had not altogether forgotten this is represented by the braying of the ass in Part Four of *Zarathustra*.

Beyond every positive doctrine enunciated by Nietzsche, whether directly or indirectly, is his fascination – one might even say obsession – with the psychology of the exceptional human being, or those to whom he refers as "the happy few." It is this fascination that serves as the basis for Nietzsche's philosophy of rank-ordering. Far more instructive than the myths of the will to power and the eternal return is Nietzsche's portrait of the philosophical nature. With all its compelling beauty and profundity, Nietzsche's portrait is a distortion of the Platonic conception he attempted to assimilate.

By his reduction of mathematics to the status of a perspective or interpretation, Nietzsche teaches us better than anyone else the consequences of the modern establishment of mathematics as the paradigm of rationality. He is entirely correct to show us that mathematics is incapable of pronouncing upon its own nobility, and so that it cannot serve as the paradigm of rationality without sundering truth and goodness. Nietzsche's anti-Platonism could be symbolized by saying that he accepts the story of Plato's lecture on the Good as devoted to geometry, and reverses the thesis to give paramountcy to poetry. The will, closely followed by the imagination, usurps the function of a reason that is incapable of asserting the goodness of reason. As we have learned to our misfortune, however, the will and the imagination are capable of providing only willful and imaginary rank-orderings. This clears the world-historical stage for the triumph of sentimentality masked as fairness.

The decisive problem for the next philosophical generation is to separate justice from pity and shame. This will not be possible without a reconstitution of reason that enables us to perceive once more the common root of truth and goodness. That root was once known as philosophy. Nietzsche bears a heavy burden of guilt for the radical deterioration in the second half of the twentieth century of our understanding of the nature of philosophy, but his guilt does not spring up *ex nihilo*. The source lies in the early-modern separation of mathematics and poetry, of which the late-modern consequence is the identification of mathematics and poetry. The problem will certainly not be resolved by a reactionary rejection of modernity and a sentimental return to the past. Man is not a crab; but neither is he a mole. It is time to reexamine the Enlightenment with open eyes, free of ideology and jargon, whether this jargon stems from poetry or mathematics. At his best, this is the direction in which Nietzsche points us. At his worst, he points us toward narcissism. As long as the higher men are hypnotized by simulacra of their own cleverness, we will continue to dwell in the epoch of the last men.

NOTES

Introduction

1. *Oeuvres,* ed. C. Adam and P. Tannery, 12 vols. (J. Vrin, Paris, 1964–74), vol. x, 213 (dating from 1619).
2. See esp. ibid., III, 297–98.
3. All citations from Nietzsche, unless otherwise indicated, are from the *Kritische Studienausgabe* of the *Sämtliche Werke,* ed. G. Colli and M. Montinari, 14 vols. (Walter de Gruyter, Berlin, 1980). Works will be cited by volume, page, and section number, together with the date of composition in the case of entries from the Notebooks. The present citation from *Götzen-Dämmerung* is from VI, 152, *Streifzüge,* 50.
4. Wolfgang Müller-Lauter was one of the first to emphasize this aspect of Nietzsche's teaching. As representative of his work, I cite "Nietzsches Lehre vom Willen zur Macht," *Nietzsche-Studien,* 3 (1974), 1–60.
5. *Menschliches, Allzumenschliches,* XI, 512, pt. II, 324; *Nachlass,* Spring 1884, XI, 69, 25 (210).
6. *Nachlass,* 1885, XI, 439, 34 (65).
7. *Jenseits von Gut und Böse,* V, 205, 9, 257.
8. *Nachlass,* 1888, XIII, 481, 15 (120).
9. IX, 306, 6 (421), and 319, 7 (14).
10. "Es giebt nichts am Leben, was Werth hat, ausser dem Grade der Macht – gesetzt eben, das Leben selbst der Wille zur Macht ist." *Nachlass,* 1886/87, XII, 215, 5 (71). Cf. *Jenseits,* V, 27, 1, no. 9, and *Der Antichrist,* V, 170, no. 2, with *Nachlass,* 1887/88, XIII, 192, 11 (414).
11. "Gesammt-Einsicht. Thatsächlich bringt jedes grosse Wachsthum auch ein ungeheures Abbröckeln und Vergehen mit sich: das Leiden, die Sympto-

251

men des Niedergangs gehören in die Zeiten ungeheuren Vorwärtsgehen."
Nachlass, 1887, XII, 468, 10 (22). Note the generality of the formulation,
and cf. XIII, 87, 11 (226), from the *Nachlass* of 1887/88. For the relation
between nihilism and decadence, cf. *Nachlass*, 1888, XIII, 265, 14 (86),
where Nietzsche says that nihilism is the logic of decadence, with *Götzen-
Dämmerung* (VI, 134, no. 135), where he defines decadence as follows:
"Nichts ist etwas werth."

12. Alexander Nehamas is right to emphasize Nietzsche's "stylistic pluralism,"
but on my view this pluralism is not a sign of perspectivism; instead it is a
key to Nietzsche's authorial intentions. See Nehamas, *Nietzsche: Life as
Literature* (Harvard University Press, Cambridge, Mass., 1985), pp. 8, 18,
40.

13. XII, 350–51, 9 (35).

14. For Nietzsche's self-identification as a nihilist, see the *Nachlass* from 1887,
XII, 407, 9 (23). In a letter to Malwida von Meysenberg of 18 October
1888, he states that he is the most extreme instance of decadence (*Sämtliche Briefe, Kritische Studienausgabe*, 8 vols. [Walter de Gruyter, Berlin,
1986], VIII, 452; hereafter cited as *SB*). In *Der Fall Wagner* (VI, 11),
Nietzsche says that he and Wagner were both decadent children of their
age, but that he (unlike Wagner) was protected against decadence "by the
philosopher in me." In *Der Antichrist* (VI, 172, 6) he equates decadence
values with nihilism.

15. *Nachlass*, 1887/88, XIII, 189f., 11 (411). Cf. the letter to Köselitz of 13
March 1888 (*SB*, VI, 68).

16. *Die Vernunft in der Geschichte*, ed. J. Hoffmeister (Felix Meiner, Hamburg,
1955), p. 30.

17. *Nachlass*, 1885, XI, 547, 35 (82). The square brackets indicate my own
addition for syntactic clarity; the angle brackets indicate an addition by
the editors of Nietzsche's text.

18. XII, 201, 5 (71).

19. *Nachlass*, 1886/87, XII, 213, 5 (71).

20. *Nachlass*, 1883, X, 244, 7 (21).

21. Cf. the letter of 20 December 1887 to Köselitz (*SB*, VIII, 213) with
Nachlass, 1882/83, X, 109, 4 (1).

22. For characteristic statements, see *Götzen-Dämmerung*, VI, 153, *Streifzüge*, 51;
Nachlass, 1887, XIII, 194; *Ecce Homo*, VI, 259, *Vorwort* 4.

23. "Die Sprache Luthers und die poetische Form der Bibel als Grundlage
einer neuen deutschen *Poesie* – das ist meine Erfindung!" *Nachlass*, 1884,
XI, 60, 25 (173).

24. See *Götzen-Dämmerung*, VI, 86, *Moral* 5: One must be outside life in order
to touch the problem of its value. This is an extremely important indication that Nietzsche was not a prisoner of an "engaged" historical perspective.

25. Bernard Pautrat is therefore right to call our attention to "l'incohérence
ou le chaos qui règne à tous les niveaux de la langue" (*Versions du soleil*
[Éditions du Minuit, Paris, 1971], p. 195); he is thus also in principle

right to attribute an inner logocentrism to Nietzsche. I see this as a mark of Nietzsche's incoherence, whereas for Pautrat it is an (unexplained) emblem of Nietzsche's superiority as a thinker.

26. *Nachlass*, 1886, XII, 190, 5 (16). For a study that stresses the relation between the eternal return and modern physics, see Günter Abel, *Nietzsche: Die Dynamik der Willen zur Macht und die ewige Wiederkehr* (Walter de Gruyter, Berlin, 1984).

27. See Pierre Klossowski, *Nietzsche et le cercle vicieux*, rev. and corrected ed. (Mercure de France, Paris, 1975), p. 58.

28. Thus interpretations like that of Bernard Pautrat, which take their bearings by the doctrines of Derridian deconstruction, fail to exclude the philosopher, and so Nietzsche himself, from the intrahistorical "decentering" or fragmenting of the subject into a multiplicity of perspectives; see *Versions du soleil*, pp. 280f. On the other hand, Pautrat observes that whereas there are as many suns as philosophies, the "philosophy" of Nietzsche includes them all because it shows them the *règle du jeu* (p. 294).

29. Gilles Deleuze is right to emphasize the importance of genealogy for Nietzsche and the "valeur de l'origine et origine des valeurs," but by characterizing the subsequent creation as free of vengeance and ressentiment, he inadvertently collapses the difference between what he calls the "élément differentiel" (will to power in its cosmological function as differentiation of accumulations of force: pp. 2, 7) and "l'élément pratique de la *différence:* objet d'affirmation et de jouissance" (p. 10). Citations are from *Nietzsche et la philosophie* (PUF, Paris, 1962). It should also be emphasized that the concept of origination does not function in Nietzsche to validate a doctrine of radical originality in the sense endorsed by Deleuze. Genealogy is able to play its role precisely because there is a finite structure in history that renders it intelligible.

30. *Nachlass*, 1887/88, XIII, 194, 11 (415). Cf. 227, 14 (21).

31. See *Nachlass*, 1876/77, VIII, 463, 23 (159).

32. *Genoi hoios essi mathōn: Pythians* 2, 72. This expression is sometimes translated erroneously as "Become whom thou art," but *hoios* means "what sort," and *mathōn* means "by understanding." The underlying implication of the whole expression is that of fulfilling one's nature.

33. *Introduction à la lecture de Hegel* (Gallimard, Paris, 1976), p. 40.

34. As Bernd Magnus argues in *Nietzsche's Existential Imperative* (Indiana University Press, Bloomington, 1978).

35. As Abel argues in *Nietzsche*.

36. See Alastair Moles, *Nietzsche's Philosophy of Nature and Cosmology* (Peter Lang, New York, 1990), p. 295.

37. It may well be true that each artwork is unique. But each artwork is an instance of a fundamental type. To "create" oneself, assuming that this is possible, is to exemplify a type. For this reason, art remains subject to the comprehensive interpretation of the philosopher. On this point I disagree with Nehamas, *Nietzsche*, p. 8, even though I endorse his valuable observation that one cannot give general directions for becoming an individual.

Nehamas exaggerates the importance of the paradigm of the literary text for Nietzsche because he overlooks Nietzsche's continuous subordination of art to philosophy.

38. *Nietzsches Philosophie der ewigen Wiederkehr des Gleichen* (Kohlhammer, Stuttgart, 1956), pp. 13f.

39. I both agree and disagree with Gianni Vattimo when he says that the eternal return is not a concept to be analyzed logically, "ma un annuncio che propone un esperimento, un mutamento pratico radicale del modo di essere dell'uomo" (*Il soggetto e la maschera* [Bompiani, Milan, 1974], p. 274).

40. Cf. Jean Granier, *Le problème de la vérité dans la philosophie de Nietzsche* (Éditions du Seuil, Paris, 1969), p. 401.

41. I can express my fundamental difference with Lawrence Lampert's excellent study *Nietzsche's Teaching* (Yale University Press, New Haven, 1986) by denying his thesis that the eternal return gives "a new grounding of normative thinking" (p. 279).

42. For Nietzsche's Greek antecedents on this point, see my article "Suspicion, Deception, and Concealment," *Arion*, Spring 1991, pp. 112–27.

43. On this point I am in close agreement with Lawrence Lampert, despite all differences between us on the success of Nietzsche's esoteric, or comprehensive, teaching.

44. *SB*, VI, 499, May 1884, to Malwida von Meysenberg.

45. *Nietzsche*, 2 vols. (G. Neske, Pfullingen, 1961), I, 21.

46. *SB*, VI, 496.

47. *SB*, VIII, 209.

48. X, 519, 16 (60).

49. IX, 519–20, 11 (197).

50. *SB*, VI, 326.

51. I would therefore disagree with Lampert's statement that the overriding theme of Part Two is wisdom: *Nietzsche's Teaching*, p. 84.

52. *Wissenschaft der Logik*, 2 vols. (Felix Meiner, Leipzig, 1970), I, 31.

53. *SB*, VI, 445.

54. IX, 519f., 11 (97).

55. Letter to von Gersdorff, 12 February 1885, in *SB*, VII, 9. See also Montinari's philological comments on the text in vol. XIV of the *Studienausgabe;* for the present point, p. 282.

56. *SB*, VIII, 222.

57. X, 522–23, 16 (165).

58. Ibid.

59. Keith Ansell-Pearson, *Nietzsche Contra Rousseau* (Cambridge University Press, Cambridge, 1991), pp. 155f.

60. See again Montinari's notes in XIV, 280.

61. In order to appreciate the resemblance of the doctrine of the eternal return to Hegel's doctrine of the circularity of the concept, one should read the closing pages of the *Wissenschaft der Logik* and in particular the discussion of the identity of progress and return in the sequence of the process of emerging determinations of the world: "Das rückwärts gehende

Begründen des Anfangs, und das vorwärts gehende Weiterbestimmen desselben ineinander fällt und dasselbe ist," and so on (vol. II, 503). My point is of course not that Nietzsche was a Hegelian but that resonances of the central notions of Hegelianism are found in Nietzsche's most personal thoughts. Eternal recurrence is as much the condition for Nietzsche's philosophical grasp of totality as is the circularity of the concept, with its attendant notion of the completeness and repetition of history, for Hegel. But Nietzsche replaces logic by art and rhetoric; otherwise stated, he emancipates the will. One should also consider here Hegel's own statement on the role of the will: "Nur der Entschluss, den man auch für eine Willkür ansehen kann, nämlich dass man das Denken als solches betrachten wolle, ist vorhanden" (vol. I, 54). Cf. the *Enzyklopädie* of 1830 (Felix Meiner, Hamburg, 1969), p. 50, para. 17.

62. *Zur Genealogie der Moral*, V, 337, pt. II, para. 25.

63. *SB*, VI, 449.

64. *Nachlass*, 1884, XI, 83, 25 (277).

Chapter 1

1. Numbers in parentheses refer to pages of *KSA*, vol. IV, unless otherwise indicated.

2. See here *Götzen-Dämmerung*, VI, 168: Culture takes time; at thirty, one is a child.

3. One should consult here para. 30 of *Jenseits von Gut und Böse*. See also *Conversations with Nietzsche*, ed. Sander Gilman and trans. David J. Parent (Oxford University Press, New York, 1987), p. 115, where Ida Overbeck attributes the following observation to Nietzsche: "Good is nothing; what we must strive for is nobility, which also does justice to evil."

4. For a sensitive treatment of references to Zarathustra's soul, see Alan White's *Inside Nietzsche's Labyrinth* (Routledge, New York, 1990).

5. A major problem in translating *Zarathustra* into English is Nietzsche's frequent use of the familiar forms of the second person. These forms sound extremely awkward to the contemporary English-speaker and may even interfere with the easy assimilation of Nietzsche's sense. One can therefore sympathize with translators like Walter Kaufmann who avoid the familiar altogether. It is, however, not satisfactory to follow this procedure consistently when citing Nietzsche in English, as the use of the familiar may be a significant element in the sense of the passage. I have retained the familiar form whenever it seemed important to do so, and often enough to give the flavor of the original, but not consistently. Hereafter, when the sense is not an issue, I have allowed my ear, rather than the rules of grammar, to be my guide.

6. *Götzen-Dämmerung*, VI, 156.

7. "Allerdings nur solange Dasein *ist* . . . 'gibt es' Sein," *Sein und Zeit* (Max Niemeyer, Tübingen, 1977), p. 212.

8. *Metaphysics* A, 982b27ff.

9. XI, 289, 27, 60.

10. V, 336, pt. II, no. 24.

11. III, 586, no. 360.

12. V, 75–77, para. 58.

13. IX, 666, 17/43 (*Nachlass*, 1882).

14. See *Götzen-Dämmerung*, para. 7, on the thinker (VI, 109f.).

15. On the significance of music in Nietzsche, see the remarkable essay by Michael Gillespie, "Nietzsche's Musical Politics," in *Nietzsche's New Seas*, ed. Gillespie and Tracy Strong (University of Chicago Press, Chicago, 1988). Bernard Pautrat (*Versions du soleil* [Éditions du Minuit, Paris, 1971], pp. 69ff.) sees Nietzsche's praise of music as an expression of his opposition to logocentrism, but an opposition that fails to elude metaphysics because it replaces the dominance of speech by that of music. Gillespie, on the other hand, shows how music is employed by *logos* in the expression of discursive structure.

16. See *Jenseits*, pt. IV, no. 153: "Was aus Liebe gethan wird, geschieht immer jenseits von Gut und Böse" (V, 99).

17. *SB*, V, 335.

18. VI, 11.

19. XIII, 227, 14 (21) (1887/88).

20. Ibid., 194, 11 (415).

21. Cf. Eugen Fink, *Nietzsches Philosophie* (Kohlhammer, Stuttgart, 1960), p. 127.

22. See *Götzen-Dämmerung*, VI, 150, *Streifzüge*, 48, for the sense in which Nietzsche advocates a return to nature, and *Nachlass*, 1887, in XII, 42, for a remark about the denaturing of nineteenth-century humankind.

23. *Götzen-Dämmerung*, VI, 152, *Streifzüge*, 50.

24. Ibid., 144, *Streifzüge*, 43.

25. III, 480–82.

26. See Stephen R. Aschheim, *The Nietzsche Legacy in Germany, 1890–1990* (University of California Press, Berkeley and Los Angeles, 1992).

27. It is worth noting the presence of this problem in Georg Lukács's *Geschichte und Klassenbewusstsein* (Luchterhand, Neuwied, 1968). Lukács exemplifies the Marxist version of the philosopher as prophet-lawgiver who faces the problem of the relation between history and necessity and cannot resolve it. See Lukács's original assertions to the effect that there is no natural-law guarantee of the success of the revolution, but only a dialectical guarantee that must be enacted by living it and that depends on the will of the proletariat (pp. 216, 245). Compare his later recantation (pp. 18–20): In response to official party criticism, Lukács conceded that the original text suffered from the un-Marxist tendency to see Marxism exclusively as *Gesellschaftslehre* (the doctrine of society) and thus to ignore its connection to nature. The failure to bring out the mediation between nature and society in work led him to lapse into Idealism (pp. 18–20).

28. On this point, see Karl Löwith, *Nietzsches Philosophie der ewigen Wiederkehr des Gleichen* (Kohlhammer, Stuttgart, 1956), pp. 23–26.

29. *Götzen-Dämmerung*, VI, 120–21, *Streifzüge*, 14.

30. See also *Jenseits*, v, 21, 1, 9.
31. Consider the following important passage from the 1886 *Nachlass*: "Weshalb es heute nötig ist, zeitweilig grob zu reden und grob zu handeln. Etwas Feines und Verschwiegenes wird nicht mehr verstanden, selbst nicht von denen, welche uns verwandt sind. *Wovon man nicht laut spricht und schreit, das ist nicht da . . .*": xii, 41, 1 (134).
32. See *Grundlinien des Philosophie des Rechts* (Felix Meiner, Hamburg, 1955), paras. 181ff. (civil society links the family to the state) and 270 (the state is the rational actualization of the Idea).
33. *Politics,* ii, 1264a24–27.
34. The importance given to genealogy by postmodernists like Foucault cannot be explained simply by reference to Deleuze. It is in my opinion closely connected to the role played by phenomenological description in the development of postmodernism, as derived from Hegel on the one hand (via Alexandre Kojève) and a Heideggerianized Husserl on the other (one should not forget that Maurice Merleau-Ponty was a student of Kojève's). The deeper link between genealogical description and positivism also helps to explain Foucault's favorable reception by analytical philosophers.
35. E.g., x, 347, 8 (26) (*Nachlass,* 1883).
36. See, for example, xii, 41, 1 (128) (*Nachlass,* 1885/86).
37. xii, 45, 1 (154).
38. xii, 280, 7 (6).
39. See esp. xii, 468, 10 (22) (*Nachlass,* 1887), and xiii, 87, 11 (226) (*Nachlass,* 1887/88).
40. This refers, of course, not to an epochally new beginning in the Heideggerian sense but to some new version of what has occurred previously an infinite number of times.
41. *Zur Genealogie der Moral*, v, 344, pt. iii, no. 5.
42. *Götzen-Dämmerung,* vi, 127, *Streifzüge,* 24.
43. One has to distinguish between Nietzsche's global political thinking, or what I would call the *grosse Politik* of Platonism, and his various views on particular political issues of his time. The *grosse Politik* is the same as the prophetic lawgiving of the philosopher. It is not itself an artifact, but it makes use of artifacts. A useful book that approaches Nietzsche from somewhere between the two aforementioned perspectives is Henning Ottman's *Philosophie und Politik bei Nietzsche* (Walter de Gruyter, Berlin, 1987). If we understand *Kultur* as the German equivalent to the Greek *paideia,* then Ottman is right to say that "was Nietzsche suchte, war die Überwindung der Entfremdung, die Wiedergewinnung der allseitigen Persönlichkeit und der Dominanz der Kultur über Ökonomie und Politik" (p. 29). See also Ottman's remark that Nietzsche is not so far from Plato *in politicis* (p. 45).
44. See Robert Pippin, "Irony and Affirmation in Nietzsche's *Thus Spoke Zarathustra,*" in *Nietzsche's New Seas,* ed. Gillespie and Strong, pp. 50f.
45. *Jenseits,* v, 79, para. 60; cf. *Nachlass* 1883, x, 244, 7 (21).

46. *Jenseits*, v, 142f., para. 210.

47. In addition to the previously cited book by Ottman, one may recommend Leslie Paul Thiele's *Friedrich Nietzsche and the Politics of the Soul* (Princeton University Press, Princeton, 1990) and Tracy Strong's expanded edition of *Friedrich Nietzsche and the Politics of Transfiguration* (University of California Press, Berkeley and Los Angeles, 1988) for studies that place Nietzsche's political thought in a broader philosophical context. A still more general but valuable approach is to be found in the essays of Volker Gerhardt: *Pathos und Distanz* (Reclam, Stuttgart, 1988).

48. For a more elaborate account, see my book *The Question of Being* (Yale University Press, New Haven, 1993).

49. XII, 187, 5 (9) (*Nachlass, 1886/87*).

50. XI, 661, 40 (61) (*Nachlass, 1885*).

51. XIII, 261, 14 (81) (*Nachlass, 1888*).

52. XII, 119, 2 (114) (*Nachlass, 1885/86*).

53. "Es giebt nichts am Leben, was Werth hat, ausser dem Grade der Macht – gesetzt eben, dass Leben selbst der Wille zur Macht ist": XII, 215, 5 (71) (*Nachlass, 1886/87*). Cf. XII, 25, 1 (58): *"Der Mensch, als einer Vielheit von 'Willen zur Macht'. . . "* For the identity between the world as will to power and as chaos, see XI, 611, 38 (12) (*Nachlass, 1885*), and *Die fröhliche Wissenschaft*, III, 468, pt. III, para. 109.

54. *Die fröhliche Wissenschaft*, III, 422, pt. II, para. 58.

55. "Die Krankheit selbst kann ein Stimulans des Lebens sein; nur muss man gesund genug für diese Stimulans sein!" (*Der Fall Wagner*, VI, 22, para. 5).

56. See, inter alia, X, 93, 25 (314) (*Nachlass, 1884*); XII, 106, 2 (90) (*Nachlass, 1885/86*); *Götzen-Dämmerung*, VI, 76, para. 3.

57. *Jenseits*, v, 57, pt. II, para. 40.

58. I cannot resist the pleasure of citing a line by the American poet Allen Tate: "We are the eyelids of defeated caves," which expresses in unusually condensed form the decadent conclusion to the Platonic foundation of philosophical politics.

59. See my article "The Golden Apple," *Arion*, Winter, 1990, pp. 187–207.

60. *SB*, VI, 326, 10 February 1883, to Overbeck: "Alle meine menschlichen Beziehungen, mit einer Maske von mir zu thun haben." *Morgenröte*, III, 12, Preface: "Denn wer auf solchen eignen Wegen geht, begegnet Niemandem: das bringen die 'eignen Wege' mit sich."

61. See the two letters to Overbeck of 7 June and 12 November 1887, *SB*, VIII, 93 and 196.

62. In this connection, see Karsten Harries's interesting essay "The Philosopher at Sea," in *Nietzsche's New Seas*, ed. Gillespie and Strong, pp. 21–44.

Chapter 2

1. Cited from Hans Weichelt, *Zarathustra Commentar* (Felix Meiner, Leipzig, 1922), p. 17.

2. It would take too much space to consider in detail rival interpretations of the pale criminal. For a plausible alternative and/or supplement to my account, see Annemarie Pieper, *Ein Seil geknüpft zwischen Mensch und Übermensch* (Klett-Cotta, Stuttgart, 1990), pp. 170–82.

3. See *Der Fall Wagner*, VI, 11, and the letter to Malwida von Meysenberg of 18 October 1888 in *SB*, VIII, 452: "Ich bin, in Fragen der décadence, die höchste Instanz, die es auf Erden giebt." That is, he is "ein Genie der Wahrheit."

4. See the previously cited x, 244, 7 (21) (*Nachlass*, 1883).

5. Pieper, *Ein Seil geknüpft*, sees the denial of causality in these lines but misses entirely the "Platonist" intentionality that is an essential side of the figure of Zarathustra; she thus follows the majority of commentators in emphasizing the nonrationalist, or Dionysian, element in Zarathustra's teaching while in effect excluding its Apollonian element: "Was Zarathustra am Bild des roten Richters und des bleichen Verbrechers aufdecken will, ist der Grundirrtum, in dem sie sich beide befinden, wenn sie einen kausalen Zusammenhang zwischen geplanter Handlung, ausgeführter Tat und Beurteilung der Tat konstruieren" (p. 173).

6. See again *Zur Genealogie der Moral*, v, 344, pt. III, no. 5.

7. Consider passages like XIII, 631, 24 (1), no. 11 (*Nachlass*, 1888), and *Der Fall Wagner*, VI, 11.

8. See *Jenseits von Gut und Böse*, v, 60, pt. II, para. 43: " 'Mein Urtheil ist *mein* Urtheil: dazu hat nicht leicht auch ein Anderer das Recht' – sagt vielleicht solch ein Philosoph der Zukunft."

9. *Phänomenologie des Geistes* (Felix Meiner, Hamburg, 1952), pp. 112ff., esp. p. 121.

10. *Götzen-Dämmerung*, VI, 144, *Streifzüge*, 43.

11. Nietzsche understood "destruction" in a literal sense and not, like some of his contemporary admirers, as a peaceful transvaluation of values. See such passages as *Jenseits von Gut und Böse*, v, 140, pt. VI, no. 208, and XIII, 640, 25 (4) (*Nachlass*, 1888/89).

12. See *Der Antichrist*, v, 170, no. 2.

13. *Zur Genealogie der Moral*, v, 350–51, pt. III, no. 7.

14. *SB*, VI, 453, November 1883, to Malwida von Meysenberg, and *SB*, VIII, 93, June 1887, to Overbeck.

15. There seems to be a contradiction in Nietzsche on the question of nature. In a cosmological sense, nature is chaos; but from the standpoint of everyday existence, strength is closer to nature than is weakness, health than sickness, and overcoming than decadence. In other words, Nietzsche inconsistently gives the palm to accumulation as opposed to dissipation of force.

16. XI, 167, 26 (71) (*Nachlass*, 1884): "Alles Sehen ... ist schon ein Wertschätzen, ein Accetiren."

17. To say that they are the same is not to say that Dionysus predominates over Apollo in a recurring synthesis. The latter seems to be the view of Ilse Bulhof in *Apollos Wiederkehr* (Martinus Nijhoff, The Hague, 1969); see p. 128 of this useful study.

18. Ed. S. Gilman, tr. D. J. Parent (Oxford University Press, New York, 1987), p. 185.
19. Cf. Herodotus, book I, 31.
20. I do not wish to rule out the additional influence of Kierkegaard on this point in Heidegger's thinking. But Heidegger insists upon the central importance of Nietzsche's thought for his own work, whereas he assigns an altogether subordinate role to Kierkegaard, whom he calls a *Schriftsteller* rather than a *Denker.*

Chapter 3

1. *Republic,* II, 377a5–d4; III, 389b2–9; 413b8–414c11.
2. *Nietzsche,* 2 vols. (G. Neske, Pfullingen, 1961), II, 314–33. See my discussion in *The Question of Being* (Yale University Press, New Haven, 1993).
3. XII, 280, 7 (6) (*Nachlass,* 1886/87): "Meine Philosophie ist auf Rangordnung gerichtet: nicht auf eine individualistische Moral. Der Sinn der Heerde soll in der Heerde herrschen, aber nicht über sie hinaus greifen . . ." Cf. XIII, 481, 15 (120) (*Nachlass,* 1888). The evidence on this point is so clear-cut that one must regard those who ignore it as either incompetent or dishonest.
4. See X, 244, 7 (21) (*Nachlass,* 1883).
5. See *Götzen-Dämmerung,* VI, 59, *Sprüche und Pfeile,* no. 3: "Um allein zu leben, muss man ein Thier oder ein Gott sein – sagt Aristoteles. Fehlt der dritte Fall: man muss Beides sein – Philosoph."
6. Hans Weichelt, *Zarathustra Commentar* (Felix Meiner, Leipzig, 1922), p. 107.
7. (Yale University Press, New Haven, 1985), chap. 16.
8. See my essay on this term, "Poetic Reason in Nietzsche: *Die dichtende Vernunft,*" *The Ancients and the Moderns* (Yale University Press, New Haven, 1989), chap. 11.
9. See Heidegger's essay "Der Spruch des Anaximanders," *Holzwege* (Klostermann, Frankfurt, 1950).

Chapter 4

1. The pros and cons of the scientific basis for the eternal return are thoroughly canvassed in the previously cited books by Abel and Moles. Interesting as it may be in itself, the entire discussion seems to me to be largely irrelevant to an understanding of Nietzsche, for whom physics is a human interpretation of chaos.
2. See the fine observation on the reversal of "Thou or I" into "I or Thou" by Karl Löwith, *Nietzsches Philosophie der ewigen Wiederkehr des Gleichen* (Kohlhammer, Stuttgart, 1956), p. 73.
3. VI, 127, *Streifzüge,* 24.
4. *SB,* VI, 449, 22 October 1883.
5. Part One, sect. 15 ("Of a Thousand and One Goals"), p. 75.

Chapter 5

1. (Felix Meiner, Hamburg, 1952), pp. 486, 563. See also *Die Vernunft in der Geschichte* (Felix Meiner, Hamburg, 1955), p. 92 (times of happiness are empty pages in world history) and p. 100 (the world-historical individual is not happy in the usual sense of the term).
2. *Jenseits von Gut und Böse*, VI, 21f., pt. I, no. 9.
3. Kaufmann mistranslates this line.
4. When used to designate the gateway, *Augenblick* has no hyphen (see IV, 200).
5. *Ecce Homo*, VI, 286.
6. Consider *Republic*, II, 372d4ff. There is no meat, but also no war or philosophy, in the first sketch of the city offered by Socrates and called by him "the true city" at e6–8 in response to Glaucon's characterization of it as a city fit for sows.
7. See vol. XIV.

Conclusion

1. *Die Philosophie Platons* (taken from *Vorlesungen über der Geschichte der Philosophie*) (Freies Geistesleben, Stuttgart, 1962), p. 17.

INDEX

(In the case of constantly recurring terms like art, decadence, nihilism, philosophy, and rhetoric, only substantive or pivotal passages are listed.)